# Knowledge, Education and Social Structure in Africa

## Edited by

## Shoko Yamada, Akira Takada and Shose Kessi

In collaboration

Langaa RPCIG
Mankon Bamenda

CAAS
Kyoto University

*Publisher:*
*Langaa* RPCIG
Langaa Research & Publishing Common Initiative Group
P.O. Box 902 Mankon
Bamenda
North West Region
Cameroon
Langaagrp@gmail.com
www.langaa-rpcig.net


In Collaboration with
The Center for African Area Studies, Kyoto University, Japan


Distributed in and outside N. America by African Books Collective
orders@africanbookscollective.com
www.africanbookscollective.com


*ISBN-10: 9956-551-21-x*

*ISBN-13: 978-9956-551-21-7*


© Shoko Yamada, Akira Takada and Shose Kessi 2021

# Notes on Contributors

**Akiyo AMINAKA** is a Research Fellow at the IDE-JETRO (Institute of Developing Economies – Japan External Trade Organization). She has written various articles in both Japanese and English, including 'Mobility with vulnerability of Mozambican female migrants to South Africa: Outflow from the periphery', in Y. Kodama (ed.) *International Migration of African Women* (IDE 2020, in Japanese). Her first book entitled *Colonial Rule and Development: Mozambique and the South African Gold Mining Industry* (Yamakawa-Shuppansha 2014, in Japanese) was awarded a prize by the Japan Association for African Studies in 2015. Her current interests lie in labour migration, state building of post-conflict countries and development scheme transplantation with particular focus on Mozambique and Angola.

**Josephine CORNELL** is a PhD candidate of Psychology at the University of Cape Town and a researcher of the Institute for Social and Health Sciences at the University of South Africa and the South African Medical Research Council – University of South Africa's Masculinity and Health Research Unit. Her research interests include identity, higher education transformation, protests and visual methods.

**Morie KANEKO** is Associate Professor of the Graduate School of Asian and African Area Studies, Kyoto University. Her main research topics are the cultural transmission of techniques of body and technological innovation in Africa and the formation of African local knowledge in a global context. Her recent works include: *Reconsidering Local Knowledge and Beyond* (co-edited, Kyoto University 2020), 'ZAIRAICHI (local knowledge) as the manners of co-existence: Encounters between the Aari farmers in southwestern Ethiopia and the 'other''(co-authored, Langaa 2017), and *The Ethnography of Pottery Making* (Showado 2011, in Japanese).

**Shose KESSI** is Dean of the Faculty of Humanities at the University of Cape Town, Associate Professor in the Department of Psychology and co-director of the Hub for Decolonial Feminist Psychologies in Africa. Her research centres on social and political psychology, community mobilisation and social change, exploring issues of identity, such as race, class and gender, and how these impact on people's participation in transformation efforts. A key focus is the development of Photovoice Methodology as a participatory action research tool that can raise consciousness and mobilise community groups into social action.

**Motoji MATSUDA** is Professor of Sociology and Anthropology at Kyoto University, Japan. His research fields are Nairobi and Western Kenya. His research topics are urbanisation, migration and conflict. His major works include: *Urbanisation from Below* (Kyoto University Press 1998); *The Manifesto of Anthropology of the Everyday Life World* (Sekai Shisosha 2008, in Japanese); *African Virtues in the Pursuit of Conviviality: Exploring Local Solutions in Light of Global Prescriptions* (co-edited with Itaru Ohta and Yntiso Gebre, Langaa RPCIG 2017) and *The Challenge of African Potentials: Conviviality, Informality and Futurity* (co-edited with Yaw Ofosu-Kusi, Langaa RPCIG 2020).

**Sethunya Tshepho MOSIME** has held a PhD from the University of KwaZulu Natal, Centre for Communication, Media, and Society since 2007. Currently, she is a Senior Lecturer and Head of the Department of Sociology at the University of Botswana. Her research and teaching interests include the rights of political and social minorities across ethnicity, gender and sexuality, and African social thought. She has authored many academic articles, such as 'Botswana: Africa's democratic developmental state or outright flattery', (co-authored with G. Kaboyakgosi) in G. Kanyenze et al. (eds) *Towards Democratic Developmental States in Southern Africa* (Weaver Press 2017).

**Nagisa NAKAWA** is Associate Professor of the School of Architecture and Environmental Design at Kanto Gakuin University, Japan. She has been engaged in mathematics education research since 2005 and has worked in Zambia and Kenya. As her lifework, she has been learning various African traditional dances. Her major works include 'Proposing and modifying guided play on shapes in mathematics teaching and learning for Zambian preschool children', *South African Journal of Childhood Education* 10 (1): 1–10 (2020) and 'Current situations and challenges on mathematics lessons in early childhood care, development and education in urban areas of Lusaka, Zambia', *Africa Education Research Journal* 9: 23–38 (2018).

**Asayo OHBA** is Associate Professor of International Education and Development with a special focus on Africa at Teikyo University, Japan. Her research fields are informal settlements in Nairobi and other regions of Kenya. Her major works include: 'Addressing inclusive education for learners with disabilities in the integrated education system: The dilemma of public primary schools in Kenya', *Compare: A Journal of Comparative and International Education* (co-authored with Francis Likoye Malenya, 2020) and 'Why do some children still leave primary school early? Comparing reasons in three regions of Kenya', *Africa Education Review* 17 (2): 33–49 (2020).

**Kopano RATELE** is the Director of the South African Medical Research Council Masculinity & Health Research Unit and Professor at the University of South Africa where he runs the Transdisciplinary African Psychologies Programme. He has published extensively and his books include: *There Was This Goat: Investigating the Truth Commission Testimony of Notrose Nobomvu Konile* (co-authored with Antjie Krog and Nosisi Mpolweni, University of KwaZulu-Natal Press 2009), *Liberating Masculinities* (Human Sciences Research Council 2016), *Engaging Youth in Activism, Research and Pedagogical Praxis: Transnational and Intersectional Perspectives on Gender, Sex, and Race* (co-edited with Jeff Hearn, Tammy Shefer and Floretta Boonzaier, Routledge 2018) and *The World Looks Like This From Here: Thoughts on African Psychology* (Witwatersrand University Press 2019).

**Nobuhide SAWAMURA** is Professor of Education and International Development in the Graduate School of Human Sciences at Osaka University, Japan. His academic career began at the Center for the Study of International Cooperation in Education (CICE) at Hiroshima University and he was a founding member of the centre. He holds an M.Phil. from the University of Edinburgh and a Ph.D. from Osaka University. His first exposure to Africa was in 1982–84, as a secondary school science teacher of the Japan Overseas Cooperation Volunteers in Malawi. He then worked for the Japan International Cooperation Agency (JICA) for 11 years. He has carried out research on a wide range of educational issues in developing countries. His recent interest is the multiple realities and meanings in primary schooling in sub-Saharan Africa, particularly in Kenya.

**Kazuro SHIBUYA** is Director of Basic Education Group, Human Development Department at the Japan International Cooperation Agency (JICA). His major works include: 'Community participation in school management from the viewpoint of relational trust: A case from the Akatsi South District, Ghana', *International Journal of Educational Development* 76 (2020) and 'Community participation in school management, relational trust, and teacher motivation toward pupils' learning outcomes: The case study from Ghana', in M. Nishimura (ed.) *Community Participation with Schools in Developing Countries: Towards Equitable and Inclusive Basic Education for All* (Routledge 2020).

**Masayoshi SHIGETA** is Professor of African Area Studies at the Graduate School of Asian and African Area Studies, Kyoto University. His main research interests extend from agricultural science, ethnobiology and crop evolution to African area studies, anthropology, studies on sleep and society and studies on development issues. His recent works include: 'ZAIRAICHI (local knowledge) as the manners of co-existence: Encounters between the Aari farmers in southwestern Ethiopia and the "other" (co-authored, Langaa 2017) and 'Reshaping the future of ethnobiology research after the COVID-19 pandemic' (co-authored, 2020).

**Akira TAKADA** is Associate Professor of Graduate School of Asian and African Area Studies at Kyoto University, Japan. His academic interests include the influence of Christianity and Western education on indigenous societies, transformation of ethnicity in the contact zone and language socialisation in caregiver–child interaction. He has conducted intensive field research in Namibia, Botswana and Japan. He has published a number of books and articles including *Narratives on San Ethnicity: The Cultural and Ecological Foundations of Lifeworld among the !Xun of North-Central Namibia* (Kyoto University Press & Trans Pacific Press 2015) and *The Ecology of Playful Childhood: Caregiver-Child Interactions among the San of Southern Africa* (Palgrave Macmillan 2020).

**Machiko TSUBURA** is a Research Fellow of the African Studies Group in Area Studies Center at the IDE-JETRO (Institute of Developing Economies – Japan External Trade Organization). She holds a PhD in Development Studies from the University of Sussex in the United Kingdom. Her research interests lie in democracy, elections and political parties in sub-Saharan Africa with a focus on Tanzania.

**Shoko YAMADA** is Professor of Comparative Education and African Studies at Nagoya University, Japan. She has conducted various researches on educational policy-making and implementation in Africa, both in the historical and present-day contexts. She is also interested in the African traditional epistemology and social meaning of knowledge. Her major works include: *Dignity of Labour for African Leaders: The Formation of Education Policy in the British Colonial Office and Achimota School on the Gold Coast* (Langaa RPCIG 2018) and *Post-Education-For-All and Sustainable Development Paradigm: Structural Change and Diversifying Actors and Norms* (Emerald 2016).

# Table of Contents

Series Preface: African Potentials
for Convivial World-Making ......................................... xv
*Motoji Matsuda*

Introduction: Knowledge, Education
and Social Structure in Africa ....................................... 1
*Shoko Yamada, Akira Takada and Shose Kessi*

PART I: Education as a Mode of Transmitting Values

1. Knowledge and Views of Tanzanian
   Youth Regarding *Ujamaa*:
   A Case Study of Students at the
   University of Dar es Salaam ....................................... 25
   *Machiko Tsubura*

2. The Medium of Instruction
   for School Education in Southern Africa:
   Historical Analyses of South African
   and North-Central Namibian Cases ........................... 53
   *Akira Takada*

3. Constructing Places of Belonging
   and Exclusion: A Spatial Reading of
   South African University Students'
   Affect and Identity ........................................... 83
   *Josephine Cornell, Shose Kessi and Kopano Ratele*

PART II: School Credentials versus Knowledge for Use

4. Skills Development Paths Chosen
   by Learners: The Case of Students
   Studying Automotive-Related Subjects
   in Technical and Vocational Education
   and Training Institutions in Kumasi, Ghana .............. 127
   *Shoko Yamada*

5. Formation of Local Knowledge
   through Experiences of School Education
   and Livelihood Activities in Southwest Ethiopia ......... 157
   *Morie Kaneko and Masayoshi Shigeta*

6. Education and Employment:
   Genesis of Highly Educated Informal
   Workers in Mozambique .............................................. 179
   *Akiyo Aminaka*

PART III: Politics and Interactions among People Surrounding
the School

7. Managing Conflicts within School
   Communities in Ghana: Focusing on
   the Art of Conviviality .................................................. 215
   *Kazuro Shibuya*

8. Community Schools Providing the
   Tools for Conviviality in Urban Kenya ....................... 247
   *Asayo Ohba*

9. Examining International Aid and
   Community Self-Help Initiatives
   from a Conviviality Perspective:
   Unrecognised Low-Fee Private Schools
   in a Slum Area of Nairobi, Kenya ................................. 271
   *Nobuhide Sawamura*

PART IV: Knowledge Acquisition as a Subjective Process

10. Investigating Mathematical
    Activities in Zambian Children's Play
    from the Perspective of Mathematics Education ......... 297
    *Nagisa Nakawa*

11. Bringing Ali Mazrui's Epistemic
    Eclecticism into Classroom Praxis:
    *Morero* as Pedagogic Eclecticism
    for Teaching African Potentials .................................... 327
    *Sethunya Tshepho Mosime*

Index ............................................................................... 357

# African Potentials for Convivial World-Making

*Motoji Matsuda*

## 1. The Idea of 'African Potentials'

The *African Potentials* series is based on the findings since 2011 of the African Potentials research project, an international collaboration involving researchers based in Japan and Africa. This project examines how to tackle the challenges of today's world using the experiences and wisdom (ingenuity and responsiveness) of African society. It has identified field sites across a variety of social domains, including areas of conflict, conciliation, environmental degradation, conservation, social development and equality, and attempts to shed light on the potential of African society to address the problems therein. Naturally, such an inquiry is deeply intertwined with the political and economic systems that control the contemporary world, and with knowledge frameworks that have long dominated the perceptions and understanding of our world. Building on unique, long-standing collaborative relationships developed between researchers in Japan and Africa, the project suggests new ways to challenge the prevailing worldview on humans, society and history, enabling those worldviews to be relativised, decentred and pluralised.

After the rose-coloured dreams of the 1960s, African society entered an era of darkness in the 1980s and 1990s. It was beleaguered by problems that included civil conflict, military dictatorship, national economic collapse, commodity shortages, environmental degradation and destruction, over-urbanisation and rampant contagious disease. In the early 21st century, the fortunes of Africa were reversed as it underwent economic growth by leveraging its abundant natural resources. However, an unequal redistribution of wealth increased social disparities and led to the emergence of new forms of conflict and discrimination. The challenges facing African society appear to be more profound than ever.

The governments of African states and the international community have attempted to resolve the many problems Africa has experienced. For example, the perpetrators of crimes during times of civil conflict have been punished by international tribunals, support for democratisation has been offered to states ruled by dictators and despots and environmental degradation has been tackled by scientific awareness campaigns conducted at huge expense.

Nonetheless, to us – the Japanese and African researchers engaging with African society in this era – the huge monetary and organisational resources expended, and scientifically grounded measures pursued, seem to have had little effect on the lives of ordinary people. The punishment of perpetrators did not consider the coexistence of perpetrators and victims, while the propagation of democratic ideals and training to raise scientific awareness was far removed from people's lived experiences. Nevertheless, while many of these 'top-down' measures prescribed to solve Africa's challenges proved ineffective, African society has found ways to heal post-conflict communities and to develop practices of political participation and environmental conservation.

Why did this happen? This question led us to examine ideas and practices African society has formulated for tackling the contemporary difficulties it has experienced. These were developed at sites where ordinary Africans live. 'African Potentials' is the name we gave to these home-grown ideas and the potential to engender them.

## 2. African Forum: A Unique Intellectual Collaboration between Japan and Africa

As the concept of African Potentials emerged, it required further reflection to develop ideas that could be applied in the humanities and social sciences. The context for these processes was the African Forum: a meeting held in a different part of Africa each year where African researchers from different regions and Japanese researchers studying in each of those regions came together to engage in frank discussion. The attendance of all core members of the project sympathetic to the idea of African Potentials ensured the continuity of the discussions at these African Forums. The core members who drove the project forward from the African side included Edward Kirumira (Uganda and South Africa), Kennedy Mkutu (Kenya), Yntiso Gebre (Ethiopia), the late Samson Wassara (South Sudan), the late Sam Moyo (Zimbabwe), Michael Neocosmos (South Africa), Francis B. Nyamnjoh (Cameroon and South Africa) and Yaw Ofosu-Kusi (Ghana). The researchers from Japan specialised in extremely diverse fields, including political science, sociology, anthropology, development economics, education, ecology and geography. As they built creative interdisciplinary spaces for interaction across fields over the course of a decade, project members have produced many major outcomes that serve as research models for intellectual and academic exchange between Japan and Africa, and experimental cases of educational practice in the mutual cultivation and guidance of young researchers.

African Forums have been held in Nairobi (2011), Harare (2012), Juba (2013), Yaoundé (2014), Addis Ababa (2015), Kampala (2016), Grahamstown (now Makhanda, 2017), Accra (2018) and Lusaka (2019). These meetings fostered deeper discussion of the conceptualisation and generalisation of African Potentials. This led to the development of a framework for approaching African Potentials and its distinguishing features.

## 3. What are African Potentials?

The first aim of African Potentials is to 'de-romanticise' the traditional values and institutions of Africa. For example, when studying conflict resolution, members of African Potentials are not interested in excessive idealisation of traditional means of conflict resolution and unconditional endorsement of a return to African traditions as an 'alternative' to modern Western conflict-resolution methods, because such ideas fix African Potentials in a static mode as they speak to a fantasy that ignores the complexities of the contemporary world; they are cognate with the mentality that depreciates African culture.

Rendering African culture static displaces it from its original context and uses it to fabricate 'African-flavoured' theatrical events, as we have seen in different conflict situations. Typical of this tendency is the 'theatre' of traditional dance by performers dressed in ethnic costume and the ceremonial slaughter of cows in an imitation of the rituals of mediation and reconciliation once observed in inter-ethnic conflicts. In our African Forums, we have criticised this tendency as the 'technologisation' and 'compartmentalisation' of traditional rituals.

Naturally, a stance that arbitrarily deems certain conflict-resolution cultures to be 'subaltern', 'backward' or 'uncivilised' needs to be critiqued and it is important to re-evaluate approaches that have been written off in this way. This does not mean that we should level unconditional praise on a fixed subject. With globalisation, African society is experiencing great changes brought about by the circulation of diverse ideas, institutions, information and physical goods. African Potentials can be found in the power to generate cultures of conflict-resolution autonomously under these fluid conditions, while re-aligning elements that were previously labelled 'traditional' and 'indigenous'. In the African Potentials project, we call this the power of 'interface function': the capacity to forge combinations and connections within assemblages of diverse values, ideas and practices that belong to disparate dimensions and different historical phases. In one sense, this is a kind of 'bricolage' created by dismantling pre-existing values and institutions and recombining them freely. It is also a convivial process in the sense that it involves enabling the coexistence of diverse, multi-dimensional elements to create new strengths that are used in contemporary society. The terms 'bricolage' and 'conviviality' are apt expressions characterising the 'interface functions' of African Potentials.

Following this outline, we can identify two features distinguishing African Potentials. First, African Potentials comprise not fixed, unchanging entities but, rather, an open process that is always dynamic and in flux. To treat African traditions and history as static is to fall into the trap of modernist thinking, in which Africa is scorned as barbaric and uncivilised, and the knowledge and practices generated there treated as subaltern and irrational – or a diametrically opposed revivalist mindset that romanticises traditions unconditionally and imbues them with exaggerated significance.

The second feature of African Potentials is its aspiration to pluralism rather than unity. For example, a basic principle of modern civil society is that conflict resolution should occur in accordance with law and judicial process. This principle is deemed to be based on common sense in our society, which means that any resolution method that runs counter to the principle is regarded as 'mistaken' from the outset. This constitutes an aspiration toward unity. It supposes that there is a single way of thinking in relation to the achievement of justice and deems all other approaches peripheral, informal and inferior. The standpoint of Africa's cultural potential, however, renders untenable the idea of a single absolute approach that represents all others as mistaken or deserving of rejection. Here, we can identify a pluralist aspiration that embraces both legal/judicial approaches and extrajudicial solutions.

An aspiration to unity, reduced to the level of dogma, can find eventual culmination in beliefs about 'purity'. In other words, thoughts, values and methods can be regarded as an absolute good, while any attempt to incorporate other (impure) elements is stridently denounced as improper behaviour that compromises purity and perfection. In direct contrast, African Potentials affirm the complexity and multiplicity of a range of elements, and attach value to that which is incomplete. This signifies a more tolerant, open attitude to ideas and values, one that differs from those of the more developed world. African Potentials are grounded in this kind of openness and tolerance.

As we have seen, African cultural potentials are distinguished by their dynamism, flexibility, pluralism, complexity, tolerance and openness. These features are completely at odds with the notion that there is a perfect, pure, uniquely correct mode of existence that competes with others in a confrontational, non-conciliatory manner – one that repels, subordinates and controls them, and occupies the position of an absolute victor. African Potentials can lead us to worldviews on humans, society and history that differ from the hegemonic worldviews that dominate contemporary realms of knowledge.

## 4. The African Potentials Series

In this way, the concept of African Potentials has enabled researchers from Japan and Africa to organise themselves and pursue activities in multidisciplinary research teams. The products of these activities have been classified into seven different fields for publication in this series. The authors and editors were selected by and from both Japanese and African researchers, and the resulting publications advance the research that has grown out of discussion in the African Forums. The overall structure of the series is as follows:

### Volume 1

Title: *African Politics of Survival: Extraversion and Informality in the Contemporary World*

Editors: Mitsugi Endo (The University of Tokyo), Ato Kwamena Onoma (CODESRIA) and Michael Neocosmos (Rhodes University)

### Volume 2

Title: *Knowledge, Education and Social Structure in Africa*

Editors: Shoko Yamada (Nagoya University), Akira Takada (Kyoto University) and Shose Kessi (University of Cape Town)

### Volume 3

Title: *People, Predicaments and Potentials in Africa*

Editors: Takehiko Ochiai (Ryukoku University), Misa Hirano-Nomoto (Kyoto University) and Daniel E. Agbiboa (Harvard University)

### Volume 4

Title*: Development and Subsistence in Globalising Africa: Beyond the Dichotomy*

Editors: Motoki Takahashi (Kyoto University), Shuichi Oyama (Kyoto University) and Herinjatovo Aimé Ramiarison (University of Antananarivo)

## Volume 5

Title: *Dynamism in African Languages and Literature: Towards Conceptualisation of African Potentials*

Editors: Keiko Takemura (Osaka University) and Francis B. Nyamnjoh (University of Cape Town)

## Volume 6

Title: *'African Potentials' for Wildlife Conservation and Natural Resource Management: Against the Images of 'Deficiency' and Tyranny of 'Fortress'*

Editors: Toshio Meguro (Hiroshima City University), Chihiro Ito (Fukuoka University) and Kariuki Kirigia (McGill University)

## Volume 7

Title: *Contemporary Gender and Sexuality in Africa: African-Japanese Anthropological Approach*

Editors: Wakana Shiino (Tokyo University of Foreign Studies) and Christine Mbabazi Mpyangu (Makerere University)

## Acknowledgements

This publication is based on the research project supported by the JSPS KAKENHI Grant Number JP16H06318: 'African Potential' and Overcoming the Difficulties of Modern World: Comprehensive Area Studies that will Provide a New Perspective for the Future of Humanity.

# Introduction

## Knowledge, Education and Social Structure in Africa

*Shoko Yamada, Akira Takada and Shose Kessi*

### 1. Metaphysics of 'African Potentials' and African Phenomena

What is 'African Potentials? As the series editor mentioned in his preface, we should abstain from falling into a simplistic definition. On the one hand, it has been necessary to examine colonial mentality critically, which accepts Western modernity as being superior to ideas and practices rooted locally. While on the other hand, simple rejection of Eurocentricity and praise of African-ness do not lead to a better grasp of African Potentials. Both attitudes rely on the West–Africa dichotomy, which places the diverse and fluid realities of Africa into a unified category.

Then, how do we theorise African Potentials while avoiding the pitfalls of generalisation and fixation? This task would prove highly metaphysical. Meanwhile, most research consisting of area studies are field-oriented, which aim to construct an understanding of the culture and social dynamics through the viewpoints of the people in context. Similar to other volumes of this series, the research sites and topics that are the focus of the authors of this volume are diverse. Geographically, the chapters focus on people, communities and institutions in different parts of East, South, and West Africa. Some are historical studies, while the majority deal with contemporary issues. Overall, given the diversity, it is difficult to identify particular empirical features as the source of African Potentials. To overcome such difficulty of developing the common ground, the authors went through a process of sharing their theoretical bases by jointly reviewing key literature and commenting on each other's works. For example, we discuss the concept of 'conviviality' and its implications in relation to the theme in this volume, namely, education and knowledge.

Conviviality is the concept proposed by Ivan Illich (1973) as a departure from a highly institutionalised and technology-dependent perspective to one through which autonomous individuals could regain self-reliance. The dictionary definition of the term is 'friendliness' or 'merry company', originating from the Latin word *convivium* meaning 'banquet' (Oxford Dictionary 2013). Illich used this uncommon word to propose a novel approach, based on multi-faceted human relationships to overcome the restrictions imposed by the excessive standardisation of values in the modern industrialised world. This concept became particularly relevant to us because Francis Nyamnjoh, a philosophical stalwart of the African Potentials project, extended Illich's notion to comprehend the constant flux of relationships in Africa, not only among people but also between humans and nature, animals and supernaturals (Nyamnjoh 2017). According to Nyamnjoh, what we see as reality is a snapshot of a temporal state of being, which keeps changing from moment to moment. Since it continues to flow, there is no point of blaming its 'incompleteness'. Africa has been victimised by European colonists and by technocrats from aid-providing agencies, for being underdeveloped and requiring modernisation. However, such a static and distant view of the state of development does not allow us to grasp the real nature of human existence and the relationships in African societies. Nyamnjoh's interpretation of conviviality appears to be more communal and relational than that of Illich, who emphasised the autonomy of individuals, although they both seek the potency of the society in its dynamic. Nyamnjoh also considers a broader scope of the relationships than Illich, as traditional African epistemology does not draw a clear boundary between the world of humans and that of plants, animals and, even, ancestors.

There is a fundamental challenge to applying the concept of conviviality, and particularly that of Nyamnjoh, as a framework for empirical analysis. According to Nyamnjoh, 'Everyone can act and be acted upon, just as anything can be subject and object of action, making power and weakness nimble-footed, fluid and situational, and giving life more a character of flux and interdependence than permanence' (Nyamnjoh 2017: 260–61). If this is the case, the realities that scholars attempt to illustrate through observations and conversations with subjective agents are mere temporalities, which may or may not, have existed in the past. Such is the inherent discrepancy between the metaphysics of conviviality and the phenomena that are to be described. Because of this, it is sometimes difficult for empirical analysts to avoid the pitfall of simplification. In other words, they tend to reduce this concept to label anything that seems to be communal, African or traditional, rather than individualistic, Western or formal. This convenient use of the term 'conviviality', and probably also that of 'African Potentials', ends up returning us to the static dichotomy of the West and Africa, from which we have aimed to move away.

Even with this difficulty, an understanding of these philosophical works helped the authors of this volume to examine the research more profoundly at the theoretical level. In the following part of this introductory chapter, we describe some underlying themes – both conceptual and empirical – that cut across the chapters. These themes allow us to view the findings and implications of each chapter from multiple angles and, in doing so, we are able to describe the wide range and great depth of African Potentials at this crucial turning point when the world is facing a global pandemic.

As the title describes, this volume aims at considering the relationships between knowledge, education and social structure from multiple angles. Most people would agree that education and knowledge are the keys to understanding the characteristics of both an individual and a society.

As stated by existentialist philosophers of education, human beings are born to learn (Kauka 2018). From birth, if not before, a baby starts to acquire new knowledge through interacting with his/her intimate circle of people and surroundings (Takada 2020). According to this intuitive concept of learning, there is no restriction on when and where a person learns. Also, learning is entirely dependent on the self-motivation of the learners in terms of what they want to learn and how they make sense of this acquired knowledge. At the same time, to maintain unity and order, societies are oriented to educate their new members – either children or adults who have joined from elsewhere – of the values, norms and information that constitute the basis of their collective identities.

For postcolonial scholars in Africa, education studies have had a special meaning, as the colonists are said to have used education as an effective means to consolidate their rule over the colonial subjects. On the one hand, they developed the school system to equip the people with the skills needed for governing the colonies. But on the other hand, they carefully managed the development of personalities at the schools so as not to alienate the educated Africans from the masses and to be willing mediators between the Europeans and Africans (Yamada 2018). There is a common struggle for many postcolonial scholars and writers. Once they were trained to think using the language and logic of the colonisers, the minds of the Africans were also governed by colonisers. Then, it was difficult for them to break away from this way of thinking (for example, Ngugi 1986; Appiah 1992). Given such fundamental importance of education in shaping the mind of people, the studies on it were among the major approaches to elaborate on what it means to be independent in post-independence Africa. At the basis of this approach lies a thirst for understanding the unique African self and identity that is devoid of colonial bias. Given this background, it is no coincidence that contemporary African educational institutions, and particularly universities, have often become sites of controversy over the boundaries between different identity groups such as gender, race, ethnicity and class.[1] The dialogue on post-coloniality continues to re-emerge in Africa and is inseparable from concepts and practices in education.

## 2. Education as a Mode of Transmitting Values

Although the chapters in this volume highlight the considerable diversity of the topics and geographic foci, we can traverse them using four main perspectives.

The first perspective is the attention paid to the role of education in shaping the collective imagination of society and individuals' sense of identity. As mentioned above, this perspective has a historical basis. It is often suggested, not only during the colonial period but also in contemporary contexts, that powerful elites knowingly manipulate these functions of education to control the minds of the general public. At the same time, more frequently than not, education ends up contributing to value formation without overt intentions. For example, it is often the attitudes of teachers and peers that transmit the values of the greater imagined society. Children from minority backgrounds, either ethnically, linguistically or socially, may be treated as inferiors, not because of their cognitive capacities, but because of their lack of exposure to the dominant values and their inability to behave 'properly' according to these values. While the absence of such 'cultural capital' (Bourdieu 1984) disadvantages those minorities, the school has the effect of transmitting the social norms associated with cultural capital and indirectly drives the learners to conform to them; this is known as a 'hidden curriculum' (Jackson 1968). Whether it is through formal schooling, informal apprenticeship or interactions with families or communities, the inherent nature of education is to prepare the members of a society to fit into a cultural and normative framework, although the values that constitute the collective identity are not static, as argued by Nyamnjoh.

To strengthen the people's collective identity, which is believed to be important in the process of nation building, politicians have often relied on a vernacular concept. Tsubura (Chapter 1 of this volume) focuses on the concept of '*ujamaa*' (meaning 'familyhood' in Swahili), which was promoted by Julius Nyerere, the first president of Tanzania, as the fundamental principle of African socialism. As Nyerere considered education a means of promulgating *ujamaa* philosophy and practices in building the newly independent country, *ujamaa* was positioned at the core of education policies and practices during the socialist period between 1967 and the mid-1980s. However, after Nyerere retired from the presidency, the government began promoting political and economic liberalisation which minimised the emphasis on *ujamaa* in schools. Against this backdrop, Tsubura examines how young Tanzanians who have no lived experiences of the socialist period have become familiar with *ujamaa* and how they perceive it in relation to political and socioeconomic conditions in Tanzania today. Through analysis of interviews with academics and students at the University of Dar es Salaam (UDSM), Tsubura's study suggests that, while knowledge of *ujamaa* acquired from textbooks in schools is relatively limited, students at UDSM have had opportunities to learn about *ujamaa* from school activities, their families, communities and various media. Without standardised formal education on *ujamaa*, their views on the relevance of *ujamaa* to Tanzania today – more broadly, their ideological beliefs – are varied and mixed and cannot necessarily be categorised into orthodox ideologies. Nevertheless, Tsubura argues that *ujamaa* still holds as a reference point for the country's educated youth in reflecting on the characteristics of contemporary Tanzania.

Based on the above considerations, some chapters in this volume have attempted to capture the shifting boundaries between social groups within an imagined community, such as a nation state (Anderson 1983), or the changing attitude of individuals toward values transmitted through education. Takada's longitudinal study (Chapter 2) discusses the politics of identity, which are closely linked with the teaching methodologies at schools in South Africa and today's north-central Namibia. Under the apartheid regime, South Africa implemented the 'Bantu education' policy, which stipulated Afrikaans as the medium language of instruction for most non-white people, as an attempt to favour Afrikaners, who had been suppressed by the predominant Anglophone residents. However, this led to resistance from black South Africans and international communities and, eventually, to the government being overthrown. South Africa also applied the Bantu education policy to Namibia (known as South West Africa at that time), where the context of school education differed considerably from that in South Africa. This practice resulted in a number of Ovawambo people, who were educated in mission schools, taking up central roles in the liberation movement against South African control. Their memorable victory shaped the narratives of those who played central roles in the liberation movement as being the legitimate memories of 'national heroes'. However, it should be remembered that there were also a significant number of San living in north-central Namibia. The history of the educational policy applied to the San in Ovamboland differed significantly to that applied to the Ovambo. In this chapter, Takada reconsiders regional history from the perspective of the oppressed people and pursues the African Potentials of education in restructuring social organisation. Takada's study indicates that, in the historical context of southern Africa, education has been a major device for creating and maintaining social and economic disparities among the diverse peoples.

In South Africa, particularly, a number of black South Africans believe that the structure of colonial rule persists and remains embedded in various spheres of society. Cornell, Kessi and Ratele (Chapter 3) focus on the 'spaces' – both physical and mental – at the campus of the University of Cape Town (UCT). In South Africa, the higher education system is characterised by persistent inequality. As a result of the enduring legacy of colonialism and apartheid, as well as processes of neoliberalism and globalisation, students with certain identities are marginalised, whereas others are privileged. Intersections of identity, such as race, class, ability and gender function as the axes of the power dynamics in differential experiences of space. Students' experiences of spatialised belonging and exclusion at the UCT are examined through a multimodal discourse analysis of their reflective mind maps of the campus, which was historically a 'whites-only' South African University. The analysis illustrated that students experience class, race and gender alienation in particular campus locations, but that they also successfully created their own places of affirmation, connection and belonging. These particular affective constructions of the campus were shaped by salient elements of the students' intersecting identities and, in turn, enabled or undermined the performance of specific student identities. Examining how students experience the campus space helps to illuminate the processes of privilege and exclusion on campus and highlights students' agency in the complex, contested and ongoing transformation process.

## 3. School Credentials versus Knowledge for Use

While we have carefully avoided equating schooling with education, it is essential to examine the school as an institution that is part of the national public system. Above, we discussed how education ensures that members of society follow the rules and the ways of thinking, highlighting how education affects the minds of learners. Even so, however significant the education may be, it cannot coerce individuals into adopting particular attitudes. Meanwhile, school forms a part of the national education system that is accredited by the national government, and it follows the national curriculum by employing teachers who were trained to teach this curriculum. Therefore, even though variations in educational experiences exist in each classroom and school, caused by the contexts and subjectivities of the students and teachers, its impact as a formally authorised institution, cannot be overlooked.

Two years before publishing *Tools for Conviviality*, Ivan Illich published his book *Deschooling Society* (Illich 1971). He argued that the school serves as the mechanism of authorising knowledge that is selected to be taught while sidelining other kinds of knowledge. Furthermore, the more society is systematised, the more the professional workers require licences and specialised knowledge, which precondition the learning at specific types of schools. At the same time, the discrepancy between those who are privileged and the rest increases, caused by inequality of opportunities to learn through the school system. Therefore, Illich claimed that knowledge and learners should be freed from school, and that learners should be matched with those who have experience and knowledge of the things that they would like to learn. This argument proposed by Illich anticipated his theory of conviviality as an analytical tool, which offers a perspective antithetical to that of the over-standardised industrialised societies.

Lave and Wenger (1991) also indicated that school education has two values; namely, those of exchange and use. For example, the type of school from which a person graduates significantly impacts his/her employment opportunities and positions offered post-school. It is a matter of the exchange value of the education credentials, which is independent of the knowledge learned in the course of school education and how useful such knowledge is (use-value).

In this volume, several authors are interested in the differential impacts of knowledge and the credentials of school education in students' lives after graduation. For example, Yamada's (Chapter 4) analysis of the strategies adopted by students in four Technical and Vocational Education and Training (TVET) institutions is particularly pertinent. In the mid-2000s, the Ghanaian Government undertook a major reform of the TVET system, shifting the emphasis from theoretical learning to practical experience in the industry to cultivate learners' competencies in problem solving in work and real-life settings. Students taking automotive-related courses found different exchange and use-values at the four TVET institutions in Kumasi: Kumasi Vocational Training Institute (KVTI), Kumasi Technical Institute (KTI), Kumasi Senior Technical High School (KSHS) and Kumasi Polytechnic (KP). The KSHS is more of an academic institution and provides more options for continuing education, leading to university and the KP. The KTI awards its graduates the senior technical certificate, which leads only to the KP. Meanwhile, the KVTI is not linked to a specific route for post-secondary education. The analysis also shows that the paths chosen by the students are not linear; instead, they are formed of multiple trajectories as the students move between the workplace and school, and back again. In Kumasi, there are diverse routes to learning the skills needed for a career in vehicle repair, and the learners assign various roles to the schools. Although the learners perceive the aims of the governmental TVET reforms as unrealistic, they make their own decisions about their career development based on their assessment of the environment, their aptitude and their self-esteem. This study provides a firm basis in the search for African Potentials, and as a way to understand the diversity of learners' subjectivities and experiences.

Kaneko and Shigeta (Chapter 5) also aimed to investigate the effect of school education – either certificate or knowledge – on the life course of graduates at South Aari *woreda* in the South Omo Zone, which was relegated to the periphery in Ethiopia's education policy. Since formal schooling was first introduced in the 1970s, the social situation in terms of school education has changed drastically in this region. The Aari began to accept the written knowledge in the textbook as the new type of knowledge in contrast to the operational knowledge acquired through the direct interaction with the real world. Consequently, people start forming unique life trajectories. The authors analysed the life history of two men, Mr Y and Mr A, who established an agricultural association in village D, to examine how their school experiences influenced the establishment of this association. The analysis revealed that their experiences of school education guided them to relativise their cultural practices as the Aari, and to explore their own way of life after graduation. In this regard, the activity of association, such as raising poultry, and the relevant knowledge accumulated among the members can be regarded as a new form of local knowledge that realises African Potentials to reorganise pre-existing social relationships and create novel communities.

The exchange and use-values of school education are sometimes realised in an unexpected manner, not envisaged by politicians. Almost 30 years after regime change and the end of the civil war in Mozambique, entrepreneurship and employment in the informal sector are increasing among highly educated young people, such as university students and graduates. This contradicts the conventional assumption that people aspire to go on to higher education to gain better formal-sector employment. Aminaka (Chapter 6) investigates the causes of this unexpected trend. As a result of the post-war reconstruction of the society and the people's desire for educational opportunities, the number of highly educated people greatly increased in Mozambique. However, due to the lack of posts in the formal sector, the question arose as to whether they could find jobs that were commensurate with their educational backgrounds. The case of Maria, a young woman, highlights this situation. Although she attended university, she quit after two years and concentrated on working in the informal cross-border trade (ICBT) as a trader. The underlying reasons for this were the disparity between the expansion of higher education institutions and the 'jobless growth' of economy in Mozambique, forcing Maria to seek economic independence as a young entrepreneur in the informal sector. However, Maria's academic career worked in her favour, because today's ICBT activities require a level of competency in understanding the political economy to be able to react to the changing custom conditions and maximise the profit margins. Thus, the informal sector acts as an arena to satisfy the socioeconomic needs of highly educated people in Mozambique today. At the same time, as the government has increased regulations on trade activities, the informal nature of ICBT has become more formal. It is important to keep monitoring the development of the relationship between the state and society.

## 4. Politics and Interactions among People Surrounding the School

The third perspective, which is shared by several authors in this volume, is the socio-political meaning of school as a local entity. Since each school operates within a particular local society, it forms a nexus of local power relationships among stakeholders such as parents, students, teachers, communities and the government.

Over the last two decades, the number of schools has increased significantly in Africa, being supported by a push from international organisations. Global agendas such as 'Education for All' adopted in 1990 or the 'Millennium Development Goals' adopted in 2000 unanimously promoted the idea of 'universal education', initially at the primary level, and later up to the junior secondary level. Accordingly, the amount of financial aid from international donors into the sub-sector of basic education increased massively in the 2000s. At one point, basic education consumed 60–70 per cent of the total governmental education budget in many African countries (Yamada 2005). During this period, many communities in poor urban neighbourhoods or remote rural areas found new schools established by the government, the numbers of which had previously been limited. Before this, many people in these communities did not attend school, and issues related to schooling mostly concerned only the local elite and the parents who could afford the time and expense of educating their children. However, with the expansion of the school system, expectations surrounding schools changed fundamentally, and most local communities became aware of the resources required to manage the schools.

Another significant factor that arose in tandem with the increase in the number of schools was the excessive burden of administering the rapidly expanding school system due to the limited capacities of the governments, both financially and operationally. Similar to many other sectors, decentralisation was introduced as a sticking plaster to patch up the wounds in the education system. One method of decentralisation was the transfer of authority for planning, financial management and implementation to the school level (AusAID 2011: 2–9; Winkler and Gershberg 2003: 13–4).

Along with the move to transfer responsibility and authority to schools, it was suggested that decision making within the schools should not rest solely with the principals and teachers, but that parents and community representatives should participate in decision-making processes. Gradually, School Management Committees (SMC) became popular administrative tools – often compulsory – as effective means of administrative and financial decentralisation and community participation. Naturally, the establishment of SMCs and their efficacy attracted much attention from international experts and scholars on educational development.

Shibuya (Chapter 7) sought to identify the root causes of success or failure of SMCs in the relationships among local participants, who had interacted with each other since before the establishment of SMCs. Based on two basic public schools (schools A and B) in Akatsi South district, Ghana, Shibuya investigated how school communities managed conflicts concerning pupil discipline, against the backdrop of the legitimacy of traditional chiefs, headteachers' working attitudes and the school's financial management. This study revealed that although both schools were socioeconomically vulnerable, they experienced different levels of conviviality, which the author defined as the art of managing conflicts through interdependent relationships among those participating in the school management. School A was able to promote pupil discipline through dialogue between the school-level stakeholders: they bridged the gaps in opinion surrounding pupil discipline and adjusted the obligations between the school and the school community, teachers and parents. Conversely, school B could not establish a space for dialogue to discuss pupil discipline because the local community had a dispute over the legitimacy of the chief. Therefore, it can be seen that the availability of conviviality determines how conflicts that occur in school communities are managed. To date, most studies of educational development have accepted SMCs as given institutions and have examined their functions without considering each locality. In contrast, this chapter is unique in that it aimed to capture how SMCs are embedded in the dynamic socio-political relationships among the local participants.

The increase in schools also led to the rapid expansion of low-cost private schools in poor communities. Contrary to popular assumptions that private schools are expensive and exclusive, private schools in developing countries often have very low fees. Analysts suggested that this is caused by high levels of dissatisfaction with the quality of education available in public schools (Heynemann and Stern 2014). It is widely believed that, as the number of public schools increased, the quality of education they provided deteriorated. Parental interest in their children's education has increased, partly because of the mass campaign for universal education. However, they remain dissatisfied with the public schools for many reasons. In this context, the chapters by Ohba (Chapter 8) and Sawamura (Chapter 9) both look at low-cost private schools (i.e., unrecognised private schools) in an urban slum in Nairobi, Kenya, and unravel the local politics surrounding the schools.

According to Ohba, community schools in the West have often been discussed in relation to school choice, and are considered as complementary to formal schools. In contrast, the role of unrecognised private schools in Africa, which are a type of community school, is much broader than that of a learning institution. As primary schooling has become more widespread across Africa, unrecognised private schools in urban slums have also been the focus of attention. Accordingly, Ohba explored how frontier urban community schools functioned in their wide-ranging role, based on data collected in the Mathare slum in the capital of Kenya, Nairobi, where the inhabitants originated from different parts of the country. Ohba visited 20 schools to understand what they offered to meet the needs of the local children. The findings indicated that these schools functioned not only as learning institutions but also as places of shelter and sources of food and clothes for poor and vulnerable children. The study also revealed that those schools had established a network to negotiate with the government for formal registration. The author argued that a growing number of community schools provided support for those who are in need, in the form of the tools required for conviviality, in the context of cosmopolitan urban slums. As society became more diverse due to globalisation, migration and urbanisation, the ill-constructed and poorly-performing community schools accommodated the various needs of vulnerable children, other than learning. She argues that without these schools, the contemporary education system would have further increased socioeconomic inequality.

Similar to Ohba, Sawamura focused on the capabilities of local urban communities in relation to providing educational support. His study was aimed at rethinking the relationship between international aid and self-help initiatives undertaken by the local population. Sawamura based his research on two unrecognised, low-fee private schools located in the Kibera slum of Nairobi, Kenya. The study showed that the schools in the slums were often established under initiatives driven by the local people. Managing the schools in this way enabled the poorest members of the community to access education. In other words, those schools served as platforms for local people to help one another and contribute to the development of their communities. As the teachers lived in the same community as the students, they felt a strong sense of duty that strengthened their motivation to work. Therefore, the school trustees and teachers often worked for the welfare of the people they served rather than for the salaries they received. The key to understanding the unique operation of these schools lies in the concept of conviviality. That is to say, sustainability and interdependence in a convivial society appear to be different from those values seen in an aid-linked society. Today, increased access to the internet makes it possible for individuals to form long-lasting relationships and mutual trust across international borders. Therefore, according to Sawamura, human connections rather than institutional ties may enable conviviality to become the mainstream principle for international development and cooperation in the future.

As described above, Ohba, Sawamura, and Shibuya all highlighted the local relationships among participants. Their interests converged in the concept of conviviality as the force that compensated for the weaknesses of the existing system. The education system tends to be top-down that is often insensitive to the context of the local population. In one way, the concept of conviviality revitalises interests in a collective orientation that is assumed to be rooted in African tradition and shared across different African societies. The attraction of this concept of conviviality appeals not only to Africanist scholars but also to those interested in other issues, such as new leadership styles or human coexistence with robots. This suggests that disillusionment with bureaucracy or the tightly-controlled system that originated from the West will lead to the desire for a less organised but more dynamic explanation of the human world.

## 5. Knowledge Acquisition as a Subjective Process

Last, we recognise that knowledge formation is a subjective process. Education scholars tend to see teaching and learning as inseparable, like two sides of a coin. While *teachers* have intentions and plans, which they implement in the process of education, *learners* construct their knowledge according to their subjective motivation.

Therefore, mutual coordination between teachers and learners is necessary for both the teaching and learning processes. Here we use the word 'teacher' in a much broader sense than solely signifying those who are licensed and practise their vocation in an established school. We consider master craftsmen or elders as equally important facilitators of knowledge construction from whom young people learn about production skills or how to become mature members of society.

There exist different conceptions about learning among educationalists, which naturally result in different ideas about the role of teachers, the character of learners and the meaning of the teaching and learning processes. If it is believed that there are truths that are legitimised by the authorities or by a supernatural presence, like a god, then the process of learning is simply to absorb these legitimate truths. In this case, the role of the teacher is to convey these truths effectively and accurately to the obedient learners. Since the collective truths are exogenously determined, the learning process is treated as a functional procedure, and learning becomes a task to be performed by the learners (Saeki 1975: 24). Against such a functionalist perspective of education, there are those who promote constructivism. Constructivism considers that learning is a subjective process in which the learners garner information from their environment and construct their own knowledge set. In this sense, the self-motivation of the learners and their interactions with their environment and teachers are the keys to education. Since there is no standardised process or set knowledge to be learned, the role of teachers is to facilitate this process rather than to transmit pre-packaged knowledge effectively. There are some variations within this constructivist set of beliefs. For example, existentialists highlight the inherent nature of human beings to want to learn (Kauka 2018). Meanwhile, experientialists emphasise the experiences through which learners acquire knowledge (Dewey 1929).

The conventional school curriculum is typically based on the functionalist assumption, particularly the core subjects such as mathematics or science. However, learning is a process of both subjective construction of knowledge and socialisation. Learners pick up information that interests them from the surrounding world and that connects with their existing knowledge. In the process of reacting to new stimuli and assimilation with their existing cognitive schema, learners increase their range of responsibility toward the people and environment that surround them, making them part of society (Takada 2020). In this sense, subjectivity and socialisation are inseparable constructs of learning for human beings in their living context. Therefore, it is reasonable that several chapters in this volume are aimed at incorporating into education the demands related to socialisation that have been cultivated historically and culturally in that society. Accordingly, several authors stress the limitations of the functionalist perspective of education, which considers that legitimate knowledge should be transmitted with minimum variations.

To consider this type of standardised curriculum fully, Nakawa (Chapter 10) explored the potential of mathematics education, based on observations of various types of play among children in a community at Mazabuka in the Southern Province of Zambia. Through observing and participating in the children's play activities, Nakawa identified 17 types of play. Among these, 15 types of play were further analysed with reference to the five types of universal activity in mathematics: counting, locating, measuring, designing and explaining. The analysis demonstrated that the play activities of these children contained an inherent sense of mathematics. Furthermore, Nakawa advocated the following points. First, children's play that involves hand clapping and the singing of songs is very complicated and facilitates children thinking and acting logically. This can be associated with them beginning to learn mathematics in school. She suggested that the primary curriculum for mathematics was developed with an emphasis on this type of play activity. Second, female children often engage in play that involves physical movement. They are capable of handling complicated rhythms and dealing with three-dimensional space. This could help children to grasp the fundamental notions of space if they are appropriately incorporated into primary school mathematics. Nakawa's results and suggestions allow us to conceive a unique type of mathematics education that develops different features from those required of a Eurocentric curriculum. It is an ambitious endeavour to establish an ethnomathematics curriculum that is based on culturally distinctive children's play.

Mosime (Chapter 11) introduces a unique pedagogical practice based on Botswana's traditional approach of building consensus. In contrast to Nakawa, who focused on the content of learning, Mosime sought alternative teaching methods, which would encourage diversity within unity. Alongside her colleagues, Mosime explored the possibility of the revival of Mazrui's (1976) eclecticism in her course on 'African Social Thought' in the Department of Sociology at the University of Botswana. She proposed to adopt *morero*, Botswana's indigenous consensus-building process, as a possible methodology for unlocking African Potentials for addressing global issues. According to Mosime, premising consensus as the starting point toward meaningful and mutually constructive social interaction, *morero* has facilitated diverse ethnic groups in Botswana, mutually and continuously, to redefine the rituals around the rites of passage in ways that eclectically combine elements of each culture, to achieve both horizontal and vertical cultural integration. The same process has been adapted into Botswana's governance. Mosime's efforts to balance conventional lecture-based higher education with a traditional African approach further develop Mazrui's (1976) eclecticism and unlock the African Potentials in ways that do not romanticise, dismiss or threaten the integrity of local knowledge. Mosime claims that the very act of writing the chapter is eclectic because the topic shifts between disparate notions of pedagogy and *morero* to fill the incompleteness, which is the condition of the African Potentials.

In summary, this volume sheds light on the fact that education and knowledge are fundamentally intertwined with political, social, economic and cultural issues in African societies. Although it is beyond the means of each author to cover the relevant topics exhaustively, the entire volume will map out the issues related to education at different levels, from macro-continental to the national education system, schools and local communities. Illich (1973: 21)

18

envisioned a convivial society that would expand the range of human abilities, management and initiatives, in contrast to societies that alienate humans through modernisation. The rich ethnographic materials presented in this volume suggest that education and knowledge acquisition that is sustained through a sense of the 'mutuality of being' (Sahlins 2013: iv) can work as tools for conviviality to regain a sense of the solid reality of life, even under the turmoil created by rapid institutional and environmental changes that confront African societies. The tools for conviviality facilitate negotiations between the incompleteness of the past and the present in the interest of the future (Nyamnjoh 2017: 267), which is where African Potentials lies.

**Endnotes**

[1] For example, the #RhodesMustFall movement which arose in 2015 at the University of Cape Town in South Africa referred to the statue, on campus, of Cecil Rhodes, the British politician and imperialist, as the symbol of institutional racism.

**Acknowledgements**

This work was supported by JSPS KAKENHI Grant Number JP16H06318.

**References**

Anderson, B. (1983) *Imagined Communities: Reflections on the Origin and Spread of Nationalism*, London: Verso.

Appiah, K. A. (1992) *In My Father's House: Africa in the Philosophy of Culture*, New York: Oxford University Press.

AusAID (2011) *Current Issues in Education: School Grants and School-Based Management*, Canberra: AusAID.

Bourdieu, P. (1984) *Distinction: A Social Critique of the Judgement of Taste*, translated by R. Nice, London: Routledge & Kegan Paul.

Dewey, J. (1929) 'My Pedagogical Creed', *Journal of National Education Association*, Vol. 18, No. 9, pp. 291–5.

Heynemann, S. and Stern, J. M. B. (2014) 'Low cost private schools for the poor: What public policy is appropriate?', *International Journal of Educational Development*, Vol. 35, pp. 3–15.

Illich, I. (1971) *Deschooling Society*, New York: Harper & Row.

———— (1973) *Tools for Conviviality*, New York: Harper & Row.

Jackson, P. W. (1968) *Life in Classrooms*, New York: Holt, Rinehart and Winston.

Kauka, E. O. (2018) 'An analysis of the nexus of existentialism in education', *International Journal of Research and Innovation in Social Science*, Vol. 2, No. 12, pp. 228–32.

Lave, J. and Wenger, E. (1991) *Situated Learning: Legitimate Peripheral Participation*, Cambridge: Cambridge University Press.

Mazrui, A. (1976) 'Eclecticism as an ideological alternative: An African perspective', *Alternatives*, Vol. 1, No. 4, pp. 465–86.

Ngugi, wa Thiong'o (1986) *Decolonising the Mind: The Politics of Language in African Literature*, London: James Currey, Heinemann.

Nyamnjoh, F. (2017) 'Incompleteness: Frontier Africa and the currency of conviviality', *Journal of Asian and African Studies*, Vol. 52, Issue 3, pp. 253–70.

Oxford Dictionary (2013) *Oxford English Dictionary*, Oxford: Oxford University Press.

Saeki, Y. (1975) *The Structure of 'Learning'*, Tokyo: Toyokan Shuppan (in Japanese).

Sahlins, M. (2013) *What Kinship Is - and Is Not*, Chicago: The University of Chicago Press.

Takada, A. (2020) *The Ecology of Playful Childhood: Caregiver-Child Interactions among the San of Southern Africa*, Cham: Palgrave Macmillan.

Winkler, D. R. and Gershberg, A. I. (2003) *Education Decentralisation in Africa: A Review of Recent Policy and Practice*, unpublished manuscript.

Yamada, S. (2005) 'Educational finance and poverty reduction: The cases of Tanzania, Kenya, and Ethiopia', *GRIPS Development Forum*

*Discussion Paper Series*, No. 8, pp. 1–26.

————— (2018) *'Dignity of Labour' for African Leaders: The Formation of Education Policy in the British Colonial Office and Achimota School on the Gold Coast*, Bamenda: Langaa RPCIG.

# Part I

# Education as a Mode of

# Transmitting Values

# Chapter 1

## Knowledge and Views of Tanzanian Youth Regarding *Ujamaa*: A Case Study of Students at the University of Dar es Salaam

*Machiko Tsubura*

## 1. Introduction

In Tanzania, *ujamaa* (meaning 'familyhood' in Swahili) – a socialist ideology introduced by the first president Julius Nyerere – was central to education policies and practices during the socialist period between 1967 and the mid-1980s. President Nyerere considered education a means of disseminating the *ujamaa* philosophy and practices in building the newly independent country. After Nyerere retired from the presidency in 1985, the country shifted to a liberal economy and a multi-party democracy in the mid-1980s and early 1990s. Consequently, new education policies and school curricula were introduced, and many topics pertaining to *ujamaa* were omitted from the education provided in schools. However, as Fouéré (2014) has argued, the moral principles advocated by *ujamaa* appear to have re-emerged in Tanzanian society amidst growing economic inequality, threats to national cohesion and political corruption since the 2000s. This has undoubtedly shaped the perspectives of ordinary Tanzanians, including the young people who were born after the socialist period. The proportion of young people in Tanzania's population has remained high owing to the sustained high fertility rate,[1] and they contribute significantly to the country's politics, economy and society. Against this backdrop, the present study examines how young Tanzanians who have no lived experiences of the socialist period have acquired knowledge of *ujamaa* and how they perceive it in relation to the country's current political and socioeconomic situation. This study was aimed at deepening our understanding of the influence of school education on the formation of Tanzanians' ideological knowledge and views, which underpin the country's political and social structure today.

The study is focused on students at the University of Dar es Salaam (UDSM), the oldest and largest public university in Tanzania, with a particular interest in the influence of school education on the views of young people and whether and how school education has shaped their knowledge and views of *ujamaa*. Students at UDSM were selected as samples for the study on the assumption that they would have relatively sound knowledge obtained from formal schooling and that their political thinking would have been developed under the significant influence of school education.

The present study is guided by the idea of 'conviviality' (Nyamnjoh 2017), which values the recognition of the incompleteness of reality in scholarship. Thus, the study posits that people's ideological views may constantly be in flux and ambiguous and cannot necessarily be categorised into existing ideologies, such as capitalism, liberalism, socialism or, even, Tanzania's *ujamaa*. Furthermore, the study is based on the expectation that the knowledge and views of individual students at the UDSM regarding *ujamaa* may be incorrect, incoherent or contradictory. Owing to the present study's exploratory nature, it employs a qualitative research methodology, and its analysis is based on (1) secondary sources (i.e., academic literature, newspapers, textbooks); (2) interviews with four academics at UDSM specialising in *ujamaa* or education in November 2019; and (3) group interviews or focus group discussions with 39 undergraduate and postgraduate students at UDSM in November 2019 (See Appendices for the list of interviewees and the guiding questions for interviews with students at UDSM; see Appendix A for the differences between group interviews and focus group discussions). The present study suggests that, while the knowledge of *ujamaa* that students at UDSM have acquired from textbooks is limited in comparison to that contained in textbooks used during the socialist period, they have had opportunities to learn about *ujamaa* from school activities, their families, communities and various media. Due to the limited coverage of *ujamaa* in school textbooks, variation characterises Tanzanian youth's knowledge and perception of *ujamaa* and, more broadly, their ideological views, depending on their personal backgrounds, experiences and interests. Nevertheless, for educated young people in Tanzania, *ujamaa* is not merely a factor of their historical past but a reference point for reflection on the characteristics of contemporary Tanzania.

This chapter is organised into five sections. Following the introductory section, the second section reviews the literature on socialism in sub-Saharan Africa (hereinafter Africa); the third summarises the historical background of Tanzania with a focus on President Nyerere and his socialist ideology, *ujamaa*, education on *ujamaa* and the University of Dar es Salaam (UDSM).[2] The fourth section explores the knowledge and views of students at UDSM regarding *ujamaa* based on interviews with Tanzanian academics specialising in *ujamaa* and education and with students at UDSM, along with an examination of some secondary school civics textbooks. The chapter concludes by summarising the study's findings.

## 2. Evolution of Socialism in Africa

Political ideologies in Africa have been shaped by complex interactions between indigenous cultures and regional, continental and global influences (Hendrickson and Zaki 2013). Following the attainment of independence from colonial rule in the late 1950s and 1960s, African leaders pursued nationalism, a broad and inclusive ideology that contained more narrowly defined ideologies, such as African socialism, African populism and African Marxism (Martin 2012: 2; Thomson 2016: 36–7). Socialism was a dominant ideology in many post-independent African countries; no fewer than 35 of 53 countries in the region adopted socialist policies between the 1950s and the 1980s, albeit with varying interpretations of and adherence to socialism (Pitcher and Askew 2006: 1–2).

Rather than adopting the socialism prescribed by the Soviet Union, African leaders developed their own versions of socialism by emphasising traditional values in their countries. On the premise that Africans had lived in classless and egalitarian communities prior to colonial rule, African socialism sought to recover traditional values in combination with modern production methods and state institutions.

27

The state played a central role politically and economically in the achievement of socialist goals. The private sector was largely nationalised, agricultural products were bought by marketing boards and international trade was controlled by governments. Most African countries, including Tanzania, adopted one-party systems to build national unity rather than encouraging political competition through multi-party systems. However, many socialist experiments in the region failed for various reasons, including the influence of the international economy and governments' inability to mobilise rural populations (Thomson 2016: 38–9).

Despite the ideological transitions in most African countries in the 1980s and 1990s, the extant literature broadly suggests that Africans today have mixed or unclear ideological orientations (Wiafe-Amoako 2016). This is partly attributable to their past experiences of socialism. For example, Pitcher and Askew (2006: 11) demonstrate that Africans and their governments have been influenced by the legacies of socialism in reflecting on their pasts and contemporary lives. Consequently, 'postsocialist transition in Africa has produced novel re-combinations of the old (socialism) with the new (neo-liberalism)' (Pitcher and Askew 2006: 11). By analysing the Afrobarometer survey data, Conroy-Krutz and Lewis (2011) demonstrate that neither political parties nor citizens in Africa have clearly coherent ideological views. Rather, they find that the median attitudes of major African political parties cannot be distinguished from one another in terms of their views on the role of the state in the economy or support for democratic norms. Similar results are found for the views of African citizens in their analysis. The findings are consistent across subgroups divided by sex, partisanship, education, media access, urban-rural settings, political knowledge and political interests. Conroy-Krutz and Lewis (2011: 25) argue that this finding contradicts studies on advanced democracies that suggest that the better educated tend to have more coherent attitudes.

In fact, incoherent ideological views may be characteristic not only of Africans but also of the global population. Freeden (2019), a leading scholar in the field of political ideologies, points to the ongoing realignment of the characteristics of various ideologies. He states that ideologies tend to be studied today as immediate responses

28

to recent political and ideological crises (e.g., populism, the far right) and that a 'fixed ideological structure, displaying a high degree of internal coherence and systematisation, is vanishing' (Freeden 2019: 7). He then suggests that 'the newer modes of delivering ideology are far more elusive to observe and discern' (Freeden 2019: 7). Drawing on these studies, highlighting mixed or incoherent ideological views of people in Africa and worldwide, the present study explores ideological views of some of Tanzania's educated youth with a focus on *ujamaa*.

## 3. History of *Ujamaa*, Education and the University of Dar es Salaam (UDSM) in Tanzania

Tanzania is among the African countries in which government policies, including those in education, have been significantly affected by ideological transitions. The first part of this section reviews the history of the *ujamaa* philosophy and policies developed by President Nyerere, and the re-emergence of *ujamaa* as a set of moral principles in society during the post-socialist period. The second part summarises the history of education on *ujamaa* and the role played by UDSM in it.

### 3-1. President Julius Nyerere and Ujamaa

Following Tanganyika's liberation from British colonial rule in 1961, the United Republic of Tanzania was formed by the merger between Tanganyika and the islands of Zanzibar in 1964. Tanzanian society is diverse, including over 120 ethnic groups, as well as Asians and Arabs, who practise Islam, Christianity or adhere to traditional beliefs. Therefore, after independence, the initial task facing President Nyerere and the ruling party – the Tanganyika African Nationalist Union (TANU), later *Chama Cha Mapinduzi* ('Party of Revolution'; CCM) – was to build a nation by enhancing unity among Tanzanians. Nyerere viewed capitalism as an inappropriate ideology for generating economic development. Neither did he believe that Soviet-style socialism based on class struggle would be suitable for Tanzania's development. Instead, he developed his own socialist ideology, *ujamaa* ('familyhood'), based on the traditional society that had existed in Tanzania before colonial rule (Thomson 2016: 49–51). With the idea that 'all able-bodied men and women, regardless of race or ethnicity, were conceived to be members of the same extended family' (Melchiorre 2020: 638), *ujamaa* was aimed at achieving 'common ownership and production as well as equal distribution of goods among people of common descent' (Hyden 1975: 54).

President Nyerere announced the Arusha Declaration, which provided an overall framework for *ujamaa* policies, along with the leadership code in 1967 and the party guidelines, called *Mwongozo*, for TANU in 1971. The leadership code and *Mwongozo* were aimed at controlling the behaviour of political leaders; they were advised to be peasants or workers, and any association with capitalist practices – such as holding shares or directorships in private companies, receiving multiple salaries and renting houses to others – was strictly prohibited (Hyden 1980: 156–60; Shivji 1976: 126; Yeager 1989: 73). President Nyerere also adopted a one-party system and ensured that TANU would establish its dominance in the country (Tripp 1992: 229; Hirschler 2006: 3). His government then formulated domestic and foreign policies and nationalised economic sectors, collectivised agriculture and promoted South Africa's liberation from apartheid (Ibhawoh and Dibua 2003; Hendrickson and Zaki 2013: 616; Thomson 2016: 49–51).

Nyerere's emphasis on the importance of rural development in achieving socialist goals was materialised in his policy of building *ujamaa* villages across Tanzania (Lal 2015). It was a resettlement scheme that employed capital-intensive techniques, including concentrating resources in selected areas in the fertile part of the country (Okoko 1987: 89–90). Agricultural production was expected to thrive in *ujamaa* villages through the collective cultivation of common land that would provide both subsistence for the villagers and a surplus. Furthermore, the vision of *ujamaa* villages extended beyond mere communal production: it was a style of living that offered 'a cooperative and imaginary way of putting a community's resources, skills, and enthusiasm at the service of the development of all of its members' (Schneider 2004: 349). While some voluntarily moved to *ujamaa* villages by supporting socialist ideas, others sought benefits provided to the villages, such as tax exemption, access to schools and clinics and subsidised seeds and fertilisers. During the programme's later stages, reluctant peasants were moved coercively to *ujamaa* villages. By 1975, most of Tanzania's rural population had resettled in approximately 7,000 villages across the country (Schneider 2004: 345; Thomson 2016: 52–3).

Despite the massive investments in rural areas, Tanzania failed to expand its national economy through *ujamaa* policies and villagisation, which led to the government's liberalisation of economic policies by accepting a structural adjustment programme devised by the International Monetary Fund (Gibbon 1995). Hyden (1980) attributes villagisation's failure to the government's inability to 'capture' the peasantry. Tanzanian peasants did not adopt modern agricultural production methods or the custom of collectively farming communal land. Rather, their first priority was to farm their individual plots using their own methods to ensure their subsistence, while collective farming comprised supplementary activities aimed at generating additional income (Thomson 2016: 53–4). More fundamentally, Nyerere's perception of the traditional egalitarian society that had existed in pre-colonial Tanzania was inaccurate; in reality, many of the diverse forms of society in the country were not necessarily egalitarian (Spalding 1996; Edwards 1998: 41).

Although an ideological shift occurred in political and economic policies in the 1980s and 1990s, Tanzania's government did not officially abandon the *ujamaa* philosophy. Socialism and self-reliance have remained in Tanzania's Constitution as guiding principles for the socioeconomic activities of the country (United Republic of Tanzania 2005; *The Citizen* 2015). Makulilo (2012: 8171) thus questions the constitutionality of the government's current liberal policies, which appear to contradict the Constitution. At least, the country's official ideological direction seems to be inconsistent across different public domains today.

In tandem with *ujamaa*'s continuity in the Constitution, Fouéré (2014: 2) points out that a modified version of *ujamaa* has re-emerged in Tanzania since the 2000s as a set of moral principles in a society 'characterised by increasing concerns about economic inequality, threats to national cohesion, and the high visibility of corruption in the political sphere' (Fouéré 2014: 2). However, Fouéré (2014) and other scholars suggest that the re-emergence of *ujamaa* does not necessarily suggest the return of a socialist ideology to the country. For example, Askew (2006) examines the popular songs composed in commemoration of Nyerere immediately after his death in 1999, 14 years after he resigned from the presidency, and finds that the term *ujamaa* or his socialist policies were rarely mentioned in the songs, while other aspects of his philosophy, such as peace, unity, solidarity and the elimination of tribalism and religious divisiveness, were frequently invoked. Thus, the moral principles promoted by Nyerere have been disconnected from the historical experience of socialism in the country (Askew 2006). The lack of a socialist dimension to the return of *ujamaa* in contemporary Tanzania seems to be in accordance with the inconsistent political attitudes among Africans identified by Conroy-Krutz and Lewis (2011), as noted in Section 2. These studies of ideologies and socialism in Africa in general and Tanzania today indicate that students at UDSM might also value moral principles advocated by *ujamaa* while neglecting its socialist dimension.

### 3-2. Education on Ujamaa and UDSM

In Tanzania, education was critical in the implementation of *ujamaa,* and UDSM played a central role during the socialist period. President Nyerere was particularly keen on using education to mobilise citizens toward socialist goals and objectives (Cliffe 1973; Okoko 1987: 41–2). During the colonial period, few Africans received formal schooling in Tanzania, while most received only one or two years of basic education, such as reading, writing and arithmetic. Post-elementary education consisted mainly of manual vocational training, such as carpentry, road construction and farming. After independence, the school system was integrated to eliminate racial barriers and incorporate all children (Mbilinyi 1979: 98–9). Soon after the proclamation of the Arusha Declaration in 1967, Nyerere issued a policy statement called Education for Self-Reliance (ESR) to ensure that educational institutions would support the socialist ideology (Mbilinyi 1979: 101).

Under the ESR policy, several education reforms were undertaken by the government. In 1968, the subject of *siasa* ('politics'), or political education, replaced civics in the curriculum at all levels of the education system to teach students *ujamaa* philosophy and practices (Mbilinyi 1979: 105; Mmari 1979: 120; United Republic of Tanzania 2011: 13, 29–30). *Siasa* was aimed at developing students' political consciousness so that they would understand and facilitate the implementation of the government's policy of socialism and self-reliance (Komba 1996: 109). The Education Act of 1969 nationalised all schools that were formerly run by voluntary organisations, and the Ministry of National Education came to manage schools, including the recruitment of teachers and control over curricula (Mbilinyi 1979: 101).

Tanzania's education sector under the ESR policy was characterised by its emphasis on equality in education. In 1974, TANU's national leaders met in Musoma and issued a directive, known as the Musoma Resolution, to accelerate the ESR's implementation, which led to the expansion of the number of primary schools across the country in a bid to achieve Universal Primary Education by 1977 (Siwale and Sefu 1977: 52). In the mid-1970s, the quota system for secondary schools was introduced to establish equality in education by mitigating regional and gender disparities in the number of students entering secondary schools. Under the quota system, diverse students were selected from various regional groups to attend secondary schools according to certain selection procedures for different districts and regions and for girls and boys. The quota system was abolished by the government in the late 1980s (Puja 2008: 98–102).

The philosophy of ESR was also founded on the idea that education must be directly related to the particular societies in which students lived. Thus, practical skills related to their livelihoods were emphasised in school education. For example, the subject of agriculture was introduced to the primary school curriculum, and each school had a farm and/or workshop to integrate school activities into those of the communities in which the schools were located. Furthermore, one-year national service for secondary school graduates was introduced by the Musoma Resolution in 1974; after national service, graduates were required to work before they would be admitted to any post-secondary education (Siwale and Sefu 1977: 37–52; Biswalo 1985: 75).

When the *ujamaa* period ended in the mid-1980s, major changes were made to school systems and curricula. *Siasa* was renamed 'civics', and several topics, including the history of TANU/CCM, the Arusha Declaration and socialism in other parts of the world, were omitted from the subject (Komba 1996: 114–5; United Republic of Tanzania 2011: 14). The content of the civics curriculum does not appear to have been standardised, and the subject was taught in an uncoordinated manner until the 2000s (United Republic of Tanzania 2011). The knowledge and views of *ujamaa* among young Tanzanians today are likely to have been influenced by the subject's transition from *siasa* to civics (Chachage 2017).

During the socialist period, UDSM occupied a unique position as an interface between politics and education (see, for example, Melchiorre 2020). While Tanzania's socialism was advanced centrally by President Nyerere and TANU (and later CCM), lively intellectual debates on *ujamaa* and other socialist ideologies were held among Tanzanian and foreign scholars at UDSM in the 1960s and 1970s. UDSM was established in 1961 as a college of the University of London, becoming a constituent college of the University of East Africa in 1963 and an independent national university in 1970. It was closely related to TANU/CCM and the country's ideology during the 1970s. The party made strong efforts to control the university by, for example, offering its headquarters for use by the university college until 1964, when it moved to the campus in the northwest of Dar es Salaam. A former executive secretary of TANU/CCM was appointed to the position of Vice-Chancellor of UDSM in the 1970s. Mandatory courses in development studies were introduced to students of all disciplines to instil TANU's ideology in them in 1969 (McCormick 1980: 171) (or in 1971 according to Burton 2020: 216). Initially, the university was relatively free to determine admission conditions, course content and methods of assessment. For example, admission was mainly based on students' performance at advanced level. Yet, as noted earlier, since the Musoma Resolution in 1974, eligibility for higher education came to be limited to those who had completed one-year compulsory national service and had work

34

experience for two years or more with recommendations from their employers and TANU (Mkude, Cooksey and Levey 2003: 1–2). However, UDSM provided a relatively open forum for debate on *ujamaa* and other socialist ideologies and became a hub of intellectuals in the 1960s and 1970s (Shivji 1993).

UDSM has maintained its strong linkages with Nyerere and *ujamaa* to the present day. For example, in 2008, the position of Julius Nyerere Chair in Pan-African Studies, popularly known as *Kigoda* (meaning 'small three-legged stool'), was created at UDSM to restore the university as a centre of public debate (Sabatho 2015). Since then, UDSM has annually organised the Mwalimu Julius Nyerere Intellectual Festival, chaired by the Julius Nyerere Chair in Pan-African Studies (Mwanziva 2016). Additionally, Issa Shivji, former law professor at UDSM and the first Julius Nyerere Chair in Pan-African Studies, and two current and former prominent academics at UDSM thoroughly researched Nyerere's life and published a series of his comprehensive biography in 2020 (Yahya-Othman, Kamata and Shivji 2020). Materials collected for their research were archived at the newly established Nyerere Resource Centre, which organised various events commemorating Nyerere, including a photography exhibition, public lectures and a round-table discussion in 2015 (Shivji 2016). Thus, Shivji and other senior academics at UDSM have been central to the maintenance and revival of the debates on *ujamaa*.

In addition to academics, student activism at UDSM has closely been associated with the rise and fall of *ujamaa*. While Melchiorre (2020) demonstrates how TANU/CCM institutionalised its control over the organisation of leftist students during the 1970s and 1980s, Provini (2014) highlights the legacy of socialism in student protests against the government's neo-liberal education policies at UDSM in the 1990s and 2000s, particularly in response to the government's cost-sharing policy. A combination of the re-emergence of moral principles advocated by *ujamaa* in society since the 2000s and UDSM's historical linkages with *ujamaa* have created a unique environment in which its students can learn about and reflect on *ujamaa* today, as discussed in the section that follows.

## 4. Knowledge and Views of Students at UDSM Regarding *Ujamaa*

According to interviews with academics and students at UDSM held in November 2019, the knowledge and views of *ujamaa* that students at UDSM have gained and developed have been shaped by both school education and their experiences outside school. Thus, this section begins with an overview of how they have learned about *ujamaa*, first from formal school education and secondly from their experiences outside school. This is followed by an analysis of their views on *ujamaa* in relation to the current political and socioeconomic conditions in Tanzania today.

### 4-1. *Students' Knowledge of* Ujamaa

Since the early 1960s, the education system in Tanzania has been based on a 7-4-2-3 system, consisting of seven years of primary school (from Standard One to Seven); four years of secondary school, or Ordinary Level (from Form One to Form Four); two years of high school, or Advanced Level (from Form Five to Form Six); and three to four years of college (Athuman 2018: 246; Asante Sana for Education 2014). While the knowledge of *ujamaa* that students at UDSM have acquired from textbooks is generally limited,[3] interviews with students at UDSM suggest that it varies depending on their majors, experiences and interests. Overall, the interviews suggest that they learned about *ujamaa* from one or some of the following subjects and activities in school: vocational skills in primary school, history and civics in secondary schools, general studies in high schools, and development perspectives and other undergraduate courses at university. Only two out of 39 students in the interviews said that they had never learned about *ujamaa* in school.[4]

As noted in Section 3-2, political education was central to introducing students to *ujamaa* philosophy and practices during the socialist period. In contrast, Nyerere and *ujamaa* are only briefly mentioned in the civics textbooks used in secondary schools today. For example, among the *Civics for Secondary Schools* textbooks for Form One to Form Four published by the Oxford University Press Tanzania, a major multinational publishing company in Tanzania

(Languille 2015: 82), *ujamaa* is mentioned only once, without any explanation of the concept, under the topic of the structure of Tanzania's Constitution in the section entitled 'Government' in the textbook for Form Two (Abeid and Olotu 2009: 10). The Arusha Declaration is briefly mentioned as part of Tanzania's history in the section entitled 'Poverty' in the textbook for Form Three (Nchimbi et al. 2012: 100). The Arusha Declaration and Tanzania's socialist economy are also briefly referred to in the Form Three civics textbook published by the Kenyan Longhorn Publishers (Nshimba and Sanya 2015: 87). Overall, *ujamaa* and the Arusha Declaration are only briefly mentioned either as part of the explanation on the Constitution or in relation to Tanzania's history, and civics textbooks for secondary school have little content on the subject. Furthermore, according to Emmanuel Mollel, who is an Assistant Lecturer in the School of Education at UDSM, while teachers in secondary and high schools have opportunities to receive training on teaching, they rarely receive training specifically on how to teach *ujamaa* today.[5]

Some students in the interviews pointed out that pupils attending primary schools run by the government and taught in Swahili tend to have more opportunities to learn about *ujamaa* and socialism than those attending private primary schools taught in English.[6] Yet, they also noted that there are no major differences in the opportunities to learn about *ujamaa* in secondary schools. At the level of high school, the extent to which students learn about *ujamaa* largely depends on their selection of majors and subjects; as anticipated, those who study history have more opportunities to gain knowledge of *ujamaa* and socialism in general.[7] One student added that high school graduates also learn about *ujamaa* from Tanzania's national service, which has a programme on the topic.[8]

Some students in the interviews recalled that they had learned about the moral principles advocated by the *ujamaa* philosophy (e.g., self-reliance, work ethic) practically through school activities. For example, students are assigned cooking, cleaning and farming as part of the vocational skills curriculum, known as *Stadi za Kazi* ('Study of Work'), in government primary schools.[9] As noted in Section 3.2, vocational skills originated in Tanzania's education policy that emphasised the importance of practical skills during the socialist period. The subject was created by merging five subjects – agriculture, music, arts and crafts, physical education and domestic science – as part of the education reforms of the mid-1980s (Athuman 2018: 248). Several of the students interviewed recalled experiences of cultivating plots of school farms in primary or secondary school.[10]

Although the number of students interviewed in this study is too small to generalise about the students at UDSM as a whole, students majoring in political science, economics, history or development studies generally demonstrated greater interest in *ujamaa* than those who majored in business-related subjects (i.e., business administration, human resource management). As mentioned in Section 3-2, all students, regardless of their majors, were required to take courses on development studies to learn about *ujamaa* at UDSM in the 1970s. The practice persists at the university up to the present, though the content of the courses was changed in the early 1990s by removing socialist slogans and adopting a more neutral stance on socialism as an alternative development strategy (Komba 1996: 18). Nonetheless, all first-year undergraduate students at UDSM take mandatory courses that cover *ujamaa*, entitled Development Perspectives I and II, offered by the Institute of Development Studies (Melchiorre 2020: 639; University of Dar es Salaam 2020).[11]

Additionally, postgraduate students in the interviews noted that they had learned about *ujamaa* in undergraduate courses in political science, economics, sociology and business administration at the university. For example, in one course in economics, Nyerere's development policies during the socialist period were assessed from various economic perspectives.[12] Generally, however, individual lecturers vary with respect to how much time they spend and the emphasis they place on teaching *ujamaa* in their classrooms at UDSM. Armstrong Matogwa, Assistant Lecturer at the Department of Sociology and Anthropology at UDSM, stated that some lecturers teach *ujamaa* as an aspect of Tanzania's history, while others teach it as an active idea or as part of the Tanzanian way of life.[13] Indeed, some faculty members at UDSM sympathise strongly with Nyerere and the *ujamaa* philosophy. Among them, staunch socialists, called *wajamaa* ('people of *ujamaa*'), embody *ujamaa* by living humble lives without wearing extravagant clothes, using mobile phones or driving private cars.[14] Furthermore, UDSM is a unique place where students have frequent opportunities to hear about *ujamaa* from, for example, public lectures organised as part of the annual Mwalimu Julius Nyerere Intellectual Festival, as mentioned in Section 3-2. Several students who demonstrated a good understanding of *ujamaa* expressed their views that *ujamaa* should be taught in greater depth in formal education so that Tanzanian youth may learn more from the country's experience of *ujamaa*.[15]

Students at UDSM also hear about or experience *ujamaa* in their daily lives. For example, mass media (i.e., television, radio) and social media have, for many, been the primary sources of information on *ujamaa* (for the media coverage of Nyerere and *ujamaa* in post-socialist Tanzania, see Fouéré 2014: 8, 2019).[16] Some students learned about *ujamaa* from their parents and relatives.[17] For example, one student, who said that he had never learned about *ujamaa* in school, heard from his parents about their experiences of having been relocated to a different village as part of villagisation.[18] Furthermore, another student mentioned that the practice whereby students share their space and belongings with other students in dormitories at secondary and high schools and universities (e.g., rooms, buckets for bathing, toothpaste) represents *ujamaa*. Another student added that he hears the word '*ujamaa*' from his friends; for example, when his friend came and took water from his room, the friend said, 'We are *ujamaa*'.[19] As such, *ujamaa* is not merely something from their historical past as taught to them in school; it is part of the language that they hear from the media and use in conversation with their families and friends.

### 4-2. Students' Views on Ujamaa

The UDSM students expressed various views on *ujamaa* in relation to the country's current political and socioeconomic situation in the group interviews. Most of the students and several scholars expressed the view that some aspects of *ujamaa* are still alive in Tanzania today, to varying degrees across the country.[20] Many students noted that people in rural areas still live communal lives by helping each other in cultivating their farms or raising livestock together, though they do not necessarily call their lifestyles *ujamaa*.

One student added that some people in rural areas still believe that Nyerere is alive and do not know about the political evolution in the country. By contrast, *ujamaa* is less evident in large cities such as Dar es Salaam. A student noted that some people in Dar es Salaam do not know who their neighbours are because their social interaction is different from that in rural areas.[21] Another student who majored in human resource management opined that *ujamaa* is not applicable to educated people.[22] However, some students also noted that mutual cooperation embodying *ujamaa* has not disappeared completely, even in large cities, particularly when social events are organised; people make voluntary contributions to weddings and funerals, regardless of their social status.[23]

Interestingly, in discussing how *ujamaa* might be revived in contemporary Tanzania during a focus group discussion among postgraduate students majoring in business administration, a student who claimed that she had never learned about *ujamaa* in school suggested that groups on WhatsApp – a popular free mobile messaging and calling service – might constitute a new form of *ujamaa*. Her suggestion was echoed by her fellow students, and they explained how widely they are connected with their friends through dozens of WhatsApp groups and the common use of them for mobilising financial contributions to social events such as weddings.[24] Given that the student mentioning WhatsApp groups as an example of modern *ujamaa* was the same student who had claimed that she had never learned about it in school, she might have conceptualised *ujamaa* simply as social connection rather than as a political ideology, based on the earlier discussion among her fellow students.

Several students referred to the stipulation of *ujamaa* in the Constitution, as noted in Section 3-1. While some mentioned it as an example of the relevance of *ujamaa* to contemporary Tanzania, others consider the reference to *ujamaa* in the Constitution to be problematic and incongruous with the reality of present-day Tanzania.[25] Some students mentioned the current government, stating that President John Magufuli is trying to industrialise Tanzania with the aim of making the country self-reliant and independent of foreign companies.[26] It is also noteworthy that, while many students observed that *ujamaa* contributed to unity among Tanzanians regardless of their ethnic or religious differences, several interviewees invoked *ujamaa* to describe certain religions or ethnic groups; for example, an undergraduate student mentioned that Muslims refer to the word *wajamaa* as people who share the same religious beliefs.[27] These interviews demonstrate the wide variation in what the term *ujamaa* means to UDSM students, ranging from the Constitution to their religious communities.

While none of the students interviewed reported that Tanzania is or should return to pure socialism, most think that *ujamaa* is important to the political and socioeconomic conditions of the country today. Many students argued that *ujamaa* should be partially implemented in Tanzania so that it could create a mixture of a socialist and capitalist economy.[28] A few of the students who demonstrated broad knowledge of the history of government policies of *ujamaa* specifically argued that the Tanzanian government should apply *ujamaa* to their management of natural resources and strengthen their control of it.[29] In contrast to the student who claimed that she had never learned about *ujamaa* in school and suggested WhatsApp groups as an example of modern *ujamaa*, these students' perspectives seem to have been informed by their knowledge of *ujamaa* obtained from school, including secondary and high schools and university. For example, one of the students who stated that the government should engage more with the management of natural resources was the postgraduate student in economics who had analysed Nyerere's development policies during the socialist period as part of her undergraduate studies at UDSM.

Interviews with several scholars further suggest that the ideological orientations of young people and, more broadly, all Tanzanians, should not be considered only from orthodox ideologies. Mbwana Mohamed Kitendo, a PhD Candidate at UDSM's Department of Political Science and Public Administration, pointed out that African countries have historically had mixed ideologies, indicating that it is natural for Tanzania to have several concurrent ideologies.[30] Thus, some students seemed to be comfortable discussing a mixture of socialist and capitalist economic policies for the country's development.

Only a few students majoring in business-related fields stated that *ujamaa* is irrelevant to Tanzania today. An undergraduate student majoring in human resource management noted that, although the idea of *ujamaa* is good, it is difficult in reality to compel wealthy people to share with others.[31] A postgraduate student majoring in business administration contended that *ujamaa* and other forms of socialism exist only in theory in Tanzania and worldwide, citing China as another example of having shifted from socialism to capitalism.[33] Even those interviewees who considered *ujamaa* irrelevant to contemporary Tanzania did not necessarily reject ideas of *ujamaa*, but they highlighted the reality as being far from the *ujamaa* philosophy.

## 5. Conclusion

The present study demonstrated that the knowledge and views regarding *ujamaa* that students at UDSM have gained and developed are shaped by both school education and their experiences outside school. The interviews with academics and students at UDSM suggested that they have various sources of information on *ujamaa*; while knowledge of *ujamaa* acquired from textbooks in schools is relatively limited, students at UDSM have had opportunities to learn about *ujamaa* from school activities, their families, communities and various media. The study also found that *ujamaa* is not merely an aspect of Tanzania's historical past, as taught in schools; it is part of the language heard in the media and used in daily conversations.

Without standardised formal education on *ujamaa*, the students' views on the relevance of *ujamaa* to Tanzania today are varied. Many students opined that Tanzania should pursue a mixture of socialist and capitalist economic policies. Thus, their ideological views cannot be categorised into orthodox ideologies, such as liberalism and socialism. This finding coincides with the notion that Africans, including Tanzanians, have incoherent ideological orientations or a novel recombination of socialism and neoliberalism, as discussed in the extant literature. Thus, the present study provides an interesting case for academic debate on political ideologies and conviviality. While the literature on political ideologies suggests that ideologies have become less cohesive and less systematised, the idea of conviviality helps us to understand the unconventional ideological views of Tanzanians as influenced by the *ujamaa* philosophy.

Despite the limited number of interviews undertaken by the present study, the results indicate that, while textbook content on *ujamaa* is relatively limited and the sources of information on *ujamaa* are varied today, students who have established their knowledge of the history of government policies based on *ujamaa* through their school education tended to appreciate the socialist dimension of *ujamaa* and expressed their views on the role of the government in the economy more clearly than others. Nonetheless, as Matogwa noted that *ujamaa* is still generally important for Tanzanians as a means of reflecting on themselves,[34] the interviews with scholars and students at UDSM demonstrate that the moral principles advocated by *ujamaa*, such as self-reliance and mutual cooperation, seem to have remained an important reference point for educated young people in Tanzania as they reflect on the characteristics of contemporary Tanzanians.

## Endnotes

[1] The proportion of young people in Tanzania's population did not change significantly between the 1980s and the 2010s. Approximately half of the population (50.1 per cent) were aged under 18 years and one-fifth (19.1 per cent) were aged between 15 and 24 years in 2012 (United Nations Association of Tanzania 2014).

[2] An earlier version of the literature review in the second and third sections was published as an IDE Discussion Paper (Tsubura 2019).

[3] Interview, Matogwa (2019).

[4] Interview, postgraduate students in Public Administration and Business Administration (2019).

[5] Interview, Mollel (2019).

[6] See Mushi (2009: 186–7) for the development of private primary schools in Tanzania.

[7] Interview, postgraduate students in Research and Public Policy, Economics and Public Administration (2019).

[8] Interview, an undergraduate student in International Development (2019). While the one-year compulsory national service was abolished in

1994 due to lack of funding, it was revived in 2013 for a six-month period (Success 2013).

[9] Interviews, Matogwa (2019), postgraduate students in Research and Public Policy and Public Administration, and undergraduate students in Linguistics (2019).

[10] Interviews, postgraduate students in Research and Public Policy and Public Administration and an undergraduate student in History (2019).

[11] Interviews, Matogwa (2019) and an undergraduate student in Linguistics (2019).

[12] Interviews, postgraduate students in Economics, Research and Public Policy and Business Administration, and Matogwa (2019).

[13] Interview, Matogwa (2019).

[14] Interviews, Matogwa (2019), Kitendo (2019) and undergraduate students in International Development (2019).

[15] Interviews, a postgraduate student in Economics and an undergraduate student in International Development (2019).

[16] Interviews, postgraduate students in Research and Public Policy and Public Administration, and an undergraduate student in History (2019).

[17] Interviews, undergraduate students in Sociology, Political Science and Public Administration and Human Resource Management (2019).

[18] Interview, a postgraduate student in Public Administration (2019).

[19] Interview, an undergraduate student in Political Science and Public Administration (2019).

[20] Interviews, Mollel (2019), Matogwa (2019), Kitendo (2019), postgraduate and undergraduate students in all the majors (2019).

[21] Interview, a postgraduate student in Business Administration (2019).

[22] Interview, an undergraduate student in Human Resource Management (2019).

[23] Interviews, undergraduate students in International Development (2019) and postgraduate students in Business Administration (2019).

[24] Interviews, postgraduate students in Business Administration (2019)

[25] Interviews, undergraduate students in International Development, Political Science and Public Administration, and Economics (2019).

[26] Interview, a postgraduate student in Research and Public Policy (2019).

[27] Interview, an undergraduate student in Sociology (2019).

[28] Interviews, a postgraduate student in Economics and undergraduate students in International Development, Political Science and Public

44

Administration and Human Resource Management (2019).

[29] Interview, a postgraduate student in Economics and an undergraduate student in International Development (2019).

[30] Interview, Kitendo (2019).

[31] Interview, an undergraduate student in Human Resource Management (2019).

[32] Interview, postgraduate student in Business Administration (2019).

[33] Interview, Matogwa (2019).

**Acknowledgements**

This work was supported by JSPS KAKENHI Grant Number JP16H06318. The author wishes to thank Charity Mapamba and Leiyo Singo for excellent research assistance and interviewees for their valuable contributions to the present study.

**References**

Abeid, R. S. and Olotu, S. R. (2009) *Civics for Secondary Schools: Form Two*, Dar es Salaam: Oxford University Press Tanzania.

Asante Sana for Education. (2014) 'Tanzania education system' (https://www.asantesanaforeducation.com/tanzania-education-system-) (accessed: 28 August 2020).

Askew, K. M. (2006) 'Sung and unsung: Musical reflections on Tanzanian postsocialisms', *Africa*, Vol. 76, Issue 1, pp. 15–43.

Athuman, J. J. (2018) 'Education programmes and curriculum reforms in Tanzania: A comparative review of education for Self Reliance and Poverty Reduction (PR) programmes', *International Journal of Science and Research*, Vol. 8, Issue 9, pp. 246–53.

Biswalo, P. M. (1985) 'A study of the impact of the Musoma Resolusion on student personnel services at the University of Dar es Salaam', *Utafiti*, Vol. 7, No. 2, pp. 75–81.

Burton, E. (2020) 'Engineering socialism: The faculty of engineering at the University of Dar es Salaam (Tanzania) in the 1970s and 1980s', in D. Matasci, M. B. Jerónimo and H. G. Dores (eds)

*Education and Development in Colonial and Postcolonial Africa: Policies, Paradigms, and Entanglements, 1890s–1980s*, Cham: Palgrave Macmillan, pp. 205–33.

Chachage, C. (2017) 'Growing up with the Arusha Declaration', *Udadisi* (http://udadisi.blogspot.com/2017/03/growing-up-with-arusha-declaration.html) (accessed: 28 August 2020).

Cliffe, L. (1973) 'Socialist education in Tanzania', in L. Cliffe and J. S. Saul (eds) *Socialism in Tanzania Vol 2. Policies*, Dar es Salaam: East African Publishing House.

Conroy-Krutz, J. and Lewis, D. (2011) 'Mapping ideologies in African landscapes', *Afrobarometer Working Paper*, No. 129, Afrobarometer.

Edwards, D. M. (1998) 'Matetereka: Tanzania's last Ujamaa village', *CAS Occasional Papers*, No. 77, Centre of African Studies, Edinburgh University.

Finch, H. and Lewis, J. (2003) 'Focus groups', in J. Ritchie and J. Lewis (eds) *Qualitative Research Practice: A Guide for Social Science Students and Researchers*, London: Sage Publications, pp. 170–98.

Fouéré, M. (2014) 'Julius Nyerere, Ujamaa, and political morality in contemporary Tanzania', *African Studies Review*, Vol. 57, No. 1, pp. 1–24.

————— (2019) 'Commemorating Nyerere, celebrating Magufuli in Tanzania', *Mambo*, Vol. 16, No. 11 (Translated by G. Darbon and revised by S. Dubord) (https://mambo.hypotheses.org/2043) (accessed: 28 August 2020).

Freeden, M. (2019) 'Editorial: The coming realignment of ideology studies', *Journal of Political Ideologies*, Vol. 24, Issue 1, pp. 1–10.

Gibbon, P. (1995) 'Merchantisation of production and privatisation of development in post-Ujamaa Tanzania: An introduction', in P. Gibbon (ed.) *Liberalised Development in Tanzania*, Uppsala: Nordiska Afrikainstitutet, pp. 9–36.

Hendrickson, J. and Zaki, H. (2013) 'Modern African ideologies', in M. Freeden and M. Stears (eds) *The Oxford Handbook of Political Ideologies*, Oxford: Oxford University Press, pp. 708–31.

Hirschler, K. (2006) 'Tanzania in transition: Violent conflicts as a result of political and economic reform', in L. Gerhardt, H. Möhle and J. Ossenbrügge (eds) *Umbrüche in Afrikanischen Gesellschaften und Ihre Bewältigung* [Changes in African Society and Their

Management], Berlin: Hamburg University.

Hyden, G. (1975) 'Ujamaa, villagisation and rural development in Tanzania', *Development Policy Review*, Vol. A8, Issue 1, pp. 53–72.

——— (1980) *Beyond Ujamaa in Tanzania: Underdevelopment and Uncaptured Peasantry*, London: Heinemann.

Ibhawoh, B. and Dibua. J. I. (2003) 'Deconstructing ujamaa: The legacy of Julius Nyerere in the quest for social and economic development in Africa', *African Journal of Political Science*, Vol. 8, No. 1, pp. 59–83.

Komba, W. L. M. (1996) 'Changing politics and political culture in Tanzania: The impact of political education and civics curricula 1967-1994', unpublished Ph.D. thesis, University of London Institute of Education.

Lal, P. (2015) *African Socialism in Postcolonial Tanzania: Between the Village and the World*, New York: Cambridge University Press.

Languille, S. (2015) 'The scramble for textbooks in Tanzania', *African Affairs*, Vol. 115, Issue 458, pp. 73–96.

Makulilo, V. B. (2012) 'What is socialism in Tanzania?', *Elixir Social Science*, No. 46, pp. 8170–80.

Martin, G. (2012) *African Political Thought*, New York: Palgrave Macmillan.

Mbilinyi, M. J. (1979) 'Secondary education', in H. Hinzen and V. H. Hundsdorfer (eds) *Education for Liberation and Development: The Tanzanian Experience*, London: Evans Brothers Limited, pp. 97–113.

McCormick, R. (1980) 'Political education as moral education in Tanzania', *Journal of Moral Education*, Vol. 9, Issue 3, pp. 166–77.

Melchiorre, L. (2020) '"Under the thumb of the party": The limits of Tanzanian socialism and the decline of the student left', *Journal of Southern African Studies*, Vol. 46, Issue 4, pp. 635–54.

Mkude, D., Cooksey, B. and Levey, L. (2003) *Higher Education in Tanzania: A Case Study*, Oxford: James Currey Limited.

Mmari, G. R. V. (1979) 'Teacher training in Tanzania', in H. Hinzen and V. H. Hundsdorfer (eds) *Education for Liberation and Development: The Tanzanian Experience*, London: Evans Brothers Limited, pp. 119–31.

Mushi, P. A. K. (2009) *History and Development of Education in Tanzania*,

Dar es Salaam: Dar es Salaam University Press.

Mwanziva, V. (2016) 'Julius Nyerere intellectual festival: *"Kigoda cha mwalimu"* overview', 30 June 2016 (https://victoriamwanziva.wordpress.com/2016/06/30/julius-nyerere-intellectual-festival-kigoda-cha-mwalimu-overview/) (accessed: 28 August 2020).

Nchimbi, J. J., Mafiga, M. R., Abeid R. S. and Olotu, S. R. (2012) *Civics for Secondary Schools: Form Three*, Dar es Salaam: Oxford University Press Tanzania.

Nshimba, D. J. M. and Sanya, E. (2015) *Fundamentals of Civics Form 3*, Dar es Salaam: Longhorn Publishers.

Nyamnjoh, F. B. (2017) 'Incompleteness: Frontier Africa and the currency of conviviality', *Journal of Asian and African Studies*, Vol. 52, Issue 3, pp. 253–70.

Okoko, K. A. B. (1987) *Socialism and Self-Reliance in Tanzania*, London and New York: KPI Limited.

Pitcher, M. A. and Askew, K. M. (2006) 'African socialisms and postsocialisms', *Africa*, Vol. 76, No. 1, pp. 1–14.

Provini, O. (2014) 'The University of Dar es Salaam: A post-Nyerere institution of higher education? Legacies, continuities and changes in the institutional space (1961-2012)', in Fouéré, M. (ed.) *Remembering Nyerere in Tanzania: History, Memory, Legacy*, Dar es Salaam: Mkuki na Nyota, pp. 279–304.

Puja, G. K. (2008) 'Gender, post-secondary education, and employment opportunities for women in Tanzania', in Nombuso, D. (ed.) *New Directions in African Education: Challenges and Possibilities*, Calgary: University of Calgary Press, pp. 95–120.

Sabatho, N. (2015) 'A life of critical engagement: An interview with Issa Shivji', *Global Dialogue*, Vol. 5, No. 1, pp. 10–2.

Schneider, L. (2004) 'Freedom and unfreedom in rural development: Julius Nyerere, *Ujamaa Vijijini*, and villagization', *Canadian Journal of African Studies*, Vol. 38, No. 2, pp. 344–92.

Shivji, I. G. (1976) *Class Struggles in Tanzania*, London: Heinemann.

———— (1993) *Intellectuals at the Hill: Essays and Talks 1969-1993*, Dar es Salaam: Dar es Salaam University Press.

———— (2016) 'Appeal to friends of Nyerere Resources Centre', *Review of African Political Economy*, 5 June 2016 (http://roape.net/2016/06/05/appeal-to-friends-of-the-nyerere-resource-centre/) (accessed: 28 August 2020).

Shivji, I. G., Yahya-Othman, S., and Kamata, N. (2020) *Development as Rebellion: A Biography of Julius Nyerere*, Dar es Salaam: Mkuki na Nyota.

Siwale, E. W. and Sefu, M. M. (1977) *The Development of Primary Education in Tanzania*, Ontario: Brock University.

Spalding, N. (1996) 'The Tanzanian peasant and Ujamaa: A study in contradictions', *Third World Quarterly*, Vol. 17, No. 1, pp. 89–108.

Success, E. (2013) 'JKT training is no longer relevant?', *The Citizen*, 7 May 2013.

The Citizen (2015) 'Katiba review special: Why capitalist Katiba won't serve purpose', *The Citizen*, 4 January 2015.

Thomson, A. (2016) *An Introduction to African Politics, Fourth Edition*, London and New York: Routledge.

Tripp, A. M. (1992) 'Local organizations, participation and the state in urban Tanzania', in G. Hyden and M. Bratton (eds) *Governance and Politics in Africa*, Boulder and London: Lynne Rinner Publishers, pp. 221–42.

Tsubura, M. (2019) 'Ideological orientation of the educated youth in Tanzania: A literature review', *IDE Discussion Paper*, No. 746 (https://www.ide.go.jp/English/Publish/Download/Dp/746.html) (accessed: 28 August 2020).

United Nations Association of Tanzania (2014) 'Fact sheet: Youth in Tanzania' (http://una.or.tz/young-people-in-tanzania-a-summary-fact-sheet/) (accessed: 15 March 2019).

United Republic of Tanzania (2005) 'The constitution of the United Republic of Tanzania of 1977' (https://www.wipo.int/edocs/lexdocs/laws/en/tz/tz008en.pdf) (accessed: 28 August 2020).

————— (2011) 'National strategy for civic education (draft)' (http://planipolis.iiep.unesco.org/sites/planipolis/files/ressources/tanzania_ur_national-strategy-for-civic-education_2011_draft.pdf) (accessed: 28 August 2020).

University of Dar es Salaam (2020) 'Seminars', Institute of Development Studies (IDS), University of Dar es Salaam (https://www.udsm.ac.tz/web/index.php/institutes/ids/seminar

s) (accessed: 28 August 2020).

Wiafe-Amoako, F. (2016) 'Political ideologies and democratic consolidation in Africa', in A. A. Mazrui and F. Wiafe-Amoako (eds) *African Institutions: Challenges to Political, Social and Economic Foundations of Africa's Development*, Maryland: Rowman and Littlefield, pp. 37–52.

Yeager, R. (1989) *Tanzania: An African Experiment*, Boulder: Westview Press.

# Appendices

## Appendix A: List of Interviewees at the University of Dar es Salaam (UDSM)

(1)    Four scholars were interviewed in English at UDSM between 11 and 13 November 2019. Their names, except that of the last interviewee, and affiliations are listed below, with the interview dates in parentheses. Charity Mapamba, research assistant, participated in all the interviews.

   (a)  Mr Emmanuel Mollel, Assistant Lecturer, School of Education, UDSM (11 November 2019)
   (b)  Mr Armstrong Matogwa, Assistant Lecturer, Department of Sociology and Anthropology, UDSM (12 November 2019)
   (c)  Mr Mbwana Mohamed Kitendo, PhD Candidate, Department of Political Science and Public Administration, UDSM (13 November 2019)
   (d)  A lecturer, Department of Educational Foundations, Management and Lifelong Learning, School of Education, UDSM (13 November 2019)

(2)    Seven sets of interviews with 39 students in total were conducted in English at UDSM between 12 and 14 November 2019. The interviews with undergraduate students turned out to be 'group interviews' (Finch and Lewis 2003: 171) in which students

individually expressed their views mainly in response to the guiding questions listed in Appendix B. The interviews with postgraduate students were 'focus group' (Finch and Lewis 2003: 171) discussions, in which students frequently interacted with one another and modified their answers in line with the conversation during the interviews. Their years and majors are listed below, with the numbers of students in square brackets and interview dates in parentheses. Charity Mapamba, research assistant, participated in all the interviews.

(a) Undergraduate students [33 in total]
   (i) Second-year students in International Development [5] (12 November 2019)
   (ii) Third-year students in Sociology [6] (13 November 2019)
   (iii) Second- and third-year students in History [4], Education [6], Linguistics [1] and Education in Adult and Community Education [1] (13 November 2019)
   (iv) Second- and third-year students in Political Science and Public Administration [4] and Economics [3] (14 November 2019)
   (v) Third-year students in Human Resource Management [3] (12 November 2019)

(b) Postgraduate students [6 in total]
   (i) Second-year students majoring in Economics [1], Research and Public Policy [1] and Public Administration [1] (12 November 2019)
   (ii) First-year students majoring in Business Administration [3] (14 November 2019)

## Appendix B: Questions for Interviews with Students at the University of Dar es Salaam (UDSM)

The following questions were used as guiding questions for interviews with students at UDSM.

(1)   How have you learned about *ujamaa* (a) in school (e.g., secondary schools, universities) and (b) outside school (e.g., from families, neighbours, religious organisations)?

(2)   What is *ujamaa*? How would you explain it to foreigners who do not know about it?

(3)     Do you hear about *ujamaa* in your daily lives? If so, how (e.g., mass media, social media, conversations with lecturers and fellow students, student organisations)?

(4)     What do you think about *ujamaa* (a) during the socialist period (mid-1960s–mid-1980s) and (b) in the post-socialist period (mid-1980s–present)? Is it still relevant to the Tanzanian government and/or the current political, economic and social situation in the country? If so, how?

# Chapter 2

## The Medium of Instruction for School Education in Southern Africa: Historical Analyses of South African and North-Central Namibian Cases

### *Akira Takada*

### 1. From a Newspaper

On 24 June 2016, *New Era*, one of the major national newspapers in Namibia, asked Mr Usko Nghaamwa, the governor of Ohangwena Region in north-central Namibia, the following question: 'Your region is one of few regions in the country that have [sic] a large number of marginalised San people. What are you doing to address their plight?' Replying to this question, the governor asserted: 'The San community can only be integrated into the society if we start with the children. Children at a very young age need to be taken to boarding schools far from their parents, where they will mingle with children from other tribes.' The following question was then posed: 'Are you saying San people cannot take care of themselves?' The governor answered: 'No, I'm saying San people are just victims of colonialism.' (*New Era* 2016). The interview certainly reflects the image of the San held by the Ovawambo, the absolute majority in the area. To understand what led the governor to make the above statement, we should take the turbulent history of the area into consideration. Thus, this chapter examines the education history for: (1) black South Africans (Section 2), (2) Ovawambo in north-central Namibia (Section 3) and (3) San in the present-day Ohangwena region of Namibia (Section 4), paying special attention to the medium of instruction, which is closely associated with interethnic relationships in the region, and their changes. To achieve this, I will clarify the relative centre-periphery relationships and marginalisation processes among these groups. The Bantu education system was implemented with the strong support of Afrikaners, who feared being marginalised by the British colonists and oppressed black South Africans. The system was also introduced in north-central Namibia, which was regarded as a territorial frontier of South Africa. This led to the liberation movement of the Ovawambo from the control of South Africa. After gaining independence for Namibia, the Ovawambo have increasingly applied political and economic pressure on the San who are the minority group in the area. To understand fully the linkages among these cases, a timetable of the major events mentioned in this chapter is provided in Table 1. Additionally, the research areas of this study are shown in Figure 1. These interrelated case studies will allow us to reconsider the regional history from the perspective of the oppressed people, and will lead to the identification of an 'African Potentials'. Accordingly, based on this analysis, I will re-examine the role of education in reproducing or restructuring the social organisation of the region (Section 5).

**Table 1. Timetable of major events mentioned in this chapter**

| Line | Year | Black South Africans | Ovawambo | San |
|------|------|---------------------|----------|-----|
| 1 | Mid-19th century | Mission schools promoted the education of local South Africans. | | |
| 2 | 1870 | | The FMS held its first literacy classes targeting the Ovawambo. | |
| 3 | 1879 | | | A Rhenish missionary attempted travel to the Kalahari Desert in pursuit of the San. |
| 4 | 1884 | | The German colonial government colonised South West Africa (~1915). | |
| 5 | 1913 | | A training school for priests and educators was established in north-central Namibia. | |

| | | | | |
|---|---|---|---|---|
| 6 | 1926 and 1930 | | | Strong pleas for a 'Bushman Mission' were made at the annual conference of Lutheran missionaries. |
| 7 | 1930s | | The South African Government strengthened regulations on schools, and about 40% of mission schools closed in north-central Namibia. | |
| 8 | 1935 | | | The head of the Rhenish Missionary Society argued for the creation of reserves for the San. |
| 9 | 1953 | The Bantu Education Act was enacted. | | |
| 10 | 1954 | | The translation of the Bible to Ondonga was completed and the ELOC was established. | The ELOC began engaging in outreach activities among the San in north-central Namibia. |
| 11 | 1959 | | The Union of South Africa agreed to assume management of the schools in north-central Namibia. | |
| 12 | 1961 | The Republic of South Africa was established. | | |
| 13 | 1960s | | | A San school was established by the missionary organisations. |
| 14 | 1963 | | Leonard Auala was appointed as the first Ovambo ELOC bishop. | |

| 15 | 1966 |  | The SWAPO launched an armed struggle. |  |
|---|---|---|---|---|
| 16 | 1972 | The government of South Africa increased the budget for education. |  |  |
| 17 | 1974 |  | The Bible was published in Oshikwanyama, and the New Testament in Kwangali. | The SAA began recruiting the San to fight against the SWAPO. |
| 18 | 1976 | The Soweto Uprising occurred. |  |  |
| 19 | 1984 |  | The ELOC was renamed the ELCIN. |  |
| 20 | 1990 |  | Namibia became independent. | Resettlement projects of the San started in the West Caprivi, north-central Namibia and in South Africa. |
| 21 | 1992 |  | The first NLBA was conducted nationwide. |  |
| 22 | 1994 | Black people voted and Nelson Mandela was elected president. |  |  |
| 23 | 2015 | The #RhodesMustFall protest began at the upper campus of the University of Cape Town. |  |  |
| 24 | 2016 |  |  | Mr Usko Nghaamwa gave a statement about the San in the Ohangwena region. |

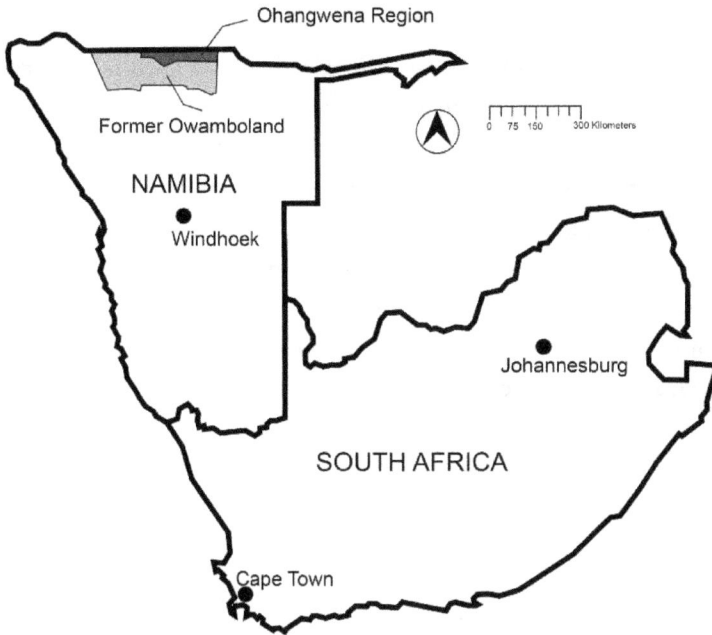

**Figure 1. Research areas**

## 2. An Overview of Education History for Black South Africans

South Africa's education policy has had an enormous impact on educational practices not just within South Africa but all over southern Africa (Figure 1). Therefore, before discussing the educational practices in Namibia, I provide an overview of the history of South Africa's education policy, paying special attention to the Bantu education system (see Gerhart 1979; Brookes 1987; Hyslop 1999; Yamamoto 2004 for more details). In particular, I note that the birth and death of Bantu education is inseparable from South Africa's distinctive social organisation, in which Dutch-originated Afrikaners had been suppressed by British colonists.

From the mid-19th century to the first half of the 20th century, mission schools were the main conduit of education for black South Africans (Table 1: line 1). The mission schools were influenced by British and American missionary organisations (Du Rand 1990: 12–38). The teachers typically offered enthusiastic and liberal education in the context of their time, and formed close relationships with the students (Gerhart 1979; Hyslop 1999: 9–13). In the mission schools, the medium of instruction was usually English. In addition, some schools adopted mother tongue education in the early educational stages. In this regard, these mission schools anticipated the later educational policies applied in Namibia. However, mission school education had serious restrictions, such as its small scale and low budget (Brookes 1987). Consequently, it was available only to privileged people. Among black South Africans, only the elite minority could attend secondary schools (Brookes 1987; Du Rand 1990: 47). Moreover, the content and quality of education lacked uniformity across the mission schools (Yamamoto 2004: 13). Mission schools could not therefore meet the expectations and demands of the majority of local residents, and gradually lost their trust and declined in popularity.

In the second half of the 1940s a change occurred. With the rapid urbanisation of South Africa due to development led by the mining industry, politicians, bureaucrats and capitalists began to argue for the necessity of mass education to provide sufficient semi-skilled African labourers (Kallaway 1987; Hyslop 1999: 5–7). Moreover, ethnic nationalism was growing among black South Africans at this time. The colonial government was wary of this movement. In particular, the Afrikaners, who had originated from Dutch settlers, were experiencing a crisis due to their declining status in society after losing a power struggle with the British colonists. Subsequently, at the request of the Afrikaners, the government issued the Bantu Education Act in 1953 (Table 1: line 9). The control of the education of black South Africans was transferred from the provinces to the central government, with the Department of Native Affairs acting as the executive body (Du Rand 1990: 139, 146–7). Under this act, the use of ethnic languages in primary education and the use of half English and half Afrikaans (the fifty-fifty English-Afrikaans policy) in secondary education began to be applied to local students (Manyike and Lemmer 2014). The fifty-fifty English-Afrikaans policy aimed to increase the number of semi-skilled African labourers as well as improve the status of Afrikaans, the language of Afrikaners.

Initially, a considerable number of black South Africans expected that the Bantu Education Act would expand their educational opportunities. As a direct result of this education system, the number of schools increased drastically during this period (Du Rand 1990: 147–8). Moreover, most teachers were relatively conservative and did not raise their voices against the imposition of the Bantu Education Act in its early stages (Hyslop 1999: 24, 43–4). It is understandable that even teachers who understood the enormity of the colour bar were reluctant to lose one of the few prestigious professions for educated black South Africans. In addition, since the mission school era, except for a few politically conscious teachers, many teachers had been accustomed to keeping a distance from politics and tried to direct their enthusiasm to less political activities, such as choral competitions (Hyslop 1999: 107–13). The African National Congress (ANC) political party was initially established to defend the rights and freedoms of black South Africans, and it tried to establish an independent educational system that would provide a 'people's education', in the 1950s. However, it soon faced serious difficulties with respect to budgets, human resources and institutional support (Benson 1966; Hyslop 1999: 65–7). Meanwhile, the racist underpinnings and institutional problems of the Bantu Education Act soon came to the surface. Most capitalists, who were largely white people, were unwilling to pay taxes for the social services of their labourers, most of whom were black people. Consequently, the government education budget did not increase from 1955 to 1972. As an alternative, the government tried to cover the increasing expenditure for the education of black South Africans with their own tax income (Hyslop 1999: 55–6). However, black South Africans, whose wages were kept low, could not afford increased taxes. As a result, the educational environment for black South Africans deteriorated rapidly.

Under the Bantu Education Act, school boards and committees had a massive influence over how education was implemented. The government often appointed conservative traditional authorities as members of the school boards and committees, rather than educational specialists (Yamamoto 2004: 18). Therefore, the government tried to integrate the education sector into the divide-

and-rule policy to control local people. As the school boards and committees increased their power over the schools in the mid-1960s to 1970s, the tyranny and corruption of the school boards and committees became apparent (Hyslop 1999: 122–7). Local people increasingly criticised the government, who used Bantu Education as a tool to increase the power of the ruling ethnic group and to create low-wage labourers.

Consequently, the Bantu Education policy did not acquire the support of local people. The ANC responded to the Bantu Education Act by calling for the boycott of schools. The mission schools in the Cape Province also deployed protest movements against the school boards and committees. Additionally, the liberal South African press vigorously opposed the policy (Du Rand 1990: 157–9). Afrikaners, who had felt oppressed by the British colonists, became increasingly frustrated by this situation and pushed the government to strengthen the enforcement of the Bantu Education policy. This made the situation worse and the educational environment for black South Africans deteriorated, despite the demands for human resource development from industry. The government could not help but increase the budget for education, and implemented education reform in 1972 (Hyslop 1999: 134–5; Table 1: line 16). Consequently, the number of secondary schools rapidly increased. This led to further unexpected results for the government (Yamamoto 2004: 18). An increasing number of students began to criticise the government's racial policy. Additionally, many teachers who were required to improve their teaching skills in both English and Afrikaans were confused. Their smouldering complaints erupted into mainstream society during the Soweto Uprising in 1976 (Hyslop 1999: 150–2; Table 1: line 18). Strikes began at Sowetan schools against the further imposition of Afrikaans as the medium of instruction and rapidly expanded to other areas. Students themselves played a prominent role in the struggle for a better education system (Thobejanea 2013). The government hastily announced that the decision of the medium of instruction would be left to the discretion of school principals. However, the strikes did not subside, but, rather, led to a nationwide resistance movement against racist policies and 'The People's Education' finally gained public support.

After the democratic government was established in 1994 (Table 1: line 22), the learning of African ethnic languages, English and Afrikaans (among the 11 official languages) was promoted (Davenport and Saunders 2000). However, critical questions about people's social identity remained unanswered. While the importance of English as the medium of instruction further increased over time, it has remained difficult for many black South Africans to acquire sufficient English skills to meet societal demands (Thobejanea 2013: 9–10; Manyike and Lemmer 2014: 253–4). Afrikaans has rapidly lost its influence. The other official languages have largely retained their position as simply nominal official languages or common languages in particular geographical areas, due to the lack of financial, educational and human resources (Yamamoto 2003). As a result, many black South Africans, as well as the Afrikaners, are not satisfied with the government's education strategy and the practical situation regarding their language (Manyike and Lemmer 2014: 254–5).

In the historical context of South Africa, school education has been a major device for creating and maintaining social and economic disparities among various peoples. The medium of instruction used in school education has been crucial to the use of education as such a device, and has simultaneously acted as an important tool that enables the device to work. In this respect, the medium of instruction is inseparable from people's social identity. Moreover, a number of black South Africans believe that the structure of colonial rule is still present. Dissatisfaction over the stagnation of 'decolonisation' and slow socioeconomic transformation has continued to prevail among them. On 9 March 2015, a so-called #RhodesMustFall protest began at the upper campus of the University of Cape Town, where a statue of Cecil Rhodes was located (Nyamnjoh 2016: 16; Table 1: line 23). The resistance movement then expanded to other universities, and issues of identity politics (e.g., racism and xenophobia) over social capital and power resurfaced. For example, several distinguished universities that used to be for 'whites' decided to discontinue the use of Afrikaans as the main language of instruction (see Davenport and

Saunders (2000), and Nyamnjoh (2016) for the details).

In summation, the history of Bantu education reflects South Africa's distinctive social organisation. Although Afrikaners constituted the majority of the white population in South Africa, for a long time they had been suppressed by the predominant Anglophone residents in both the politico-economic and linguistic-cultural spheres. The Bantu Education Act was designed as a remedial strategy to favour Afrikaners (Hyslop 1999: 158–64; Yamamoto 2004: 9). At the same time, it was an attempt to maintain social organisation, with the core aim of distinguishing between white and non-white individuals. The government thereby tried to make a future that would reproduce the high social status and economic interests of white people. However, this attempt led to resistance not only from black South Africans but also international communities, leading to a coalition between them and the eventual overthrow of the government. It can be said that this unexpected result is one manifestation of African Potentials, namely, 'a dynamic entity produced through contact, negotiation and compromise with state and global political mechanisms in the context of the contemporary world (Matsuda 2019a)'. However, as the #RhodesMustFall protest showed, the negotiations toward peace and reconciliation never ended and have been repeatedly revived as dynamic and flexible responses to real-life issues (Matsuda 2019b).

## 3. The History of Education for the Ovawambo in North-Central Namibia

Although the Bantu Education Act had a big influence on a vast area of southern Africa, considerable diversity has also been recognised in the educational practices of this area. From this perspective, educational practices in north-central Namibia (formerly Owamboland)[1] merit particular attention (Figure 1). Namibia became independent in 1990, relatively late among the African nations, from the de facto colonial rule of South Africa, the regional giant. Under South African rule, north-central Namibia was regarded as a territorial frontier of South Africa as well as an important source of cheap labour. At the same time, north-central Namibia is home to many Ovawambo (consisting of subgroups such as the Ovakwanyama, Aandonga and Aakwambi), who were the major forces pushing for independence. It was also a stronghold of the Southwest African People's Organisation (SWAPO), who are the ruling party of Namibia today. Reflecting differences in the socio-cultural context, the trajectory of educational practices in north-central Namibia differed significantly from that in South Africa (see Hellberg 1997; Peltola 2002; Takada 2013, 2015 for further details).

In the latter half of the 19th century, north-central Namibia became deeply incorporated into the global system. As the shadow of colonisation was being cast upon the area, it was missionary organisations who had the most direct and strongest influence on the establishment of an educational system within the local society. The Finland Missionary Society (FMS) held its first literacy classes targeting Ovawambo in 1870 (Lehtonen 1999: 14; Table 1: line 2). Reflecting the nationalist movement in its home country,[2] the FMS activities clearly differed from the imperialistic and racial policies that were then dominant in southern Africa. Constructing close relationships with the local people, the FMS pursued 'genuine conversion', while emphasising the training of local leaders. Most Finnish teachers adopted English as the medium of instruction. Some Ovawambo also learned the Finnish language. In 1913, a training school for priests and educators was established in north-central Namibia (Table 1: line 5). Ovawambo gradually came to shoulder propagation activities (Hellberg 1997: 207–13; Peltola 2002: 216).

In contrast to missionary organisations, such as the FMS, the colonial governments were initially uncooperative with educational reforms in north-central Namibia. The German colonial government, which colonised South West Africa (today's Namibia) from 1884 until 1915, did not accomplish a significant reform of the educational system in Owamboland (Lehtonen 1999: 31, 105; Table 1: line 4). Similarly, the South African Government, which took over the administration of South West Africa from Germany after World War One, did not supervise the education provided by the FMS for many years. Only in the 1930s, did the South African Government put pressure on schools that did not meet the standards set by the government, and about 40 per cent of mission schools had to close in north-central Namibia (Lehtonen 1999: 76–81, 96–7; Table 1: line 7). Nevertheless, the missionaries patiently continued their activities. In 1954, the translation of the Bible in Ondonga (a major Oshiwambo language) was completed and the Evangelical Lutheran Ovambo-Kavango Church (ELOC), an indigenous church, was also established (Table 1: line 10). The ELOC made a considerable effort to develop the region, which set it apart from the government of South Africa, which sought to strengthen the control of local residents by white settlers. The ELOC also enthusiastically promoted the education of local leaders. In 1963, Leonard Auala was appointed as the first Ovawambo ELOC bishop (Table 1: line 14; Figure 2).

**Figure 2. Leonard Auala, who became the first Ovambo ELOC bishop in 1963** (courtesy of the National Achive of Namibia)

Even after the establishment of the ELOC, the FMS continued to support its activities (Hellberg 1997: 207–13; Peltola 2002: 323–5). Following repetitive requests from the FMS and ELOC, the Union of South Africa gradually increased its financial support for educational activities in the area. They finally agreed to assume management of the schools in this area in 1959 (Table 1: line 11). The Republic of South Africa, which was established in 1961 (Table 1: line 12), introduced the 'Bantu education' framework into the schools in north-central Namibia (Lehtonen 1999: 135–9). Consequently, the fifty-fifty English-Afrikaans policy was also promoted in this area. Officially, this policy remained largely intact until the government of independent Namibia adopted English as the medium of instruction. The South African Government encouraged the use of Afrikaans, which strengthened the influence of the white population in South Africa and South West Africa. However, most schools could not adequately meet the requirements, particularly the fifty-fifty English-Afrikaans policy, due to a lack of human, material and financial resources. Local people, especially the SWAPO, immediately began to oppose the introduction of Bantu Education.

At this time, the SWAPO asked for cooperation from the United Nations, who were in conflict with the South African Government over the governance of South West Africa. The United Nations began to support the SWAPO's activities. The SWAPO established bases outside the country and launched an armed struggle in 1966 (Table 1: line 15). Socialist bloc members, including Cuba and East Germany, who aimed to expand their influence in Africa under the Cold War, also supported the SWAPO. Consequently, from the mid-1970s to 1980s, the liberation movement intensified. The intention was to achieve a new political regime after independence. Educational activities were flourishing among the exiles in countries like Angola, Cuba and East Germany, with support from old socialist camps and the United Nations (Takada 2015: 69). These educational activities were conducted in Oshiwambo, Spanish, English and other languages. The experiences learned together during this difficult time enhanced the consciousness of the exiles as compatriots and enabled them to form a solid network after independence. The FMS and the ELOC (which was renamed the Evangelical Lutheran Church in Namibia (ELCIN) in 1984) (Table 1: line 19) were sympathetic to the liberation movement (Nambala 1994: 165). The ELOC leaders had become the leaders of the people in north-central Namibia and were in close contact with the SWAPO. They regarded the control of South Africa's apartheid regime over South West Africa as a serious violation of human rights. Thus, despite opposition from other churches that claimed to keep a distance from politics, the FMS and the ELOC/ELCIN publicly declared their support for the liberation movement from the start (Hellberg 1997: 220–1). During this time, the FMS and the ELOC/ELCIN also promoted missionary work in local African languages. For example, the Bible in Oshikwanyama (another major Ovawambo language) and the New Testament in Kwangali (a major Kavango language) were published in 1974 (Table 1: line 17). The missionary organisations were also engaged in literacy education and gospel translation in San languages (see the next section).

The liberation movement gained international support, and Namibia achieved independence from the Republic of South Africa in 1990 (Table 1: line 20). After independence, the new government as well as a number of local people who could not have obtained a satisfactory education under the apartheid regime showed a great interest in reforming the educational system. The government was extremely active in promoting reforms, including primary education (up to Grade 3) in the pupils' 'mother tongue', the adoption of English (not Afrikaans, which was promoted before independence) as the official language and as the medium of instruction for higher education, literacy education for adults whose educational opportunities had been limited, and human rights education to utilise the principles of the Constitution, which was claimed to be the most advanced in the world at that time.

As the starting point of these reforms and to understand the actual situation and issues regarding education in Namibia, the National Learner Baseline Assessment (NLBA) has been conducted nationwide for students in grades 4-7 since 1992 (Table 1: line 21). This survey clearly showed the 'north-south disparity' in education, namely, the degree of learning achievement in northern Namibia, where many local non-white Namibians (e.g., Ovawambo) lived, was significantly lower than that in southern Namibia, where many whites lived and included the capital, Windhoek (MCC, Florida State University, and Harvard University 1994). This is considered to be a result of the Bantu education system, which had kept the quality of education for local non-white Namibians low under the South African regime. However, the study also demonstrated a large variance in academic performance in north-central Namibia, suggesting that there was a diverse range of education and learning opportunities in this area, and some schools, particularly mission schools, had promoted advanced education (MCC, Florida State University, and Harvard University 1994: 72–3).

Since independence, the government of Namibia has made great efforts to provide quality education nationwide, and to make education accessible to all citizens irrespective of ethnicity, locality and social class. For example, national standards have been established to improve teaching and learning quality. Figure 3 shows examples of standard textbooks currently (in 2017) used in Namibian elementary schools. From the unified covers of these textbooks, it is clear that there is an intention to treat languages with diverse backgrounds as equally as possible. Nevertheless, many schools, particularly schools in rural areas, including north-central Namibia, have faced a number of challenges and hardships in fulfilling this goal. These schools have suffered from a lack of human, material and financial resources (Shikalepo 2020). Consequently, the school performance in rural Namibian schools has not been very impressive

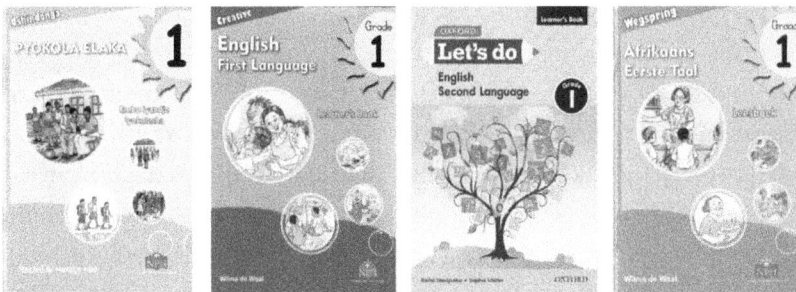

**Figure 3. Examples of standard textbooks for Grade 1 students (from left to right, Oshingonga, English as first language, English as second language and Afrikaans) in Namibian elementary school** (photo taken by the author in 2017)

(Namwandi 2014). Various NGOs and international organisations have supported moves to improve teaching and learning conditions in rural Namibian schools. For example, the Japan International Cooperation Agency (JOCV) has sent a number of young volunteers to support educational activities in rural Namibian schools (Figure 4).

**Figure 4. A local teacher and a Japanese volunteer jointly teaching computer science in Etosha Secondary School, located in north-central Namibia** (photo taken by the author in 2017)

To summarise, the FMS and the ELOC/ELCIN promoted missionary and educational activities, with the aim of a 'genuine conversion' of local residents in north-central Namibia, and trained church leaders from local church members. In this attempted national development, unlike most South African influential churches, the FMS was not backed by the colonial policy of the home country. In this respect, among the European churches that had expanded into southern Africa, the FMS established an exceptional relationship with the colonial governments. This relationship was incompatible with the Bantu Education framework, which aimed to facilitate the divide-and-rule of local residents. Hence it was a logical consequence that these missionary organisations' language policies (e.g., the use of

English and Oshiwambo as the medium of instruction, Bible translation and literacy education in people's mother tongue) led the liberation movements. The liberation movement, which is a good example of an African Potential as an opposing force to global inequality and oppression (Matsuda 2019a), gained international support and the collective agency of these organisations led to the independence of Namibia.

## 4. The History of Education for the San in the Ohangwena Region

After the independence of Namibia, some narratives, such as those of the SWAPO, who played a central role in establishing the new state, have achieved the status of being authentic and legitimate memories of 'national heroes' (Dobell 2000). On the other hand, other narratives have been proposed or suppressed within the regional societies. In this respect, it should be remembered that several groups of San-speaking people, who are known as indigenous hunter-gatherers, have lived in north-central Namibia for a long time, particularly the Ohangwena region, (Figures 1 and 5; Takada 2015). In this section, by unravelling the stories of the educational history of the San, I will reveal the 'social facts' that comprise their authentic and legitimate memory, from the perspective of a tiny minority at both regional and national levels, and reconsider the basis of the regional and national societies.

Missionary organisations have long shown a special interest in missionary work among the San. It is documented that the FMS missionaries encountered San people during their very first visits to north-central Namibia (Peltola 2002: 48). In 1879, a Rhenish missionary made an attempt to travel to the Kalahari Desert in pursuit of the San, and discussed the establishment of a mission station for them (Table 1: line 3). One motivation for missionary organisations to establish a missionary station for the San was their remoteness from the Christian world. Although this plan was not realised, due to the lack of stability in their domestic situation, missionary activities for the San gradually progressed. At the

**Figure 5. San children in the early 20th century at Manutoni, on the edge of Etosha Pan** (courtesy of the National Achieve of Namibia)

beginning of the 20th century, in the white settlements in the southern part of the country, some San people were converted to Christianity (Gordon and Douglas 2000: 64–5). At the annual Lutheran missionary conferences held in 1926 and 1930, there were strong pleas for a 'Bushman Mission' (Gordon and Douglas 2000: 144; Table 1: line 6). Also, at the hearings of the South West Constitutional Commission held in 1935, Heinrich Vedder, the head of the Rhenish Missionary Society at that time, argued for the creation of two reserves for the San further south, one for the Haiǁom (also known as ǂAkhoe) (Takada 2015) and one for the !Kung (also known as Juǀ'hoan and !Xun) (Takada 2015; Dieckmann 2007: 135; Table 1: line 8).

In the 1950s, in cooperation with the FMS, the ELOC began engaging in activities aimed at the marginalised San in north-central Namibia (Table 1: line 9). Around that time, most of the San (!Xun, ǂAkhoe, etc.) moved around the Ovawambo villages, with whom they had established close ties, and also spent time in the bush for hunting and gathering. Finnish missionaries played a central role in the introduction of permanent settlements and residential concentration

70

for the San. Many Ovawambo who had close relationships with the ELOC also took part in this programme. The inducements of the missionary organisations were successful and large numbers of San moved to the settlements established by the ELOC (Gordon and Douglas 2000; Peltola 2002; Widlok 1999, 2003; Dieckmann 2007; Takada 2013, 2015: 62–5). Missionary organisations placed a high value on agriculture, literacy education and psychological care (Jansen, Pradhan and Spencer 1994).

In the 1960s, a school exclusively for the San was built, and many San children and young people started attending it (Lehtonen 1999: 147; Table 1: line 13). The missionary organisations provided hostels for children and minors attending the San school, although they returned to their parental homes at weekends and on school holidays. As a result, the lives of the children and minors were, to some extent, separate from their family-centred lives. At the hostel, the boys and girls lived in separate buildings and plentiful amounts of nutritious food were provided. In the !Xun and ǂAkhoe languages, folktales were compiled, a book of the Bible (Luke) was translated and literacy education was conducted. The missionary organisations educated promising San individuals, training them to become local religious leaders at the schools in which the Ovawambo learned. The church committee selected the San individuals to be sent to these schools, based on the recommendation of the pastors. The missionary organisations paid almost all the fixed tuition costs. As a consequence of these activities, some San individuals became pastors or their assistants. These local leaders began to work to educate and enlighten the local residents, including both San and Ovawambo. Under the missionary organisations, they engaged in Bible classes, Sunday meetings, agricultural promotion and literacy education. Literacy education was conducted for each of the Oshikwanyama, !Xun and ǂAkhoe. The teaching materials in the !Xun and ǂAkhoe languages were made mainly by Finnish linguistic experts and taught by Ovawambo teachers and their !Xun assistants who were trained in literacy education. Both the !Xun and ǂAkhoe participated in the Oshikwanyama class. Additionally, !Xun, and ǂAkhoe participated in the !Xun and ǂAkhoe classes, respectively. It was reported that 40 to

50 students attended the classes, which were held twice a week (Takada 2013, 2015: 65–8).

However, from the 1970s to 1980s, as the liberation movement intensified, the missionary organisations' activities among the San were hindered (Jansen, Pradhan and Spencer 1994: preface). South African soldiers often entered the San villages established by the missionary organisations and obstructed their activities (Berger and Zimprich-Mazive 2002: 21). Many San got through this difficult time by strengthening their relationship with the Ovawambo or reactivating hunting and gathering. Because many Ovawambo who joined the liberation movement were in exile at that time, it is likely that the San who remained in north-central Namibia made up for the labour shortage (Takada 2015: 74–5).

On the other hand, the South African Army (SAA) started to recruit San to fight against the SWAPO in 1974 (Lee and Hurlich 1982: 333; Table 1: line 17). Although many San empathised with the SWAPO in north-central Namibia, the SAA's enormous financial power attracted some San individuals. Even more San were recruited from Kavangoland, Bushmanland and Angola, where connections with the Ovawambo were weaker. The SAA brigaded San battalions for bush-fighting in guerrilla warfare (Uys 1993: 99–100, 145–75). The SAA strategically made use of common images of the San, namely, the regimentation of San battalions and alleged 'magical skills' of 'Bushmen' (Widlok 1999: 234–6) in bush war, with the aim of intimidating the Ovawambo, who constituted most of the SWAPO members. Furthermore, the SAA aimed to create a public image that the Republic of South Africa was supporting the indigenous San who stood up to fight against communist guerrillas. By creating such an image, they tried to 'Africanize' the war (Gordon and Douglas 2000: 2, 185). Consequently, even San who were sympathetic towards the SWAPO feared that SWAPO soldiers might suspect them of being spies for South Africa.

The fear of being accused a spy has continued to some extent after independence. Many San who had been hired by the SAA were afraid of retaliation from the SWAPO, which became the ruling party in the new government. Thus, at the initiative of the Lutheran World

Federation, which is the superior body of the ELCIN and FMS, activities were launched to resettle former San soldiers in camps established in West Caprivi, north-central Namibia or in South Africa (Table 1: line 20). Later, the management and operation of the camps within Namibia were handed over to the government, with the Ministry of Lands, Resettlement and Rehabilitation (MLRR)[3] acting as the executive body. San children and minors started to attend local schools (Figure 6). Although a policy to use the 'mother tongue' in primary education (up to Grade 3) was implemented, it was Oshiwambo (mainly Oshindonga) that was adopted as the medium of instruction in north-central Namibia. Education programmes for the San led by the missionary organisations ended, while San developmental support activities by international agencies and NGOs increased (Jansen, Pradhan and Spencer 1994; Berger and

**Figure 6. San children in Ekoka village, which was originally established by the missionary organisations** (photo taken by the author in 2004)

Zimprich-Mazive 2002; Takada 2013, 2015: 81–2). As the government has promoted various projects for the development and welfare of the San, the pressure to integrate the San socio-culturally into the Ovawambo regional majority has increased.

The FMS and ELOC/ELCIN literacy and development projects for the San were an extension of those provided to the Ovawanbo, with the aim of realising a 'genuine conversion'. Literacy education in San languages and the establishment of a San school were designed to coordinate the missionary and educational activities with the distinctive lifestyle of the San. Moreover, the philanthropic and Protestant morals of Christianity matched well with the San egalitarian principles of subsistence based on cooperative labour, delayed returns and sharing among community members (Takada 2015: 132–3). Consequently, a unique community based on San languages was created as a realisation of African Potentials. The traditional and customary San methods for living an orderly livelihood were reorganised through contact, negotiation and compromise with global and national organisations (Matsuda 2019a). The projects were very different from those of the development policies that the (colonial) governments have implemented in various parts of southern Africa for San groups such as ǂAkhoe (Widlok 1999; Dieckmann 2007), G|ui or Gǁana (Takada 2002; Sapignoli 2018) and Ju|'hoan (Hays 2016). The San groups in these projects have struggled with inadequate procedures and a lack of legitimacy regarding the development policies, particularly language policies and resettlement projects. It cannot be denied that there is a considerable gap in the understanding between the missionaries and San regarding educational activities. Nevertheless, the missionaries respected San languages and cultures, used their voice to introduce innovation into educational activities and elicited the San's active involvement. These characteristics made a big difference in the responses of the San to missionary and government actions. However, after the government took control of the education and development activities, the policies for the San changed fundamentally, and new oppressions and affirmative actions were enacted against them in north-central Namibia. The resilience and endurance of San culture and society, as an important touchtone of African Potentials (Matsuda 2019b), is being tested, again.

## 5. Understanding History and Education from the Perspective of the Marginalised

Government action for the San described in the previous section has focused on poverty reduction and regional development in north-central Namibia. The activities of the government have been based on a significantly different principle from those of missionary organisations. Furthermore, the government has reduced the personnel, budgets and support systems used to implement these activities. Having seen these changes, an Omuwambo man, who was formerly in charge of literacy education for the San under the missionary organisations, commented, 'Since independence, the government has had projects for the San, at least on paper. But in reality, the missionary organisations have left and the government doesn't pay adequate attention to the San. The San have been abandoned to suffer' (Takada 2015: 80).

On the other hand, the government has struggled to steer the nation due to its limited budget and resources. From their perspective, the San are bothersome minorities who do not readily follow their policies. The concept of the 'nation' won by the liberation movement might be threatened by minorities who cannot easily be absorbed into the rhetoric of sacrifice embedded in the memory of the liberation movement.[4] In other words, the San make the government and its supporters realise that the programme of nation building remains unfinished. In this respect, the San are not merely tiny minorities in north-central Namibia but also have a significant existence that continuously reminds government of the 'fear of small numbers' (Appadurai 2006). To overcome such unease and fear, the holders of power frequently and fiercely oppress and exclude minorities.

The statement made by the governor of the Ohangwena region that was presented at the beginning of this chapter was made in this context (Table 1: line 24). He clearly advocated the integration of the San community into society by way of separating San children from their parents and promoting the education of those children. Although this education policy may aim to nurture people's self-awareness as Namibian nationals, we should be cautious about whether the image of 'society' here is biased to that of the Ovawambo, as the regional and national majority. Consequently, the integration policy led to a greater awareness of the differences between the Ovawambo and the San. This is particularly so for the San themselves, as well as the people and organisations who support the San. Such 'politics of difference' (Young 1990) have become a big issue with respect to the relocation policy of the San from their 'traditional' area in Botswana (Takada 2002; Sapignoli 2018). Similar to other disadvantaged social groups (Frazer and Honneth 2003), their affirmative action has required the government to recognise their minority culture and their identity, and to properly distribute natural resources and social capital to them. Whether or not these actions are earnestly done will indicate the state's capability to build a fair nation.

Understanding history and educational policies from the perspective of the marginalised is important not only in north-central Namibia and the nation of Namibia but also across the broader area of southern Africa. The liberation movement from South Africa's apartheid regime in north-central Namibia, which was regarded as a territorial frontier of South Africa, not only led to the independence of Namibia but also had a big impact on the restructuring of the South African political system. This demonstrates that the perspectives and activities of people oppressed on the periphery often anticipate or sharpen the problems of the core structure and indicate potential solutions.

In the globalising world, methods and mediums by which oppressed people can raise their voices have been rapidly increasing (e.g., international conferences, mass media and social media). The socio-political situation strengthens the fear of the holders of power and often results in an escalation of intimidation of the oppressed people. It is not clear whether such a situation provides hope for democracy or threatens its foundations, because democracy is a regime that was born in an era that did not adopt such methods and mediums as a basic premise. A promising solution may be discovered from education and learning based on African Potentials, where the incompleteness of various stakeholders provides the power to establish linkages among them and create new provisions (Nyamnjoh 2016). The San school established by the missionaries, the SWAPO's educational activities in exile and the resistance movements derived from schools operating against South Africa's apartheid regime exemplify the fruits of African Potentials, with convivial activities emerging from the difficult situation at that time. However, in the present-day globalising world, we need new and creative realisations of African Potentials that meet the current situation.

Together with the phrase 'rainbow nation' coined by Archbishop Desmond Tutu (Tutu 1994), the phrase 'unity in diversity', which originated in the proverb of ǀXam[5] came to be widely known due to a speech delivered by Nelson Mandela, and is written in the preamble to South Africa's Constitution. Some other states, such as the Republic of Indonesia, have also adopted it as a guiding principle for recognising differences in a multicultural society and for making harmony and constructiveness possible (The Minister of Culture and Tourism, Republic of Indonesia 2002).

However, in reality, it is by no means easy to turn a beautiful rainbow glimpsed after a furious storm into the solid foundation for a long-lasting social life. Rather, the fear and unease brought about from both inside and outside society have repeatedly caught up with us in different forms. In such a process, people who have been oppressed may become oppressors themselves. To overcome past errors and construct a better future, we should improve the education system to enhance the active learning of accumulated knowledge, skills and wisdom, and to create new forms of unity in diversity continuously that are contingent on changing social situations. This difficult task will be facilitated by one of the most important characteristics of African Potentials, namely acknowledging the hybrid and mixed properties of various elements, and attaching value to the character of incompleteness (Matsuda 2019b).

## Endnotes

[1] Also spelled as Ovamboland, reflecting German orthography. Throughout this chapter, I use the spelling 'Owamboland' for consistency.

[2] From 1809 Finland became a self-governing state, but was placed under Russian influence. In the latter half of the 19th century, the principle of national self-determination surged in Europe. The nationalist movement led to the independence of Finland in 1917.

[3] The MLRR was reconstructed and changed its name to the Ministry of Lands and Resettlement in 2005.

[4] The concept was also threatened by the voices rising from some church members who supported the liberation movement. After independence, they questioned SWAPO's 'human rights abuses perpetrated against large numbers of their own followers' during the liberation movement and prompted a reconsideration of the role of churches in the new era (Lombard 2001).

[5] The |Xam is one of the San groups that lived in South Africa. They were driven to extinction by the settlement of white and Bantu peoples.

## Acknowledgements

This work was supported by JSPS KAKENHI Grant Numbers JP16H06318, JP16H02726 and JP17KT0057.

## References

Appadurai, A. (2006) *Fear of Small Numbers: An Essay on the Geography of Anger*, Durham: Duke University Press.

Benson, M. (1966) *South Africa: The Struggle for a Birthright*, Harmondsworth: Penguin.

Berger, D. J. and Zimprich-Mazive, E. (2002) *New Horizons for the San: Participatory Action Research with San Communities in Northern Namibia*, Windhoek: UNESCO Windhoek Office.

Brookes, E. (1987) *A South African Pilgrimage*, Johannesburg: Ravan Press.

Davenport, T. R. H. and Saunders, C. (2000) *South Africa: A Modern History (5th edition)*, New York: St. Martin's Press.

Dieckmann, U. (2007) *Haiℓℓom in the Etosha Region: A History of Colonial Settlement, Ethnicity, and Nature Conservation*, Basel: Basler Afrika Bibliographien.

Dobell, L. (2000) *SWAPO's Struggle for Namibia, 1960–1991: War by Other Means (2nd edition)*, Basel: P. Schlettwein Publishing.

Du Rand, S. M. (1990) 'From mission school to Bantu education: A history of Adams College', M.A. thesis submitted to the Department of History, University of Natal, Durban.

Frazer, N. and Honneth, A. (2003) *Redistribution or Recognition? A Political-philosophical Exchange* (translated into English by J. Golb, J. Ingram and C. Wilke), New York: Verso.

Gerhart, G. M. (1979) *Black Power in South Africa: The Evolution of an Ideology*, Berkeley: University of California Press.

Gordon, R. J. and Douglas, S. S. (2000) *The Bushman Myth: The Making of a Namibian Underclass* (2nd edition), Boulder: Westview Press.

Hays, J. (2016) *Owners of Learning: The Nyae Nyae Village Schools over Twenty-Five Years*, Basel: Basler Afrika Bibliographien.

Hellberg, C.-J. (1997) *Mission Colonialism and Liberation: The Lutheran Church in Namibia 1840–1966*, Windhoek: New Namibia Books.

Hyslop, J. (1999) *The Classroom Struggle: Policy and Resistance in South Africa 1940–1990*, Scottsville: University of Natal Press [Hyslop, J. (2004) *The Educational History of Apartheid*, (Japanese Translation, T. Yamamoto) Yokohama: Shumpusha Publishing (in Japanese)].

Jansen, R., Pradhan, N., and Spencer, J. (1994) *Bushmen Ex-servicemen and Dependents Rehabilitation and Settlement Programme, West Bushmanland and Western Caprivi, Republic of Namibia: Evaluation, Final Report, April, 1994*, Windhoek: Republic of Namibia.

Kallaway, P. (1987) 'Education and the state: From mass education to people's education: Some preliminary notes', in D. Young and R. Burns (eds) *Education at the Crossroads*, Rondebosch: School of Education, University of Cape Town, pp. 20–56.

Lee, R. B. and Hurlich, S. (1982) 'From foragers to fighters: South Africa's militarisation of the Namibian San', in E. B. Leacock and R. B. Lee (eds) *Politics and History in Band Societies*, Cambridge:

Cambridge University Press, pp. 327–47.

Lehtonen, L. (1999) *Schools in Ovamboland from 1870 to 1970*, Helsinki: The Finnish Evangelical Lutheran Mission.

Lombard, C. (2001) 'The detainee issue: An unresolved test case for SWAPO, the churches and civil society', in I. Diener and O. Graefe (eds) *Contemporary Namibia: The First Landmarks of a Post-apartheid Society*, Windhoek: Gamsberg Macmillan Publishers, pp. 161–84.

Manyike, T. V. and Lemmer, E. M. (2014) 'Research in language education in South Africa: Problems & prospects', *Mediterranean Journal of Social Sciences*, Vol. 8, No. 5, pp.251–8.

Matsuda, M. (2019a) *File 1: The Experiences of the Five African Forums of the First Phase (2011-2016)*, unpublished manuscript.

———— (2019b) *File 2: Expressions of African Potentials*, unpublished manuscript.

MCC (The Ministry of Education and Culture), Florida State University, and Harvard University (1994) *How Much do Namibia's Children Learn in School? Findings from the National Learner Baseline Assessment*, Windhoek: New Namibia Books.

Nambala, S. (1994) *History of the Church in Namibia*, Grand Rapids: Lutheran Quarterly.

Namwandi, D. (2014) 'Rural learners taught by unqualified teachers', *Namibian Sun*, 2 June 2014 (https://www.namibiansun.com/news/rural-learners-taught-by-unqualified-teachers) (accessed: 10 May 2020).

New Era (2016) 'Nghaamwa on the state of Ohangwena', *New Era*, 24 June 2016 (https://neweralive.na/posts/nghaamwa-state-ohangwena) (accessed: 7 December 2020).

Nyamnjoh, F. B. (2016) *RhodesMustFall: Nibbling at Resilient Colonialism in South Africa*, Bamenda: Langaa RPCIG.

Peltola, M. (2002) *Nakambale: The Life of Dr. Martin Rautanen*, Helsinki: Finnish Evangelical Lutheran Mission, Printed by Natal Witness Commercial Printers (Pty) Ltd., Pietermaritzburg.

Sapignoli, M. (2018) *Hunting Justice: Displacement, Law, and Activism in the Kalahari*, Cambridge: Cambridge University Press.

Shikalepo, E. E. (2020) 'Improving the quality of education at rural schools in Namibia', *International Journal of Research and Innovation in Social Science*, Vo. 4, No, 2, pp. 62–8.

Takada, A. (2002) 'Social changes among the Central Kalahari San: The analysis of population dynamics, subsistence activities, and child weight', *Journal of African Studies (Africa-Kenkyu)*, Vol. 60, pp. 85–103 (in Japanese with English abstract).

————— (2013) 'A study on educational reform in Namibia: Educational practices for the !Xun San in Owamboland', *Africa Educational Research Journal*, Vol. 4, pp. 19–34 (in Japanese).

————— (2015) *Narratives on San Ethnicity: The Cultural and Ecological Foundations of Lifeworld among the !Xun of North-central Namibia*, Kyoto and Melbourne: Kyoto University Press and Trans Pacific Press.

The Minister of Culture and Tourism, Republic of Indonesia (2002) 'Unity in diversity: One world with culture and environment diversity', paper presented at *World Ecotourism Summit*, Quebec, 19–22 May 2002.

Thobejanea, T. D. (2013) 'History of apartheid education and the problems of reconstruction in South Africa', *Sociology Study*, Vol. 3, No. 1, pp. 1–12.

Tutu, D. (1994) *The Rainbow People of God: A Spiritual Journey from Apartheid to Freedom*, Cape Town: Double Storey Books.

Uys, I. (1993) *Bushman Soldiers: Their Alpha and Omega*, Germiston: Fortress publishers.

Widlok, T. (1999) *Living on Mangetti*, Oxford: Oxford University Press.

————— (2003) 'The needy, the greedy, and the state: Dividing Haillom land in the Oshikoto region', in T. Hohmann (ed.) *The San and the State*, Cologne: Rüdiger Köppe Verlag, pp. 87–119.

Yamamoto, T. (2003) 'The English language as the medium of instruction: The case of South Africa', *Bulletin of Institute of Japanese Language Soka University*, Vol. 15, pp. 28–49 (in Japanese).

————— (2004) 'To understand this book', in J. Hyslop, *The Educational History of Apartheid* (Japanese Translation, T. Yamamoto), Yokohama: Shumpusha Publishing, pp. 7–35 (in Japanese).

Young, I. M. (1990) *Justice and the Politics of Difference*, Princeton: Princeton University Press.

# Chapter 3

## Constructing Places of Belonging and Exclusion: A Spatial Reading of South African University Students' Affect and Identity

*Josephine Cornell, Shose Kessi and Kopano Ratele*

## 1. Introduction

In South Africa, the higher education landscape is marked by persistent and inherent inequalities, manifested both in who is able to access higher education and which students are privileged once they are enrolled within higher education institutions (HEIs). The enduring legacy of colonialism and apartheid, during which education was used to control indigenous people and support white supremacy, is still felt within universities today (Le Grange 2016; Sehoole 2006). At HEIs, students from certain categories of identity often experience marginalisation and exclusion, whereas others are privileged (SAHRC 2016). As Soudien (2008: 674) remarks, 'The character of the university ... produces particular identity outcomes, particularly amongst people who have existed on the margins of privilege who work with their identities and have their identities worked upon in a range of interesting ways.'

An important element of these dynamics of power and identity in HEIs, which is not often considered, is space (Cox, Herrick and Keating 2012). Space is rarely neutral and instead always already racialised, sexualised, gendered, classed and 'identified' in other ways. Operating in intersection with each other, these categories of identity (mapped onto and constituted through space) are axes of power in individuals' differential experience of space (Massey 1994; Valentine 2001). Identities are 'spatially and geographically contingent, not developed in a physical or material vacuum' (Paechter 2004: 307). Through the organisation, design and management of campus space, HEIs send out messages about the dominant hierarchical structures on campus and reproduce particular power relations (Cox 2011). Rather than a fixed state, students' sense of belonging is an ongoing, interactional process, involving interaction between students' identities and the spaces they occupy (Samura 2016). Thus, in seeking to understand identity in education contexts, it is vital to consider the space in which identities are formed and sustained (Paechter 2004).

At the same time, space is always open to re-negotiation and re-configuration (Cox 2011). Although students' identities may be shaped by the different spaces they occupy at different times, they can also change, challenge or reproduce normative spaces. There is a 'constant, subtle interplay between space and the people in it' (Temple (ed.) 2014: xxvii). Neither university spaces nor the identities of the people who occupy them are stable, singular or permanent (Massey 1994; Valentine 2001), but instead are in a mutually 'constitutive state of becoming' (Acton 2017: 4).

Drawing on a tradition of critical approaches to space (see Kobayashi 2005; Massey 1994, 2005; Neely and Samura 2011; Rose 1993), we understand 'space' as both material and socially produced and productive; as fluid, open to negotiation, and yet also rooted in layers of historical meaning. We consider space as infused with power and power relations as implicitly spatialised; and importantly, we hold that discourses, meanings and experiences inform ways of making, negotiating and organising space. From these conceptualisations of space, we then understand 'places' as 'formed out of the particular set of social relations which interact at a particular location' (Massey 1994: 168). Places are continually reproduced environments-in-the-making (Knowles 2003; Massey 1994), which must be actively imagined and continually invented (Matus and Talburt 2009). Simply put, space is a physical, geographic location but it is influenced by broader discourses and the socio-political processes that occur within it.

There are always 'ideological and political processes involved in the production and maintenance of places (and the people in them)' (Gray and Manning 2014: 642). University places are thus formed through the daily and ongoing contestation and negotiation between the varied trajectories of the students in these places, as well as these

84

broader multimodal discourses that circulate about the area. Attempts to 'secure the identity of places' are 'attempts to stabilise the meaning of particular envelopes of space-time' (Massey 2005: 5). This is not to say that campus places are necessarily always consciously and intentionally co-constructed, but the identity of campus place is always a collective achievement formed through a range of daily practices and underpinned by broader ideological processes (Massey 2005).

Through a multimodal discourse analysis of university students' representations and constructions of campus places, this chapter examines students' experiences of spatialised belonging and exclusion at the University of Cape Town (UCT), a historically 'white-only' South African university and how these relate to students' intersecting identities. The chapter begins with a brief review of the literature on higher education transformation in South Africa, with a focus on research into students' experiences in higher education in the country, followed by research on space in higher education, before reporting on our study.

## 2. Higher Education Transformation in South Africa

It has been more than two decades since the dismantling of apartheid and yet the transformation of the higher education landscape is incomplete and contested. Since the advent of non-racial democracy in 1994, the national government has introduced policies to redress the colonial and apartheid inequalities and injustice entrenched within the higher education system (Odhav 2009). These national policies, as well as those developed by individual HEIs, promised redress and equity; however, their actual implementation has often been uneven and profoundly inadequate. These policies are framed within broader social and economic processes, such as globalisation and neoliberalism, which contradict many of the goals of transformation and seek to entrench the privilege of the global elite (Badat 2016; Le Grange 2016). In many cases, these transformation policies have failed to shift and, at times, even actively obscured and reproduced historical power relations and inequalities

(Badat 2016; SAHRC 2016; Soudien et al. 2008).

The concept of 'transformation' in the higher education landscape has generally been 'hollowed out' to a focus on numbers and changing the demographics of student bodies (Badat 2016). Widening participation in higher education from a more diverse group of students is seen as one of the most significant transformation successes. The increase in the proportion of black[1] students is undoubtedly significant (Cloete 2002). However, concerns have been raised about the nuances of these demographic changes, which have been described as a 'skewed' and 'stalled' revolution (Cooper 2015). Additionally, questions have been broached regarding the throughput and support of black students once they are accepted into undergraduate degrees (Akoojee and Nkomo 2007; Petersen, Louw and Dumont 2009).

The South African Human Rights Commission (SAHRC) reports that despite some transformation successes 'patterns of systemic exclusion, marginalisation and discrimination persist' (SAHRC 2016: viii). As the widespread student movements such as #RhodesMustFall and #FeesMustFall that have swept this country since 2015 indicate, there have not been sustained changes wrought on the Euro-American-centric, hetero-patriarchal, middle class, white, cisgendered status quo within the dominant institutional cultures of most South African HEIs (Badat 2016; Msibi 2013; SAHRC 2016; Steyn and Van Zyl 2001). These student movements have centred on calls to decolonise or Africanise (rather than 'transform') higher education. Although academic theorising on decolonisation and Africanisation has been well established over the years (e.g., Ndlovu-Gatsheni 2013; Nakusera 2004; Nyamnjoh 2012), there has been a growth in conceptual reflection on the decolonisation of higher education since the start of the student protests in 2015 (e.g., Heleta 2016; Mamdani 2016; Mbembe 2016). Indeed, the concept of decolonising education has been increasingly drawn on by students, academics and higher education institutions in South Africa to denote a wide range of concerns around institutional, curricula, economic and pedagogical redress (Morreira, Taru and Truyts 2020). Similarly, there has been a resurgence of claims for Africanisation in education and knowledge, taken to refer, among other things, to a reflection of African experiences and realities in ontologies, institutional cultures, curriculum and epistemologies (Lebakeng, Phalane and Dalindjebo 2006; Letsekha 2013). In this dynamic social and educational context, amongst other issues, the student movements have problematised the demographic composition of academic staff, the outsourcing of workers, the Euro-American focus of curricula, the predominance of English and rising tuition fees, and have called for free higher education (Badat 2016). These student movements have been instrumental in the recently renewed and expanding interest in writing and debate on the state of higher education in South Africa.

## 3. Research into Students' Experiences in Higher Education in South Africa

Research into higher education transformation in South Africa is a growing area of study. An important avenue in this body of literature examines the experiences of the students who study within these contexts, highlighting the need and importance for including students' voices and experiences in a nuanced understanding of the South African higher education landscape. Within this literature, a selection of studies has examined the identity or subjectivity of students. This research has examined identity in relation to sexuality (e.g., Hames 2007); race (e.g., Walker 2005); gender (e.g., Walker 1998); language (e.g., Parkinson and Crouch 2011); disability (e.g., Isaacs 2020; Mutanga 2013); and intersections of some or all of these aspects of identity (e.g., Soudien 2008). Within these explorations of identity, few of these (discussed below) have considered spatial or material dimensions.

## 4. Space and Research into Higher Education

Although the social sciences began to consider the importance of space as a theoretical concept in the 1990s, it is only comparatively recently that space has been thought relevant in research into education (Vavrus 2016). Often when space is considered, it is in the use of spatial language, in which space is mainly employed as a metaphor (Gulson and Symes 2007). Looking beyond the use of spatial vocabulary, a critical spatial lens can help deepen understandings of the formation of subjectivities and structures of power. A spatial lens can locate and highlight how broader ideologies and discourses manifest in the lived experiences and materiality of higher education (Robertson 2010; Samura 2016). The 'spatial framings of inequality and exclusion' in education are an essential area of critical research in education (Fenwick, Edwards and Sawchuck 2011: 159). Theorists have highlighted the need to consider the connection between space and issues of justice, participation and exclusion in education (Andersson, Sadgrove and Valentine 2012). A growing body of critical research in education explores and exposes these power dynamics and processes (e.g., Hopkins 2010; Muñoz 2009; Samura 2016; Wee 2019).

Perhaps the most established body of research that has examined space in South African higher education has been concerned with the racialised segregation of universities (e.g., Durrheim et al. 2004; Moguerane 2007). At UCT specifically, numerous studies have documented the deeply racially segregated nature of the student body (Alexander 2007; Alexander and Tredoux 2010; Tredoux et al. 2005). These studies illustrate that the powerful but implicit set of values, assumptions and norms that govern the use of space in higher education institutions in South Africa are difficult to disrupt. Alexander (2007), for example, found that even when there are numerous opportunities for intergroup contact, racial segregation between students remains deeply entrenched. Moguerane's (2007) study of segregation at a postgraduate student residence at a historically white-only Afrikaans university concluded that the status quo remained in the residence spaces which were skewed to privilege white Afrikaans students. Nevertheless, black students were able to use space to mediate feelings of alienation and powerlessness in residences by creating spaces of belonging for themselves in communities of students with shared experiences of 'blackness'.

Other research, although not focusing only or specifically on racial segregation in space, has similarly examined spatialised inclusion and exclusion on university campuses. Jagessar and Msibi (2015: 70), for example, examined homophobia in residence spaces at a university in KwaZulu-Natal. They found that homophobia is normalised through the use of violence and mob power, which is enabled through 'the instrumental colonisation and use of certain spaces which secure the mob, giving it power to act'. Higham (2012) similarly examined university students' experiences of exclusion and inclusion at two South African universities. His findings elucidated how variations in exclusion can overlap in one location and how exclusion and inclusion can stem from institutional as well as broader societal processes. Importantly, Higham elucidates that internal institutional norms and practices leave the responsibility for inclusion on new entrants rather than dismantling existing systems. Higham concludes by arguing that his findings 'suggest "place" and "space", conceived geographically, rather than solely in term of access, can offer additional insights into how politics of identity and difference impact upon inclusive education' (Higham 2012: 499).

Dixon and Janks (2018) also provide a spatial reading of a South African university campus. They demonstrate that university spaces – at both the micro and macro arrangement – produce embodied subjectivities, and they highlight the necessity of 'reconceptualising spatial arrangements in higher education institutions as part of the process of transformation' (Dixon and Janks 2018: 95). Their findings indicate that students typically spend their free time relegated to liminal campus spaces which are typically segregated along racial lines and that students generally felt unwelcome and isolated in spaces on this campus. Dixon and Janks's (2018) study demonstrates the insights around power and hierarchy that can be gained from a close spatial reading of university campuses and offers useful insights into students' use of space and the importance of considering space in the process of transformation.

Although, of course, identity is implicated in all of the studies discussed above, there have also been a few studies that specifically considered the dynamics of space in identity construction on campus. Bangeni and Kapp (2005), for example, examined black undergraduate students' identities in transition at UCT. They explored different spaces – home and university – in relation to the participants' identities. Students' identities were found to be challenged by rejection from their communities when they went home, and dominant institutional discourses resulted in the sense of being 'unhomed'. However, they suggest that being 'unhomed' is symbolic of the ambivalent space inhabited by black students who straddle these different and contradictory discourses. They hold that the experience of being 'unhomed' does not result in a loss of identity as much as an ongoing and fluctuating repositioning of these students' identities as they encounter these varied discourses.

Similarly, Gibson and Macleod (2012) examined the sexual identity narratives of lesbian women at a historically white-only South African university. They explored the 'interpretative repertoires drawn on in relation to these women occupying particular geographical, institutional, and familial spaces' (Gibson and Macleod 2012: 463). The participants in this study continuously (re)negotiated their sexual identities across the multiple classed and raced, familial and institutional spaces they have variously inhabited.

These studies highlight the interesting potential for spatial theorising in research into higher education and in particular, how space mediates students' identities and their experiences of belonging and exclusion.

## 5. Study Context: The University of Cape Town

UCT is a historically 'white only' English-medium university based in Cape Town, South Africa. It was founded in 1829 initially as a private high school for white, Christian boys. Under the apartheid regime, 'white only' institutions, such as UCT, were prohibited from admitting black students or employing black staff without special permission, and from teaching material the government considered 'subversive' (Davies 1996). Although UCT was one of the 'open universities' that opposed academic segregation from the 1950s onwards, it should also be noted, that UCT at times colluded with the apartheid government (Davies 1996; Phillips 2019; Steyn and Van Zyl

2001). UCT and the other English-speaking universities were often focused more on academic freedom and their own institutional autonomy than the rights of black South Africans (Davies 1996; Phillips 2019) and considered these as separate matters. It was not until the 1980s that any tangible attempts were made to admit black students to the university. UCT was one of the first universities to desegregate in a meaningful way, although the numbers of black students remained relatively low. In 1989, a few years shy of the official dismantling of apartheid in 1994, black students constituted 24.7 per cent of the student population at UCT, and by 1993 black student enrolments had increased to over a third of the student population (Luescher 2009).

Post-1994, UCT implemented an affirmative action or so-called 'race-based' admissions policy, which was utilised until the end of 2015.[2] In an attempt to redress the racist admissions policies of the past, applicants' race was considered when selecting students. In the more than two decades since the dismantling of apartheid, the demographic breakdown of the student body has indeed shifted substantially. Black students at UCT are now in the majority. The most recently available statistics for 2018 indicate that 45 per cent (12,423) of the student body is classified as 'generic black' ('black South Africans', 'coloured', 'Indian' and 'Chinese' South Africans), 22 per cent (6,211) as 'white', 18 per cent (5,005) are identified as 'racially other', 15 per cent (4,268) as 'international' (UCT 2018).

Despite great leaps in the demographic change since 1994, transformation at UCT more broadly has followed a haphazard trajectory. The dominant university experience for many black and LGTBIQ+ students in the two decades since apartheid has often been one of marginalisation and stigmatisation (Boonzaier and Mkhize 2018; Kessi and Cornell 2015). This growing sense of alienation among the student body culminated in student, Chumani Maxwele, symbolically flinging faeces at the statue of the colonialist Cecil John Rhodes on Upper Campus (see Maxwele 2016), followed by months of sustained student protests that grew into the #RhodesMustFall and #FeesMustFall student movements. The institutional culture of the university has faced fierce criticism.

Specifically, the university has been criticised for the Eurocentric focus in curricula, the predominance of English on campus, the paucity of black academic staff, the dominance of racialising stereotypes of black students and staff, rising exclusionary tuition fees, the outsourcing of workers, a lack of material change in the artwork and symbols around campus and colonial architecture, as well as cisgender and heterosexual bias (Boonzaier and Mkhize 2018; Steyn and Van Zyl 2001; Kessi and Cornell 2015). This is not to say that there have not been transformation successes or significant changes wrought to the UCT educational landscape since 1994. Particularly since the start of the protests in 2015, various noteworthy transformation endeavours have been implemented, and students and staff have expended substantial effort in putting transformation on the agenda. However, in the 25 years since the dismantling of apartheid, ultimately the process of transformation has been and continues to be deeply contested, uneven and sporadic.

## 6. Visual Research Methods in Education

Visual research methods are an important technique for research into higher education, as HEIs are intrinsically visual spaces (Metcalfe 2016), which can be seen, for example, in the increased use of visual approaches and digital technologies within higher education processes and practices (such as PowerPoint in classrooms; interactive online resources; image-heavy university websites; and institutional branding and marketing). Moreover, in the South African context, the visual – in the form of photographs, video, signs, placards, performance art, body art, clothing – featured strongly in the recent student movements and protests aimed at decolonising higher education in South Africa (see Thomas 2018 for visual analysis of photographs taken by students during these protests). Indeed, students' engagement with and participation in higher education is increasingly complex and visual. As Howes and Miles (2015: 16), conclude:

Images are used in the process of mediating conversations across linguistic, cultural and across boundaries between experience and inexperience, explicitly serving the role of facilitating and promoting conversation and communication, directly creating the possibility of encounters between people otherwise constrained and limited by social conventions, positions of power, and hierarchy.

Hence, visual methods, particularly when used in participatory ways, have the potential to transcend cultural conventions between researchers and participants (Malherbe et al. 2016) and are therefore particularly useful in contested contexts such as transformation in higher education spaces.

Studies in social psychology have also recognised the importance of the visual in the development of identity (Forrester 2000; Frith et al. 2005; Reavey and Johnson 2017). Social representations research, for example, has highlighted how images circulating in the public sphere about particular individuals or groups have an impact on identity construct as identities are fundamentally social and co-constructed in relation to others (Howarth 2002). Our own prior research about black students in higher education has shown how stigmatising images of blackness impact on students' sense of self-esteem and denies them the symbolic resources for positive identity construction (Kessi and Cornell 2015). Nevertheless, the construction of images through the research process itself is an emerging area of study for psychological research.

Furthermore, visual methods are an often neglected approach in the study of higher education (Metcalfe 2016). De Lange, Moletsane and Mitchell (2015) suggest that it can be challenging to convince educational research scholars of the power of visual research methods. Most research tends to rely on non-visual data collection encompassing textual practices, such as the analysis of transcribed interviews. While these methods are undoubtedly important, the dominance of text-centric research may hinder a thorough exploration and deeper engagement with the progressively more multimodal higher education environment (Metcalfe 2016).

Furthermore, visual research methods are useful for research into space because it can be challenging for participants to articulate experiences of institutional space (Cox 2011) without recourse to visual resources. Drawing on Massey (2005), Beyes and Michels (2014) suggest that since space is mimetically unrepresentable, more unusual methods are necessary in research and writing on space, including, for example, drawings of mental maps of space. Considering that spatial analysis of education is still relatively recent, it is vital to utilise a range of methodological tools that may help understand how space matters in educational contexts (Ferrare and Apple 2010).

## 7. Data Collection: Reflective Mental Maps

Considering the central focus on space in the study, visual methods were deemed most appropriate in exploring students' identities and affective experiences of campus spaces. Thirty-eight students at UCT from across all faculties and a range of disciplines participated in this study. The only inclusion criteria were that the participants were registered as full-time students at the time of their participation in the study. The sample of student participants was heterogeneous in terms of race, gender, sexuality, language, ability, religion and class. Students from a range of intersecting identities needed to be included as it illuminated the differential and skewed experiences of privilege and oppression that are related to different intersecting identities. Students were recruited through the Department of Psychology's Student Research Participation Programme (SRPP).[3] Due to space limitations, this chapter looks specifically at the maps produced by five students; Zoliswa, Kate, Maria, Nicole and Anele. Table 1 outlines these participants' demographic details as per their own self-descriptions.[4]

Participants were asked to draw reflective mental maps of the University. At the simplest level, these maps constitute the participants' representation of the UCT campus. More specifically, the participants were requested to document how they experience, use, perceive and feel within the different campus spaces using drawing and writing. This task was open to the participants' interpretation, and a range of different kinds of maps were produced.

**Table 1. Participants' details**

| Pseudonym | Self-described identity | Faculty | Discipline | Level of Study |
|---|---|---|---|---|
| Zoliswa | 'Black, queer and a traditionalist' | Humanities | Environmental and Geographical Sciences & Psychology | 3rd year |
| Kate | 'South African, white, female' | Law | Law | 1st year |
| Maria | 'Mixed race but, for demographic purposes, a coloured female' | Humanities | Gender Studies, Social Development, & Psychology | 3rd year |
| Nicole | 'My kind of identity is more shaped around my personality and my mind' | Humanities | Psychology and Sociology | 2nd year |
| Anele | 'I'm the light in this University. I'm a flower that's blooming' | Humanities | Psychology, Social Development and Social Work | 2nd year |

For example, some participants relied on text more than others. Some participants documented only certain places on campus, whereas other participants drew the campus as a whole. Some maps were detailed, while other maps were minimalistic.

In previous research in education, mental maps have been used successfully to examine education spaces (e.g., Beyes and Michels 2014; Brunn 2012; Gieseking 2007; Rohleder and Thesen 2012). Maps can be understood as a symbolic depiction of particular a territory, in this instance, the University of Cape Town (Machin and Mayr 2012). As such, maps are not exact, neutral representations of the physical characteristics of a landscape. Instead, the meaning and structure of a map are influenced by the specific social intentions of its creator (Fowler 1991). We thus understand these reflective mental maps to constitute spatial representations of the creators' associations with particular places, as well as the features they consider important to their experience of these places and spaces (Brunn 2012). As Brunn (2012: 100) suggests, 'these highly personal maps are considered extensions of the person who prepared or drew the map'. These maps are visual testimonies illustrating how people see themselves and the spaces and places that they occupy (Brunn 2012). When seeking to understand and interpret these maps, we must consider the various semiotic resources the creator includes in the map, that is, the visual elements and text that give the map meaning. Importantly, an analysis of these maps should consider which semiotic resources the creator has emphasised and highlighted, and which have been minimised or excluded and why (Machin and Mayr 2012).

## 8. Data Analysis

The data in this study were analysed using multimodal discourse analysis, a form of critical discourse analysis (CDA). CDA seeks to capture the interrelationship between power, ideology and language (Fairclough 1992). The principal concept underlying CDA is that power relations are implemented and negotiated through discourse. Within mainstream research into education, positivist and so-called replicable and objective means of analysis are often given preference, while critical analysis that attends to matters of privilege and inequality are often neglected. CDA can offer a more complex and nuanced understanding of practices and processes within education (Rogers (ed.) 2004). CDA can take many forms, as Van Leeuwen (2006: 291) suggests, 'there is no theoretical orthodoxy in critical discourse analysis'. Ultimately, the different approaches to CDA are united by a shared focus on critiquing the hegemonic discourses underpinning and shaping systems of inequality, injustice and oppression (Van Leeuwen 2006).

Traditionally, CDA was focused purely on the analysis of language; however, theorists began to consider that meaning is communicated through other semiotic modes in addition to language (Machin and Mayr 2012). These modes include, for example, images, sounds and movement (O'Halloran 2011). In particular, Kress and van Leeuwen (2001) argued for the need to analyse visual features in much the same way that CDA traditionally studied language. They coined the term 'multimodal analysis' to describe the analysis of other semiotic modes that extends beyond the study of language. Language and text can still be analysed, but in *combination* with these other phenomena (O'Halloran 2011). The inclusion of a multimodal analysis can offer CDA a more comprehensive set of tools to encourage a systematic analysis of data (Machin and Mayr 2012). A multimodal discourse analysis thus involves the elucidation of the semiotic resources people choose to utilise to realise particular communicative aims. In this chapter, we analysed the semiotic choices (both textual and visual) participants made in constructing their maps which allowed us to draw out the broader discourses connoted throughout the maps. These discourses signify and enable particular identities and actions (Machin and Mayr 2012). Specifically, this involved coding the textual and visual semiotic resources present in the maps. We then organised the delineated codes into thematic categories, which were then used to derive two discourses, namely: *Places of Exclusion and Alienation;* and *Places of Belonging, Connection and Affirmation.* We then examined how these two discourses relate to students' intersecting identities and affective experiences on campus.

## 9. Findings and Discussion

We have conducted a multimodal discourse analysis of the discourse students produce for particular places on campus, specifically, places of exclusion and belonging across their reflective mental maps of campus. An affective state of belonging or exclusion is spatialised. Drawing on an understanding of affect here that views the sources of emotions as outside rather than *within* individuals, affect is engendered within 'settings that choreograph trajectories for bodies and shape the nature of social encounters and exchanges' (Durrheim et al. 2013: 45). Affect is thus located in the interconnections between bodies and the materialities of time and space. Importantly, however, as Durrheim et al. (2013) assert, particularly in the process of discourse analysis – the theoretical coordinates of which view meaning making as a fluid, relational but embedded process – although not located within people – affect is ultimately connected to thought by people as they talk about, write about and, indeed, draw their daily lives. As they suggest, 'affect is inextricably linked to meaning making because it is "enfolded in action"' (Durrheim et al. 2013: 46). The affective potentialities of campus places, in turn, influence the types of identities students embody across campus. We will examine, in particular, the maps produced by Zoliswa, Kate, Maria, Nicole and Anele (see Figures 1–5).[5]

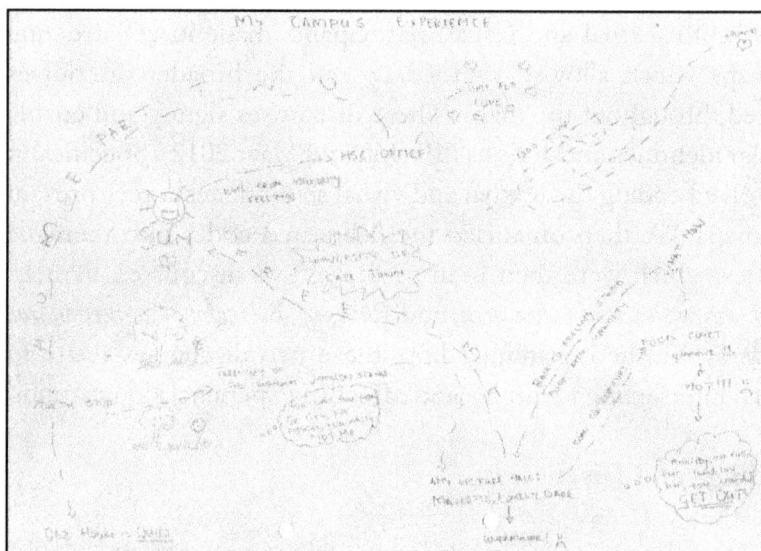

**Figure 1. Zoliswa's reflective map**

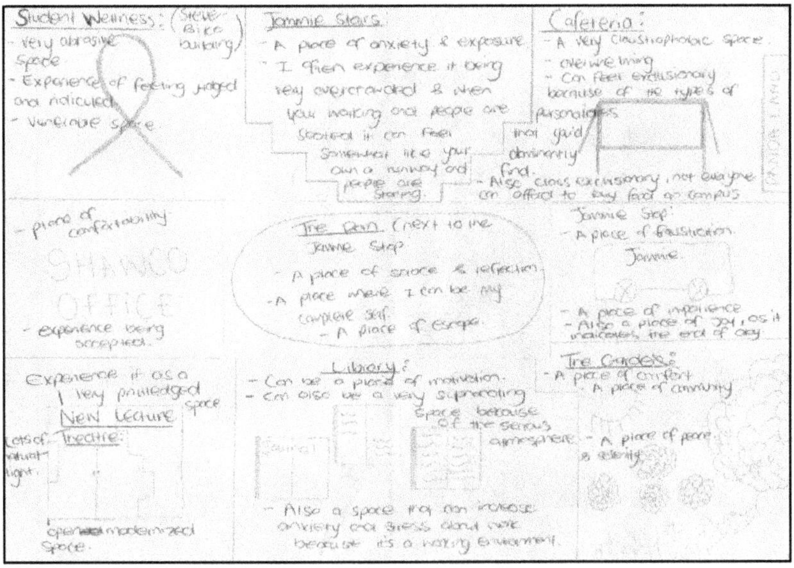

Figure 2. Maria's reflective map

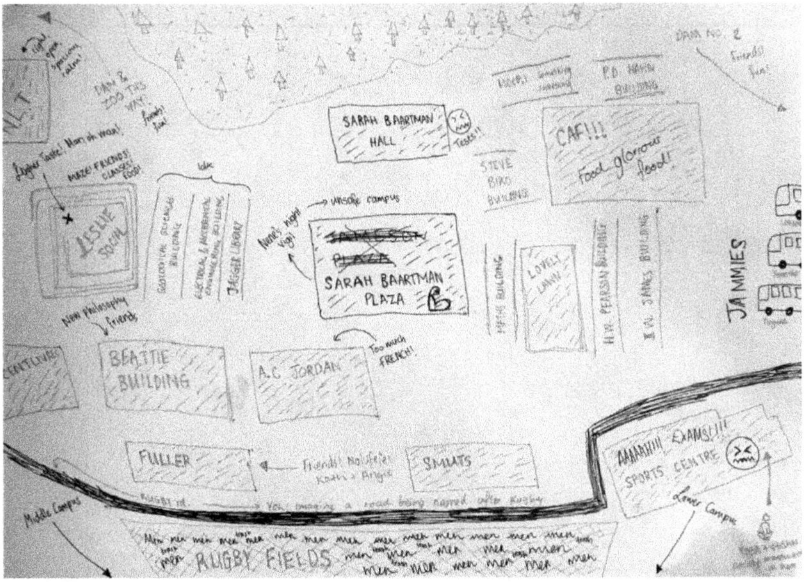

Figure 3. Kate's reflective map

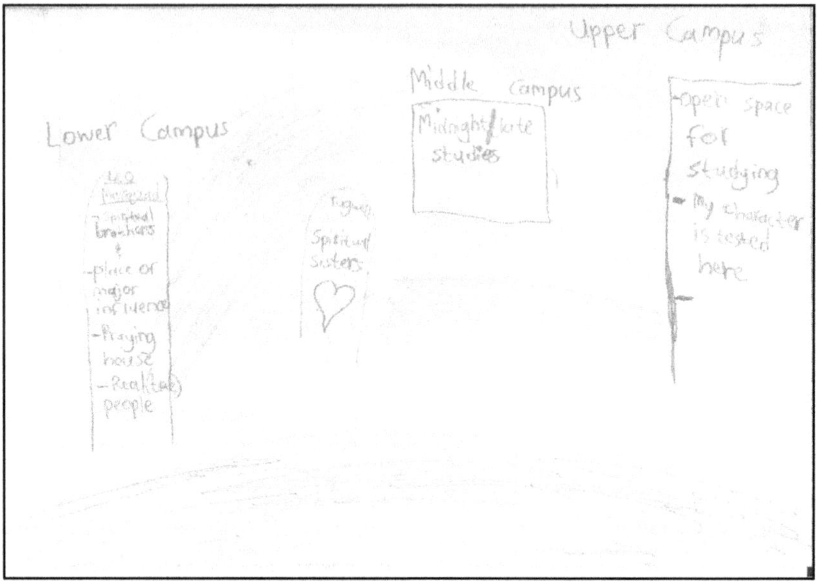

**Figure 4. Anele's reflective map**

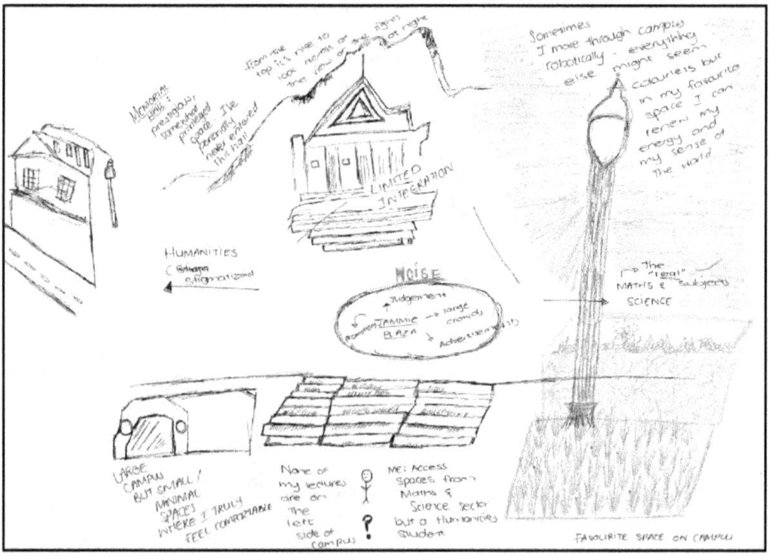

**Figure 5. Nicole's reflective map**

## 10. Places of Exclusion and Alienation

Students across all of the maps documented places of exclusion and alienation on campus. These particular affective constructions of campus space were shaped by salient elements of students' intersecting identities and in turn, enabled or undermined the performance of specific student identities. In Zoliswa's reflective map (Figure 1), for example, she constructs three locations on campus as places of exclusion and alienation: the Jameson Plaza, the Food Court and lecture theatres. In her depiction of the Jameson Plaza on the map, for example, Zoliswa labels this place, an otherwise blank area, 'territory of the unknown' (see Figure 6).

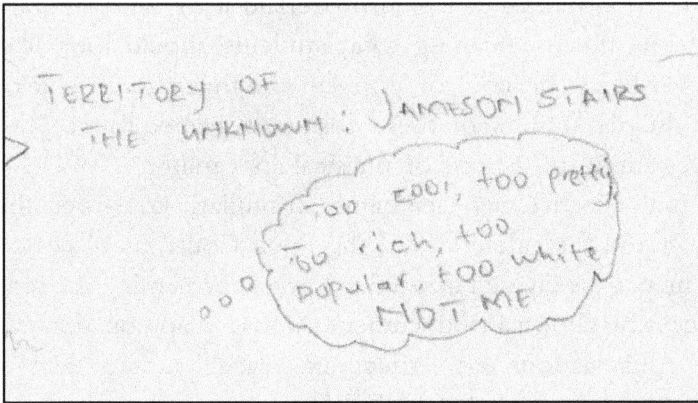

**Figure 6. Close up of Jameson Plaza on Zoliswa's map**

The Jameson Plaza[6] is considered 'the epicentre of the upper campus' (Tredoux et al. 2005: 417) and is a frequent and busy gathering spot for students. It is noted, however, for high levels of racial self-segregation between students, and black students often report feelings of discomfort and judgement when using this space (see Alexander and Tredoux 2010). On her map, Zoliswa uses the full name 'Jameson Stairs' rather than the more common and colloquial 'Jammie Stairs', which hints at distancing and a lack of ownership over this place. The use of the word 'territory' is suggestive of boundaries and borders, invoking a sense of a place that is governed by laws, not a place that is open and easily accessible. The boundaried construction of the plaza is reinforced by the thought bubble she draws hovering over the plaza on the map, which highlights that these are boundaries that are classed and raced. Zoliswa fills the thought bubble with the text 'too cool, too pretty, too rich, too popular, too white. NOT ME' (see Figure 6). The repetition of the word 'too' – both textually and visually – evokes a sense of being overwhelmed in this space. The implication here is that Zoliswa's intersecting identities are 'not enough' for the Jameson Plaza. She cannot enact a legitimate and affirming student identity in this space. She represents with this speech bubble an active alienation from the plaza space. This alienation relates, on the one hand, to the identities that the plaza was built for, the student envisioned by the architect, the young, white men of the Cape Colony. But it is also overlaid with contemporary iterations of the norms dictating what students should look like, dress like, speak like to be 'cool' or 'popular' and thus comfortable or welcome on the plaza. Some of these norms are related to race, but also wealth, clothing and aspects of physical appearance.

Maria, in her reflective map (see Figure 2) similarly constructs the Jameson Plaza and the cafeteria (i.e., the Food Court) as places of exclusion. The page is divided into a 3 x 3 grid representing the nine campus spaces she chooses to document. Maria's map constitutes a mosaic of constructions of 'affect in place', rather than a cartographic representation of the UCT campus as with most of the other maps featured. Although not explicitly linked to race and class on her map, the affective state she connects to the plaza specifically mirrors the discomfort Zoliswa documents in her representation. The density of the text in this section could be seen as a mimetic representation of the bustling overcrowding of the space that Maria describes. In the content of this text, Maria elucidates the passive trajectory of 'being watched' which connects to the rigid spatialised norms Zoliswa depicts in her map. The affective identity discourse thus produced for the Jameson Plaza – which she textually places the top of the plaza section of her map – is as 'a place of anxiety and exposure' (see Figure 7).

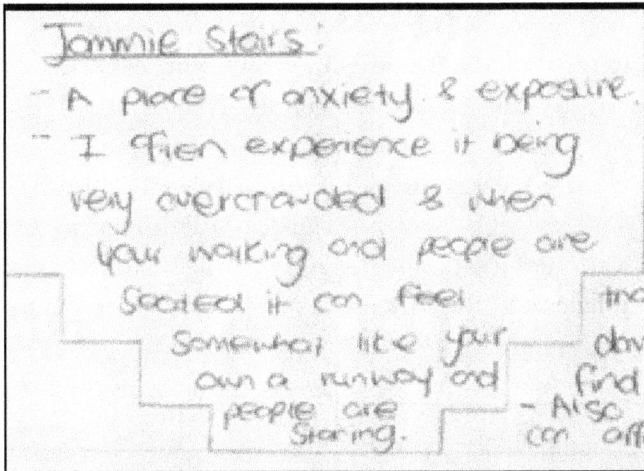

**Figure 7. Close up of Jameson Plaza on Maria's reflective map**

In her construction of the cafeteria space, however, Maria is more explicit in connecting experiences of alienation to classed identities (see Figure 8).

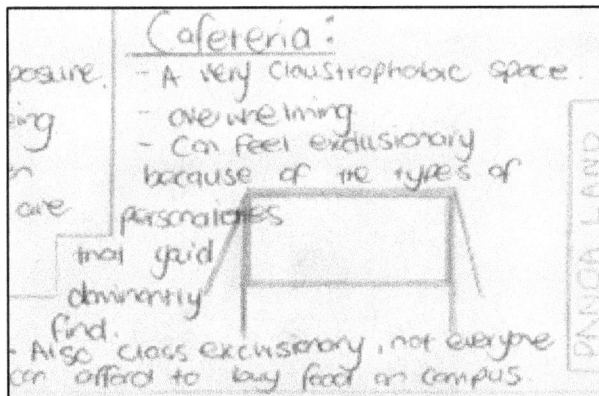

**Figure 8. Close up of the cafeteria on Maria's reflective map**

Her construction of the cafeteria as a place of exclusion is premised on three intersecting socio-spatial dynamics or as Massey (2005) would term, geometries of power: firstly, the claustrophobic physical design of the space; the identity performances of the other students occupying that space which Maria experiences as alienating; and the prohibitively high price of campus food for many students.

103

Maria's depiction connects to Zoliswa's construction of the Food Court (i.e., the cafeteria), with the affective state she experiences described as 'Anxiety, too full, too loud, too hot, too crowded. GET OUT!'. Zoliswa emphasises the ambivalence of the cafeteria – supposedly a place for refreshment and leisure ('yummie', 'ROAD TO COMFORT', smiley face) – which is swiftly undermined by the changing arrow direction, the sarcastic insertion of the word 'NOT!!', the frowning pencil faces and the lament, 'WHAT NOW' (see Figure 9).

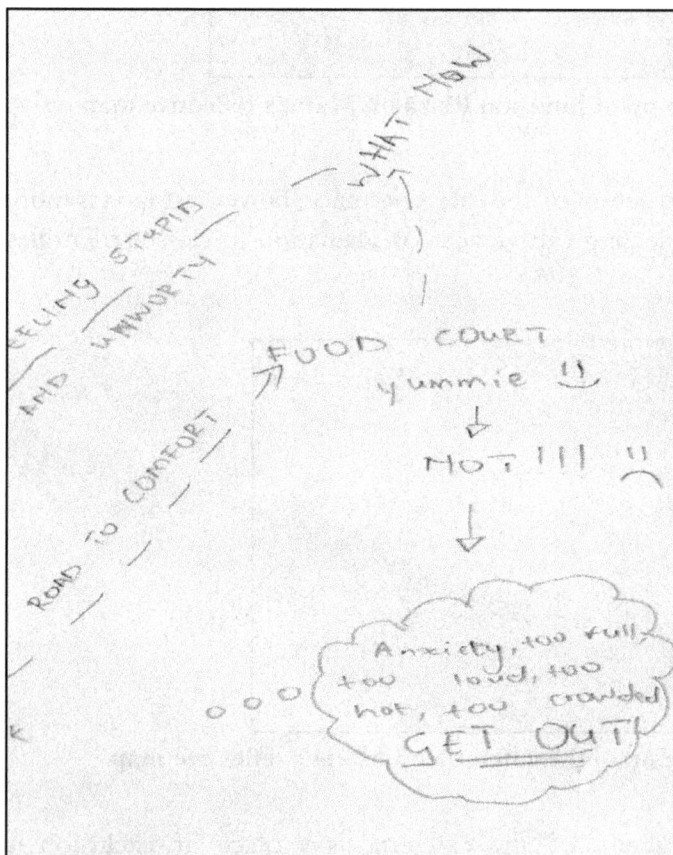

**Figure 9. Close up of the food court (cafeteria) on Zoliswa's map**

Maria and Zoliswa's depictions of the cafeteria contrasts with Kate's map (see Figure 3) – as a middle class, white student – with her positive construction of the cafeteria as premised entirely on the easy availability of food ('CAF!!! Food glorious food!') (see Figure 10 for close up).

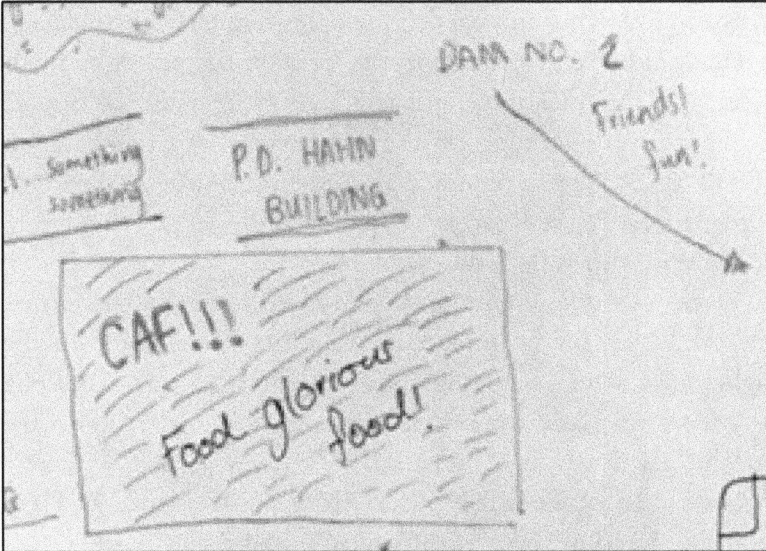

**Figure 10. Close up of the cafeteria on Kate's reflective map**

Where race and class are salient in Zoliswa and Maria's experience of marginalisation in space, in Kate's reflective map (Figure 3), gendered exclusions are considered. Kate draws the rugby fields which take a prominent place in the Upper Campus cartography and, using black pen, fills the space with repetitions of the word 'men', representing mimetically perhaps the male bodies of the rugby players crowding the field (see Figure 11).

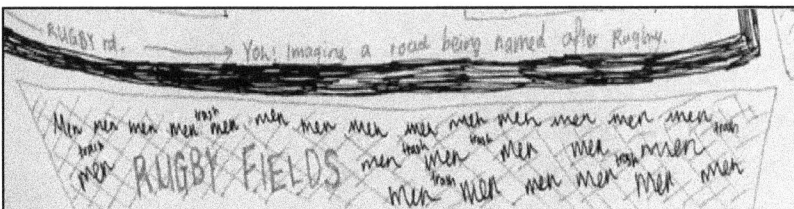

**Figure 11. Close up of the rugby fields on Kate's map**

UCT has a strong culture of rugby and is known for its rugby team, the Ikey Tigers. Arguably, the university has privileged rugby (and the men's rugby team in particular) over other sports which have a more diverse following and participation, both in terms of race and gender. This can be seen spatially in the location of the rugby fields in the heart of Upper Campus and as Kate highlights in the orange text on her map, the naming of the ring road above the fields as Rugby Road (this has been renamed as Madiba East but is frequently still referred to as 'Rugby Road').

Kate continues to reflect the gendered dimensions of exclusion in other places she documents on her map. In her construction of the Jameson Plaza, for example, she links the plaza space to the candlelight vigil ('Nene's night vigil') held for first-year UCT student, Uyinene Mrwetyana, and the protest activities that occurred on the plaza around her death. In August 2019, Uyinene went to collect a parcel from a post office a few blocks from her residence and was raped and murdered in the post office by a post office worker. Her murder sparked a broader wave of protest against gender-based violence in South Africa (Lyster 2019) and the University held a week of mourning and reflection with several memorial services, vigils and protest events taking place on the plaza (Davids 2019). Although Uyinene was not murdered on campus, there have been many other incidences of gender-based violence on and around the university campus. Between December 2015 and April 2016, for example, a serial rapist attacked six UCT students around campus and the surrounding suburbs, particularly at Rhodes Memorial (Petersen 2016). The affect Kate links to the plaza (and ultimately the campus in its entirety) here is a state of grief and danger, in particular a gendered danger. However, Kate overlays this particular state of affect with semiotic representations of strength and resistance. She draws a raised fist and clenched arm, a universal symbol of resistance (see Davidson and Blair 2019) and enacts her own renaming of the plaza, scribbling across and crossing out the 'Jameson Plaza' label on her map (see Figure 12).

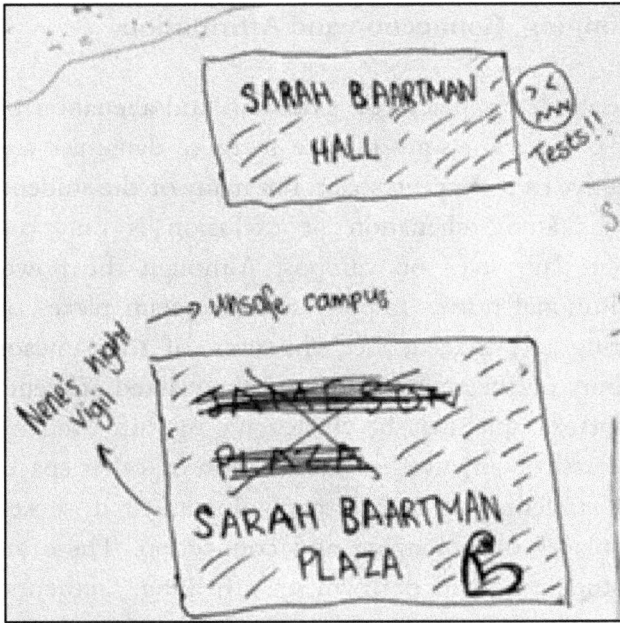

**Figure 12. Close up of the Jameson Plaza on Kate's map**

It is noteworthy that Kate's act of obliteration of the plaza toponym is included on the map. Kate could have simply written 'Sarah Baartman Plaza',[7] but she moves through the process of writing down the 'Jameson Plaza' label, documenting its erasure. Embodied within commonly recognised place names are the histories of the relationships between humans and those places (see Takada 2016). Indeed, the name 'Jameson Plaza', after the British colonialist Leander Starr Jameson, is a signifier of the history of the university's colonial connections. Kate's counter-naming of this plaza is a form of 'toponym opposition' to this legacy of colonialism within the university and is one of the many ways the identities of places are contested (Guyot and Seethal 2007: 56). The Jameson Plaza has as yet not been renamed, and most likely will not officially be renamed the Sarah Baartman Plaza. Kate's reference to Sarah Baartman in her counter-naming here, with the arrow connection to Uyinene's vigil in this space, invokes a palimpsest memorial to black South African women and the historical echoes of gender-based violence throughout South Africa's broader active spatial archive (see Knowles 2003).

107

## 11. Places of Belonging, Connection and Affirmation

Although students depict places of exclusion and alienation on their campus maps, there is always nuance to these dynamics and processes and affective experience in space. For many of the students participating in this study, alienation or exclusion is only one dimension of their daily lives on campus. Although the power relations and institutional norms implicit within certain places on campus are enduring and, indeed, the 'whiteness' of the Jameson Plaza, the masculinity of the rugby fields and the classed affluence of the cafeteria, for example, may be challenging to shift, students are agentically and actively involved in the creation of other spaces on campus. The students' reflective maps documented several constructions of places of belonging and connection. These are places in which students could perform an affirming, 'authentic' student identity.

For many students, such as Kate and Zoliswa, spaces of belonging are created through the connection to other people, both as friends and partners, in specific places on campus. These are spaces which make possible other affective states for students. Zoliswa depicts on her map (in Figure 1), for example, her student leadership office ('HSC Office') about which she writes that she 'runs from feelings of inferiority' (see Figure 13 for close up) engendered within other places on campus, such as the Jameson Plaza and the lecture theatres.

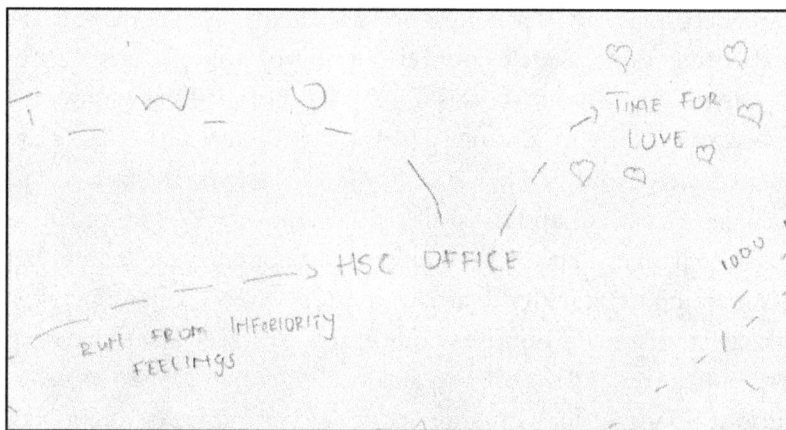

**Figure 13. Close up of Zoliswa's place of belonging**

This place is thus, in some ways, a retreat, created through an act of withdrawal, but simultaneously an insertion into the heart of campus space (an office connected to a leadership position no less) for a 'time of love', visually underscored by the collection of hearts circling her text. This is an office space in which Zoliswa spends time and connects with her partner and performs her student leadership role and thus enacts an affirming, validating student identity. Kate similarly documents spaces of connection with others on her map (Figure 3), but unlike Zoliswa, Kate's connection to friends is illustrated in more frequent and more public spaces across campus, such as different lecture theatres and residence spaces. Kate reads and experiences much of campus space through the lens of the friendships she associates with particular places, engendering, despite her considerations of gendered exclusion, and an overwhelming sense of belonging across the entire campus. It is arguably notable that the one student to depict such a campus-wide experience of spatialised belonging is white and middle-class.

In addition to the connection to other people on campus, students also sought to create refuge places in which they could nurture spiritual connection and reflection – often with and through other people. In Anele's reflective map (Figure 4), for example, he associates his residence on Lower Campus with spirituality and discursively constructs it as a place of prayer, labelling it as a 'praying house', whereas Middle and Upper Campus are exclusively framed as places of study. The spiritual dimensions of his identity which are neglected on Upper Campus are fostered in these spaces, and thus the residence is central to the co-constitution of an affirming student identity (*'place of major influence'*). Close, familial (*'spiritual brothers/spiritual sisters'*) and 'authentic' (*'real (true) people'*) subject positions are created for the other students in his residence and the students in the female residence next door (see Figure 14).

In contrast to the authenticity and influence he ascribes to the Lower Campus residence spaces in this map, Upper Campus is constructed as a place that undermines and challenges his 'true' identity (*'my character is tested here'*) (see Figure 15).

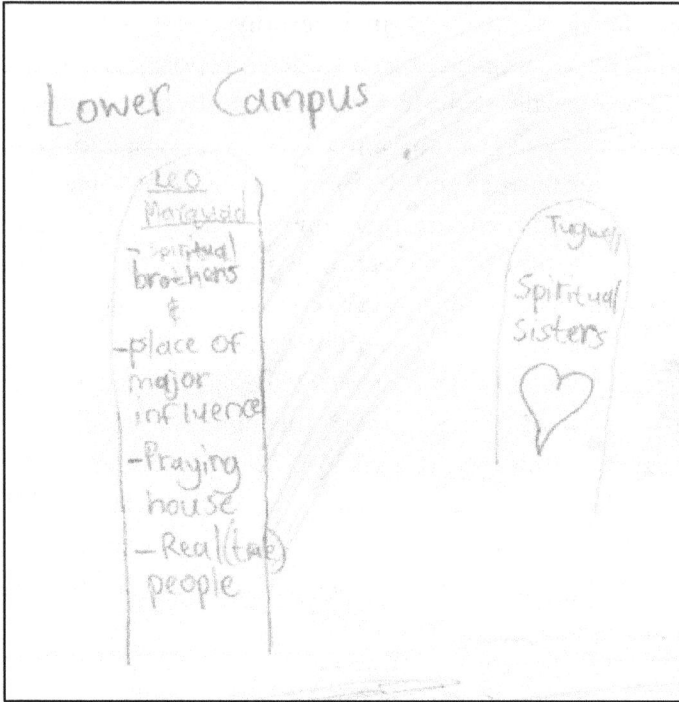

**Figure 14. Close up of Anele's map**

That is not to say, however, that Anele does not strive and succeed in the academic spaces of Upper and Middle Campus or indeed that he is unable to occupy an 'academic identity'. Indeed, his self-described identity as 'a blooming flower' and a 'light in the university' are affirming and confident self-descriptions. Instead, this map illustrates to an extent that Anele's student identity is geographically fractured, with his 'spiritual identity' constituted in residences spaces and an 'academic identity' located on Upper and Middle Campus. For Anele, these two particular identities may be broadly incompatible, but he abandons neither and finds places on campus in which enactments of both are possible.

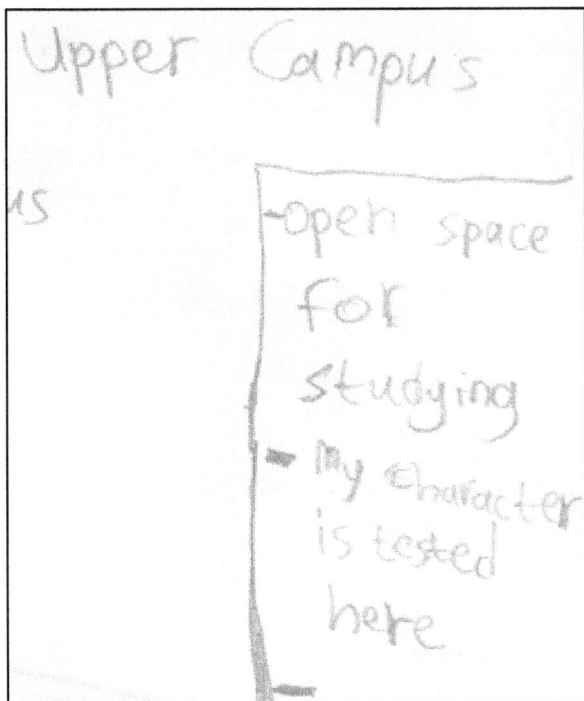

**Figure 15. Close up of Anele's map**

Students also seek refuge and belonging within the pockets of nature on campus. Much like Anele constructs his residence as a place that allows for the enactment of a particular kind of 'true' spiritual identity, Maria and Nicole construct places of nature on campus as engendering the enactment of an 'authentic self' in comparison to other places on campus. On Maria's reflective map (see Figure 2), for example, she documents her reflections on 'The Dam': 'a place of solace and reflection. A place where *I can be my complete self*. A place of escape' (see Figure 16).

Similarly, on Nicole's reflective map (see Figure 5) about her favourite place on campus, a small patch of lawn, she writes that she can 'renew my energy and *my sense of the world*' (see Figure 17).

It is unsurprising then that, despite typically being located on the edges of Upper Campus or tucked away in corners and crevices, these places take up much space on the students' maps. Indeed, size is frequently used to indicate salience in visual semiotic resources (**Machin and Mayr 2012**). Although geographically located

111

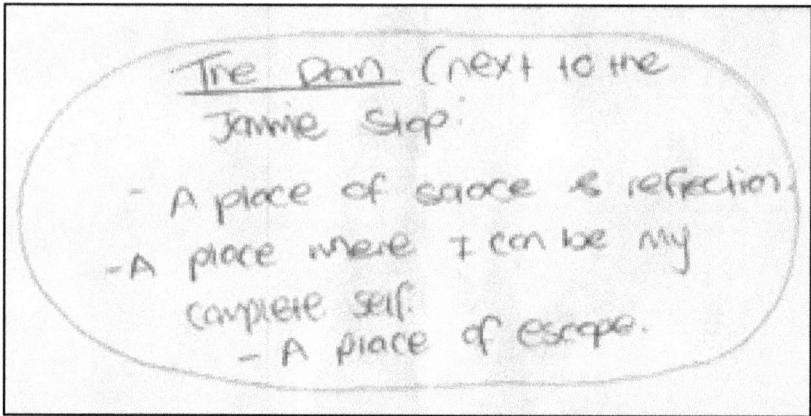

**Figure 16. Close up of the Dam on Maria's reflective map**

peripherally on Upper Campus, Maria centres and encircles the dam on her map. Similarly, Nicole's favourite place (see Figure 17) takes up a third of her map and while in reality, it comprises a few square meters. Both Nicole and Maria construct these favourite locations as places to escape into nature. Notably, a place that allows for an expression of an identity they feel is authentic is one that is a place that offers an oasis within wider campus space, the construction of this identity only achievable in peripheral locations on campus. These places, however, also function to 'recharge' students' affective states of belonging on campus to potentially mediate and enable students to cope with experiences of alienation within other places on campus. Nicole, for example, writes on her map that she will often 'move through campus robotically, everything else might seem colourless' (see Figure 17). This apparent disengagement from broader campus space is further represented with her use of colour in her map. Her favourite space, on the other hand, is rendered brightly in colour. These places function as a site of renewal which is linked to various intersecting dimensions of this space: elements of the natural materiality (e.g., sun, fresh air); quiet; lack of other people; and within this the scope for embodying particular identities. To 'be yourself' in some places, for certain times builds tolerance and mediates the dissonance and alienation of 'not being themselves' or 'feeling uncomfortable' in other places, at other times.

112

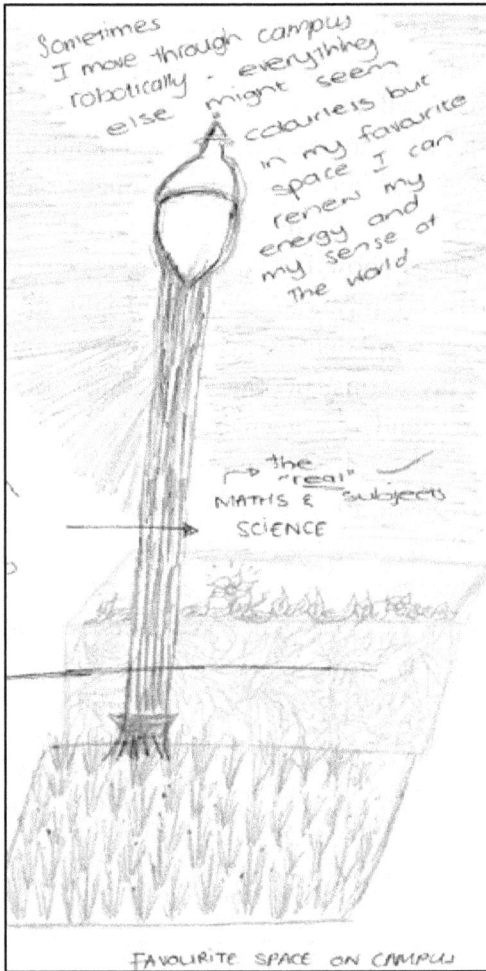

Sometimes
I move through campus
robotically . everything
else might seem
colourless but
in my favourite
space I can
renew my
energy and
my sense of
the world.

→ the
"real" —
MATHS &   subjects
SCIENCE

FAVOURITE SPACE ON CAMPUS

**Figure 17. Close up of Nicole's favourite place on campus**

## 12. Conclusion

Inequality and exclusion are embedded within the fabric of South African higher education institutions. These institutions were built under colonial and apartheid systems of oppression to educate a very particular student, representing intersections of white, male, middle-class, heterosexual, able-bodied, cisgender identity. The widening participation of students from a diverse range of identities and the establishment of national and institutional policies aimed at redress

113

demonstrates an important transformation success, however hierarchical arrangements of privilege within these spaces of education persist. Students' experiences of alienation or belonging on campus are varied, multifaceted and crucially, spatialised. A multimodal discourse analysis of the reflective maps students produced to depict campus space is able to elucidate the nuances of students' experiences of affect in space and the construction of particular identities. Students' maps show both places of exclusion and belonging across campus and provide valuable insight into students' spatialised affective experiences on campus and contextually contingent identity constructions. Students may experience classed, raced and gendered alienation in particular campus places, but also successfully and simultaneously create their own places of affirmation through, for example, connection to others and nature in place. Examining how students experience campus space helps illuminate processes of privilege and exclusion on campus and foregrounds students' agency; however, the creation of inclusionary campus places should not be the sole responsibility of students. The institution, more broadly, and all those who work within it should be accountable for working to create welcoming spaces for all students.

**Endnotes**

[1] The term 'black' in this chapter is used in the inclusive sense to refer to people classified as 'black', 'coloured' and 'Indian' under the apartheid regime.

[2] From 2016 onwards, the admissions policy considers a hybrid three mechanisms when selecting applicants: the applicant's Admissions Points Score (calculated from their school-leaving results); their scores on entrance examinations; and a Weighted Points Score (calculated using the 'disadvantage factor' applicable to each applicant).

[3] SRPP is a points system used to promote and facilitate student involvement as participants in the research activities of the Department of Psychology. Undergraduate students are required to sign up as participants

for a certain number of research studies per course, for which they receive points which go towards their final course grades.

[4] As a central theoretical assumption of this study is that identities are fluid, flexible and constructed, participants were asked to self-identify rather than to tick off specific race, class, gender or sexuality categories. Table 1 thus outlines participants' self-described identities. In most cases, participants utilised relatively conventional identity categories, but some students provided other self-descriptors (e.g., 'I'm a flower that's blooming') which defied more traditional categorisation. In many instances, these identities were elaborated on in later stages of the broader study not covered in this chapter. For example, the student who described himself as a blooming flower also discussed at length elsewhere his experience of being a black, first-generation student. However, this table provides only the identities given by the students when asked outright to self-identify, and not those other identity descriptors that emerged in later aspects of the data collection.

[5] All names used in this chapter are pseudonyms.

[6] It is a paved plaza situated on the university's main campus flanked above and below by a series of stone steps known as the Jameson Stairs and the site of the university's main hall, the recently renamed Sarah Baartman Memorial Hall (formerly the Jameson Memorial Hall named after the British colonialist, Leander Starr Jameson).

[7] Sarah Baartman was a South African Khoi woman born in 1789 who was enslaved and exhibited across Europe in the 19th century as part of various 'freak show' attractions and 'scientific' displays. Upon her death, her brain, skeleton and sexual organs were put on display in a French museum and returned to South Africa only in 2002 (see Gordon-Chipembere [ed.] 2011; Gqola 2008).

**Acknowledgements**

This work was supported by JSPS KAKENHI Grant Number JP16H06318 and the National Research Foundation, the Hub for Decolonial Feminist Psychology in Africa, and the University of Cape Town.

# References

Acton, R. (2017) 'Place-people-practice-process: Using sociomateriality in university physical spaces research', *Educational Philosophy and Theory*, Vol. 49, No. 4, pp. 1441–51.

Akoojee, S. and Nkomo, M. (2007) 'Access and quality in South African higher education: The twin challenges of transformation', *South African Journal of Higher Education,* Vol. 12, No. 3, pp. 385–99.

Alexander, L. (2007) 'Invading pure space: Disrupting black and white racially homogenised spaces', *South African Journal of Psychology*, Vol. 37, No. 4, pp. 738–54.

Alexander, L. and Tredoux, C. (2010) 'The spaces between us: A spatial analysis of informal segregation at a South African university', *Journal of Social Issues,* Vol. 66, No. 2, pp. 367–86.

Andersson, J., Sadgrove, J. and Valentine, G. (2012) 'Consuming campus: Geographies of encounter at a British university', *Social & Cultural Geography*, Vol. 13, No. 5, pp. 501–15.

Badat, S. (2016) 'Deciphering the meanings, and explaining the South African higher education student protests of 2015–16', *Pax Academica,* Vol. 1, pp. 71–106.

Bangeni, B. and Kapp, R. (2005) 'Identities in transition: Shifting conceptions of home among "black" South African university students', *African Studies Review*, Vol. 48, No. 3, pp. 1–19.

Beyes, T. and Michels, C. (2014) 'Performing university space', in P. Temple (ed.) *The Physical University: Contours of Space and Place in Higher Education,* Oxon: Routledge, pp. 15–33.

Boonzaier, F. and Mhkize, L. (2018) 'Bodies out of place: Black queer students negotiating identity at the University of Cape Town', *South African Journal of Higher Education,* Vol. 32, No. 3, pp. 81–100.

Brunn, S. D. (2012) 'Using cognitive maps to heal the legacies of apartheid', in B. Leibowitz, L. Swartz, V. Bozalek, R. Carolissen, L. Nicholls and P. Rohleder (eds) *Community, Self and Identity: Educating South African University Students for Citizenship*, Cape Town: HSRC Press, pp. 97–116.

Cloete, N. (2002) 'New South African realities' in N. Cloete, R. Fehnel,

P. Maassen, T. Moja, H. Perold and T. Gibbon (eds) *Transformation in Higher Education: Global Pressures and Local Realities in South Africa*, Cape Town: Juta, pp. 415–43.

Cooper, D. (2015) 'Social justice and South African university student enrolment data by "race", 1998–2012: From "skewed revolution" to "stalled revolution"', *Higher Education Quarterly*, Vol. 69, No. 3, pp. 237–62.

Cox, A. M. (2011) 'Students' experience of university space: An exploratory study', *International Journal of Teaching and Learning in Higher Education*, Vol. 23, No. 2, pp. 197–207.

Cox, A. M., Herrick, T. and Keating, P. (2012) 'Accommodations: Staff identity and university space', *Teaching in Higher Education*, Vol. 17, No. 6, pp. 697–709.

Davids, N. (2019) 'Something is deeply wrong with our society', UCT Website, 5 September 2019 (https://www.news.uct.ac.za/article/-2019-09-05-something-is-deeply-wrong-with-our-society) (accessed: 28 November 2020).

Davidson, K. and Blair, J. (2018) 'Semiotic analysis of the raised fist emoji as a sign of resilience', *Semiotics*, 2018, pp. 31–45.

Davies, J. (1996) 'The state and the South African university system under apartheid', *Comparative Education*, Vol. 32, No. 3, pp. 319–32.

De Lange, N., Moletsane, R. and Mitchell, C. (2015) 'Seeing how it works: A visual essay about critical and transformative research in education', *Perspectives in Education*, Vol. 33, No. 4, pp. 151–76.

Dixon, K. and Janks, H. (2018) 'Location and dislocation: Spatiality and transformation in higher education', in R. Pattman and R. Carolissen (eds) *Transforming Transformation in Research and Teaching at South African Universities*, Cape Town: African Sun Media, pp. 89–108.

Durrheim, K., Rautenbach, C., Nicholson, T. and Dixon, J. (2013) 'Displacing place identity: Introducing an analytics of participation' in B. Gardener and F. Winddance-Twine (eds) *Geographies of Privilege*, New York: Routledge, pp. 43–71.

Durrheim, K., Trotter, K., Manicom, D. and Piper, L. (2004) 'From exclusion to informal segregation: The limits of transformation at the University of Natal', *Social Dynamics,* Vol. 30, No. 1, pp. 141–69.

Fairclough, N. (1992) *Discourse and Social Change,* Cambridge: Polity Press.

Fenwick, T., Edwards, R. and Sawchuck, P. (2011) *Emerging Approaches to Educational Research: Tracing the Sociomaterial,* Oxon: Routledge.

Ferrare, J. J. and Apple, M. W. (2010) 'Spatializing critical education: Progress and cautions', *Critical Studies in Education*, Vol. 51, No. 2, pp. 209–21.

Forrester, M. (2000) *Psychology of the Image,* London: Routledge.

Fowler, R. (1991) *Language in the News,* London: Routledge.

Frith, H., Riley, S., Archer, L. and Gleeson, K. (2005) 'Imag(in)ing visual methodologies', *Qualitative Research in Psychology*, Vol. 2, No. 3, pp. 187–98.

Gibson, A. and Macleod, C. (2012) '(Dis)allowances of lesbians' sexual identities: Lesbian identity construction in racialised, classed, familial, and institutional spaces', *Feminism & Psychology,* Vol. 22, No. 4, pp. 462–81.

Gieseking, J. (2007) '(Re) constructing women: Scaled portrayals of privilege and gender norms on campus', *Area,* Vol. 39, No. 3, pp. 278–86.

Gordon-Chipembere, N. (ed.) (2011) *Representation and Black Womanhood: The Legacy of Sarah Baartman,* Basingstoke: Palgrave MacMillan.

Gray, D. and Manning, R. (2014) '"Oh my god, we're not doing nothing": Young people's experiences of spatial regulation', *British Journal of Social Psychology,* Vol. 53, No. 4, pp. 640–55.

Gulson, K. N. and Symes, C. (2007) 'Knowing one's place: Space, theory, education', *Critical Studies in Education*, Vol. 48, No. 1, pp. 97–110.

Guyot, S. and Seethal, C. (2007) 'Identity of place, places of identities: Change of place names in post-apartheid South Africa', *South African Geographical Journal,* Vol. 89, No. 1, pp. 55–63.

Gqola, P. D. (2008) '"Crafting epicentres of agency": Sarah Bartmann and African feminist literary imaginings', *Quest: An African Journal of Philosophy,* Vol. 20, No. (1–2), pp. 45–76.

Hames, M. (2007) 'Sexual identity and transformation at a South African university', *Social Dynamics,* Vol. 33, No. 1, pp. 52–77.

Heleta, S. (2016) 'Decolonisation of higher education: Dismantling epistemic violence and Eurocentrism in South Africa', *Transformation in Higher Education,* Vol. 1, No. 1, pp. 1–8.

Higham, R. (2012) 'Place, race and exclusion: University student voices in post-apartheid South Africa', *International Journal of Inclusive Education,* Vol. 16, No. 5-6, pp. 485–501.

Hopkins, P. (2010) 'Towards critical geographies of the university campus: Understanding the contested experiences of Muslim students', *Transactions of the Institute of British Geographers,* Vol. 36, pp. 157–69.

Howarth, C. (2002) 'Identity in whose eyes?: The role of representations in identity construction', *Journal for the Theory of Social Behaviour,* Vol. 32, No. 2. pp. 145–62.

Howes, S. and Miles, A. (eds) (2015) *Photography in Educational Research: Critical Reflections from Diverse Contexts,* Oxon: Routledge.

Isaacs, D. (2020) '"I don't have time for this": Stuttering and the politics of university time', *Scandinavian Journal of Disability Research,* Vol. 22, No. 1, pp. 58–67.

Jagessar, V. and Msibi, T. (2015) '"It's not that bad": Homophobia in the residences of a university in KwaZulu-Natal, Durban, South Africa', *Agenda,* Vol. 29, No. 1, pp. 63–73.

Kessi, S. and Cornell, J. (2015) 'Coming to UCT: Black students, transformation and discourses of race', *Journal of Student Affairs in Africa,* Vol. 3, No. 2, pp. 1–16.

Knowles, J. (2003) *Race and Social Analysis,* London: Sage.

Kobayashi, A. (2005) 'Anti-racist feminism in geography: An agenda for social action', in L. Nelson and J. Seager (eds) *A companion to Feminist Geography,* Oxford: Blackwell Publishing, pp. 32–40.

Kress, G., and van Leeuwen, T. (2001) *Multimodal Discourse: The Modes and Media of Contemporary Communication,* London: Hodder Arnold.

Lebakeng, J. T., Phalane, M. M. and Dalindjebo, N. (2006) 'Epistemicide, institutional cultures and the imperative for the Africanisation of universities in South Africa', *Alternation,* Vol. 13, No. 1, pp. 70–87.

119

Letsekha, T. (2013) 'Revisiting the debate on the Africanisation of higher education: An appeal for a conceptual shift', *The Independent Journal of Teaching and Learning*, Vol. 8, No. 1, pp. 5–18.

Le Grange, L. (2016) 'Decolonising the university curriculum', *South African Journal of Higher Education*, Vol. 30, No. 2, pp. 1–12.

Luescher, T. M. (2009) 'Racial desegregation and the institutionalisation of "race" in university governance: The case of the University of Cape Town', *Perspectives in Education*, Vol. 27, No. 4, pp. 415–25.

Lyster, R. (2019) 'The death of Uyinene Mrwetyana and the rise of South Africa's "Am I Next?" Movement', *New Yorker*, 12 September 2019 (https://www.newyorker.com/news/news-desk/the-death-of-uyinene-mrwetyana-and-the-rise-of-south-africas-aminext-movement) (accessed: 28 November 2020).

Machin, D. and Mayr, A. (2012) *How to Do Critical Discourse Analysis: A Multimodal Introduction*, London: Sage.

Malherbe, N. Suffla, S. Seedat, M. and Bawa, U. (2016) 'Visually negotiating hegemonic discourse through Photovoice: Understanding youth representations of safety', *Discourse & Society*, Vol. 27, No. 6, pp. 589–606.

Mamdani, M. (2016) 'Between the public intellectual and the scholar: Decolonisation and some post-independence initiatives in African higher education', *Inter-Asia Cultural Studies*, Vol. 17, No. 1, pp. 68–83.

Massey, D. (1994) *Space, Place and Gender*, Cambridge: Polity Press.
——————— (2005) *For Space*, London: Sage.

Matus, C. and Talburt, S. (2009) 'Spatial imaginaries: Universities, internationalisation, and feminist geographies', *Discourse: Studies in the Cultural Politics of Education*, Vol. 30, No. 4, pp. 515–27.

Maxwele, C. (2016) 'Black pain led me to throw Rhodes poo', *Business Day Live*, 16 March 2016 (https://www.businesslive.co.za/bd/opinion/2016-03-16-black-pain-led-me-to-throw-rhodes-poo/) (accessed: 28 November 2020).

Mbembe, A. J. (2016) 'Decolonising the university: New directions', *Arts and Humanities in Higher Education*, Vol. 15, No 1, pp. 29–45.

Metcalfe, A. S. (2016) 'Visual methods in higher education' in F. K. Stage and A. S. Metcalfe (eds) *Research in the College Context: Approaches and Methods*, New York: Routledge, pp. 111–27.

Moguerane, K. (2007) 'Post-apartheid politics of integration at a residential student community in South Africa: A case study on campus', *African Sociological Review*, Vol. 11, No. 2, pp. 42–63.

Morreira, S., Taru, J. and Truyts, C. (2020) 'Place and pedagogy: Using space and materiality in teaching social science in Southern Africa', *Third World Thematics: A TWQ Journal*, pp. 1–17 (https://doi.org/10.1080/23802014.2020.1747944) (accessed: 7 December 2020).

Msibi, T. (2013) 'Queering transformation in higher education', *Perspectives in Education*, Vol. 31, No. 2, pp. 65–73.

Muñoz, F. M. (2009) 'Critical race theory and the landscapes of higher education', *The Vermont Connection*, Vol. 30, No. 1, pp. 53–62.

Mutanga, O. (2013) '"I am a university student, not a disabled student": Conceptualising identity and social justice in South African higher education through the capabilities approach lens', *Journal of Educational Studies*, Vol. 12, No. 1, pp. 76–88.

Nakusera, E. (2004) 'Rethinking higher education transformation in terms of an African (a) philosophy of education: Perspectives on higher education', *South African Journal of Higher Education*, Vol. 18, No. 3, pp. 127–37.

Ndlovu-Gatsheni, S. J. (2013) 'Decolonising the university in Africa', *The Thinker*, Vol. 51, pp. 46–51.

Neely, B. and Samura, M. (2011) 'Social geographies of race: Connecting race and space', *Ethnic and Racial Studies*, Vol. 34, No. 11, pp. 1933–52.

Nyamnjoh, F. B. (2012) '"Potted plants in greenhouses": A critical reflection on the resilience of colonial education in Africa', *Journal of Asian and African Studies*, Vol. 47, No. 2, pp. 129–54.

Odhav, K. (2009) 'South African post-apartheid higher education policy and its marginalisations: 1994-2002', *SA-EDUC Journal*, Vol. 6, No. 1, pp. 33–57.

O'Halloran, K. L. (2011) 'Multimodal discourse analysis', in K.

Hyland and B. Paltridge (eds) *The Bloomsbury Companion to Discourse Analysis*, London: Bloomsbury, pp. 120–37.

Paechter, C. (2004) 'Space, identity and education', *Pedagogy, Culture and Society*, Vol. 12, No. 3, pp. 307–8.

Parkinson, J. and Crouch, A. (2011) 'Education, language, and identity amongst students at a South African university', *Journal of Language, Identity, and Education*, Vol. 10, No. 2, pp. 83–98.

Petersen, C. (2016) 'Serial rapist strikes again at UCT', *Independent Online*, 11 March 2016 (https://www.iol.co.za/capetimes/news/serial-rapist-strikes-again-at-uct-1996483) (accessed: 28 November 2020).

Petersen, I., Louw, J. and Dumont, K. (2009) 'Adjustment to university and academic performance among disadvantaged students in South Africa', *Educational Psychology: An International Journal of Experimental Educational Psychology*, Vol. 29, No. 1, pp. 99–115.

Phillips, H. (2019) *UCT under Apartheid Part 1 1948-1968: From Onset to Sit-in*, Auckland Park: Fanele.

Reavey, P. and Johnson, K. (2017) 'Visual approaches: Using and interpreting images', in C. Willig and W. Stainton Rogers (eds) *The SAGE Handbook of Qualitative Research in Psychology*, London: Sage, pp. 354–73.

Robertson, S. L. (2010) '"Spatializing" the sociology of education', in M. W. Apple, S. J. Ball and L. A. Gandin (eds) *The Routledge International Handbook of the Sociology of Education*, Oxon: Routledge, pp. 15–26.

Rogers, R. (ed.) (2004) *An Introduction to Critical Discourse Analysis in Education*, Mahwah: Lawrence Erlbaum.

Rohleder, P. and Thesen, L. (2012) 'Interpreting drawings: Reading the racialised politics of space', in B. Leibowitz, L. Swartz, V. Bozalek, R. Carolissen, L. Nicholls and P. Rohleder (eds) *Community, Self and Identity: Educating South African University Students for Citizenship*, Cape Town: HSRC Press, pp. 87–96.

Rose, G. (1993) *Feminism and Geography: The Limits of Geographical Knowledge*, England: Polity Press.

SAHRC (South African Human Rights Commission) (2016)

*Transformation at Public Universities in South Africa*, SAHRC Report, Johannesburg: SAHRC.

Samura, M. (2016) 'Remaking selves, repositioning selves, or remaking space: An examination of Asian American college students' processes of belonging', *Journal of College Student Development*, Vol. 57, No. 2, pp. 135–50.

Sehoole, C. (2006) 'Internationalisation of higher education in South Africa: A historical review', *Perspectives in Education*, Vol. 24, No. 4, pp. 1–13.

Soudien, C. (2008) 'The intersection of race and class in the South African university: Student experiences', *South African Journal of Higher Education*, Vol. 22, No. 3, pp. 662–78.

Soudien, C., Michaels, W., Mthembi-Mahanyele, S., Nkomo, M., Nyanda, G., Nyoka, N., Seepe, S., Shisana, O. and Villa-Vicencio, C. (2008) *Report of the Ministerial Committee on Transformation and Social Cohesion and the Elimination of Discrimination in Public Higher Education Institutions*, Pretoria: Department of Education.

Steyn, M. E. and Van Zyl, M. (2001) '"Like that statue at Jammie stairs": Some student perceptions and experiences of institutional culture at the University of Cape Town in 1999', Cape Town: Institute for Intercultural and Diversity Studies of Southern Africa.

Takada, A. (2016) 'Unfolding cultural meanings: Wayfinding practices among the San of the Central Kalahari', in W. Lovis and R. Whallon (eds) *Marking the Land: Hunter-Gatherer Creation of Meaning in Their Environment*, New York: Routledge, pp. 180–200.

Temple, P. (ed.) (2014). *The Physical University: Contours of Space and Place in Higher Education*, Oxon: Routledge.

Thomas, K. (2018) 'Decolonisation is now: Photography and student-social movements in South Africa', *Visual Studies*, Vol. 33, No. 1, pp. 98–110.

Tredoux, C., Dixon, J., Underwood, S., Nunez, D. and Finchilescu, G. (2005) 'Preserving spatial and temporal dimensions in observational data of segregation', *South African Journal of Psychology*, Vol. 35, No. 3, pp. 412–32.

UCT (University of Cape Town) (2018) *Transformation Report - 2018*,

Cape Town: UCT.

Valentine, G. (2001) *Social Geographies: Space and Society,* Essex: Pearson Education.

Van Leeuwen, T. (2006) 'Critical discourse analysis', in K. Brown (ed.) *Encyclopedia of Language and Linguistics*, Boston: Elsevier, pp. 290–4.

Vavrus, F. (2016) 'Topographies of power: A critical historical geography of schooling in Tanzania', *Comparative Education*, Vol. 52, No. 2, pp. 136–56.

Walker, M. (1998) 'Academic identities: Women on a South African landscape', *British Journal of Sociology of Education*, Vol. 19, No. 3, pp. 335–54.

————— (2005) 'Rainbow nation or new racism? Theorising race and identity formation in South African higher education', *Race Ethnicity and Education*, Vol. 8, No. 2, pp. 129–46.

Wee, A. (2019) 'Space and identity construction: A study of female Singaporean undergraduates in the UK', *Journal of International Students*, Vol. 9, No. 2, pp. 384–411.

# Part II

# School Credentials versus Knowledge

# for Use

# Chapter 4

## Skills Development Paths Chosen by Learners: The Case of Students Studying Automotive-Related Subjects in Technical and Vocational Education and Training Institutions in Kumasi, Ghana[1]

*Shoko Yamada*

## 1. Introduction

In many African countries, including Ghana, there is a deeply-rooted belief that vocational education has a lower value than academic education (Eichhorst et al. 2012: 4–9). This perception is based on the historical roots of school-based education, which was introduced to provide staff for Christian missions, European firms and colonial governments, with a literary education. In this context, the notion that school education leads to white-collar jobs became prevalent, and education that was oriented to equipping learners with manual skills tended to be looked down on (Foster 1965).

However, this attitude toward vocational education does not mean that skilled jobs and the training needed for them are not respected. Across West Africa, including Ghana, there exist highly developed apprenticeship systems, although these are often informal arrangements (Hart 1970; Anokye et al. 2014; Sonnenberg 2012). Because of the high regard for apprenticeships and the craftsmen who were trained via this system, it is not unusual for graduates from formal secondary schools, who are likely to be better educated than the majority of apprentices, to take up apprenticeships. For example, according to the study by Fluitman (1992: 3–4) in Ibadan, Nigeria, 36 per cent of apprentices held a high school diploma.

In the 60 years since independence, the Ghanaian government has initiated several reforms for technical and vocational education and training (TVET). There has been an ongoing argument in support of TVET, not only in Ghana but also globally. For example, it was said that TVET would combat youth delinquency caused by unemployment, and that training of the labour force should be based on a detailed assessment of the needs of the labour market and manpower plans. However, efforts to reinvent TVET have often been met with opposition that has pushed education back toward more general, literary goals, and these forces may be rooted in the public mistrust of vocational education (Yamada 2001).

In 2007, the Ghanaian government began a large-scale TVET reform, the largest after that introduced in 1986.[2] At first glance, many of the arrangements and their justifications appeared to reiterate those that were already in place. However, a significant characteristic of the current reform is that it emphasises the cultivation of the learners' competencies in problem solving in work and life settings. In other words, the attention has shifted from improving the educational system to enhancing the knowledge and skills acquired by the learners. Accordingly, TVET curriculums prioritise the need for more practical training and industrial attachment (IA)[3] over theoretical lectures. Also, to be certified as having attained specific levels and types of vocational skills, students have to pass practical tests, regardless of whether they completed the school curriculum. Therefore, theoretically, it is possible for apprentices without a TVET diploma to obtain a skills certificate at the same level as those from TVET.

Because of its massive scale, the reform process has caused a great deal of confusion, and it will take a while for the reform to be reflected in the daily practice of schools (Kumasi Technical Institute 2011; Owusu-Acheampong et al. 2014). As a result, the author's interviews showed that students did not recognise the changes implemented by the reforms. The career decisions after basic education (primary and junior secondary school) are diverse for young people who do not come from privileged households. To earn a living, they have to work. At the same time, to be effective in work, they have to acquire skills, whether via a formal school or in the workplace. The locations and modes of training chosen by the young people depended on the realities they faced and the options that they considered optimal in their contexts. It is not unusual for young

128

Ghanaians to start to work first, and then return to school later in life. This shows that learning is not reserved only for students in a school setting, to acquire knowledge and skills to enhance their work-related capacity, but it is also chosen subjectively. In over-institutionalised societies, the level of the school certificate determines the value of the holder in the labour market, almost as if the amount and quality of knowledge the person has gained are represented by the school diploma that they hold. Besides, it is assumed that the educational process is linear from primary school to university, in which those who fail to proceed smoothly along the educational ladder do not have the opportunity to resume learning at a later stage. However, the ways in which Ghanaian young people combine different learning modes, often very creatively, provide us with an opportunity to consider 'African Potentials' as a way to deconstruct the notion of learning and education from the perspective of the learners, and to examine the role of schooling critically.

This chapter is aimed at capturing the elements that constitute learners' motivations, future aspirations and paths followed in accumulating skills. I conducted a questionnaire survey with students from four different types of TVET institutions in Kumasi city to compare patterns of the subjective decisions made in terms of skills development. The institutions were Kumasi Vocational Training Institute (KVTI), Kumasi Technical Institute (KTI), Kumasi Senior Technical High School (KSHS) and Kumasi Polytechnic (KP). In total, 494 participants completed questionnaires and all were second-year students learning vehicle repair skills, such as vehicle mechanics, electrics, auto-body repairs and welding. Except for the polytechnic, the other three schools require a basic education certificate for entry. In this sense, KVTI, KTI and KSHS are the options available to graduates of basic education and KP is the option for those with more experience, knowledge and diplomas. By comparing the records of training and work among the students at VTI, TI and STHS, the post-basic education institutions, with those in KP, one can highlight the different skills development paths taken and the reasons underlying these differences. In this chapter, I describe the movements of young people between multiple channels of education and work. In terms of educational sites, schools and informal apprenticeships are considered equal, as they have different advantages for the learners beyond the required marks of the Basic Education Certificate Examination.

## 2. Academic Context of This Study

### 2-1. Global Discourse on Skills Development and TVET Reforms in Ghana

Since the Education for All (EFA) goals were unanimously adopted by the member states of the United Nations Educational, Scientific and Cultural Organization (UNESCO) and multilateral organisations in 1990, the major focus of global discussions on educational development has been the expansion of access to basic education. Thanks to the concerted efforts of the international community, opportunities for schooling have significantly increased in many developing countries. Moreover, the increased numbers of students enrolled were seen as a triumph for the human right to education.

At the same time, with the majority of young people attending school, at least at the basic level, new issues emerged (UNESCO 2012). Up until the start of the 2020s, there was the rather simple assumption that universal basic education would contribute to reducing poverty. However, after several decades of focused intervention, no clear evidence was found that further schooling contributed to either better learning outcomes or increased employment and, hence, a reduction in poverty. Knowledge and skills are essential to getting a decent job and leading a stable life. However, they cannot necessarily be gained by sitting in a classroom or memorising the curriculum content that is considered important by Ministry of Education (MOE) experts. Over the last decade, there has been an increasing awareness that school education should be more relevant, making the transition from school to work smoother and enabling graduates to apply their knowledge more effectively in their work. It was, therefore, considered important to reflect the

130

voices of the private sector in decisions made about educational content (King and Palmer 2013). Based on neoliberal economic theory, international specialists argued that the primary role of the government should be to bridge the gap between the supply and demand of a trained workforce. Therefore, external advisors encouraged governments to establish an independent agency to coordinate between the training providers, industries that employ graduates and the various ministries involved. In other words, the role of the government was envisaged more as a catalyst than a direct training provider, with the private sector expected to drive the competitive training market (Eichhorst et al. 2012: 4–9; Yamada and Mazda 2009: 130–5).

In Africa, South Africa was the first to adopt TVET reforms based on this framework, and Ghana is among the first group of sub-Saharan African countries to follow suit, with growing support from donor organisations (Allais 2007). Following the internationally promoted model to establish an independent coordination agency, the national parliament of Ghana passed the Council for TVET (COTVET) Act in 2007, and comprehensive reforms of the formal and informal skills development systems have been undertaken under the COTVET initiative. The COTVET also took the lead in developing Occupational Standards for vocational skills, a National TVET Qualification Framework, and an Accreditation Standard for education and training providers (Darvas and Palmer 2014: 5; Government of Ghana 2014a: ix; COTVET 2012). With support from donors such as the World Bank, the Africa Development Bank and bilateral aid agencies in Germany, Belgium and Denmark, the skills development fund was established in 2012 to implement so-called competency-based training (Darvas and Palmer 2014: 5; Government of Ghana 2014a: ix; COTVET 2012).

## 2-2. Labour Market and Youth Skills Development in Ghana

In 2012, the commercial production of oil started in Ghana, which boosted the economy and improved the employment situation. In 2001, 10 per cent of the labour force was unemployed, and the unemployment rate of young people aged between 15 and 24 was at

15.9 per cent. However, these rates dropped to 2.4 per cent and 3.3 per cent respectively by 2014 (World Bank 2016). At the same time, the manufacturing sector shrunk from around 10 per cent to 8.1 per cent, in contrast to the service sector, which expanded with the oil boom (Aryeetey et al. 2014: 233). This suggests that oil export raised domestic consumption in the short term, but has not strengthened the basis of value-added production and that the relative contribution of manufacturing to the national income has fallen. It also suggests that the current growth is fragile, and depends on the export price of the raw materials. The development of mid- to high-level technicians is now more vital than ever to ensure long and stable economic growth.

Compared to other African countries, Ghana has had a relatively high level of educational achievement, as it was the educational centre of British West Africa. As of 2005, its gross primary school enrolment rate was 83.4 per cent, rising to 108.5 per cent in 2014.[4] Also, the percentage of primary school students transitioning to junior high school (JHS) – the level to which education is compulsory – was 93.8 per cent. However, the percentage who progressed from JHS to senior high school (SHS) fell sharply to 45.8 per cent. Despite this representing an improvement from 25.5 per cent in 2005, there remains a significant bottleneck between JHS and SHS, and many JHS graduates choose other career tracks rather than attending SHS (Ghana Education Service 2006, 2015). While approximately half of JHS graduates do not proceed to SHS, only 12 per cent enrol in TVET institutions. There is no accurate data for other non-schooled young people; however, it is assumed that they are either in apprenticeships, informal employment, household work or are not in education, employment, or training (NEET) (Government of Ghana 2014a: 2–11). It is estimated that more than 440,000 young people are learning their skills in informal apprenticeships. If this is true, the ratio of apprentices to TVET students is 4:1 (Darvas and Palmer 2014: 6; Palmer 2009: 32).

The informal sector covers a large proportion not only of skills development but also of employment. According to the 2010 national census, 93 per cent of employment was in the private sector, of which 86.1 per cent was informal. Thus, formal private sector employment accounted for only 7 per cent (Government of Ghana 2010), and the majority of TVET students conducted industrial attachments (IAs) in the informal sector. Moreover, it is not very common for TVET graduates to obtain formal sector employment, at least not immediately after school. To bridge the polarised economy and widen the basis of formal sector employment, the government expected TVETs to take on active roles (Government of Ghana 2014b). In this situation, TVET institutions promoted entrepreneurship for students rather than encouraging their aspirations to be employed by private companies or governmental bodies. Accordingly, there is grant support available for those TVET graduates who fulfil certain conditions and set-up a business (Government of Ghana 2014a: ix–2).

Students do not arrive at the TVET with a comprehensive knowledge of the labour market conditions or policies. According to the interviews I conducted, students knew that the time allocated for IAs had increased compared to a few years ago, when the idea of competency-based training was not prevalent. However, other influences were not well-known; the decision to enrol at a specific TVET institution was made independently of the policy, and was based on students' self-motivation and judgement of the career opportunities offered.

## 2-3. Factors Affecting Career Choice

There are various theories that try to explain the factors that influence individuals' career choices. Sociologists and economists tend to highlight the antecedents that condition the attainment of social status. They try to find patterns in the relationship between career choices and social, economic and educational factors. Many studies have demonstrated that education reproduces the social inequality of access to different types of occupations, caused by educational attainment and economic status of the household, ethnicity, gender and other socioeconomic factors (Bowles and Gintis 1976; Pascarella and Terenzini 1991; Croll 2008; Hossler et al. 1999).

In contrast to studies focusing on the external conditions affecting individuals' career options, other theories have examined the relationship between subjectivity and career choice. Social learning theorists consider that an individual learns from interaction with the environment and other people, and the experiences and knowledge acquired as such become the basis of their subjective career decisions (Bandura 1986; Holland 1997). Based on a common understanding of the importance of social learning, diverse theories have tried to specify the constructs of environmental and personal conditions that influence personal career decisions and their degrees of importance. There are factors outside of the control of the individual, such as economic conditions or societal industry structure, which either encourage or discourage students from choosing certain types of careers. At the same time, each individual believes in their capacity to work at their designated level of performance, which Bandura defines as the sense of 'self-efficacy'. According to Super (1990), satisfaction in work and life depends on the levels at which a person finds an adequate position in which their abilities, interests, values, personality traits and self-esteem are expressed.

Lent et al. (1994: 79–80) proposed a social cognitive framework of career development, which is composed of three mutually related domains. First, each person forms and elaborates their career-relevant interests. Second, they select their career options and, third, pursue them with perseverance and continued performance. In summary, having been conditioned by environmental factors, which include socioeconomic status and interactions with others, individuals develop their interests in specific career options. During this period, while they are developing their interests, values and personalities, their sense of self-efficacy comes into play. Once an aspiration develops, the process to actualise it follows with continuous practice and the accumulation of experience and knowledge.

With significant exceptions (Areetey et al. 2013; Langevang and Gough 2012; Osuji 1976), few studies exist on career decision making by mid- to low-skilled workers in developing countries, and especially not in sub-Saharan Africa. Models developed in Europe and North

America cannot easily be applied to Africa. However, it is important to consider the cognitive and socio-emotional dimensions of young people in formal and informal vocational training, in addition to socioeconomic and school factors, to examine their career trajectories. In doing so, it becomes possible to capture, in full, the roles played by the TVET and its reforms.

## 3. Overview of the Research Site and Sample Population

### 3-1. *Kumasi City in the Ashanti Region*

Ashanti is one of the ten regions in Ghana, located in the mid-south of the country. It has a population of 4.5 million, which constitutes 14.8 per cent of the total population, and is even bigger than the Greater Accra Region, where the national capital is located. The city of Kumasi is the regional capital and has a population of 1.73 million people, constituting over a third of the total population of the region (Government of Ghana 2010). The biggest ethnic group is the Asante, of the Akan language group, whose supreme chief still has the royal court of its chieftaincy in Kumasi. As a legacy of its rule and cultural influence across West Africa, there is a network of major roads leading to the palace. The market in Kumasi, which is said to be the biggest in West Africa, attracts many traders.

The literacy rate of the region is 60.5 per cent, which is higher than the national average of 53.4 per cent, but the intra-regional gap is significant: it is highest in Kumasi at 74 per cent, while in the Ejura/Sekyedumase District, it is as low as 35.3 per cent. Nearly half of the population are engaged in agriculture (44.5 per cent), followed by trading (18.4 per cent) and manufacturing (12.2 per cent) (Government of Ghana 2010). In Kumasi, women also take part in economic activities, particularly in petty trading in the market and on the streets (Clark 1994).

As mentioned earlier, Kumasi has long been known as a hub for manufacturing. Modern factories, most of which have been built with foreign investment, are concentrated in the coastal areas. However, the Ashanti region contains mineral mines (mostly gold) and their processing bases. Kumasi is also known for the Suame Magazine, which is an old industrial cluster composed of several thousands of informal workshops.[5] While the Suame Magazine and its high level of skills are widely known both inside and outside of Ghana, these skills are not based on modern technologies or high productivity. Rather, they are adaptive skills, where the workforce excels in repairing vehicles without having adequate equipment and/or the genuine parts from the original manufacturer companies.

Christianisation during the colonial period has resulted in 77.5 per cent of the regional population being Christian, followed by 13.2 per cent who are Muslim (Government of Ghana 2010). However, there are many settlements of Muslim migrants from the north who live in the northern part of Kumasi, and these areas are known as 'Zongos'. These migrant Muslims own or work in many of the workshops in the Suame Magazine. According to the author's interviews with the workshop owners, the ratio of Muslims in the Suame Magazine is around 50 per cent, which is much higher than the average in Kumasi city. In fact, in some areas of the Suame Magazine where the northern migrants are concentrated, Hausa, the lingua franca of the Muslims in West Africa, is spoken in their daily operations.

### 3-2. The TVET System in Ghana and Sample Schools and Students

In Ghana, there are more than 200 public TVET institutions run by the government, and this does not include the private TVETs. Figure 1 shows the major categories of TVET institutions. After completion of the basic education at JSH level, students' educational paths become diverse, even among those who continue with their schooling. As mentioned previously, only about 45 per cent of JHS graduates proceed to SHS. Others will go to one of the TVET institutions, informal skills training or become NEETs. In Figure 1, the shaded horizontal area shows the TVET institutions that can be selected by JHS graduates. In addition to the technical and vocational courses of SHS, the Ministry of Education (MOE) runs Technical Institutes (TIs) for those with basic education certificate. The TIs are oriented toward training mid-level technicians and they allocate more time for practical training and theory for specific vocational fields,

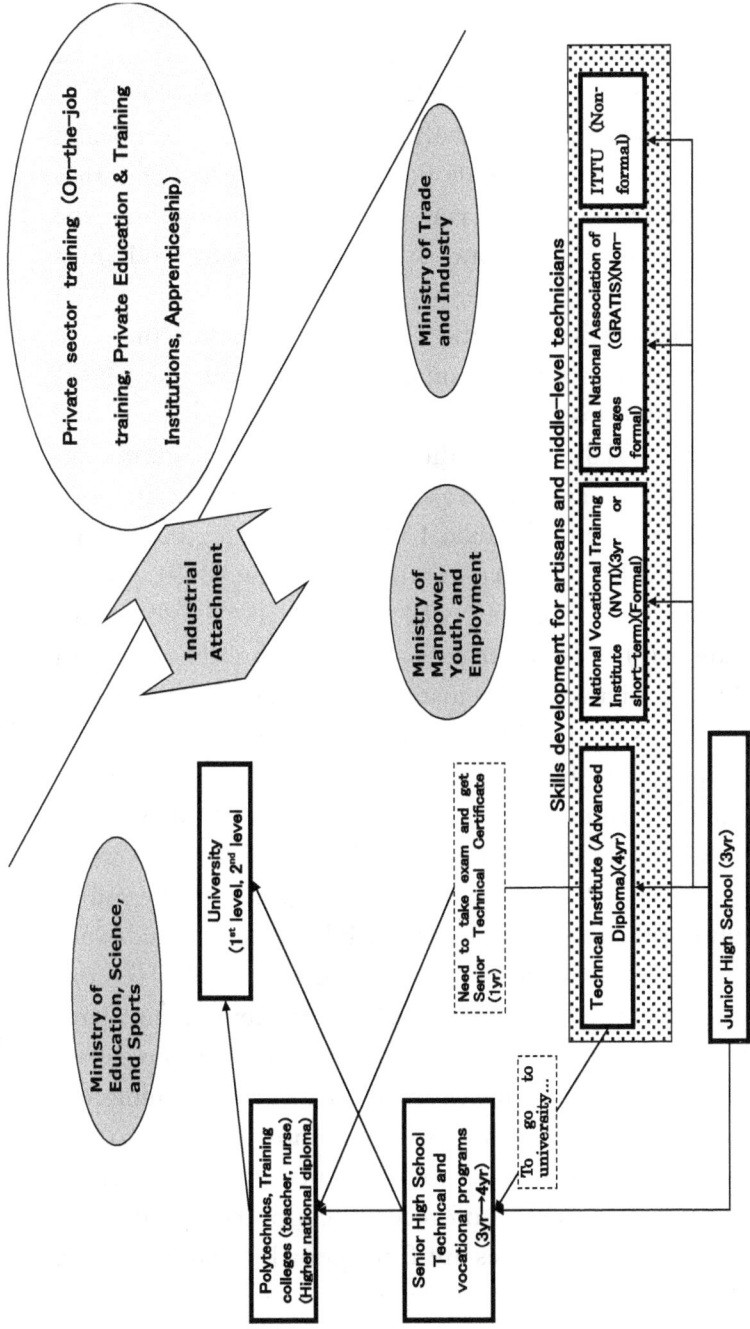

Figure 1. The skills development system in Ghana

Source: Compiled by the author based on interviews and official documents

137

rather than the technical and vocational courses offered by SHS. On graduation from a TI, students obtain a senior technical certificate, which is different from the SHS diploma. To proceed on to a polytechnic, which represents tertiary education along the technical/vocational route, students require either a SHS diploma or a senior technical certificate. The SHS graduates can also apply to universities, while TI graduates with senior technical certificates cannot apply to universities directly but have to go via a SHS or a polytechnic. There are 45 public TIs in Ghana and, among them, the Kumasi Technical Institute is one of the top-ranking and most competitive.

One of the characteristics of the TVET system is that there are many institutions that are run by ministries other than the MOE. There are 116 institutions run by the Ministry of Employment and Labour Relations (MELR), and these are the most numerous. However, most of them are run on a small scale. Therefore, in terms of enrolment, 70 per cent of public TVET students are in TIs that are supervised by the MOE (Darvas and Palmer 2014: 48–9). Among the TVET institutions under the MELR, the National Vocational Training Institutes (NVTIs) are the most widely distributed and best known. KVTI, one of the sample institutions included in this study, is part of the NVTI system. There are also institutions that fall under the supervision of the Ministries of Youth and Sports, Trade and Industry, Local Government and Rural Development, Fisheries and Aquaculture Development, and Roads and Highways, among others.

While Figure 1 shows only the selected categories of the public TVET institutions, the private sector is much larger and includes not only privately run TVET institutions but also corporate TVETs, on-the-job training and informal apprenticeships. Apprenticeships have the highest number of learners. Entry into an apprenticeship is easy because it does not require any formal certificates or minimum educational level. Although it has been common practice to pay initiation fees to the business owner to commence an apprenticeship, their collection is not as strictly enforced as school fees, particularly when the prospective apprentices are from poor households or are relatives of the owner.

138

This complicated picture of skills development highlights the variety of routes that can be taken by young people after JHS, up to which level access to formal education is almost universal. With this in mind, I conducted questionnaire surveys at different types of TVET institutions to compare student expectations in terms of their schooling, future aspirations and the socioeconomic factors that affect their skills development trajectories. The questionnaires were conducted between October and December 2013 and included 494 students who were studying vocational skills related to vehicle repair at four different types of TVET institutions in Kumasi city. These included KVTI, KTI, KSHS and KP. As explained above, KVTI is one of the NVTIs under the jurisdiction of the MELR. Meanwhile, the TIs, SHS and KP are under the jurisdiction of the MOE. Among these three, KTI and KSHS require a basic education certificate for admission, while KP requires a senior technical certificate or above.

Since Kumasi has the second-highest population after the capital, Accra, and has been an established centre for learning manufacturing skills, the technical and vocational schools in this city tend to date back further than those in other locations. The Kwame Nkrumah Science and Technology University, the first and most prestigious higher education institution which has engineering courses, was established in Kumasi in 1951, even before the country's independence in 1957. The KP was established in 1954, also before Ghana's independence. All of the sample institutions were established over 40 years ago, except for the KSHS, which is 25 years old. Questionnaires were given to all second-year students who were present on the days the survey was undertaken, in relevant programmes. Second-year students were selected for the following reasons: first, first-year students have spent only a couple of months in school and would have had limited experience of the school; second, third and fourth-year students tended to be on IAs (in-firm practical training), particularly at KTI and KVTI. Reflecting the sex bias of the student population in the fields of electrics, mechanics, welding and autobody repairs, 96.8 per cent of respondents were male. Besides the questionnaire survey, interviews were also conduct-

# Table 1. Data of sample schools and participants

| | School information | | | | Questionnaire respondents | | | | | | | | |
| --- | --- | --- | --- | --- | --- | --- | --- | --- | --- | --- | --- | --- | --- |
| | | | | | Motor vehicle mechanics | | | Electricals | | | | | |
| | Year established | Total enrolment | Number of courses | Total number of grades | Small-duty mechanics | Heavy-duty mechanics | Motor vehicle electricals | Electrical machine rewinding | Electrical installation | Motor vehicle (auto) body repairs | Welding and fabrication | N/A* | Total |
| Kumasi Polytechnic | 1954 | 6,634 (AY 2012) | 27 | 3 years (Higher National Diploma) + 1.5 years (Bachelor of technology; Bachelor of science) | 65 | 9 | 0 | 15 | 23 | 3 | 0 | 42 | 157 |
| Kumasi Technical Senior High School | 1991 | 2,511 (AY 2012) | 9 | 4 years | 93 | 4 | 1 | 1 | 0 | 7 | 1 | 2 | 109 |
| Kumasi Technical Institute | 1977 | 1,358 (AY 2012) | 15 | 4 years | 5 | 36 | 0 | 26 | 64 | 18 | 0 | 0 | 149 |
| Kumasi Vocational Training Institute | 1973 | 1,098 (AY 2012) | 8 | 3 years | 23 | 15 | 15 | 0 | 1 | 8 | 17 | 0 | 79 |
| Total | | | | | 186 | 64 | 16 | 42 | 88 | 36 | 18 | 44 | 494 |

*N/A the respondent did not report the courses they were enrolled in on the questionnaire, although they belonged to one of the listed courses

(Source: The author)

ed with 40 apprentices and 13 business owners in the informal auto-repair workshops in the Suame Magazine. The findings from the interviews in the informal sector will be presented elsewhere (Yamada 2020).

## 4. Analysis

### 4-1. Characteristics of the Students in the Respective TVET Institutions

Earlier, I explained that all the sample schools, except for KP, are potential options for young people who have completed their basic education. This does not necessarily mean that all these young people will proceed to these schools immediately after graduation from basic school. Generally, there is an interval of one to three years between basic school graduation and students entering KTI, KVTI or KSHS, while the period before entering KP is nine years on average. Accordingly, many students have work experience after their basic education (59.2 per cent at KP, 35.4 per cent at KTI, 30.9 per cent at KVTI and 26.7 per cent at KSHS).

The young Ghanaians found it difficult to separate and report on their experiences of work and apprenticeships. Traditionally, apprentices start after being introduced to the business owner through personal connections and after bringing the basic tools and initiation fees (Jaarsma et al. 2011: 443). Since this system relies heavily on human relationships, there are many cases where the owners accept relatives or penniless young men without charging them any fees. In workshops over a certain size and with stable cash revenues, the apprentices often receive pocket money and are made responsible for tasks depending on their skill level. However, in micro workshops with just a few workers, the training is not systematised, and the distinctions between training and employment or between free labour and care taking are ambiguous. As mentioned previously, apprentices do not necessarily become independent or open their own workshops, even after acquiring the skills (Yamada 2020). In the Suame Magazine, many 'apprentices' stay on for many years without any prospect of buying land or the machinery needed to start a

141

business, while some leave after a few years.

To my question, 'What kind of work did you do before starting at your current school?' the most frequent answer was, 'Factory or workshop, in the same technical field as the one I specialise in now at school', and 54.5 per cent of respondents had had work experience. The highest percentage of students with work experience were among those attending KTI (65.9 per cent), followed by KP (54.9 per cent), KVTI (50 per cent) and KSHS (40 per cent). In summary, except for KSHS, which is a high school where the students are more geared toward attending university, over half of the students had work experience, and the technical specialisation in the school matched the work experience.[6] Since it is difficult to distinguish between training and work, particularly in the informal sector, the years of work before school should not be considered an interruption to learning but, rather, as part of a continuum. Our study also suggests that young Ghanaians move between formal schooling and informal work (apprenticeships) over several years.

It should be noted that the longer the interval between graduating from basic schools, the less socioeconomic background influenced the school choice, and the higher the likelihood that the school specialisation matched the work experience. For example, the years after basic school correlated negatively with the father's level of education (-.146; significant at $p<.01$) and economic status (-.169, $p<.01$). Also, the results of the Basic Education Certificate Examination were less important as the number of years after completing basic school increased. Meanwhile, the proportion of respondents with work experience matching their current specialisation increased when we focused on those with more than eight years' experience (64.1 per cent) compared to the overall proportion (54.5 per cent). In summary, people who returned to school following a longer interval chose to do so based on their conviction that they needed a formal qualification for their work and did so without family support. Also, their past academic performance did not influence their decision to re-enter formal education.

As mentioned previously, as part of the TVET reforms in Ghana, the required period for IAs increased and became compulsory for the

142

TVET diploma. Since opportunities to undertake IAs in formal sector companies are limited, most of the TVET students conduct IAs in the informal sector. It has been a long-lasting voluntary practice of Ghanaian young people to strategically combine the theoretical learning in school with practical work-based training in informal sector workshops. Therefore, the new TVET system endorses the status quo rather than introducing any change. At the same time, it is increasingly difficult to distinguish between students on IAs, apprentices and casual helpers in the informal workshops, as their activities are similar. In this situation, what aspect of schooling attracts those young people who transition back and forth between school and the informal sector?

## 4-2. Student Perceptions about Their Education and Future Careers

To understand how the participating students felt about their experiences in their respective TVET institutions, we asked 17 relevant questions (S1-S17, see Table 2). The answers were on a Likert scale of one-five levels of satisfaction from five ('very good/ useful') to one ('very bad/ not useful at all'). I also asked the respondents to rank their top three likely careers after graduating from the TVET institutions (F1-F8, Table 2) and the top three reasons for choosing their current TVET institution (R1-R9).

Since there were many items to consider, and to reduce the number of variables for further analysis, a principal component analysis (PCA) was conducted to identify the underlying relationships among the measured variables. The PCA was conducted separately for perceptions about education (S-variables), future aspirations (F-variables) and the reasons for selecting the current school (R-variables). For respective categories of variables, PCA yielded two components each to represent the latent patterns in the participants' responses. Regarding the school and its teachers, the first criterion of students' evaluation seemed to be the diploma that they could obtain on graduation and the links that the school helped them to establish through industrial placement. This component was named 'Satisfaction_diploma & industry link', and its overall factor loading

143

# Table 2. Descriptive statistics of questions related to students' perceptions and socioeconomic backgrounds

| | Question items | Frequency | Mean | Standard Deviation | Minimum | Maximum |
|---|---|---|---|---|---|---|
| | Perceptions about the school and its teachers (5-level Likert scale) | | | | | |
| S1 | How useful were the core subjects? | 469 | 1.28 | 0.67 | 1 | 5 |
| S2 | How useful were the theories' courses? | 443 | 1.46 | 0.80 | 1 | 5 |
| S3 | How useful were practicals? | 460 | 1.35 | 0.79 | 1 | 5 |
| S4 | How useful were attachments? | 394 | 1.28 | 0.59 | 1 | 5 |
| S5 | How useful was the teachers' guidance? | 427 | 1.68 | 0.88 | 1 | 5 |
| S6 | How useful were school events? | 388 | 2.06 | 1.06 | 1 | 5 |
| S7 | How useful were the relationships with other students? | 422 | 1.86 | 0.93 | 1 | 5 |
| S8 | How useful were the relationships with private company developed in the school? | 438 | 1.62 | 0.85 | 1 | 5 |
| S9 | How useful is the diploma from the school? | 447 | 1.27 | 0.72 | 1 | 5 |
| S10 | Does the teacher give you printed papers to help your understanding? | 460 | 2.02 | 1.26 | 1 | 5 |
| S11 | Does the teacher use the machine models to help your understanding? | 453 | 2.32 | 1.41 | 1 | 5 |
| S12 | Does the teacher use other equipment and materials to help your understanding? | 454 | 2.16 | 1.28 | 1 | 5 |
| S13 | Does the teacher pose questions for you to express your ideas? | 450 | 1.59 | 0.91 | 1 | 5 |
| S14 | Do "practicals" help you understand how to apply theories? | 451 | 1.51 | 0.92 | 1 | 5 |
| S15 | Do you have enough tools for everyone? | 447 | 3.58 | 1.35 | 1 | 5 |
| S16 | Does the teacher give you opportunities for working on the machine by yourself? | 458 | 2.75 | 1.44 | 1 | 5 |
| S17 | Does the teacher show you the way of doing things by demonstrating? | 458 | 1.93 | 1.17 | 1 | 5 |
| | Most likely career after graduation (Ranking top 3) | | | | | |
| F1 | Go to Polytechnic | 494 | 1.49 | 1.43 | 0 | 3 |
| F2 | Go to University | 494 | 1.45 | 1.25 | 0 | 3 |
| F3 | Go to Training college (teacher, nurse) | 494 | 0.25 | 0.65 | 0 | 3 |
| F4 | Go to post-secondary education institutions other than Polytechnic, University, and Training college | 494 | 0.10 | 0.44 | 0 | 3 |
| F5 | Work in the same field as my current specialization | 494 | 1.00 | 1.14 | 0 | 3 |
| F6 | Work in a field different to my current specialization | 494 | 0.24 | 0.70 | 0 | 3 |
| F7 | Help family work | 494 | 0.10 | 0.34 | 0 | 3 |
| F8 | Others | 494 | 0.09 | 0.36 | 0 | 3 |
| | Reason for choosing the current school (Ranking top 3) | | | | | |
| R1 | I can commute from my parents' (relatives') house | 494 | 0.20 | 0.63 | 0 | 3 |
| R2 | I wanted to learn the trade | 494 | 0.82 | 0.87 | 0 | 3 |
| R3 | My exam score was suited for this school | 494 | 0.40 | 0.85 | 0 | 3 |
| R4 | The tuition was affordable | 494 | 0.35 | 0.83 | 0 | 3 |
| R5 | The facilities and equipment of this school are good | 494 | 0.81 | 1.07 | 0 | 3 |

| | | | | | | |
|---|---|---|---|---|---|---|
| R6 | I wanted to learn from the instructors/teachers of this school | 494 | 0.55 | 0.96 | 0 | 3 |
| R7 | I heard good things about this school | 494 | 0.59 | 1.06 | 0 | 3 |
| R8 | I can achieve a high income after graduating from this school | 494 | 1.44 | 1.31 | 0 | 3 |
| R9 | Others | 494 | 0.08 | 0.40 | 0 | 3 |
| Socio-economic characteristics of students | | | | | | |
| Score of Basic Education Certificate Examination | | 464 | 0.06 | 0.02 | 0.03 | 0.17 |
| Father pays school fees (3= fully; 2= mostly; 1= partially) | | 489 | 1.97 | 1.36 | 0 | 3 |
| Years after graduating the Junior High School | | 484 | 4.82 | 3.92 | 1 | 16 |

Source: Compiled by the author

was 20.3 per cent. The second component that determined the students' level of satisfaction was the availability of practical training and hands-on experience during their time as students. This component was named 'Satisfaction_practical training', which contributed 17.9 per cent to the overall explanation of the students' perception of the school and its level of education.

I extracted two components for the career prospects. One was to continue education and, particularly, to proceed to KP. This component was named 'Future_polytechnic', and its factor loading was 16.5 per cent. The second component was to work in their field of specialisation ('Future_work', 16.1 per cent). As the factor loadings for the two components indicated, the career patterns of students were evenly divided into two groups; either to proceed on to further education or to start work.

Two components were extracted from questions R1–R9, which indicate the reasons why the students selected their current school. Table 2 shows that the average points the respondents allotted were highest on the questions about the prospect of future income (R8, 1.44), the learning of skills (R2, 0.82), and the facilities and equipment that enabled them to learn the skills (R5, 0.81). However, since most of the respondents indicated the importance of skills learning and income, these questions did not contribute to highlighting the differential patterns in the responses. As a result, the two PCA components did not relate to the educational content or

145

the respondents' aspirations. Instead, they represented opportunistic conditions, such as commuting distance or exam scores ('School choice_feasibility', 14.8 per cent) or the cost of schooling ('School choice_cost', 14.0 per cent).

Based on student perceptions, I investigated how the learners' subjectivities would relate to other factors, such as work experience, prior education and family socioeconomic background. By comparing the differential patterns across the students at the four sample TVET institutions, I show how decisions are made about learning trajectories and work among Ghanaian young people who are studying automotive-related vocational skills.

### 4-3. Factors Determining School Choices and Career Paths

Table 3 shows the logistic regression results. The dependent variables of the four models are the enrolment status at the respective sample TVET institutions, and this enables the comparison of the determinants underlying school choice. The independent variables used for these models are the same. The six component-variables representing the respondents' perceptions about the educational strengths of their school, their futures and the reasons for choosing the school are included. Furthermore, to examine the impact of the socioeconomic and educational backgrounds of the individuals, I included variables on the Basic Education Certificate Examination scores, the number of years after graduating from JHS and a dummy variable to show whether the respondent's father pays for the tuition fees. In Ghana, when the biological father does not have the financial means, the cost of schooling is typically paid for by other members of the extended family or by the students themselves. Therefore, the fact that the father pays the fees indicates a relatively high economic status for the household.

As mentioned previously, KP is the only post-secondary educational institution, whereas the other three are post-basic level institutions. Therefore, the required entrance diploma, students' age and years of experience clearly differed for KP compared to the other three institutions. Accordingly, in terms of the number of years after graduating from basic school, students at KSHS, KTI and

146

**Table 3. Logistic regression models to demonstrate the socio-economic and motivational characteristics among students of different TVET institutions**

| | Polytechnic | KSHS (Technical High School) | KTI (Technical Institute) | KVTI (Vocational Training Institute) |
|---|---|---|---|---|
| Satisfaction_diploma & industry link | 0.252 | -0.022 | 0.517** | -0.704** |
| | (0.252) | (0.207) | (0.189) | (0.232) |
| Satisfaction_practical training | 0.232 | -0.091 | -0.251 | -0.024 |
| | (0.271) | (0.244) | (0.221) | (0.194) |
| Future_polytechnic | -1.454*** | -0.542* | 0.479* | 0.664** |
| | (0.339) | (0.264) | (0.236) | (0.249) |
| Future_work | 0.935** | -0.766** | -0.190 | 0.174 |
| | (0.357) | (0.262) | (0.216) | (0.215) |
| School choice_feasibility | -0.053 | 0.121 | -0.450* | 0.300 |
| | (0.280) | (0.188) | (0.179) | (0.203) |
| School choice_cost | 0.340 | 0.245 | -0.130 | -0.491* |
| | (0.268) | (0.181) | (0.179) | (0.203) |
| BECE score | 9.397 | 21.047** | 12.533 | -81.409*** |
| | (12.261) | (7.952) | (8.699) | (17.197) |
| Father pays school fees | -0.094 | 0.289* | 0.188 | 0.079 |
| | (0.213) | (0.143) | (0.140) | (0.155) |
| Years after graduating JHS | 0.764*** | -0.543*** | -0.550*** | -0.106 |
| | (0.126) | (0.140) | (0.139) | (0.072) |
| (Constant) | -6.114*** | -0.364 | -0.564 | 2.725** |
| | (1.334) | (0.723) | (0.764) | (0.962) |
| R-Sq. | 0.709 | 0.259 | 0.307 | 0.337 |
| N | 254 | 254 | 254 | 254 |

Source: Compiled by the author

KVTI reported significantly fewer years than did KP students.

For the majority of students, KP represents the final stage of their formal education,[7] and they foresee that they will return to work after graduating (with a coefficient of 0.935 and significance at a level of $p<.001$). This is in stark contrast to KSHS students, who do not aspire to go to KP (-0.542, $p<.05$) or work (-0.766, $p<.01$). This shows that KSHS students consider themselves to be headed for university. As mentioned previously, early academic performance (the BECE score) does not influence the decision of students to enrol at KP, as they are older and have more work experience. They are mostly self-funded and did not choose the school for opportunistic reasons such as proximity or low tuition fees. This suggests that the typical KP student is a mature technician who is dedicated to developing his career.

The question remains as to what these students have been doing during the years before enrolling at KP? The answer lies in the regression models of the students who attended KTI and KVTI. Both models demonstrate a strong desire to proceed to the Polytechnic (0.479, $p<.05$; and 0.664, $p<.001$, respectively). However, a comparison of the average gap in years after JHS among the KP students (9.09 years), and that of KTI and KVTI students shows a much shorter gap among the latter (2.53 and 3.57 years, respectively). This implies that despite their aspirations, some students tend not to be able to enrol at KP immediately after graduation but, instead, they (re)enter the world of work. Some maintain the aspiration to attend KP and realise it after some years, while others may choose other career trajectories. The students' attitudes toward these two schools differ; the KTI students express relatively positive opinions about the diploma and the opportunities afforded by the school to work in industry (0.517, $p<.01$), whereas the KVTI students are more critical of their school (-0.704, $p<.01$). The KTI students chose their school, not because of convenience or financial reasons, but proactively, for the opportunity to learn the skills offered by the school (-0.450, $p<.05$). On the other hand, the KVTI students claim that they did not choose their school because of the low tuition fees (-0.491, $p<.05$). This result endorses my observation that many KVTI students have experience of apprenticeships in informal workshops and make money or receive financial support from their relatives before proceeding to KVTI. It also explains why they are slightly older than the KTI and KSHS students, who went on to attend the post-primary institutions straight away.

## 5. Conclusion

This study found that among students who study at the four different TVET institutions in Kumasi, the longer the interval between leaving JHS to entry into the TVET, the more the student's choice of school was determined by factors other than family background. Instead, they recognise the importance of schooling for their career development. Therefore, older students are more likely to have work experience in the same professional fields as those they specialise in at school. For them, schooling helps to top up their knowledge and achieve accreditation for their accumulated expertise, and to enhance their efficacy in the same vocation. Among the school options available for holders of the basic education certificate (KSHS, KTI or KVTI), KSHS is attended by those with higher academic scores and from relatively better off socioeconomic households. Unlike KTI and KVTI, KSHS is more of an academic institution and provides more options for continuing education, leading to university and KP. KTI awards its graduates the senior technical certificate, which leads only to KP. Meanwhile, KVTI is not under the auspices of the MOE and is not linked to a specific route for post-secondary education.

Meanwhile, many students of KTI and KVTI have selected 'learning of skills' as an essential reason for making their choices. The interviews showed that some students started their professional careers either as KVTI students or apprentices and went on to attend KTI or even KP. Therefore, KTI and KVTI provide schooling that is more focused on a career continuum in which learners accumulate knowledge and skills more gradually.

Among the TIs in Ghana, KTI is highly regarded, particularly for its diverse programmes and its high-level equipment, indicating that the students appreciate the quality of the practical education offered. On the other hand, their evaluation of the theoretical teaching at KTI was low. Among the three TVET institutions for basic education graduates, KVTI was supposedly the one that most directly contributed to the formation of employable skills. However, despite their desire to learn these skills, KVTI students expressed discontent with their school and teachers. This suggests that, despite the best intentions of the Ministry of Manpower, Youth and Employment, the role of the Vocational Training Institutes (VTIs) should be reconsidered to ensure that they can fully contribute to promoting employment opportunities for skilled workers.

In West Africa, and particularly Kumasi, traditional apprenticeships are highly sophisticated and well-established. Therefore, for those wanting to learn the skills and follow in their predecessors' footsteps, having an apprenticeship in the Suame Magazine suffices. Also, the reputation of the Suame Magazine and the networks with customers and supporting industries are important social capital that cannot be gained at school. As I discussed previously (Yamada 2020), this is one of the reasons why students from the polytechnics also come to the Suame Magazine for training. Nevertheless, young people still aim to go back to school. Naturally, the timing of their return to school, and the type of school they choose, are determined by many factors. As mentioned earlier, in choosing career options, both external and internal factors come into play. Those from better socioeconomic family backgrounds tend to follow more linear career-development paths. In this study, a large number of the KSHS students fell into this group. However, in Ghana, as of 2015, the net enrolment at SHS was as low as 25 per cent (World Bank 2016). After JHS, only a minority of students proceed to SHS, and that includes those on a technical track. As explained earlier, 86.1 per cent of employment in Ghana is in the informal sector and this sector absorbs a large number of JHS graduates who did not go to SHS. Informal sector employment is unstable, and workers frequently move from job to job. In such a situation, aspiring and competent young people try to accumulate skills, together with financial and social capital, to move up the career ladder, albeit gradually. Along with this type of long-term strategy, young Ghanaians return to school expecting to gain assets that are not available in their workplace.

In Kumasi, there are a number of diverse routes to learning the skills needed for a career in vehicle repair. In this context, learners assign various roles to the schools, such as temporary respite after JHS, a place to learn practical skills, somewhere to acquire theoretical knowledge and certification, and a step to the next level of education. Seen from the learners' perspective, the aims of the governmental TVET reforms appear to be remote and unrealistic. However, based on their own assessment of the environment, their aptitude and self-esteem, young people make their own decisions about their career

150

development. The question is, what type of value can schools add to this process? This study suggests that, from the learners' perspective, there is a need to revisit the idea of a top-down reform of the education system. While the government TVET system is often criticised for being slow to adapt to technological change, the learners' expectations for learning skills are based on their experiences of working on the ground. Therefore, it would be useful for the government to set aside its ideas of manpower planning and a curriculum-based education for national economic growth and, instead, lower the boundaries between the various TVET institutions and apprenticeships, so that learners have the flexibility to move between the different learning modes according to their needs. The system would be more effective if it aligned with the existing learning routes and the subjective motivations of the learners.

The study also hints that an analysis of these career development strategies and learning trajectories would open the way for us to consider 'African Potentials' in education and learning, freeing ourselves from rigid assumptions about the legitimacy of school as a linear track of career and knowledge formation. Ivan Illich (1971) suggested that schooling creates a class of people who proceed through the hierarchy of educational institutions and reach high-status positions in society. He stated that as schools' function of tracking social classes becomes more intense, it also becomes less relevant to the world outside the school. Because of this disconnection, skills and knowledge should not be restricted or defined by schools if they are to maintain relevance. Illich (1973) proposed the notion of conviviality as a tool to break down the standardised social framework and reconceptualise it, based on the relationships between our autonomous selves. Such attitudes share a basis with the search for 'African Potentials', which transcends this series of publications. The starting point for such an endeavour should be the subjectivity and experience of the individual, which this chapter has consistently pursued.

151

## Endnotes

[1] This chapter is a modified version based on the author's paper that was previously published in Japanese (Yamada 2017).

[2] As a part of the 1986 education reform, Integrated Community Centers for Employable Skills were built all around the country. Also, the National Coordinating Committee on Technical and Vocational Education and Training (NACVET) was established to coordinate between the labour market and the education and training institutions, which initiated various measures to improve the relevance of the TVET to the labour market needs (Akyeampong 2005). Replacing the NACVET, which wasn't very successful, the Council of TVETs (COTVET) was established in 2007, with similar objectives, although some specific programmes that it implements follow more recent trends.

[3] Industrial attachment is a Ghanaian term for an internship that is required as a part of the TVET curriculum.

[4] Gross enrolment rate uses the total population within the range of standard enrolment ages as the denominator for the actual enrolment. Therefore, when there are enrollees who are outside the standard ages, the gross enrolment rate may exceed 100 per cent.

[5] According to the study conducted by McCormik, there were approximately 4,000 metal processing factories and 5,000 vehicle repair factories (McCormik 1998). Currently, the total population of the Suame Magazine is said to be around 80,000 (Adeya 2006: 3).

[6] While 54.5 per cent of the respondents with work experience have specialised in the same field as in school, 13.3 per cent have worked in factories or workshops in different technical fields, 8.3 per cent were street vendors, 5.5 per cent were involved in farming, 3.5 per cent undertook household work and 14.9 per cent were doing other types of work.

[7] Since they are currently enrolled at the Polytechnic, the prospect of going back to the Polytechnic is low (-1.454, $p<.001$).

## Acknowledgements

This work was supported by JSPS KAKENHI Grant Number JP16H06318.

# References

Akyeampong, A. (2005) 'Vocationalisation of secondary education in Ghana', in J. Lauglo and R. Maclean (eds) *Vocationalisation of Secondary Education Revisited, Technical and Vocational Education and Training: Issues, Concerns and Prospects (1)*, Dordrecht: Springer, pp. 149–227.

Adeya, N. (2006) 'Knowledge, technology and growth: The case study of Suame Manufacturing Enterprise Cluster in Ghana', unpublished manuscript, WBI Africa Cluster Case study.

Allais, S. M. (2007) 'Understanding the failures of the South African National Qualifications Framework as the driver of educational reform in post-apartheid South Africa', *9th UKFIET Conference 2007*, University of Oxford, Oxford, UK, 11–13 September 2007.

Anokye, P. A., Afrane, S. K. and Oduro-Ofori, E. (2014) 'The informal apprenticeship system in Ghana: Post graduation job integration and its implications for the management of urban space', *Journal of Environment and Earth Science*, Vol. 4, No. 18, pp. 84–93.

Areetey, E. B.-D., Doh, D. and Andoh, P. (2013) 'Choosing an apprenticeship: Skills preferences amongst the youth', *International Development Planning Review*, Vol. 35, No. 2, pp. 135–53.

Aryeetey, E., Baah-Boateng, W., Ackah, C. G., Lehrer, K. and Mbiti, I. (2014) 'Ghana', in H. Hino and G. Ranis (eds) *Youth and Employment in Sub-Saharan Africa: Working but Poor*, London: Taylor & Francis Books, pp. 232–302.

Bandura, A. (1986) *Social Foundations of Thought and Action: A Social Cognitive Theory*, Englewood Cliffs, Upper Saddle River: Prentice-Hall.

Bowles, S. and Gintis, H. (1976) *Schooling in Capitalist America: Educational Reform and the Contradictions of Economic Life*, New York: Basic Books.

Clark, G. C. (1994) *African Market Women: Seven Life Stories from Ghana*, Bloomington: Indiana University Press.

COTVET (2012) *COTVET, Brochure*, Accra: Government of Ghana.

Croll, P. (2008) 'Occupational choice, socio-economic status and educational attainment: A study of the occupational choices and destinations of young people in the British household panel survey', *Research Paper in Education*, Vol. 23, No. 3, pp. 243–68.

Darvas, P. and Palmer, R. (2014) *Demand and Supply of Skills in Ghana: How Can Training Programs Improve Employment and Productivity?*, Washington DC: World Bank.

Eichhorst, W., Rodriguez-Planas, N., Schmidl, R. and Zimmermann, K. F. (2012) *A Roadmap to Vocational Education and Training Systems around the World, IZA Discussion Paper Series, No. 7110*, Bonn: IZA - Institute of Labor Economics.

Fluitman, F. (1992) 'Traditional apprenticeship in West Africa: Recent evidence and policy options', *Discussion Paper Geneva*, No. 34, in Ghana Education Service (ed.) *Report on Basic Statistics and Planning Parameters for Education in Ghana 2014-5 Academic Year*, Accra: Government of Ghana.

Foster, P. (1965) 'The Vocational School Fallacy in Development Planning', in A. A. Anderson and M. J. Bowman (eds) *Education and Economic Development*, Chicago: Aldine, pp. 142–66.

Ghana Education Service (2006) *Report on Basic Statistics and Planning Parameters for Education in Ghana 2005-6 Academic Year*, Accra: Government of Ghana.

———— (2015) *Report on Basic Statistics and Planning Parameters for Education in Ghana 2014-5 Academic Year*, Accra: Government of Ghana.

Government of Ghana (2010) *Population and Housing Census 2010: Demographic, Social, Economic and Housing Characteristics Report*, Accra: Ghana Statistical Service.

———— (2014a) 'How to improve, through skills development and job creation, access of Africa's youth to the world of work', *Ghana Country Report for the 2014 Ministerial Conference on Youth Employment*, in Abidjan, Cote d'Ivoire, 21–23 July 2014.

———— (2014b) *Ghana Shared Growth and Development Agenda (GSGDA) II 2014-7*, Accra: Government of Ghana.

Hart, K. (1970) 'Small scale entrepreneurs in Ghana and development planning', *Journal of Development Studies*, Vol. 6, No. 4, pp. 104–20.

Holland, J. L. (1997) *Making Vocational Choices: A Theory of Careers (3rd edition)*, Odessa: Psychological Assessment Resources.

Hossler, D., Schmit, J. and Vesper, N. (1999) *Going to College: How Social, Economic, and Educational Factors Influence the Decisions Students Make*, Baltimore: Johns Hopkins University Press.

Illich, I. (1971) *Deschooling Society*, New York: Harper and Row.

——————— (1973) *Tools for Conviviality*, New York: Harper and Row.

Jaarsma, T., Maat, H., Richards, P. and Wals, A. (2011) 'The role of materiality in apprenticeships: The case of the Suame magazine, Kumasi, Ghana', *Journal of Vocational Education & Training*, Vol. 63, Issue 3, pp. 439–49.

King, K. and Palmer, R. (2013) *Education and Skills Post 2015: What Evidence, Whose Perspectives?, NORRAG Discussion Paper, Geneva, No. 6*, NORRAG – Network for International Policies and Cooperation in Education and Training.

Kumasi Technical Institute (2011) *Tracer Study of Industrial Attachment by KTI Students*, unpublished report.

Langevang, T. and Gough, K. V. (2012) 'Diverging pathways: Young female employment and entrepreneurship in Sub-Saharan Africa', *The Geographical Journal*, Vol. 178, pp. 242–52.

Lent, R. W., Brown, S. D. and Hackett, G. (1994) 'Toward a unifying social cognitive theory of career and academic interest, choice, and performance', *Journal of Vocational Behavior*, Vol. 45, Issue 1, pp. 79–122.

McCormick, D. (1998) *Enterprise Clusters in Africa: On the Way to Industrialization? IDS Discussion Paper, No. 366*, Nairobi: IDS (Instiutute of Development Studies).

Osuji, O. N. (1976) 'Patterns of occupational choice and aspiration in conditions of economic and technological underdevelopment', *Journal of Vocational Behavior*, Vo. 8, pp. 133–44.

Owusu-Acheampong, E., Williams, A. A. and Azu, T. D. (2014) 'Industrial attachment: Perspectives, conceptions and misconceptions of students at Cape Coast Polytechnic, Ghana', *Journal of Education and Practice*, Vol. 5, No. 37, pp. 63–7.

Palmer, R. (2009) 'Skills development, employment, and sustained growth in Ghana: Sustainability challenges', *International Journal of*

*Educational Development,* Vol. 29, Issue 2, pp. 133–9.

Pascarella, E. T. and Terenzini, P. T. (1991) *How College Affects Students: Findings and Insights from Twenty Years of Research, Volume I,* Hoboken: Jossey-Bass.

Sonnenberg, K. (2012) 'Traditional apprenticeship in Ghana and Senegal: Skills development for youth for the informal sector`, *Journal of International Cooperation in Education,* Vol. 15, No. 2, pp. 93–105.

Super, D. E. (1990) 'A life-span, life space approach to career development', in D. Brown, L. Brooks and Associates *Career Choice and Development (2nd edition),* San Francisco: Jossey-Bass, pp. 197–261.

UNESCO (2012) *Youth and Skills: Global Monitoring Report 2012,* Paris: UNESCO.

World Bank (2016) *World Development Indicators* (http://data.worldbank.org/data-catalog/world-development-indicators) (accessed: 10 April 2016).

Yamada, S. (2001) 'Perspectives on vocational education in Africa', *Journal of International Cooperation in Education,* Vol. 4, No. 2, pp. 87–98.

———— (2017) 'Skills development paths selected by learners: The case of automobile-related students in TVET institutions in Kumasi, Ghana', *Journal of African Studies (Africa-Kenkyu),* Vol. 91, pp. 1–16 (in Japanese with English abstract).

———— (2020) 'Traditional apprenticeship as an educational and life experience: Life stories of young auto repair apprentices in Kumasi, Ghana', in Y. Ofosu-Kusi and M. Matsuda (eds) *The Challenge of African Potentials: Conviviality, Informality and Futurity,* Bamenda: Langaa RPCIG.

Yamada, S. and Mazda, N. (2009) 'TVET as viewed from the education sector in Ghana, Uganda and Malawi', in S. Krishna (ed.) *Vocational Education and Training: Issues and Perspectives,* Hyderabad: Institute of Chartered Financial Analysts of India University Press, pp. 121–50.

# Chapter 5

## Formation of Local Knowledge through Experiences of School Education and Livelihood Activities in Southwest Ethiopia

*Morie Kaneko and Masayoshi Shigeta*

### 1. Introduction

This chapter is focused on how villagers have incorporated education into their own life courses since formal schooling was first introduced to the region of South Aari *woreda* (one of the administrative units in Ethiopia, equivalent to a county in English), which formed part of South Omo Zone of the Southern Nations, Nationalities, and Peoples' Region (SNNPR), in the 1970s. Before 1970, it was extremely rare for farmers in the region to send their children to school. A boy was sent to the Ethiopian Orthodox Church by his father to learn the language of the people from Northern Ethiopia who invaded the region in the late 19th century (Shigeta and Kaneko 2017). In the case of this father, the learning process began with an understanding of the concept that by living with others who were different, children would not remain ignorant. This chapter takes as its starting point the question of how individual educational histories and school experiences are now being reimagined by the first generation who had access to formal education.

According to the United Nations Educational, Scientific and Cultural Organization's (UNESCO) Bureau of Statistics data, in 2015, Ethiopia's primary education (net) enrolment rate exceeded 80 per cent, with an 87.7 per cent attendance rate for boys and an 81.4 per cent attendance rate for girls (The World Bank website). Even in rural villages in South Aari *woreda*, South Omo Zone, where this research was conducted, by 2013 primary education enrolment had reached almost 100 per cent. An elderly man living in the area said, 'It used to be said that there were as many granaries as there were children,

[children are a valuable part of the workforce and a means to enrich lives], but today our children go to school'. This man continues to send his own children to school. Both parents and children accept that attending primary school is part of the early years' life course.

Secondary school attendance in Ethiopia is, however, much lower. According to The World Bank website, in 2015, the secondary school enrolment rate was 35.6 per cent for boys and 34.2 per cent for girls. Only a limited number of villagers go on to attend secondary school, and an even more limited number continue on to higher education and professional employment. The continued stagnation in secondary school enrolment rates is a problem that Ethiopia has faced since the introduction of modern education in the 1960s (Negash 2006; Joshi and Verspoor 2012).

## 2. School Education in Ethiopia

### 2-1. Further Expansion of the Education Sector in Ethiopia and the Educational Environment in South Aari Woreda, South Omo Zone

According to Negash (2006), between 1941 and 1970, education in Ethiopia was influenced by two major ideas based on the concept that 'education is good' (Negash 2006: 13). The first was the view that modern education is the best strategy for training people to respect the king, the state and the Ethiopian Orthodox Church.[1] The second was the idea, proposed by UNESCO, that there is a direct link between investment in human development and social development.[2] This latter idea continues to be the foundation of Ethiopia's education policy today.[3] This view is largely consistent with the current tendency to view the acquisition of skills through schooling as a means of personality formation.

In the imperial era, prior to 1973, education was geared toward small numbers of students and was focused on the northern regions of the country. During the socialist era from 1974 to 1991, the government began to improve the educational environment by constructing school buildings in peripheral areas, such as South Omo Zone, where schools had not previously existed. For people living in these marginalised areas, education had been something they could only enjoy as part of their religious practices, such as in the Ethiopian Orthodox and Protestant churches. However, during the socialist regime, children had opportunities to access education through a formal education system, regardless of their religious background. The education sector expanded during the socialist regime, but without an adequate budget or resources to support it. In addition, to make the best use of the school facilities in many schools it became common to teach students in shifts.[4] In South Aari *woreda*, all primary to early secondary schools operate a morning–afternoon class shift system. The current regime introduced the transition to a federal system. As a result, Ethiopian education has been transformed again, this time with regard to a choice of the language of instruction and the expansion of school facilities (Joshi and Verspoor 2012). Primary education enrolment (net enrolment) increased from around 19.1 per cent in 1994 to 84.6 per cent in 2015 (The World Bank website). In the current regime, the Ministry of Education, in addition to making extremely efficient use of external funding, including bilateral and multilateral aid to expand the education sector further, has generally made use of community funding and building materials provided by locals to improve the educational environment, including the construction of classrooms (Yamada 2011).[5]

However, the expansion of the education sector based on the current government's education policy has been criticised for failing to link education with poverty reduction, despite the widespread belief that access to education has the potential to eradicate or alleviate poverty (Negash 2006: 23).[6] In South Aari *woreda*, the enrolment rate in primary education has increased. This has been facilitated by the continued financial support that parents and relatives provide to children in schools, and the development of an educational environment by *woreda*, villages and the community.

Despite this, some young people are unable to find employment on completing their schooling, while others drop out of school and live in their villages. A World Bank report pointed out that Ethiopia's education policy should not only pay attention to enrolment and completion rates but should also focus on providing education that enhances academic performance, with the aim of producing a skilled labour force (Joshi and Verspoor 2012: 18).

## 2-2. Objectives and Methods: A Trial to Understand the Multi-Layered Experiences of Eskan

The focus of this study was on the rural area of South Aari *woreda* in South Omo Zone, which has been relegated to the periphery in Ethiopia's education policy. The study considered experiences of school education as opportunities to learn in the classroom as well as occasions to interact with people with different cultural backgrounds. The study focused on two men, who established an agricultural association in village D, and examined how their experiences of school education may have influenced the establishment of this association.

To examine changes in life course among the Aari, this study adopted two local concepts, '*eskan*' in the Aari language (Kaneko 2014, 2016; Shigeta and Kaneko 2017), which means 'know' in English, and '*tamar*' in the Amharic language, which means 'learn in school', to analyse learning in school through social experiences. A common phrase that is expressed in the area is, 'I managed to *tamar* it, but I could not *eskan* it.' In other words, the term *eskan* includes a semantic concept that combines the act of learning knowledge with the act of being able to put that knowledge into practice and apply it. The expression *eskan* is useful when we see it as the social experience of living in a town, rather than just an experience in the classroom.[7]

The phrase '*eskan*' is also used to describe the actions of a person who practises it. A person who is able to *eskan*, 'know', is *esta-baab* in the Aari language, which means one who knows things through experience. It is used to denote a person who is capable of mature thinking. This usage shows that *eskan* is not just a verb that indicates the act of practising but also a verb that indicates the status of acquiring knowledge that can be practised through experience.[8]

This study attempted to interpret two aspects of an agricultural association based on the contrast and combination of the *eskan* and *tamar* concepts. The formation of local knowledge could be determined by examining the contrast and combination of *eskan* and

160

*tamar.*

The study was based on data from fieldwork undertaken in village D. The research period was from December 2013 to March 2014. Twenty-one heads of households were interviewed about their livelihood activities. In addition, two core members of the agricultural association, Mr Y and Mr A, were interviewed about the establishment of the association.

## 2-3. Modern School Education in the Study Area

Village D is located in South Aari *woreda* (Figure 1). The villagers live at an altitude of 2,000–3,500 metres and are engaged in enset-based agriculture.

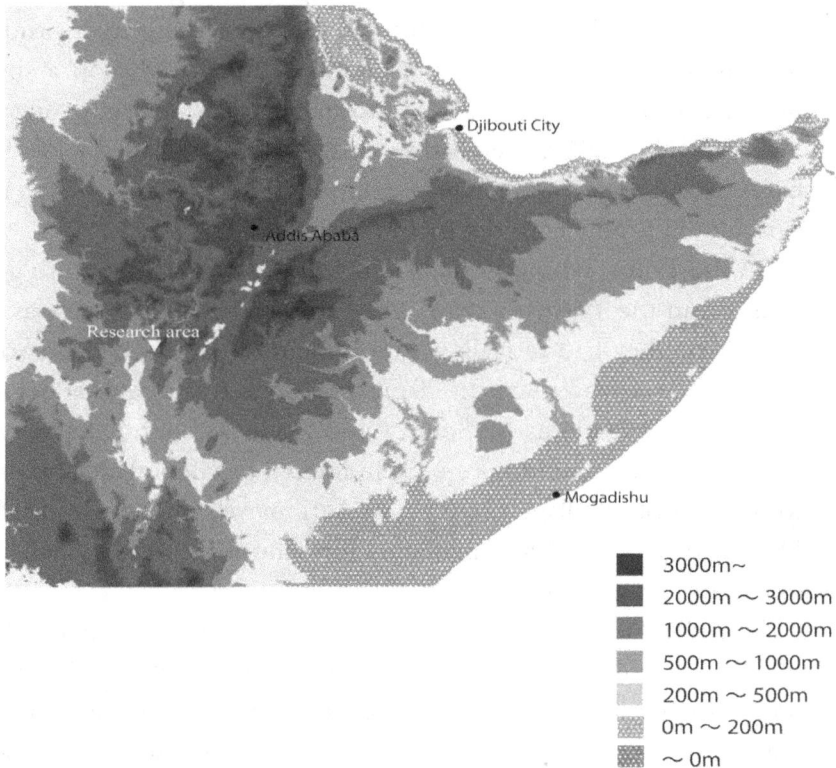

**Figure 1. Research area**

*A revision of a map (Kaneko and Shigeta 2020: 6)

Enset, one of the main staple foods in Ethiopia, also plays a cultural role that is closely tied to the life course of the Aari.[9] Other than enset, people also cultivate vegetables such as cabbages, carrots and kale, as well as cereals such as barley, wheat and maize. The nearby town G (6–7 kilometres southwest of village D, about 1,600 metres above sea level) is inhabited by northerners who invaded this area during the imperial period in the late 19th century. It was the administrative centre before city J became the capital of South Omo Zone.

Almost all merchants in town G originate from the northern part of Ethiopia and trade in cash crops, such as coffee and Ethiopian cardamom. It is one of South Omo Zone's commercial centres. Twice a week, many farmers from village D bring their agricultural products to the local market in town G. Some bring their products directly to restaurants and hotels and attempt to develop a special business relationship with them to achieve a stable cash income. Since October 2019, the road from town G to village D has been barely maintained[10] and, therefore, farmers from village D bring their agricultural products to town G on horseback.

In the 1970s, village D opened a school for students up to grade four. From the 1970s to 2016, when students enrolled in a class for grade five, they had to walk for more than two hours to and from a school in a nearby town. In 2017, after some negotiations between the local governments of South Omo Zone and South Aari *woreda*, and the chairperson in village D, additional teachers were appointed to the school in village D by South Aari *woreda*. The locals in village D provided the building materials for school facilities, which were opened to grade seven.

When students in village D travel to school from their fathers' house, they are able to balance their school attendance with farming duties for their households. In village D, during the busy farming season, the school adjusts the schedule of classes to accommodate the schedule of farm operations (Suzuki 2004). When students complete grade seven in the school of village D and move on to grade eight, they often move to town G to stay with relatives where they rent rooms in the town.

In South Omo zone, the penetration of school education has led to a high percentage of Aari people from rural villages taking up local official positions. In contrast, people from northern Ethiopia (e.g., the Amhara people), who invaded this region in the late 19th century, are mainly engaged in the local business sector.

## 3. Establishing an Agricultural Association and School Education

### 3-1. Awareness of the Importance of Eskan in the Life Course of Mr Y

This section examines the life histories of Mr Y and Mr A, who founded an association for raising poultry, and the impact of their experiences of school education on the establishment of this association. The association for raising poultry was established in 2013. Mr Y initially discussed his idea of an association for raising poultry with Mr A, and then the two of them recruited members.

Mr Y is the fifth of eleven children. His parents and his siblings believe in Protestantism. Although his father and his siblings did not complete a school education, Mr Y went to elementary school from his father's house in the late 1990s. As mentioned above, the school in village D operates a shift system that runs in conjunction with the busy farming season and off-season for farmers. Most students are engaged in agricultural work while studying, and they know how to undertake farm work [*eskan*]. Most students, including Mr Y, have been able to access learning in school and engage in enset-based agriculture at the same time. They are not deprived of the opportunity to work on farms.

At the point at which boys leave school (about 12 to 15 years old) they also leave their father's house and start preparing for independence by building their own house on land given to them by their father. They create a garden around their house and plant enset seedlings.[11] The boys then begin to prepare for their marriage as they become socially and economically independent, while developing their household livelihoods as part of their life course. When girls reach the age of 14 to 15 years, they are asked to marry by boys and then start to become socially independent and take care of family

163

issues. Mr Y excelled academically. In the fifth grade, he began to study at a primary school in a nearby village. From this point on he began to take a slightly different path from that of the traditional life course.

Around 2000, Mr Y was selected for a scholarship programme that the authors were running with a local researcher to access secondary education. At the time, without such a programme, it would have been difficult for the Aari, who made their living from agriculture, to send their children to the high school in the town. When attending the secondary school, Mr Y lived in town G. During his education he learnt about the background of the residents of town G. They were largely the descendants of people from northern Ethiopia, such as the Amhara, who have a different cultural background from that of the Aari.

Mr Y achieved excellent grades in the national examinations before graduating from high school, and then attended an agricultural college in South Omo Zone. When Mr Y attended the agricultural college, the government covered all the tuition fees. He had to cover the transportation costs between South Omo Zone and the agricultural collage, and the cost of food and school supplies during school days. After Mr Y graduated from the agricultural college, he returned to the South Aari *woreda* and started to work for the agricultural office as an extension worker. His life course was the idealised course for most students. Nevertheless, Mr Y resigned from his job because he devised a plan to establish an agricultural association through his experiences as an agricultural extension worker. Resigning from a local official position is not a common practice in this area.

The authors were told by Mr A that Mr Y had resigned his position as an agricultural extension worker and returned to the village, although he found it difficult to hold enough cultivated land in village D to maintain a livelihood. I became interested in the circumstances that led him to such an action. When the authors met with him, he was asked why he had left his job and returned to the village. We also asked him why he had established the association for raising poultry. It was hard to believe that he was in his 30s because he was of a very calm demeanour and carefully considered each question before he answered.

When I was a high school student in town G, I noticed that Amhara parents left their houses and money to their children. However, the Aari used up the resources acquired in their youth, and passed it all away. I wondered why we could not leave our property to our children. After graduation in 2008, I worked for the local government office as an extension worker supervisor in village D for three years, and then for one year in village S. During this period, almost no farmers took my suggestions to improve their agricultural practices seriously, despite the ideas being based on agricultural science. I really felt that I needed to conduct a trial to demonstrate these ideas to farmers in a local context. I resigned from my job in 2012, and I started making a living as a farmer in village D. Just after I returned to the village, I discussed my vision with Mr A. Mr A agreed with my vision, and we started this project in 2013. (This text is based on the interview with Mr Y on 9 March 2014).

Although we did not ask him about the influence of his schooling on the establishment of the association for raising poultry, he explained the significance of bringing the results of his schooling back to his hometown to apply them. When he worked as an agricultural extension worker, no one was receptive to new farming methods and knowledge. This experience led him to realise that local farmers would not accept what he had learned if he just showed it to them. Mr Y realised that they would only embrace a new technology when they could actually see it work successfully.

From the age of seven until he was in his thirties, Mr Y continued to train himself in the *tamar* system of knowledge to perceive the world. Reading books and listening to the explanations of teachers is the best way to develop in the *tamar* system. When Mr Y resigned from his position as an agricultural extension worker, it could be seen as an attempt to combine what he had learned from the *tamar* system of knowledge with the *eskan* system.

### 3-2. Mr A's Life Course in the Village

The other core member of the agricultural association, Mr A, was a farmer and one of village officers. He was based in village D. The authors and Mr A became acquainted with each other when Mr A donated numerous local varieties of enset seedlings to communal farmers who were growing local varieties. At that time, the authors were running a communal farm field with other researchers and local people. The authors started conducting field research because there were unique local varieties of enset in village D. I stayed with Mr A's family during the fieldwork.

Mr A is seven or eight years older than Mr Y. He had a wife and five children in 2013. He went to the elementary school in village D and completed his secondary education through distance learning. He owns a piece of land in the village that is large compared with other villagers. He has a home garden of about 2,500 square metres and several cereal fields. Compared with his friends in the same generation, he has a large area of cereal fields. The land he owns was cultivated by Mr A's grandfather when he settled in village D.[12] His grandfather had three boys (Mr A's father was the second son), and the land he had cultivated was given to all three of them. Mr A was the only son of his father, and he was therefore able to inherit all the land that his father had inherited.

According to Mr A, he was born after his mother had miscarried six children. She was about to give up having a child because of the series of miscarriages. However, a local diviner in the indigenous religion who could talk with God told her that her child would be the future ruler of this land. She became positive about having a child. Mr A was then born, followed by two sisters in the following years.

When Mr A was a child, his mother died from an illness. Mr A's father had more than one wife, although Mr A was his only son. Mr A therefore inherited all his father's land.

> When I was small, around three or four years old, my mother died. I grew apart from my father when I was a child. I was working for the village office when I was a small boy around twelve to thirteen years old. At that time, I started making money by selling eucalyptus and enset

166

seedlings. It was a new business at that time. At almost the same time, I became interested in protestant church activities.

I finished eighth grade by taking a correspondence course. During that period, I went to town G and I saw the Aari who worked for the Amhara as daily labourers, and became concerned that more Aari would have to work for the Amhara if we could not make independent lives from agricultural practices in the near future. I seriously considered how people could improve their lives by adopting new ideas, such as agricultural science, to our local agricultural practices. In 2012, I was elected as a chairperson in village D. I made an effort to establish an agricultural association in village D. When creating this association, I was thinking about people's lives in the village, and I also wished to keep my large property for my children.

When Mr A explained his own background, he mentioned that his family was poor (he used the term *dha,* which means 'poor' in Amharic). He continued to mention the following points, which were related to the proposition that 'his family was poor'. First, the fact that his father had a large property but failed to make use of it. In addition, Mr A was estranged from his father because his father kept his mother away from him when she was ill, and Mr A did not engage in enough farm work with his father. Mr A and his father were not sufficiently involved in farm work together. Furthermore, after his mother died, his father did not have any wives living with him long enough to make a suitable livelihood for them. Mr A learned from his childhood experiences that a large piece of property did not always make for a better life.

When he was old enough to build his own house, i.e., 12 to 13 years old, Mr A left his father's house and began to visit the village office. Then, at a fairly young age, he became a member of the village office. Mr A was also engaged in new businesses, such as selling eucalyptus tree seedlings and vermin control in enset home gardens. It was around that time that Mr A converted to the Protestant faith. According to his interviews, he was a man who took a keen interest in establishing new business opportunities from his early years. For him, school was also a place to learn new things. He attended primary

167

school and then finished his secondary education through distance learning.

In 2012, Mr A was elected a chair person in village D. For the people in village D, to achieve a better life for everyone, it was necessary to create a network of roads from the main paved road to the village and its educational environment. When he became a chairperson, Mr A went to the state government to petition for the construction of a road from the main paved road to the village and the allocation of a budget for additional teachers to be assigned to the school in village D. Within a year of becoming a chairperson, his negotiating skills led to the decision to assign an additional teacher to Village D to offer classes up to the seventh grade. In conjunction with this petition, Mr A also asked people in village D to provide materials for building the additional classrooms that were required. In addition, the village office built new houses in a communal plot near to the school, which were provided to the newly appointed teachers. Mr A promptly created an educational environment for both students and teachers in village D, with the understanding and cooperation of the villagers.

Mr A had long been engaged in political and economic activities in the village and he learned how to solve the challenges in village D through his experiences in the village office. Mr A was also an excellent listener. He found a way to collect information before he took care of issues. During the three months of fieldwork, the authors had breakfast with guests who visited Mr A's house to ask him to listen to their problems every morning. They believed that he could solve their problems or show them how to get the problem resolved.

Mr A was concerned that the youth of the village were facing a problem of land shortage. According to Mr A, there was very little new land available for cultivation in village D. The population of village D was growing and the young men were unable to own their own cultivated land or raise livestock in their fields. After taking over as a chair person in village D, Mr A had the opportunity to learn about the concept of the agricultural association from Mr Y when Mr Y returned to the village. For Mr A, who was familiar with the *eskan* system of knowledge, which was based on action and experience, Mr Y stood out as a person who could contribute *tamar* knowledge, based on his school experience, although the learning had not been put into practice.

### 3-3. The Establishment of the Association for Raising Poultry

As soon as Mr Y returned to village D, he shared his ideas with Mr A. Most importantly, Mr A and Mr Y belonged to the same Protestant church and, therefore, they had the opportunity to see each other almost every weekend. Similar to the modern school education system, the Protestant churches that had permeated the area after the 1980s provided a place to introduce new ideas and to learn from them. Gradually, the members of the church began to carry out joint labour in each other's fields and to appreciate the advantages of such a beneficial association. In the late 2010s, the church also began to function as a meeting place for members to exchange ideas on how to make a living. Just as Mr A had realised, Mr Y also noticed that many of the young men in village D, including himself, were facing land shortage problems. Mr Y believed that they would not be able to develop their own lives and those of their children if they continued to farm and raise livestock in the same way as their fathers' generation.

Mr Y proposed starting an association for the confinement rearing of chickens, enabling their eggs to be sold. He also proposed that the association could accumulate capital for new businesses through this activity. According to Mr Y, raising poultry could be started with a very small amount of money compared to dairy husbandry. The activity did not need much capital in terms of feed expenses, just the initial cost of the purchase of chickens and a place to raise them. At the same time, there was an opportunity to obtain higher profits if locals could accept and use modern agricultural technology for raising poultry. Mr Y also mentioned that the activities of the association would be diversified and members could receive a monthly salary from the new businesses in the near future. He told them, 'We are going to improve our lives together.'

Mr A had agreed with Mr Y's idea to establish an agricultural association in village D. Mr A held a meeting with Mr Y to recruit members to join the association for raising poultry. After the association started their activities, Mr A encouraged Mr Y to apply for a micro-finance programme provided by the Ethiopian government via their *woreda* office. Mr A also shared information about hybrid poultry varieties with the agricultural association members to support the development of the association.

Mr Y and Mr A held a recruitment meeting in 2013 and asked, mainly, the young men to attend and learn about the agricultural association. Because Mr Y and Mr A believed in Protestantism and attended church on a daily basis, they approached a young male in the Protestant church. According to Mr Y, they held the meeting to explain the agricultural association at a Protestant church because there were daily interactions with people in Protestant churches. However, he also confirmed that being a Protestant was not an important condition for participation in the association's activities if that person could follow the three rules listed below. Participation was open to anyone who could follow these rules, although in fact they were strongly influenced by Protestant doctrine.

In the meeting, Mr Y and Mr A asked people who were interested in joining the association to sign a pledge to keep at least three rules: (1) members put in 1,000 Ethiopian Birr (ETB), equal to c.a. 50 USD in advance, (2) do not miss work more than three times, and (3) do not fight, even if you drink. This final rule was essentially equivalent to NOT drinking. Twenty of the people who attended the meeting informed Mr Y and Mr A that they would like to participate in the group. All were Protestant. The reason for the participation of so many people is that their proposed ideas may have been seen as an attractive new activity. In addition, some of the new participants felt limited in their ability to live in the village due to the shortage of land. One week after the meeting, the twenty participants came up with the first instalment of 100 ETB each, which was paid into the group account. Then they ordered an improved chicken variety through the extension workers in the *woreda* office. It took six months for them to receive these chickens through the *woreda* office. When the *woreda* office contacted them about the delivery, all of the members attended the meeting. As soon as they were contacted, they went to the *woreda* office to receive them because the new chicken variety was unusual in the area, even though it was becoming popular among farmers. Eighteen members paid the remaining 900 ETB each, while two dropped out.

Members of the association quickly set up poultry facilities, where the chickens were to be kept after they were delivered. Land for raising poultry was provided by one of the members. Using the funds raised to join the association, a tin-roofed building was constructed. There were no roads suitable for vehicles in the area where the building was to be constructed. The members bundled a few sheets of tin purchased in town and carried them on their shoulders and heads to the proposed construction site, which took about two hours. In addition to the space where the chickens were kept, there was also space for keeping the poultry feed and agricultural tools purchased by the association, as well as for a watchman to sleep at night, and to hold meetings.

The association leased land to grow grain and grasses to obtain the poultry feed according to modern farming methods. In the traditional animal feeding context, Aari farmers put chicken to grass in the daytime, and keep chickens indoors overnight. They rarely feed them. However, members of the association worked to obtain feedstuff from agricultural products for the chickens. The 18 members continued to work on their farms to obtain the poultry feed and took turns as nightwatchmen in the new poultry facility. The authors conducted this fieldwork for one and half years after the association was established. By that time, their building was completed and they were generating income from poultry raising, which was deposited into the association's bank account controlled by the South Aari *woreda*. In 2014, the association applied for a loan from a micro finance institution through the *woreda* office to purchase more chickens and accumulate capital.

The association has not shared any of the profits made in the less than two years between the time it began its activities and the time the authors conducted fieldwork. When the authors asked if there were any problems or arguments among members about the sharing of profits, Mr Y explained that members believed that there was no point in sharing the profits at this stage and that funds should be accumulated. Members were not looking for short-term gains because they believed that they were all growing, *gapnti* in the Aari language, and changing their lives, *ookumi* in the Aari language, together.

## 4. The Combination of the Two Knowledge Systems and the Formation of Local Knowledge

This study is focused on two men, Mr Y and Mr A, who established the association for raising poultry in Village D. The study examined the impact of their experiences of school education on the establishment of the association. Following the establishment of the association for raising poultry and the rapid development of its activities, the cooperation between Mr Y and Mr A had a great influence on the association. In other words, the successful combination of the *eskan* and *tamar* systems of knowledge was crucial.

Mr Y was born and raised in village D. He left the village to attend school from grade five and finished his secondary education in the town. He then went on to attend and complete agricultural college, and he returned to South Omo Zone as an agricultural extension worker. He has spent most of his education in the *tamar* system of knowledge, i.e., learning things by reading or listening. He performed well in that system and was able to obtain a position as an extension worker. What made him a little different from most students and extension workers was that he saw and learned about the succession from parents to children among the Amhara and spent his school days wondering why the Aari did not adopt the same mode of succession as the Amhara. In addition, he also wondered why farmers did not accept the new agricultural skills that Mr Y had learned in collage, which he had tried to promote during his work for the agricultural office as an extension worker. When Mr Y started pursuing the question of why farmers did not accept new agricultural skills, he formulated a hypothesis that the farmers would accept them, if they could be convinced that they would work in the context of rural farming practices. The resignation of Mr Y from the position of agricultural extension worker can be seen as an action derived from the combination of two different systems of knowledge, i.e., *tamar* and *eskan*.

In contrast, Mr A was educated in an *eskan* system, with knowledge acquired through practice. The story of his birth and the fact that he is estranged from his father were the basis of his opting out of the life course of the so-called common Aari boy. School was a fascinating place for Mr A. However, Mr A completed his secondary education through distance learning and, therefore, his experience of school education remained as written knowledge without practical application. When Mr A saw the Aari working as servants for the Amhara in the town he began to fear that people from northern Ethiopia would once again dominate the Aari, as their ancestors had experienced in the past. When Mr A was elected as the chairperson in village D, he made a series of decisions to implement or solve specific problems for the village. He developed his system of *eskan* through his own experience of working on problems in the village office.

When Mr Y shared has idea with Mr A and they started to work together to establish the agricultural association it could be regarded as a combination of two knowledge systems, i.e., *tamar*, which is knowledge learned by reading and hearing, and *eskan*, which is knowledge acquired through practice. However, what is important here is that when Mr Y shared his ideas with Mr A, both Mr Y and Mr A recognised that there were two systems of knowledge and that each system was important in solving the problems and challenges in village D. In this situation, both Mr Y and Mr A could accept each other's views based on their systems of knowledge acquisition, and they could also combine them to prepare for the establishment of the association. Mr Y and Mr A found a way to combine different knowledge systems – commensurability – because they understood that the development of the community would allow all people in the community to live 'better' lives.

Through Mr Y's experiences of school education, he developed a belief in modern agricultural science and believed that the activities of the association would help him to pass on what he created to his children's generation. Additionally, for Mr A, the potential of modern agricultural science and the activities of the association assuaged his fears about being deprived of what he had. The combination of the two systems of knowledge, *tamar* and *eskan*, also provided a means of overcoming two different emotions, hope and anxiety.

This study regarded experiences of school education as an opportunity to learn in the classroom as well as an occasion to interact with people with different cultural backgrounds. For both men, who took on important roles in establishing the agricultural association, the experiences of Mr Y and Mr A of school education encouraged them to relativise, as Aari, their cultural practices. In this regard, experiences of school education during the life course of the Aari provide each student with an opportunity for personality formation in terms of questioning their cultural practices and exploring options for his or her own way of life in the future. In the case of Mr Y and Mr A, their experiences of school education made them aware of the importance of combining different systems of knowledge, *tamar* and *eskan*. The young men who agreed with their ideas then came together and participated in the activities of the agricultural association to develop their livelihoods.

The activities of the poultry-raising association are still in their infancy. However, the association is perceived by the villagers as a new activity, led by the young men in village D, that will create a new way of generating income based on modern agricultural technology. The activity of the association and the knowledge accumulated among its members can be regarded as the creation of a local form of knowledge with the potential to reorganise already existing social relationships and create new communities in the future.


**Endnotes**

[1] The role of religion, especially in the Ethiopian Orthodox Church, is that before modern schooling, officials were educated by the church

(Wagaw 1979).

2 This idea is strongly influenced by the results of a study by Schultz (1961) in the United States, which asserted that it is valid in a growing economy (Negash 2006: 14). However, according to the study, only when the economy is growing, will investment in education lead to higher incomes for individual investors and increased revenues for the state (Schultz 1961).

3 For example, a 2012 World Bank report mentioned the link between the quality of education and economic growth (Joshi and Verspoor 2012: 16).

4 It has been noted that during the socialist regime prior to the 1980s, education suffered from a higher student to teacher ratio than during the imperial period. This was especially apparent when compared to the northern regions and has led to a poorer educational environment (Poluha 2004).

5 In recent years, with financial support from the private sector, the government has allocated more money to higher education, leading to an increase in the number of students entering higher education. In particular, the number of women pursuing higher education has increased (Negash 2006: 23). Since 1998, the Ethiopian government has been active in improving higher education in the country, establishing regional universities and allocating a high percentage of the national budget to them. In developing countries, while human resources development through higher education is seen as essential to social development, its dissemination is not properly and effectively aligned with relevant social policies and development plans. This produces a serious qualitative gap between the human resources required by the labour market and the graduates supplied by universities (Woldegiyorgis 2015).

6 Once the international achievement goals in education are introduced to each country, their meaning changes according to the local context and the local actors involved (Yamada 2007). It is important to consider which elements of the international achievement goals change depending on the local context as certain factors come into play. In terms of primary education, a significant disparity has also been found between rural and urban areas. Except in Addis Ababa, the percentage of schoolchildren who have completed primary education is low.

[7] The meaning of '*eskan*' is ever expanding, and the word is now used to refer to knowledge learned from books, media or teachers. The Aari now use the Amharic loanword '*tamar*', which means learning, as an extension of *eskan*.

[8] *Tamar* can also be used as *tamarta-baab* (person who has studied in school) to describe a person. With the introduction of modern schooling to this region in the 1960s, *tamar* has been accepted as an alien word of Amharic origin. *Tamarta-baab* is also used separately from *esta-baab*.

[9] Among the Aari, a young man of 12 to 15 leaves his father's house and builds his own house as an act that shows he is becoming a full-fledged man. At that time, he also plants enset seedlings in his home garden. At a funeral, people bring a false stem of enset to the deceased's home and grieve the death by beating it (Shigeta 1996). Enset is thus closely tied to a person's life course.

[10] A way of only about 3 metres wide has been bulldozed down the slope. During the rainy season, heavy trucks and other vehicles have difficulty using this road.

[11] A variety of plants are grown in the home gardens, mainly enset, but also kale and other leafy vegetables (Shigeta 1996). The starch in enset's rhizomes and pseudostems is used as a food item. Depending on the variety, a household of seven (a husband and wife with five unmarried children from three to fifteen years old) will consume the starch produced from a single enset plant in about ten days to three weeks if they prepare one or two meals daily, including lunch or dinner (data from the authors in preparation). If about 20 enset plants are grown in a home garden, the household can be self-sufficient. According to the measurement results from 23 home gardens in Village D, the smallest home garden was 500 square metres. It is possible for one household, including a couple and three unmarried children (zero to seven years) to support themselves through enset production. However, young households without cereal fields have no means to earn cash, so they rent land for cereal cultivation or retail vegetables at the market to earn cash income.

[12] People in village D had started to cultivate the land more than three generations ago (Hisada 2014).

## Acknowledgements

This work was supported by JSPS KAKENHI Grant Numbers JP16H06318 and JP18H03444.

## References

Hisada, S. (2014) *Measuring the Farmland with Farmers: Engaged Area Studies on Sharing Local Knowledge by Using Participatory 3 Dimension Map*, Kyoto: Shoukadoh (in Japanese).

Joshi, R. and Verspoor, A. (2012) *Secondary Education in Ethiopia: Supporting Growth and Transformation,* Washington DC: The World Bank.

Kaneko, M. (2014) 'I know how to make pots by myself: Special reference to local knowledge transmission in Southwestern Ethiopia', *African Study Monographs, Supplementary Issue*, Vol. 48, pp. 59–75.

———— (2016) 'Variations in shape, local classification, and the establishment of a chaîne opératoire for pot making among female potters in Southwestern Ethiopia', in H. Terashima and B. S. Hewlett (eds), *Social Learning and Innovation in Contemporary Hunter-Gatherers: Evolutionary and Ethnographic Perspectives (Replacement of Neanderthals by Modern Humans Series)*, Tokyo: Springer, pp. 217–227.

Kaneko, M. and Shigeta, M. (2020) 'Introduction to this special topic "reconsidering local knowledge and beyond", reconsidering local knowledge and beyond', *African Study Monographs, Supplementary Issue*, No. 59, pp. 1–9.

Negash, T. (2006) *Education in Ethiopia: From Crisis to the Brink of Collapse,* Uppsala: Nordiska Afrikainstitutet.

Poluha, E. (2004) *The Power of Continuity: Ethiopia through the Eyes of Its Children,* Uppsala: Nordiska Afrikainstitutet.

Schultz, T. W. (1961) 'Investment in human capital', *The American Economic Review*, Vol. 51, No. 1, pp. 1–17.

Shigeta, M. (1996) 'Creating landrace diversity: The case of the Ari people and ensete (*Ensete ventricosum*) in Ethiopia', in R. F. Ellen and K. Fukui (eds), *Redefining Nature: Ecology, Culture, and Domestication*, Oxford: Berg, pp. 233–268.

Shigeta, M. and Kaneko, M. (2017) 'Zairaichi (Local Knowledge) as the manners of co-existence: Encounters between the Aari farmers in Southwestern Ethiopia and the "other", in Y. Gebre, I. Ohta and M. Matsuda (eds) *African Virtues in the Pursuit of Conviviality: Exploring Local Solutions in Light of Global Prescriptions*, Bamenda: Langaa RPCIG, pp. 311–338.

Suzuki, I. (2004) 'The transformation of children's collaborative farm work in Southwestern Ethiopia: The impact of modern school education and protestantism', Pre-doctoral thesis, Graduate School of Asian and African Area Studies, Kyoto University (in Japanese).

The World Bank website (https://data.worldbank.org/indicator/SE.PRM.ENRR.FE?locations=ET) (accessed: 20 June 2020).

Wagaw, T. G. (1979) *Education in Ethiopia, Prospect and Retrospect*, Ann Arbor: University of Michigan Press.

Woldegiyorgis, A. A. (2015) 'A glance at the Ethiopian higher education from the developmental state perspective', *Bahir Dar Journal of Education*, Vol. 15, No. 2, pp. 1–37.

Yamada, S. (2007) 'Making sense of the EFA from a national context: Its implementation, and impact on households in Ethiopia'. in D. P. Baker and A. W. Wiseman (eds), *International Perspectives on Education and Society*, Vol. 8, pp. 453–491.

——— (2011) 'Social factors determining "community participation": The tradition of community school and school management committees in Oromia region, Ethiopia', *Journal of International Development Studies*, Vol. 20, No.2, pp. 107–125 (in Japanese with English abstract).

# Chapter 6

## Education and Employment: Genesis of Highly Educated Informal Workers in Mozambique

*Akiyo Aminaka*

## 1. Introduction

The poor have always been socially powerless. The increasing reliance on institutional care adds a new dimension to their helplessness: psychological impotence, the inability to fend for themselves ... Modernized poverty combined the lack of power over circumstances with a loss of personal potency (Illich 1970: 3).

One afternoon in January 2018, 24-year-old Maria[1] was busy attending to her clients at her hair salon on a corner in the Polana Caniço zone of Maputo in Mozambique. In her spare time, she told me about her career as the owner of the hair salon in addition to running two accessories and cosmetics retail stands at the municipal markets while simultaneously being the mother to a one-year-old baby. Since 2017, she had purchased most of these goods once a month from the wholesale market of light industries at Guangzhou in China and more recently from India.[2]

It was Maria's 64-year-old father who introduced her to the author. He spoke modestly but proudly about his independent daughter's business. He also felt that he had fulfilled his responsibility as a parent, having sent all three of his children, including his eldest daughter Maria, to higher education institutions. His own educational background was limited to secondary school, and he had not attended a higher education institution.[3] This fact may have also contributed to her parents' pride in providing their children with more educational opportunities than their own parents had. Maria's

179

father belongs to Mozambique's so-called '3.8 generation (geração de 8 de Março)', who were called upon directly by the first president, Samora Machel, to contribute to nation building shortly after independence in 1975 (Notícias 2015; Rádio Moçambique 2018).

In my view, Maria is exemplary as a young female entrepreneur (Honwana 2012; Raimundo and Chikanda 2016). As well as her business success, Maria's relatively high educational background merits consideration. She left university after two years to focus on her economic activities as an informal cross-border trader (ICBT), to which she had already been committed since her first year of the economics programme at university. She went back and forth between the formal institution and informal trade for her learning and practice before deciding that the practical leaning opportunities that she required lay outside the institutionalised system.

Of course, Maria may differ significantly from the poor whom Illich observed among New York's Puerto Rican community or in Latin American society in the 1970s, considering that she lives in Mozambique's capital city in the 2000s. However, Illich's arguments may still offer an important analytical perspective on the expansion of education systems, industrialisation and job creation in Africa today. This is borne out by the fact that it is as an ICBT that Maria is realising her personal potency.

The term 'ICBT' gained academic recognition only in the 2000s. In practice, however, ICBT activities are based on the development of urban informal trade, which has been widespread in Africa since the mid-1980s, when the implementation of structural adjustment programmes sharply reduced public employment in formal sectors (Mijere 2009: 19–20; Benjamin et al. 2014: 7).[4] The World Bank's report in 2014 defines ICBT as follows:

> Its unique feature is that very close geographical proximity renders transportation cost immaterial allowing those who are able to cross borders regularly to take advantage of differences in the supply, demand and price of various goods and services available on either side of the border (Benjamin et al. 2014: 16).

This definition of 'very close geographical proximity' should be updated, as we have observed that ICBT takes place intercontinentally between Africa and Asia. The development of ICBT in Mozambique is one of the points to be explored in this chapter. Another aspect for consideration is the genesis of highly educated ICBTs, such as Maria. Attendance at higher education institutions in Mozambique is particularly low, amounting to 0.9 per cent in 2017 (INE 2019: 128). Why did Maria drop out of the university that she was so fortunate to attend, and why did she commit so deeply to ICBT? How did this society come to produce a well-educated informal sector worker?

Mijere (2009) has observed that education level had no impact on ICBT activities in the Southern African Development Community (SADC), based on research carried out between 2003 and 2004. In the intervening 15 years, the circumstances around ICBT have changed drastically in several aspects. The relevant changes have been achieved through two institutional changes. One involves the relaxation of restrictions on the movement of people, thus ensuring improved and affordable transport services combined with additional communication services to connect people across long distances. The other institutional change involves educational reform aimed at increasing the proportion of the population with relatively high educational backgrounds, who can maximise the above-mentioned changes in circumstances.

A recent report published by the World Institute for Development Economics Research at the United Nations University (UNU-WIDER) offers some insights into this case. The WIDER's report, based on quantitative research conducted among university finalists in Mozambique, highlights the following points. Underemployment and unemployment are common, and 23 per cent of graduates were unemployed 18 months after graduation. In addition, a mismatch in areas of study was observed, and many found their salaries to be lower than expected. While most graduates believe their education to have been worthwhile, half of the finalists surveyed believe that their current jobs do not require university degrees. Moreover, the provision of formal channels and services aimed at helping graduates find work is insufficient. Jobs were mainly found using informal channels and personal networks. Amongst the finalists, women took longer than men to enter the labour market and received lower salaries, despite having the same educational background (Jones et al. 2019).

The above-mentioned report posits the existence of structural factors in addition to personal factors. To identify these structural factors, this chapter aimed to propose a course of social change by exploring the genesis of relatively highly educated ICBTs in Mozambique in relation to the labour market and education, given a specific timeline.

## 2. '3.8 Generation', the Generation of Post-Independent Expectation

On 8 March 1977, several days after the third congress of the *Frente de Libertação de Moçambique* (FRELIMO) (Mozambique Liberation Front), the first president, Samora Machel, gathered the urban youth from throughout the country to assemble at Maputo. The charismatic president encouraged the secondary school-age cohort, in particular – named the '3.8 generation' – to contribute to the construction and development of their newly independent country.[5] The Mozambican government who adopted socialism after independence used financial and technical support from the former Eastern Bloc to fill the huge vacancies in the labour market following the exodus of the colonists. The colonial institution had been relevant for the Portuguese population, and access for indigenous Mozambicans had been extremely limited to a small portion of the assimilated population. Soon after independence, the Mozambican government had no immediate solution for the lack of secondary and tertiary education in the country.

From 1977, the Mozambican government recruited pupils in their late teens from all over the country and offered them the opportunity to participate in an educational programme in Cuba.[6] Among this generation, another cohort comprising 899 children in their early teens (695 males and 204 females) were selected and sent to the former German Democratic Republic (GDR) to complete six years

182

of secondary education, including two years of vocational training, between 1982 and 1988 (Müller 2010; Dorsch 2011).

Maria's father remembers those days well, as he was one of the young graduates from the secondary school in the capital city, and he belongs to the 3.8 generation. After completing his secondary education, he began to work as a civil servant at the municipal library while some of his friends went to study in Cuba.[7] Although the Council for Mutual Economic Assistance (COMECON) had rejected the Mozambican government's application for entry in 1981, the COMECON member states' economies were deeply committed to the development of natural resources in Mozambique, such as coal and natural gas, and they established joint ventures in those sectors, including professional education for Mozambicans(Müller 2010).

However, heading toward regime change near the end of the Cold War, the government was forced to turn to the International Monetary Fund (IMF) and the World Bank in 1984, as the country was experiencing a civil war between the FRELIMO and the *Resistência Nacional Moçambicana* (RENAMO) (Mozambican National Resistance) combined with the destabilisation caused by South Africa and famine in the early 1980s. Some students returning from the Eastern Bloc were assigned to coal mines at Moatize and the gas fields at Pande-Temane, but most of the students were sent to complete compulsory military service.[8] One of the informants received eight years of educational experience in Cuba in 1979 when he turned eighteen years of age. When he returned to Mozambique in 1986, he entered the military for one year. Then, after working in Maputo for several years, he began working for the National Hydrocarbon Enterprise (*Empresa Nacional de Hidrocarbonetos*: ENH).[9] Another staff member at ENH had worked through the 1980s and 1990s maintaining and distributing the gas pipelines from the gas fields at Pande-Temane in Inhambane Province to a local community at risk of a guerrilla attack.[10]

The Mozambican government decided to make a regime change from socialist to capitalist after concluding negotiations with the World Bank and IMF in 1984. The regime conversion resulted in discontinuity in professional education for Mozambicans and the

183

entire economic system at the national level. The situation subsequently deteriorated further when the Mozambican government could not offer employment to 834 students returning from the GDR to Mozambique in 1988. When the FRELIMO and the RENAMO reached a peace accord in 1992, most of the joint ventures and nationalised firms for which those trained in the Eastern Bloc were expected to work were abandoned or dissolved (Müller 2010).

The introduction of the structural adjustment programme exposed even the public administration to restructuring. Maria's father took early retirement and then entered self-employment, using his retirement allowance to start a transportation business with cars individually imported from Durban in South Africa. Around the same time, Maria's mother began to participate in street vending to supplement their household income. Maria's mother handled second-hand clothes that Asian wholesalers imported on a large scale and made substantial profits from during the 1990s and 2000s.[11] Together, they struggled to maintain their family life amidst the expansion of the informal sector common to the African countries that embraced structural adjustment policies.

## 3. The Genesis of ICBT from the 3.8 Generation

The 3.8 generation was not monolithic. The majority of those who received higher education in the Eastern Bloc turned to the Western Bloc after the end of the Cold War and proceeded toward careers as technocrats. The regime change had a severe impact on most of that generation who had received secondary education and, thus, their perspective on their government was critical. The genesis of Mozambican ICBT in the mid-1980s occurred in tandem with the approaching regime change and deteriorating war situation.

The term 'ICBT' did not gain traction in scholarship until the 2000s (Peberdy 2000). However, the Mozambican designation *mukherista*, used to refer to merchants who repeatedly cross the border, was already in use in the 1980s. The original designation *mukhero* denotes 'transport' in the local language – Shangaan – in southern Mozambique. When *mukhero* is combined with the official Portuguese suffix '–isto /-ista', indicating a person, it means 'transporter'. The fact that the commonly accepted designation of *mukerista* is a feminine noun attests that many women engaged in this business from the outset.

ICBT began in earnest when urban Mozambique suffered from serious commodity shortages along with the intensifying civil war situation in the mid-1980s. In the early 1980s, the Mozambican ICBT began with the female residents of Namaacha, a town located on the border with Eswatini (formerly Swaziland), according to the president of the first ICBT association in Mozambique, the Mukhero Association (*Associação Mukhero*) (see Figure 1). They began to supply commodities by crossing the border irregularly when they encountered shortages in supplies from Maputo, 70 kilometres away, owing to the war situation. A series of official facilities for border control, including migration and customs, were in place. However, the officials tolerated the ICBT activities and did not charge any customs because the officials themselves suffered as a result of the commodity shortages as well as the local residents. Soon, every Wednesday and Saturday become well known as cross-border purchase days among the officials and local residents. Meanwhile, the extent to which the central ministry was aware of or acknowledged the activities carried out by ICBTs remains unknown (Jairoce 2016).

Maputo's female residents soon began participating in these activities and, seeing the good profit margins, Maputo's male residents subsequently joined in on a larger scale, hiring Namaacha residents to make purchases several times a day for the capital's informal market. At that time, in the mid-1980s, Eswatini was the main supplier because it was the only country at the southern end of Mozambican territory that black Mozambicans were able to cross the border to, officially. Under the apartheid regime, South Africa did not permit the entrance of black Mozambicans, with the exception of planned migrant labour for its core industries.

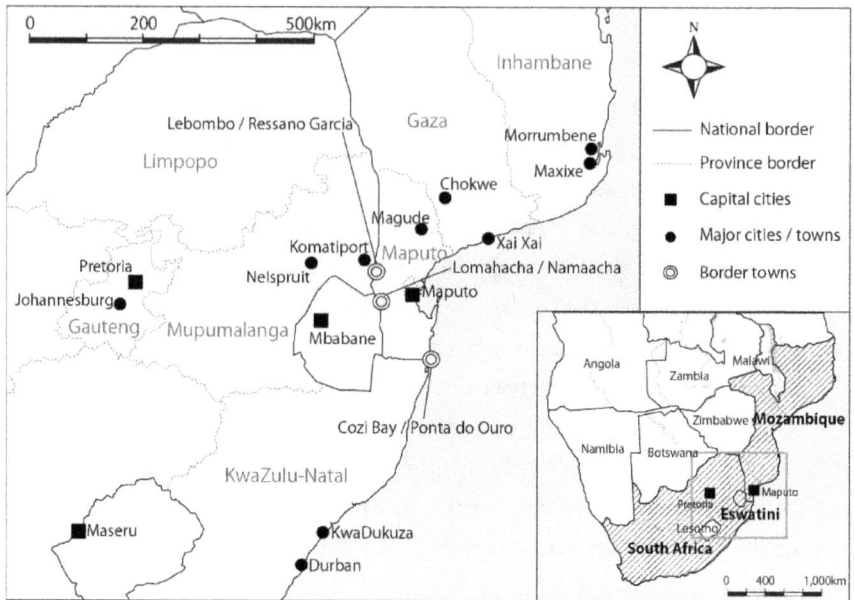

**Figure 1. Southern Mozambique and neighbouring countries**

Maputo's ICBTs, who dramatically increased the flow of materials, share some characteristics: they formerly had regular salaries while employed in a formal sector and were suddenly obliged to work in an informal sector. Those new ICBTs included ex-civil servants made redundant by privatisation and labourers who had migrated to the GDR in the 1980s and became unemployed following the regime change. The latter group, on returning to Mozambique, were called *Madgermanes*, meaning 'made in Germany'. They belong to the 3.8 generation, who had been encouraged to contribute to nation building by Samora Machel in 1977 and included the president of the ICBT association. *Madgermanes* experienced both high expectations on their departure and deep disappointment on their return, when the FRELIMO government misappropriated a portion of their wages that had been promised to them. Consequently, the *Madgermanes* formed an association and continue to demonstrate in the hope that the government will reimburse their unpaid salaries.

The second stage in the development of ICBT occurred when the South African government eased racial regulations on migration toward the end of the apartheid regime, between 1986 and 1991, allowing black Mozambican ICBTs to cross the border and pioneer new supply routes in South Africa (Peberdy and Rogerson 2000). The first supply route developed by Mozambicans was to Nelspruit in Mpumalanga Province located 100 kilometres from the Mozambican border. Subsequently, the location of main suppliers for both fresh and processed food and consumer goods was established at Komatiport in the same province but a mere four kilometres from Mozambican border. The main road between Maputo and Ressano Garcia, the border point close to Komatiport, was rehabilitated in the early 1990s, and alternative means of transportation, such as shared minibuses – more reasonable than individual forms of transportation – became available. Demand for transportation services increased at this time. In this sense, Maria's father was shrewd, having invested in transport services after taking early retirement around that time.

These logistic improvements caused the initial investment required of ICBT newcomers to decrease and, thus, the number of ICBTs rose. Although the difficulty in acquiring entry visas to South Africa continued to be a barrier for Mozambican migrants, including ICBTs, some ICBTs formed an association in 1994 to support its members' passport and visa acquisition by issuing recommendation letters bearing the association's name (Jairoce 2016).[12] The individual who took the initiative to establish the ICBT association in 1994 was one of the *Madgermanes* and is the association's current president. Having been born in 1961 at Xai Xai, the provincial capital of Gaza Province in southern Mozambique, he was 16 years old in 1977 and was thus one of the 3.8 generation. Following the application for labour migration, he spent several months undergoing basic and paramilitary training and worked in GDR for ten years from 1980 to 1990, when he returned to Mozambique.[13]

The third stage in Mozambican ICBT's development also occurred in the mid-1990s as a consequence of the changing circumstances between Mozambique and South Africa. Major South African supermarkets advanced throughout Southern Africa, not only in capital cities but also in provincial cities. For example, Shoprite opened in Maputo in 1994 and other similar mass retailers followed. According to one of the informants, this allowed customers to purchase the same products without the interposition of ICBT, regardless of where the customers lived. Along with this change, Mozambican ICBTs, who had purchased at the same shops in Nelspruit or Komatiport, lost their advantage.[14] The existing ICBT activities entered a phase of selection.

ICBTs have experienced continuous changes in their commercial environment. Small-scale ICBTs were relevant in the late 1990s and early 2000s, particularly those who crossed South Africa via the border between Ressano Garcia and Lebombo in shared minibuses. However, some lost their businesses due to the encroachment of South African supermarkets in Mozambique and the associated loss of competitiveness from 1994.[15] ICBTs cannot derive any profit if an item's unit price is low, so ICBTs must deal with considerable quantities of items to gain any benefit, and thus they require more capital. Nowadays, a division of labour exists to an extent, as follows. Middle- and large-scale ICBTs in the area of the capital who have access to transport continue to supply fresh and processed food with low unit prices but large market distribution volumes. In the process of weeding out smaller-scale ICBTs, some of them have expanded geographically, cultivating new suppliers and niche markets by actively moving between Africa and Asia.

## 4. Education and Employment for the Post-War Generation

### 4-1. Rehabilitation in Primary Education

It is imperative that education keep pace with the above-mentioned changing needs of the labour market. This section charts recent reforms in the education sector with a particular focus on tertiary education, which includes higher education and technical and vocational education. First, let us examine Mozambique's education system.

Preschool is not compulsory in Mozambique, and children commence primary education, which lasts seven years and is free of charge, at the age of six or seven. Primary education is subdivided into two levels: the first level lasts five years while the second level lasts two years.

Secondary education is offered in general schools and in technical schools for students aged between 13 and 18 years for five years. General secondary education is divided into two levels. Students sit a national exam between the first and second levels. Upon completion of the second level, some of those awarded the certificate may proceed to teacher training colleges where they may complete a two-year programme to qualify as primary school teachers.

Technical and vocational education (TVE) is offered in TVE schools and institutes and in vocational training centres (VTCs). TVE schools comprise five levels with one year per level, and the first two levels are jointly equivalent to the first level of general secondary school. Completion of the fifth level is equivalent to completion of the second level of general secondary school.

Students who complete secondary education, either general or technical, can progress to higher institutes such as universities, polytechnics, colleges or academies, where they can pursue a range of study programmes (Gondwe 2011: 14–5).

The above encapsulates the current system in 2020. However, the existence of the system and the reality of the infrastructure are separate issues. Sixteen years of civil war between the FRELIMO and the RENAMO had destroyed or closed 57.8 per cent of national-level schools by 1992. In areas that were particularly affected by the war – for example, Tete Province – the ratio was as high as 94.8 per cent, as shown in Table 1 (Van der Berg et al. 2017: 2).

Soon after the end of the civil war, the diffusion of primary education was targeted as the foremost priority with respect to the education system, in addition to being addressed in the Millennium Development Goals (1990–2015). The expansion of primary education combined with the high population growth rate made it necessary to expand secondary education in turn, as shown in Table 2 and, subsequently, post-secondary education. Thus, the section that follows charts the series of reforms in the education sector with a particular focus on tertiary education.

## Table 1. War impact on school destruction

| Region | Province | Existing in 1983 | | Destroyed or Closed by 1992 | | Population Distribution in 1997 (%) |
|--------|----------|------------------|------------------|-----------------|-------------------|---|
| | | Number | Distribution (%) | Number | Destruction (%) | |
| North | Niassa | 508 | 8.6 | 352 | 69.3 | 4.9 |
| | Cabo Delgado | 542 | 9.2 | 109 | 20.1 | 8.2 |
| | Nampula | 1,116 | 19.0 | 535 | 47.9 | 19.5 |
| Centre | Zambézia | 1,130 | 19.2 | 997 | 88.2 | 20.3 |
| | Tete | 479 | 8.1 | 454 | 94.8 | 7.3 |
| | Manica | 225 | 3.8 | 109 | 48.4 | 6.2 |
| | Sofala | 386 | 6.6 | 253 | 65.5 | 8.8 |
| South | Inhambane | 506 | 8.6 | 220 | 43.5 | 7.1 |
| | Gaza | 546 | 9.3 | 169 | 31.0 | 6.6 |
| | Maputo Province | 339 | 5.8 | 204 | 60.2 | 5.1 |
| | Maputo City | 109 | 1.9 | 0 | 0.0 | 6.3 |
| Total | | 5,886 | 100.0 | 3,402 | 57.8 | 100.0 |

Source: Van der Berg et al. (2017), INE (1997)

## Table 2. Net enrolment rate in secondary education by gender and region, 1997, 2003, 2011 (%)

| | 1st Level (3 years) | | | 2nd Level (2 years) | | |
|--------|------|------|------|------|------|------|
| | 1997 | 2003 | 2011 | 1997 | 2003 | 2011 |
| Gender | | | | | | |
| Female | 1.9 | 6.9 | 21.3 | 0.0 | 1.2 | 4.8 |
| Male | 1.7 | 7.4 | 19.9 | 0.1 | 1.3 | 6.4 |
| North | 0.5 | 4.6 | 10.9 | 0.0 | 0.5 | 3.9 |
| Centre | 1.3 | 4.8 | 18.2 | 0.1 | 0.9 | 4.2 |
| South | 3.5 | 12.7 | 39.1 | 0.0 | 2.5 | 10.3 |
| National | 1.8 | 7.2 | 20.6 | 0.0 | 1.3 | 5.6 |

Source: Van der Berg et al. (2017: 16)

Enrolment in primary education has improved remarkably in the last three decades. This fact, combined with high population growth rates, has created significant pressure to expand technical and vocational education and training (TVET) and higher education. However, considerable inequality in access to post-primary education persists. It was estimated in 2015 that the number of graduates from secondary education would be 148,000 in 2016 and would double to around 280,000 in 2020 (World Bank 2015: 4). It has been necessary to prepare TVET and higher education options for these graduates. One of the key challenges in Mozambique's education sector is the improvement of access to TVET as well as higher education.

## 4-2. Drastic Expansion of Higher Education

Undoubtedly, the education sector was afforded high priority in Mozambique's socioeconomic reconstruction following the end of the civil war. Soon after the war ended in 1992, Law 6/92 substituted a new, adjusted system for the existing education system that had been established by Law 4/83 in 1983 during the socialist regime. However, the process and progress of reform in the education sector varies across the different levels. In Mozambique, it began at both ends of the spectrum: primary education and higher education. During the 1990s, primary education received much of the attention owing to its position among the Millennium Development Goals (MDGs): UNESCO's 'Education for All' movement addressed access to primary education as one of the goals to be achieved by 2015. The Mozambican government also prioritised higher education as a means of securing human resources for management positions, not only for the public sector, which was under reform, but also for the growing private sector. However, professional education underwent modest changes during that period. Between 2006 and 2010 – that is, the period of the MDGs – almost 50 per cent of education expenditure was allocated to primary education, while secondary education received around 20 per cent, TVET received around 4 per cent and higher education received 19 per cent (Sousa Cruz et al. 2016: 36).

While TVET's specific set goals have not been determined in the

191

Mozambican context, the government once regarded higher education as an important sub-sector with the potential to contribute significantly to economic development. In 2000, the government published the *Strategic Plan of Higher Education in Mozambique 2000-2010* and decided to establish the Ministry of Higher Education, Science and Technology (MHEST) (Vogels 2002) as distinct from the Ministry of Education and Culture. Soon after the war ended in 1992, Mozambique had only three public higher education institutions (World Bank 2015: 4), which had increased to 37 institutions by 2009, as shown in Figure 2. It expanded rapidly in terms of number and geographical location, to include 49 institutions by 2014. In addition to the existing public providers, the participation of private providers caused a rapid increase in numbers.

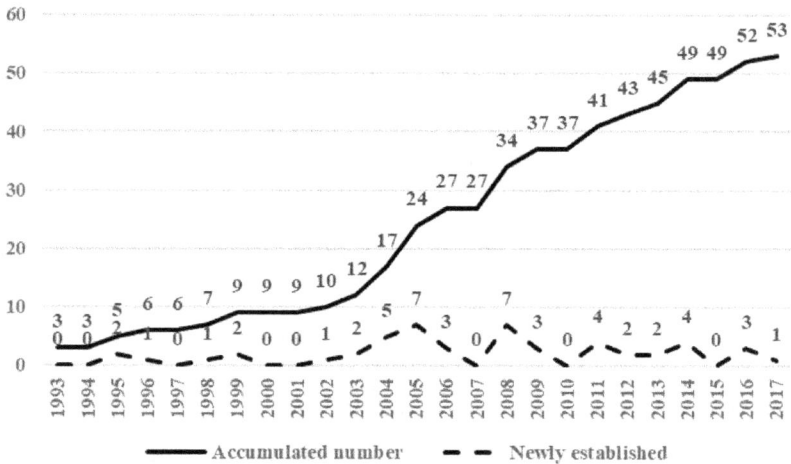

**Figure 2. Evolution of higher education institutions**
Source: Cossa et al. (2019)

Maria entered one of the newly founded private universities in 2013. The participation of private providers and the subsequent increase may be understood as demand driven but not policy driven, as the expenditure allocation provoked no drastic increase, as mentioned above. Public providers also reformed to expand geographically throughout all ten provinces, as shown in Table 3, though the service delivery had previously been almost entirely

192

concentrated in the capital city. The institutions in the capital city also diversified their pupils' geographical origins through the introduction of a quota system in 2006 that mandated a certain number of posts per province. Around the same time, Mozambique's macro economy had achieved favourable growth of 7 per cent per year throughout the 2000s, and part of the urban population enjoyed the economic boom that caused the demand-driven increase in higher education. The growth in the macro economy was the result of intense foreign direct investment directing export-oriented industries during the years after the immediate end of the civil war in 1992.

**Table 3. Evolution of enrolment to higher education by province**

| Province | 2003 | | 2012 | |
|---|---|---|---|---|
| | Number | % | Number | % |
| Cabo Delgado | 72 | 0.4 | 3,820 | 3.1 |
| Gaza | 0 | 0.0 | 6,946 | 5.6 |
| Inhambane | 93 | 0.5 | 5,590 | 4.5 |
| Manica | 180 | 1.0 | 5,671 | 4.6 |
| Maputo City | 12,808 | 74.4 | 53,239 | 43.0 |
| Maputo Province | 0 | 0.0 | 5,512 | 4.5 |
| Nampula | 1,998 | 11.6 | 12,017 | 9.7 |
| Niassa | 277 | 1.6 | 4,663 | 3.8 |
| Sofala | 1,550 | 9.0 | 12,600 | 10.2 |
| Tete | 0 | 0.0 | 6,120 | 4.9 |
| Zambézia | 247 | 1.4 | 7,601 | 6.1 |
| Total Entry | 17,225 | 100.0 | 123,779 | 100.0 |

Source: Ministério da Educação (2014)

However, the rapid expansion was not accompanied by supplementation of appropriately qualified teaching staff and adequate equipment. Around two-thirds of teachers in higher education hold bachelor's degrees (World Bank 2015: 4). The guaranteed education quality has been questioned (Langa 2012), as educational content scarcely kept pace with the labour market, which was changing daily. After the university reform, the number of institutions and students in higher education increased, but the high dropout rates persisted at more than 90 per cent through the 2010s. The high dropout rates and the quality of education were regarded with considerable concern, as the government took legal steps to inspect the conditions and ensure the quality of education by Decree 15/2018, which revoked the old decree enacted in 2011. In 2018, the government recommended the closure of 20 institutions due to their inadequate operations (RFI 2018).

### 4-3. TVET Reform: A Race against Time

During the period of favourable growth in the macro economy, the national poverty ratio deteriorated, and Mozambique's economy was criticised as consisting of jobless economic growth (Léautier and Hanson 2013). Indeed, who could be said to have benefited from the growth of the macro economy in Mozambique? The aluminium refining, liquefied natural gas, coal and heavy sand industries are all export-oriented and driven by foreign direct investment. Foreign companies recover most of the profits as new capital. The minimal profits that remain in Mozambique's domestic market mostly enrich the family businesses that Maputo's political elite have incorporated into the relevant industrial sectors (Africa Intelligence 2013), including former president Armand Guebuza (2005–2015) and the succeeding president Filipe Nyusi, who reportedly tripled the number of family businesses within the first five years of his term (2015–2019) (Carta de Moçambique 2020). These beneficiaries are distributed among the political elite as a means of consolidating their political power. This highly political circumstance is among the obstacles to the nationwide dissemination of the effects of macroeconomic growth.

Unguaranteed quality of education and high dropout rates also caused the general tendency of governments in developing countries to increasingly regard TVET as a solution for employment (Gondwe 2011: 9). The focus of the government's attention appears to have shifted from the general expansion of higher education institutions

194

to TVET, which underwent modest reforms during the 1990s. At that time, the industrial structure was in a transitional phase of political regime change, economic privatisation and information technology-related innovations. Under these circumstances, it is likely to have been extremely difficult to establish a TVET programme that met with labour market acceptance.

The Mozambican government published the *Professional Technical Education Strategy (2002–2011)*, which emphasised the need to improve the TVET system's quality to equip Mozambicans properly with updated skills that would meet the changing needs of the labour market. Its overall objective is to contribute to Mozambique's economic and social development along with the MDGs. The government announced plans to revamp the vocational school curriculum in 2003 and plans to create new courses in 2005. The pilot project was set to launch between 2010 and 2015. Fewer than 50 schools were operational, and most of these required updating with respect to facilities and/or instructor training (Sapo Notícias 2011). The government then extended the launch timeframe to 2020.

As its reform strategy aligned with the global trend of TVET system reform, it shared some similarities with other African countries, including social factors, such as pressure for job creation among the population and the bottom-up educational level of the youth. However, at the same time, differences existed with respect to sub-composition and characteristics within the same industries. For example, in Mozambique, manufacturing accounted for 14.2 per cent of the GDP in 2010 but accounted for only 3.6 per cent of the workforce. In Ethiopia, by contrast, manufacturing accounted for 4.2 per cent of the GDP and 6.3 per cent of the labour force in 2005. This shows that while Mozambique's manufacturing sector is capital intensive, Ethiopian manufacturing is more labour intensive, for example, in the leather-processing and textile industries. This is partly because foreign capitals drive manufacturing in Mozambique. Comparing agriculture, Ethiopia's agriculture, which accounts for 75.1 per cent of the labour force, accounted for 45.3 per cent of the country's GDP in 2005. In Mozambique, agriculture, which accounts for 71.5 per cent of the workforce, accounted for 24.2 per cent of the GDP in 2010 (Newman et al. (eds) 2016: 3–5). This demonstrates that Ethiopian agriculture is more export oriented and achieves higher value-added gains than Mozambique's. As this brief comparison suggests, even within the same industrial sector, each country's labour market acceptance differs depending on the characteristics of each industry. TVET, which trains human resources, must also be reformed to suit each country's circumstances.

As TVET programmes are expected to meet the changing needs of the labour market that connect to the industries, industrial policy may be instrumental in offering guidelines for programme reform. Nevertheless, in sum, Mozambican industrial policies were subject to international investment trends and lacked any long-term perspective. Sousa Cruz et al. (2016) observed the shift in industrial policy as follows. In the 1990s, the industrial policy set the goals for economic rehabilitation, modernisation and expansion after the end of the civil war, focusing on small and medium enterprises with domestic capital and enhancing linkages and diversification. Its practice was the privatisation of national companies into oligopolistic industries, such as sugar, cement and beverages. The other aspect was the invitation of foreign investment, as in the case of the first megaproject, Mozal – a joint aluminium smelter project in a newly established industrial park. The 2005 policy was aimed at attracting private, foreign investment for comparative advantages by region and also aimed to forge links with Mozal, but that vague focus resulted in the failure of linkages between biofuels and agro-industries.

Following the discovery of natural gas, the government's 2010 policy focused on multinational minerals-energy complexes in terms of capital and human resources, and derived linkages to establish various free trade zones. However, in practice, minerals-energy complexes could not forge linkages to create the desired economic spillover effect but merely enriched the family business run by the political elites, as mentioned above. The 2015 policy set the industrialisation as a solution for employment and diversification of export and substitution of import. The recent policy finally focuses on employment, but a significant gap persists between the education and industrial sectors (Sousa Cruz et al. 2016: 92–114). The long-term economic plan 'National Strategy of Development' (*Estratégia Nacional de Desenvolvimento* 2015-2035) published in 2014 also seeks macroeconomic growth with particular emphasis on megaprojects in extract industries, such as natural gas, coal, heavy sand etc. (República de Moçambique 2014). Various consultations have revealed opportunities to increase the competitiveness and productivity of local firms to supply multinationals as part of the megaprojects since the feasibility of large-scale resource development emerged in 2011 with the discovery of natural gas reserves.

In advance of the pilot implementation's conclusion in 2015, the parliament approved a new law on professional education (*Lei da Educação Profissional*) in 2014 and the government established the National Professional Education Authority (*Autoridade Nacional de Educação Profissional*), aimed at regulating qualifications in the TVET system, and disclosed its plan to establish 97 technical schools to open by 2015. The mandate on higher education and TVET was transferred from the Ministry of Education to the newly created Ministry of Science and Technology, Higher, Technical and Professional Education (MCTESTP) in 2015 (World Bank 2015).

The current Integrated Programme for Vocational Education Reform (*Programa Integrado da Reforma da Educação Profissional*: PIREP) aims to establish a labour market-driven vocational education system with the involvement of other social partners and stakeholders offering a bridge to private sectors. The PIREP is structured across three phases as follows: first, the piloting phase (2006–2011); second, the expansion phase (2012–2016); and third, the consolidation phase (2017–2021) (Nuffic 2012). Additionally, the Sustainable Development Goals (SDGs, 2016–2030) presented another phase of development in the education sector that created a bridge to employment specifically aimed at SDGs.

The development of Mozambique's TVET system is ongoing. Meanwhile, in the featured natural gas industry, the construction of facilities is underway with the expectation that production will start in 2024, albeit with potential delays as circumstances dictate. The question of whether Mozambique's TVET reforms will lead to job creation involves a race against time.

197

## 5. Education and Employment under Jobless Growth

Returning to the issue of employment, the Mozambican government developed a series of laws aimed at job creation in favour of nationals, introducing a quota system for foreign workers from 2008, when foreign direct investment to African countries, including Mozambique, drastically increased after the global financial crisis, called the 'Lehman Shock'. Since the introduction of the quota system, most foreign companies started recruiting Mozambican youth locally and conducted in-house training to remedy the lack of qualified labour.[16] The IMF has estimated that these liquefied natural gas megaprojects that are under preparation for production have already created ten to twenty thousand new posts across several sectors, including construction, metalworking, and welding in particular, and communication (Ross (ed.) 2014). However, those posts were not always filled by Mozambican labourers due to their lack of qualifications. More recently, between 2018 and 2019, the current government has emphasised job creation under the nationwide 'local context (*conteúdo local*)' campaign that is intended to promote the participation of Mozambican companies in the megaproject since the major contractor's final decision to invest in 2019. However, even ten years after the introduction of the quota system for foreign workers in 2008, remarkably few Mozambican workers are qualified in that specific area, and Mozambique's labour market has failed to meet these professional demands (Bower et al. 2010).

It is estimated that only 6.3 per cent of the economically active population worked in the formal sector in 2015. According to labour economists, in addition to this current situation, thirty thousand young workers per year will join the labour market within a short timeframe, and this number will increase to fifty thousand after 2025 (Jones and Tarp 2012). The Mozambican government set a target of inclusive economic growth and poverty reduction that would benefit more people with six key objectives: reducing poverty rates; increasing production and productivity in the agro-fisheries sector; promoting employment; human and social development;

strengthening governance; and strengthening macroeconomic and financial management. However, an evaluation by the IMF indicates that promoting employment showed the lowest achievement rate among the six above-mentioned key objectives (IMF 2014).[17]

Why have large investments not led to job creation? To answer this question, it is necessary to distinguish the different matters affecting the demand and supply sides. In the Mozambican context, the supply side cannot supply appropriately qualified labour to respond the needs of the labour market. As a temporary solution to the lack of skilled labour, foreign workers have primarily supplemented the market; as a long-term solution, it is expected that national workers will gradually take the place of foreign labour. The more critical problem is on the demand side, more precisely, the industrial policy that orients the labour demand. During the three decades since the war ended Mozambique's economy has been highly dependent on the foreign direct investment that initiated macroeconomic growth. However, this trend is not always steady, as this section examined. Thus, its macroeconomic-oriented industrial policy has been short-lived while the education that produces skilled labour is a lengthy process.

## 6. Turning to the Informal Sector

### 6-1. Development of ICBT in the 2010s

The jobless growth in Mozambique combined with population increase caused the narrow passage leading to the formal labour market to become even narrower. As the formal sector shrank and its entryways remained restricted, people turned to the informal sector. The debate on the linkage between the formal and informal sectors has developed since the 1970s along the following lines: the dual economic theory, structuralism and the theoretical approach of the rule of law. The dual economy theory views the informal sector as distinct from the formal sector and argues that it is disadvantaged (Sethuraman 1976; Tokman 1978). Structuralism, in contrast to the dual economy theory, argues that the two sectors have been intrinsically linked and that the formal sector is expanding its profit

199

margins through informal modes of production and employment (Moser 1978; Portes et al. (eds) 1989). Furthermore, the rule of law argues that capitalists and governments collude to establish 'the rules of the game' or a 'capitalist' framework' to maximise the benefits accruing to them through the relationship between the informal sector and the legal environment (De Soto 1989).

Each framework captures the characteristics of the informal sector, and they are not in conflict. In addition to these frameworks, development policy since the 2000s has focused on transforming the informal sector into the formal sector, rather than viewing it as an adjunct to the formal sector (Chen et al. 2004; Stuart et al. 2018). In the labour sector, the International Labour Organization is the leading agent. It works together with local and international civil society organisations to improve the working environment in the informal sector and to enhance the nature of employment in more public institutions.

ICBT entered a new developmental phase in the 2000s. The South African Government exempted Mozambicans from short-visit visa requirements in 2005, making it possible for Mozambicans to remain in South Africa for 30 days without any visa. This fact once again allowed traders to participate in ICBT even if they were not members of the ICBT associations mentioned above. As the dominant objective of Mozambican ICBT is the purchase of material to supply Mozambique, the traders complete their purchases and swiftly return to Mozambique. A purchase at Komatiport in South Africa's Mpumalanga Province requires only one day; a purchase at Johannesburg in Gauteng Province in South Africa takes one to several days; a trip to China or India will take five to seven days. According to Maria, she obtained information from her colleague that allowed her to access a Chinese-run wholesale store zone in Johannesburg.[18] It had been established in Johannesburg in the mid-1990s (Harrison et al. 2012).[19]

The next dimension of ICBT development was the adoption of technical innovations in communication and finance. ICBT techniques advanced drastically from 2010, when the majority of mobile phone users switched providers. Figure 3 shows the number of mobile cellular subscriptions and individual internet users in Mozambique between 2000 and 2018. The number of subscriptions and internet users increased steadily up to 2015. Additionally, in 2010, Nokia, one of the major providers that was used mainly for short messaging services, lost its share in the Mozambican market as part of a general international trend, as shown in Figure 4. Although Nokia had successfully occupied a market share of 41.76 per cent in 2010, it decreased to 2.55 per cent in 2015, while Opera, which represented the arrival of the smart phone, increased its market share by 75.59 per cent in 2016.

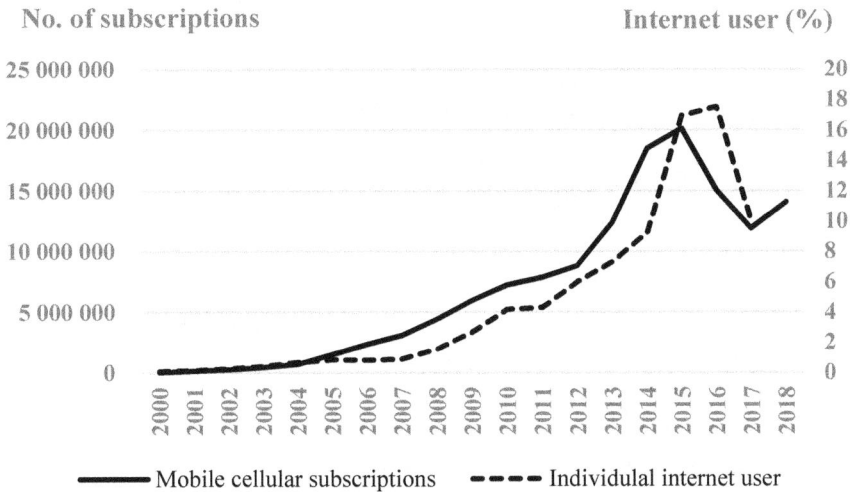

**Figure 3. Mobile cellular subscriptions and individual internet users in Mozambique**
Source: International Telecommunication Union
(https://www.itu.int/en/ITU-D/Statistics/Pages/stat/default.aspx)

In the Mozambican context, while Nokia dominated the market, people used short messaging services more than calls, but when Opera became prevalent, people began to enjoy sharing images and videos combined with the convenient internet connection. ICBTs and their customers use the messenger application WhatsApp, which began in 2009 and has accelerated its performance since 2014, to share detailed specifications of items for order purchases. The purchased item is sent to the customer via a trusted minibus service and, after receiving the item, the customer can transfer payment using the Kenyan-created electronic payment service M-Pesa, which the South African mobile phone company Vodacom brought to Mozambique in 2013. In sum, today's ICBT frontrunners – including Maria, who was born in 1994 – are digital natives, who have grown up in the digital age and develop their businesses with minimal logistical costs by making the most of external information services and investing their limited capital in purchases.

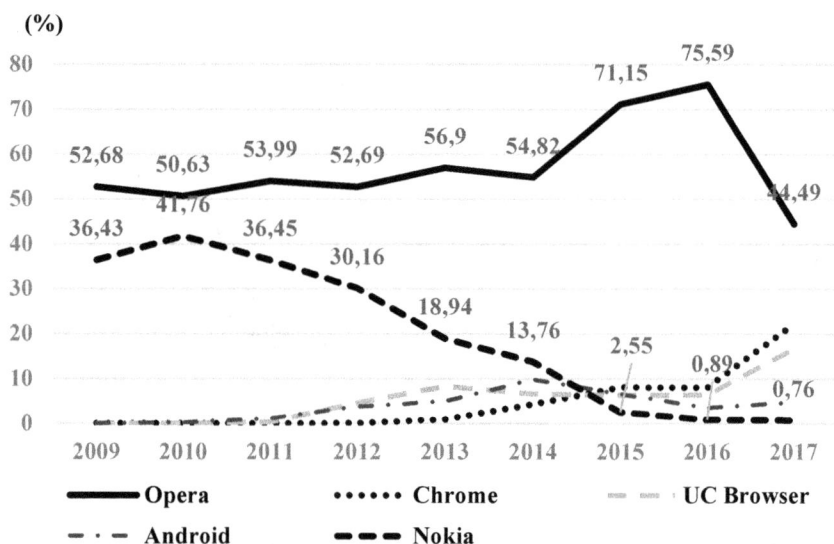

**Figure 4. Mobile browser market share in Mozambique**
Source: Statcounter Global Stats (https://gs.statcounter.com/browser-market-share/mobile/mozambique/#yearly-2009-2017)

## 6-2. Maria's Story: A Young ICBT

Let us return to Maria's experience. When we contextualise her experience within the changing environment surrounding ICBT in Mozambique, as outlined above, what implications can be derived from her experience? Maria has worked in the informal sector since her high school days, and has worked in ICBT since 2013, when she was 19 years old. In the beginning, she purchased chicken in

Komatiport in South Africa and supplied it to Mozambican wholesale markets: while Mozambique has a large chicken market, it used to produce only on a small scale. However, she switched from chicken to clothing accessories in response to the policy changes implemented by the Mozambican government to gradually increase the importation tax for chicken in 2016 and to ban its importation in 2019, in a bid to protect and encourage domestic production. As she shifted her focus, she was also obliged to shift her supply source from Komatiport to Johannesburg. Eventually in Johannesburg's wholesale markets, she found that most clothing accessories, including artificial and natural hair, originally came from China and later from India. She began to travel almost monthly to China in 2017 and to India in 2018 to purchase goods for her stands in the municipal market, which is wholly formal, and for her hair salon. Nowadays, she communicates with her business counterpart in Guangzhou via WhatsApp.[20]

Maria's reaction to the policy change demonstrates her high level of literacy with respect to the business regulatory environment. She reacts quickly to changing customs duties, carefully selects handling items and secures good suppliers through her willingness to travel. Let us examine her educational background to understand how she acquired her literacy in business regulations and the changing environment. She entered a private university in 2013, which was founded in a period characterised by the expansion of higher education. She took economics as her major but dropped out the following year. The timing coincides with the period during which the quality of higher education was questioned and marketisation was criticised (Langa 2012). Aside from the issue of the quality of education at newly established universities during that time, it is easy to imagine that the universal-standard course of study based on Western theories in the first and second years of her economics programme would normally differ considerably from the realities of the southern African economy that Maria faced. It is more reasonable to assume that her ability to cope with circumstances was probably acquired outside of an institutionalised education.

Maria's circumstances are also key factors. Her parents have been positive role models of self-employment and success in the informal sector since her high school days, and that experience led her to engage in ICBT activities soon after her entry into university. In addition, Maria reported having left university upon recognising her difficulty with the time management required to balance her studies with her business. She did not simply quit university; she chose ICBT because she had already experienced success in ICBT before dropping out. Moreover, through her economic activities as an ICBT, Maria had attained social status as a role model for young female entrepreneurs, as Honwana (2012) has described. Consequently, she chose economic independence and self-esteem over an educational career that promised no future employment.

Maria's experiences in the informal sector provided her with most of the key factors that she needed to enhance her self-esteem and, more precisely, self-efficacy: modelling, experience, social persuasion and physiological factors (Bandura (ed.) 1995). This fact shows clear affinity with the argument in favour of 'deschooling society' presented by Illich, in that Maria encountered opportunities outside of institutionalised education during her life course.

## 7. Conclusion

Mozambican ICBT has undergone several phases of new entry and selection since its genesis in the 1980s. While some ICBTs responded flexibly to changing conditions at that time, their activities have largely been replaced by relatively large-scale ICBT. It is difficult to grasp the actuality of informal workers such as ICBTs. However, their activities are not entirely informal: they often contact and negotiate with the formal framework of regulations set by the state. This is becoming increasingly prevalent as they inevitably cross borders between states. Since the 1980s, frequent changes have occurred, not only in terms of item trends but also in terms of trade and custom conditions and procedures between Mozambique and South Africa. Today's ICBT activities require greater literacy regarding the political economy to respond to the changing customs conditions and procedures, and to maximise their profit margins. At the same time, ICBT's informal character has become increasingly formal.

Maria's experience is a reflection of Mozambique's socioeconomic actuality. In the short term, it reflects the results of the bottom-up approach to secondary and tertiary education on the one hand, and the problems associated with the rapid expansion of higher education institutions on the other hand. Combined with the Mozambican labour market, described as reflecting jobless economic growth, graduates, most of whom will encounter difficulties in finding suitable employment in the formal sector, may feel as though they have been abandoned. In the longer term, Maria's experience, including that of her parents' generation, reflects almost five decades of large-scale reproduction of the informal sector in terms of the committed population and geographic range.

The upper echelons of the bloated informal sector may ride the wave of normalisation as ICBT becomes increasingly formal. However, regarding the relationship between state and society, not all informal sector workers want to be formalised, for two reasons. First, from an economic perspective, the informal sector's core characteristic is its operation outside the framework of state control in society. Thus, it is also unclear whether the tolerated strength of the informal sector as an alternative provider for socioeconomic needs will be secured after formalisation. Second, from a social perspective, the informal sector provides learning opportunities outside the institutional context. As we observed in Maria's case, the informal sector attracts resilient human resources who are not wholly reliant on formal institutions that do not always work. This reflects the unpredictable relationship between state and society. This relationship is particularly relevant in societies that are not yet entirely institutionalised. Thus, the development of this relationship is worthy of continuous observation.

**Endnotes**

[1] All individual names of the informants in this chapter have been

205

changed.

[2] Interview with a female informal cross-border trader, 15 July 2018, Maputo city, Maputo Province, Mozambique. On the earlier economic activities of Africans in Guangzhou, see Li et al. (2008).

[3] Interview with the father of ICBT Maria, 19 January 2018, Maputo city, Maputo Province, Mozambique.

[4] Mijere (2009: 20–1) also offers thought-provoking views on the genesis and continuity of cross-border trade in Africa, which is historically rooted in the society prior to the establishment of the colonial national border, combined with the nation-state regime and legal restrictions. The history of informal cross-border trade reflects the interaction between local society and legal restrictions set by the nation-state-based regime.

[5] The targeted cohort of young people were those who were of school age at that time, equivalent to those who were born in the years between 1950 and 1970. Some of them were allocated for professional education within the country and the others were sent to allied countries abroad (Notícias 2015). Interview with Maria's father, 4 March 2020, Maputo city, Maputo Province, Mozambique.

[6] No detailed data were available regarding the total number of Mozambicans sent to Cuba from the 1970s to the 1990s, but it is estimated that 3,764 were sent between 1961 and 2004 (Dorsch 2011).

[7] Ibid.

[8] Interview with a male staff member at the Inhambane branch of the ENH (*Empresa Nacional de Hidrocarbonetos*), 4 September 2015, Vilankulos, Inhambane Province, Mozambique.

[9] ENH is one of the few companies with post-independent national origins established in 1981 when the government had strong economic ties with the Eastern Bloc.

[10] Interview with a male mechanical staff member at the Inhambane branch of the ENH, 6 September 2015, Vilankulos, Inhambane Province, Mozambique.

[11] Interview with Maria's mother, 3 July 2018, Maputo City, Maputo Province, Mozambique.

[12] Interview with the president of Mukhero Association, 22 November 2018, Maputo City, Maputo Province, Mozambique.

[13] Ibid.

[14] Interview with 60-year-old ex-ICBT female, 22 August 2018, Xai Xai City, Gaza Province, Mozambique.

[15] Ibid.

[16] For example, the South African natural gas company SASOL, operating at Inhambane Province in southern Mozambique, began locally recruiting young workers who had completed the second phase of secondary education without questioning their specialities and offering in-house training. Interview with two young male SASOL workers who were recruited locally, 8 September 2015, Vilankulos, Inhambane Province, Mozambique.

[17] Policies for poverty reduction in Mozambique are based on the Millennium Absolute Poverty Reduction Action, a specific mid-term action plan for the Development Goals (MDGs) Plan (*Plano de Acção para a Redução da Pobreza*) (Absoluta: PARPA) Period I: 2001–2005, Period II: 2006–2009, followed by the most recent 'Poverty Reduction Action Plan (*Plano de Acção para a Redução da Pobreza:* PARP) 2011–2014'. The evaluation by the IMF abovementioned is for the PARP.

[18] Interview with a female informal cross-border trader, 19 January 2018, Maputo City, Maputo Province, Mozambique.

[19] According to Maria, she first accessed Chinese wholesalers in Johannesburg and subsequently obtained access to Guangzhou. The Chinese-African business network was established by West Africans in the 1990s. As Guangzhou serves as a hub for African merchants' information networks regarding their items and potential frontiers, Maria discovered that China was a processing and wholesale centre for wigs and extensions, whether natural or synthetic, provided by India or Brazil. Subsequently, she obtained information on an Indian material supplier and began travelling to India for purchases. Ibid.

[20] Interview with a female informal cross-border trader, 19 January 2018, Maputo city, Maputo Province, Mozambique.

## Acknowledgements

This work was supported by JSPS KAKENHI Grant Number JP16H06318.

# References

Africa Intelligence (2013) 'Frelimo omnipresent in the mining sector', *Africa Intelligence*, 16 December 2013 (https://www.africaintelligence.com/insiders/mozambique/201 3/12/16/frelimo-omnipresent-in-the-mining-sector/107999404-be2) (accessed: 14 August 2020).

Bandura, A. (ed.) (1995) *Self-Efficacy in Changing Societies*, Cambridge: Cambridge University Press.

Benjamin, N., Beegle, K., Recanatini, F. and Santini, M. (2014) *Informal Economy and World Bank, Policy Research Working Paper, No. 6888*, Washington DC: World Bank.

Bower, R., Brito, L. and Menete, Z. (2010) 'Educação, formação profissional e poder' in L. Brito, C. N. Castel-Branco, S. Chichava and A. Francisco (eds) *Desafios para Moçambique 2010*, Maputo: Institute of Economic and Social Studies, pp. 273–96.

Carta de Moçambique (2020) 'Familia Nyusi triplicou número de empresas nos últimos 5 anos – revela CIP', *Carta de Moçambique*, 24 February 2020 (https://cartamz.com/index.php/politica/item/4494-familia-nyusi-triplicou-numero-deempresas-nos-ultimos-5-anos-revela-cip) (accessed: 14 August 2020).

Chen, M., Vanek, J. and Carr, M. (2004) *Mainstreaming Informal Employment and Gender in Poverty Reduction: A Handbook for Policy-Makers and Other Stakeholders*, London: Commonwealth Secretariat.

Cossa, E. F. R., Buque, V. L. and Premugy, C. I. C. (2019) 'Desafios de normação do ensino superior em Moçambique e suas implicações na qualidade de ensino', Comunicação apresentado na 9.ª Conferência FORGES (Fórum da Gestão do Ensino Supeiro nos Países e Regiões da Língua Portuguesa), 20–22 November 2019, Universidade de Brasília, Brasília, Brasil.

De Soto, H. (1989) *The Other Path: The Invisible Revolution in the Third World*, New York: Harper and Row.

Dorsch, H. (2011) 'Black or red Atlantic? – Mozambican students in Cuba and their reintegration at home', *Zeitschrift für Ethnologie*, Vol. 136, No. 2, pp. 289–309.

Gondwe, M. (2011) *Alignment of Higher Professional Education with the Needs of the Local Labour Market: The Case of Mozambique*, Hague: Nuffic Netherlands Organization for International Cooperation in Higher Education.

Harrison, P., Moyo, K. and Yang, Y. (2012) 'Strategy and tactics: Chinese immigrants and diasporic spaces in Johannesburg, South Africa', *Journal of Southern African Studies*, Vol. 38, No. 4, pp. 899–925.

Honwana, A. (2012) *The Time of Youth: Work, Social Change, and Politics in Africa*, Boulder: Kumarian Press.

Illich, I. (1970) *Deschooling Society*, London: Marion Boyars.

IMF (International Monetary Fund) (2014) *República de Moçambique: Plano de Acção para Redução da Pobreza — Relatório de Progresso, Relatório do FMI, No. 14/147*, Washington DC: IMF.

INE (Instituto Nacional de Estatística) (1997) *Resultados Preliminares do II Recenseamento Geral de População e Habitação de 1997*, Maputo: INE.

_____ (2019) *IV Recenseamento Geral da População e Habitação 2017 Resultados Definitivos*, Maputo: INE.

Jairoce, J. F. (2016) 'A Mulher e o comercio informal trasnfronteirico vulgo "mukhero" no sul deMoçambique: Casos das fronteriras de Namaacha e Ressano Garcia, 1984–2016', Tese de Doutrado, Universidade Federal do Rio Grande do Sul.

Jones, S., Santos, R. and Xirinda, G. (2019) *Final Report of the Survey on the Education-Employment Transitions of University Finalists*, Maputo: The United Nations University World Institute for Development Economics Research (UNU-WIDER).

Jones, S. and Tarp, F. (2012) *Jobs and Welfare in Mozambique: Country Case Study for the 2013 World Development Report, Background Paper for the World Development Report 2013*, Helsinki: The United Nations University World Institute for Development Economics Research (UNU-WIDER).

Langa, P. V. (2012) 'A mercantilização do ensino superior e a relação com o saber: A qualidade em questão', *Revista Científica da Universidade Eduardo Mondlane, Série: Ciências da Educação*, Vol. 1, No. 0, pp. 21–41.

Léautier, F. A. and Hanson, K. T. (2013) *Jobless Economic Growth: Lessons from Africa, ACBF Working Paper, No. 25*, Harare: The African Capacity Building Foundation.

Li, Z., Xue, D., Lyons, M., Brown, A. and Braithwaite, M. (2008) 'The African enclave of Guangzhou: A case study of Xiaobeilu', *Acta Geographica Sinica*, Vol. 63, No. 2, pp. 208–18.

Mijere, N. J. N. (2009) *Informal Cross-Border Trade in the Southern African Development Community (SADC)*, Addis Ababa: Organisation for Social Science Research in Eastern and Southern Africa (OSSREA).

Ministério da Educação (2014) *Dados Estatísticos do Ensino Superior e dos Insitituições de Investigação, 2003, 2012*, Maputo: Ministério da Educação.

Moser, C. (1978) 'Informal sector or petty commodity production: Dualism or independence in urban development', *World Development*, Vol. 5, No. 9/10, pp. 1041–64.

Müller, T. R. (2010) '"Memories of paradise": Legacies of socialist education in Mozambique', *African Affairs*, Vol. 109, No. 436, pp. 451–70.

Newman, C., Page, J., Rand, J., Shimeles, A., Söderbom M. and Tarp F. (eds) (2016) *Manufacturing Transformation: Comparative Studies of Industrial Development in Africa and Emerging Asia*, Oxford: Oxford University Press.

Notícias (2015) '38 ANOS DA GERAÇÃO "8 de MARÇO": Sempre "prontos" ao chamamento da patria', *Notícias online*, 18 March 2015 (https://www.jornalnoticias.co.mz/index.php/politica/33364-38-anos-da-geracao-8-de-marco-sempre-prontos-ao-chamamento-da-patria.html) (accessed: 14 August 2020).

Nuffic (2012) *International Conference: Shaping the Future, Alignment of Capacity Development with Priority Areas – TVET Reform in Mozambique*, 2–3 July 2012, Crown Plaza Hotel Promenade, The Hague.

Peberdy, S. (2000) 'Mobile entrepreneurship: Informal sector cross-border trade and street trade in South Africa', *Development Southern Africa*, Vol. 17, No. 2, pp. 201–19.

Peberdy, S. and Rogerson, S. (2000) 'Transnationalism and non-South African entrepreneurs in South Africa's small, medium and micro-enterprise (SMME) economy', *Canadian Journal of African Studies*, Vol. 34, No. 1, pp. 20–40.

Portes, A., Castells, M. and Benton, M. (eds) (1989) *The Informal Economy: Studies in Advanced and Less Developed Countries*, Baltimore: Johns Hopkins University Press.

Rádio Moçambique (2018) 'Frelimo endereça mensagem pela passagem do 8 de Março', *Rádio Moçambique*, 8 March 2018 (https://www.rm.co.mz/rm.co.mz/index.php/sobre/item/177-frelimo-endereca-mensagem-pela-passagem-do-8-de-marco.html) (accessed:14 August 2020).

Raimundo, I. and Chikanda, A. (2016) *Informal Entrepreneurship and Cross-Border Trade in Maputo, Mozambique, SAMP Migration Policy Series, No. 73*, Cape Town: South African Migration Programme.

República de Moçambique (2014) *Estratégia Nacional de Desenvolvimento 2015–2035*, Maputo: República de Moçambique.

RFI (Radio France Internationale) (2018) 'Governo moçambicano tenciona fechar mais de 20 Universidades', *Radio France Internationale*, 2 November 2018.

Ross, D. C. (ed.) (2014) *Mozambique Rising: Building a New Tomorrow*, Washington DC: International Monetary Fund.

Sapo Notícias (2011) 'Moçambique terá 97 escolas de formação técnico profissional', *Sapo Notícias*, 11 June 2011 (https://24.sapo.pt/aim/artigo/131311062011164226.html) (accessed: 24 November 2015).

Sethuraman, S. (1976) 'The urban informal sector: Concept, measurement, and policy', *International Labour Review*, Vol. 114, No. 1, pp. 69–81.

Sousa Cruz, A., Guambe, D., Marrengula, C. P. and Ubisse, A. F. (2016) 'Mozambique's industrial policy: Sufficient to face the winds of globalization?' in C. Newman, J. Page, J. Rand, A. Shimeles, M. Söderbom and F. Tarp (eds) *Manufacturing Transformation: Comparative Studies of Industrial Development in Africa and Emerging Asia*, Oxford: Oxford University Press, pp. 92–114.

Stuart, E., Samman, M. and Hun, A. (2018) *Informal Is the New Normal:*

*Improving the Lives of Workers at Risk of Being Left Behind, Working paper, No. 530*, London: Overseas Development Institute.

Tokman, V. (1978) 'An exploration into the nature of the informal-formal sector relationship', *World Development*, Vol. 6, No. 9–10, pp. 1065–1075.

Van der Berg, S., Da Maia, C. and Burger, C. (2017) *Educational Inequality in Mozambique, WIDER Working Paper No. 2017/212*, Helsinki: The United Nations University World Institute for Development Economics Research (UNU-WIDER).

Vogels, M. (2002) 'The development of higher education in Mozambique', *EAIE 14th Annual Conference, Education in Developing Countries (Edc-Track)*, 11–14 September 2002, Porto, Portugal.

World Bank (2015) *Project Paper on a Proposed Additional Grant in the Amount of SDR 32 Million (US$45 Million Equivalent) to the Republic of Mozambique for the Higher Education Science and Technology Project, Report No: PAD1296*, Washington DC: World Bank.

# Part III

# Politics and Interactions among

# People Surrounding the School

## Chapter 7

# Managing Conflicts within School Communities in Ghana: Focusing on the Art of Conviviality

## *Kazuro Shibuya*

## 1. Introduction

Access to basic education in developing countries has expanded since the World Conference on Education for All in Jomtien, Thailand, in 1990 and the Millennium Development Goals introduced in 2000. Behind the scenes, however, there have been disagreements among national governments, communities and households regarding which organisations bear responsibility for improving engagement with public education. In sub-Saharan Africa, historically there have been so-called 'community schools', established by members of that particular geographical community (Yamada 2011b). In Ghana, which is the focus of this study, school fees were abolished under the Free and Compulsory Universal Basic Education policy. Community members have since recognised that the government provides schooling; thus, they are increasingly less actively involved with schooling (Essuman 2013).

In contrast, decentralisation of education has also been promoted in developing countries, aiming efficient use of educational finances and transparent school management, with community and parent/guardian participation in school management. School management committees (SMCs) have been established worldwide; these committees are composed of community and parent representatives that are mandated to make decisions on school management (Barrera-Osorio et al. 2009; Bruns et al. 2011; De Grauwe 2005).

However, in an effort to obtain a quality education, individual guardians and pupils tend to proactively pursue their choice of school, regardless of their residential area. Thus, the geographical community, within which households reside, and the school community, which is composed of school-level stakeholders, have not necessarily overlapped. As a result, socially and economically fragile households have been left in marginalised geographical communities, thus broadening educational disparities (Ogawa 2017).

Sub-Saharan African countries, including Ghana, have historically consisted of geographical communities led by chieftaincy, in which the chiefs are responsible for discussing and addressing school-related issues. The discussion of educational issues has been within the scope of the SMC's institutional mandate, whereas community members have continued to meet to discuss educational issues and perform related activities outside the framework of SMCs (Hirose 2011).

To analyse the realm of school management, in which various stakeholders are involved, this study focused on the concept of 'conviviality'. Nyamnjoh (2016) defines conviviality as an art by which individuals in Africa formulate community through interdependency and manage possible conflicts through dialogue. Thus, this study aimed to investigate, from the perspective of conviviality, how school communities manage conflicts over pupil discipline, in a context of the division of traditional chieftaincy, and the headteachers' questionable work ethic and financial management, with a focus on two public basic schools in Akatsi South District, Ghana.

## 2. Literature Review

Below, a literature review of community participation in school management is presented. It begins with an overview of the concepts of community, participation and conviviality. This is followed by a discussion of the context of community participation in school management in Ghana, in which the educational system, its community participation policies and societal and educational challenges are described.

## 2-1. Community Participation in School Management and Conviviality

### 2-1-1. Community

Community has been discussed in the literature from the perspective of geographical communities, defined as residential areas, cultural communities (e.g., ethnic groups and religions), and school communities composed of parents/guardians who enrol their children in school (Nishimura 2017; Rose 2003). In this study, the cultural community was regarded as being nearly homogeneous, as the majority of the population in the study area belonged to the Ewe ethnic group; this particular group practises Christianity.

In Ghana, traditionally, indigenous geographical communities have contributed to the development of schools and the establishment and maintenance of school facilities (Yamada 2011a). The traditional chieftaincy system remains in use, and there are a chief and the elders in each geographical community. Consensual democracy is emphasised, in that all of the members of a geographical community are expected to participate in meetings, discuss the issues and contribute to the decision-making process. Chiefs are responsible for promoting the development of the geographical community (Ajei 2001). The local administration is responsible for the construction and renovation of schools. However, traditional chiefs often become involved in addressing educational issues concerning pupils, teachers and guardians, as this platform provides an opportunity to show their leadership and charisma (Hirose 2011). The geographical community does not have mandates for school management; however, they are involved in establishing and renovating schools, securing land for schools and addressing schooling issues.

The school community denotes a group of people who gather and work for the purpose of school management, regardless of their geographical location or cultural backgrounds (Nishimura 2017). It has been argued in the literature that the school community may not necessarily be homogeneous or consensual in terms of support for school development. For instance, there are multi-layered

217

communities of kinship networks, physical-geographical community and guardians who enrol their children in these schools (Yamada 2011b). Among the geographical communities, there are differences in the extent of participation in school events, depending on the distance between the school and the community (Saito 2013). Within the school community, SMC executive members include local government officials, local educational administration members, community/guardian representatives and parent–teacher association (PTA) members. An SMC is a unit of local educational administration, in which member chosen by the community and parents/guardians participate in a form of representative democracy. This participation has legitimacy, in that the community and guardians have a say in school management (Edwards Jr and Klees 2015).

It has been noted in the literature that the historical commonality between geographical and school community members has dissolved. In a case study of secondary schools in Kenya, Ogawa (2017) revealed that children do not necessarily attend schools within their geographical community; instead, they tend to choose schools based on the school's characteristics rather than geographical distance. In an analysis of Ethiopia, Yamada (2011b) also found that not all children in households attend schools neighbouring their geographical community, given the expansion in school choice. Thus, children in some households attend schools outside their geographical boundaries in pursuit of a higher quality of education, whereas other children from more fragile households are left behind in marginalised geographical communities.

In this study, based on the context in Ghana, school community is defined as consisting of those who participate in the SMC executive and general meetings; geographical community refers to those residing in a particular geographical area.

## 2-1-2. Participation

The discourse of community and parent participation in school management originated in developed countries and has since been disseminated to developing countries. It is significant to embrace participatory democracy through collectives of the community (e.g., bowling clubs) in the context of developed countries (Putnam et al. 1993; Putnam 2000). Notably, Putnam asserted that face-to-face contact and socialisation are critical in participatory democracy. However, it has been pointed out that the collectives of the community require equal membership and burdens for their members, without considering their diversity, fragility or need for flexibility (Selle and Kristin 1999; Suetomi 2005).

Participatory democracy has both features of consensual democracy and representative democracy. Consensual democracy is rooted in indigenous geographical communities, as described in 2-1-1 (Ajei 2001), whereas participation in a representative democracy stresses that the decision making in school management includes input not only from the school staff but also from parents and community members, for the sake of transparency and accountability. In school-based management, in which decision-making authority in school management occurs at the school level, participation based on the principle of representative democracy has become popular. School governing bodies have been established as a means of accelerating participation in a representative democracy in which schools are held accountable to community/parent representatives for school performance (Barrera-Osorio et al. 2009; Bruns et al. 2011; De Grauwe 2005; Rose 2003). Thus, the instrumental value of community participation for optimal educational outcomes has been stressed (Edwards Jr and Klees 2015)

However, it has been argued in the literature that conflicts, differentiation and alienation among school-level stakeholders have been provoked in various developing countries that have institutionalised community participation in school management. Such conflicts include disputes over ownership of schools and land, elite capture of decision-making processes in school management and tension between community members/parents and headteacher/teachers over teachers' professional autonomy (Saito 2013; Shoraku 2008; Fujii 2010; Yamada 2011b; Essuman and Akyeampong 2011; Pellini 2005; Rose 2003).

## 2-1-3. Conviviality

Illich (1973) defined the concept of conviviality in terms of the following: human beings are not objects that are influenced by expert knowledge or an efficient mechanism of modern industrialisation; instead, they are subjects who are engaged with the world, emphasising political process with clear language, demonstrating independence and making decisions on their own. Based on this concept, Nyamnjoh (2016) redefined conviviality as the art that is used by people to prevent conflicts and pursue coexistence in the context of African society.[1] While Illich considered individuals to be independent, Nyamnjoh considered individuals to be incomplete, such that they formulate a community of interdependency.

The perspective of conviviality has been applied in various cultural and regional studies in Africa. For instance, Matsuda (2016) analysed a situation in Kenya, in which post-election violence occurred in 2007; the analysis revealed that politically hostile ethnic groups who lived within the same geographical community engaged in dialogue to protect their properties, cooperated with each other to conduct self-defence activities and managed possible conflicts. Thus, Matsuda's study demonstrates the coexistence of different ethnic groups committed to engaging in community policing. Nowicka and Vertovec (2014) argued that conviviality can be used as an analytical tool to explore ways to live together. Vigneswaran (2014) studied the case of community policing in Johannesburg, South Africa, which has seen considerable violence over the years; the study illustrated how people mitigate or ameliorate sociocultural differences through conviviality, in which cooperation stems from individuals' sense of insecurity and the search for protection in public settings. Both Nowicka and Vertovec (2014) and Vigneswaran (2014) stress that conviviality emerges not merely in a setting that is diverse ethnically, racially or religiously but also in other forms of division such as those between the vulnerable and their protectors, between newcomers and long-standing residents and between those who respect or violate the norms of civility. Thus, this literature review reveals the concept of conviviality as a reflection of how people under socioeconomically vulnerable circumstances manage conflicts originating from their sociocultural differences and depend on each other in working toward shared or compromised goals.

Schooling involves mutual dependency between pupils, teachers, principals and parents, which stems from feelings of vulnerability. When one party recognises the uncertainty of the other party and makes a conscious commitment to relieve their uncertainty, this creates a very intense and meaningful social bond among parties. For instance, poor parents who experience knowledge asymmetry with teachers, must rely on teachers in pedagogical aspects; conversely, teachers need parental support to promote children's sustained engagement with instruction (Bryk and Schneider 2002). Without mutual dependency, it is unlikely that the conflicts, differentiation and alienation among school-level stakeholders, as mentioned in 2-1-2, can be navigated successfully. In the literature, many have speculated on the triggers of conflicts, including politics within geographical communities, such as disputes over the ownership of communal land (Yamada 2011b), disruptions to communities caused by migration and disintegration of matrilineal family structures (Pryor 2005) and experiences of civil war between different ethnic groups (Komatsu 2014, 2019). With the exception of these studies, few have considered how school-level stakeholders from different sociocultural backgrounds manage conflicts over schooling. Thus, in this research, conviviality is defined as the art of how school-level stakeholders with sociocultural differences, and under socioeconomically fragile situations, manage conflicts through their interdependency with regard to community participation in school management.

## 2-2. Policies and Practices of Community Participation in School Management in Ghana

### 2-2-1. Education System
The education system in Ghana consists of six years of primary school, three years of junior secondary school, three years of senior secondary school and higher education (teacher education colleges, as well as universities and polytechnics). In junior high school (JHS),

pupils in grade three take the Basic Education Certificate Examination to proceed to senior high school (SHS). Recently, access to kindergarten (KG) has been expanded; basic education schools, in which one headteacher manages the KG, primary and JHS sections, have become typical. Enrolment rates have improved due to various interventions.[2] Greater access to higher levels of education is expected to continue based on the policy introduced by the current administration to provide free SHS beginning in September 2018.

*2-2-2. Outline of Policies of Community Participation in School Management*

In 1995 under the Ghana Education Service (GES) Act, the SMC was established as the school-level decision-making body. A free, compulsory, universal basic education programme was introduced in 1996. One of the objectives of this programme was to improve access to, and participation in, education. Therefore, the SMC was perceived as a vehicle to accelerate this objective.

An SMC is mandated to engage in the development of a school performance improvement plan (SPIP), execution of the capitation grant, use of school report cards and organisation of school performance appraisal meetings (SPAM) to hold schools accountable to parents/guardians and community members for school performance (Ghana Education Service 2012). SMCs in Ghana do not have strong mandates to recruit or dismiss teachers, nor do they have veto power regarding the SPIP.

SMC executives are composed of the following members: the District Director of Education or his or her representative, a District Assembly representative (assemblyman), a Unit committee[3] representative, the chief's representative, a PTA representative, the headteacher, two members of the teaching staff and co-opted members who perform specific functions (optional) (Ghana Education Service 2012).

There are three types of SMC meetings: general, executive and emergency. Executive meetings are based on representative democracy that SMC executive members discuss and endorse the SPIP. General meetings are based on a consensual democracy that community members have carried over, based on traditional chieftaincy.

In addition to SMCs, PTAs exist as voluntary organisations that are made up of parents/guardians and teachers. The mandate of the PTA is to support the maintenance and renovation of the school's infrastructure, promote teacher welfare, provide a conducive learning environment, and increase enrolment.

During the period of time that the field study was conducted for this research, the SMC and PTA conducted their executive and general meetings jointly to save time for those who participated in both the SMC and PTA. Thus, this study considered SMC executive and general meetings to be included in PTA meetings.

## 2-2-3. *Societal and Educational Challenges in Ghana*

Pryor (2005) argued that due to the migration and the disintegration of matrilineal family structures, the community is merely a geographical entity and does not engender a sense of collectivity. Mfum-Mensah (2004) reported that community members regarded participation in school management as an outside imposition on their community, although it was intended to empower them. Essuman and Akyeampong (2011) pointed out that conflicts have occurred between community members/guardians, who felt that they had mandates to control and monitor teachers, and the teachers, who felt threatened because their professional autonomy was called into question.

Pupil discipline has become an emerging concern for Ghanaian society; many have proposed possible reasons for this. Andrews (2017) highlighted that an extended family is associated with poverty, as it affects one's capacity to be fully involved in a child's education. Essuman (2013) asserted that many children are being fostered by relatives other than their biological parents; however, grandparents and distant relatives may not have the same degree of commitment to, or knowledge of, the child's welfare regarding education and schools, and may therefore participate less in school affairs. Sefa-Nyarko et al. (2018) pointed out that 'poor parenting' is a hindering factor contributing to a low secondary school completion rate.

Poor parenting includes a lack of support and supervision. Studies

223

have also argued that parents believe that they do not have the resources and tools necessary to educate their children and overly rely on teachers to provide the required support (Ampadu et al. 2017). Additionally, young people in poor communities are likely to be engaged with youth employment that can earn 'quick money'. 'Okada' drivers who transport passengers on motorbikes without licences, are one example (Sefa-Nyarko et al. 2018). This can lead to the problem that minors or overaged pupils drop out or work after school to earn money (Volta Online 2018).

Pupil discipline is of the highest concern for parents and teachers. It has been common practice in Africa for teachers to use a cane to discipline pupils when they misbehave (Alhassan 2013). Despite several attempts to prevent teachers from using the cane, this disciplinary tool continues to prevail in Ghana (Andrews 2017). However, in 2016, the GES passed a directive banning any form of corporal punishment, including the use of a cane. This provoked controversial discussions among school-level stakeholders as to whether they should or should not use canes to discipline children (Lartey 2019). Andrews (2017) argued that corporal punishment is a preventing factor for parent participation; however, the dichotomies of opinions between parents and teachers, in terms of the use of corporal punishment in Ghana, were also noted.

## 3. Method

### 3-1. Conceptual Framework

This study examined the process of how school-level stakeholders with socioeconomic vulnerabilities and sociocultural differences were able to manage conflicts, to establish and preserve a secure, protective environment within geographical and school communities through conviviality. Here, the focus was on how school communities deal with pupil discipline. The two schools included in this case study showed different reactions to the directive to ban the use of corporal punishment in disciplining pupils. Behind the scenes, both case study schools have experienced disputes over the legitimacy of chiefs, unreliable working practices and the mismanagement of school funds by the headteacher.

## 3-2. Research Question

How do school communities manage conflicts over pupil discipline through conviviality?

## 3-3. Research/Analytical Method

This research adopted the mixed method. The quantitative analysis aimed at investigating the collective participation based on headteacher questionnaire, and the socioeconomic status data based on additional headteacher questionnaire using the Population and Housing Census data. Based on the quantitative data, the qualitative analysis was conducted through in-depth case study of two schools.

### 3-3-1. Target Country/Area

The Akatsi South District in the Volta region of Ghana was chosen for this study. In 1995, Ghana introduced its policy regarding community participation in school management; this policy continues to place Ghana at the forefront of this educational undertaking in sub-Saharan Africa (Barrera-Osorio et al. 2009). Thus, Ghana was selected for this study because its experiences can provide insight for other countries that have introduced policies regarding the decentralisation of education and community participation in school management since 2000.

The Akatsi South District is one of the pilot districts for community participation interventions supported by the Japan International Cooperation Agency. Thus, this district was selected for this particular study because the District Director of Education was committed to the pilot activity and ensured a satisfactory level of cooperation for this study. Notably, schools for the case study were selected from those that have not been involved with the pilot activity to minimise any influence of the intervention on the research.

The Akatsi South District has a relatively prolific profile in terms of poverty indicators, compared with many of the 25 districts in the Volta region (Ghana Statistical Service 2014a). According to district officials, the major ethnic group in the district is the Ewe; this is also

225

the main ethnic group for the Volta region. In terms of religion, most of the Ewe are Christians.[4]

### 3-3-2. Case Study Schools

This study investigated case study schools in rural areas, where geographical and school communities overlap. Based on information from the Akatsi South District Education Office, two basic education schools in rural areas were selected as case study schools: one with KG and primary sections, and the other with KG, primary and JHS sections. Both schools were established approximately 70 or 80 years ago.

School A is located 30 minutes by car from the city centre of the district capital, Akatsi. It is on a dirt road, which only geographical community members use; the dirt road joins a paved main road. School B is located fewer than 20 km from Akatsi. In total, 70–80 per cent of the geographical community who enrol children in these two schools work in agriculture; more than 80 per cent have access only to sources of unsafe water, which is below the district average.[5] As shown in Table 1, School B was established in 1935, such that it is one of the oldest schools in the Akatsi South District. It has 15 teachers, of whom 12 are full-time. The socioeconomic status of both case study schools is listed in Table 2. Both schools show a lower SES than the average of the surveyed 85 schools. This means that the case study schools are not well endowed. The extent of collective participation at School A was above the district average, whereas School B had lower scores than the district average in all indicators, as shown in Table 3. Thus, the schools were selected for this analysis on the basis of the similarity of socioeconomic status and the difference in collective participation.

## Table 1. Summary of basic information regarding case study

| | Year of establishment | Place | # of teachers | KG (Note 2) | | | Primary | | | JHS (Note 3) | | | Total |
|---|---|---|---|---|---|---|---|---|---|---|---|---|---|
| | | | | M | F | T | M | F | T | M | F | T | |
| School A | 1946 | Rural | 6 (full-time) | 42 | 48 | 90 | 61 | 69 | 130 | - | - | - | 220 |
| School B | 1935 | Rural | 15 (12 full-time) | 30 | 38 | 68 | 117 | 88 | 205 | 45 | 47 | 92 | 365 |

Note 1: Data as of 2016, Note 2: Kindergarten (KG), Note 3: Junior high school (JHS), Note 4: M, male; F, female; T, total

Source: Akatsi South District Education Office

## Table 2. Descriptive statistics of socioeconomic status at Schools A and B

| | District average (SD) | School A | School B |
|---|---|---|---|
| Proportion of those that graduated from senior high school and above (%) | 11.85 (4.96) | 8.93 | 11.59 |
| Proportion of those who work for the agricultural industry (%) | 68.76 (18.27) | 69.63 | 80.49 |
| Proportion of those who have access to water sources that are not considered safe (%) | 68.82 (26.47) | 88.98 | 84.80 |
| Proportion of those who have a mobile phone (%) | 28.15 (8.82) | 29.06 | 22.14 |

Source: Additional headteacher questionnaire based on the Population and Housing Census 2010 data

### 3-3-3. Data

This field study was conducted for approximately one week each in both September 2017 and September 2018 in the Akatsi South District, in which data were obtained from the same case study schools. Semi-structured and focused group interviews were conducted with the following groups: headteachers, teachers and parents/guardians (Table 4). The interviews took place at the school compound and lasted 30 minutes to one hour for each group. Group members were asked about their history, the status quo, any challenges in relationships between the school community and the

**Table 3. Descriptive statistics of collective participation at Schools A and B**

|  | District average (SD) | School A | School B |
|---|---|---|---|
| Frequency of SMC general meetings (2016) | 3.36 (1.74) | 6 | 3 |
| Frequency of SPAM (average between 2014 and 2016) | 1.35 (1.35) | 2 | 1 |
| Average participation rate in SMC general meetings (2016; Note 1) | 35% (19%) | 24% | 10% |
| Number of resource mobilisation channels (2016) | 5.52 (2.00) | 6 | 5 |
| PTA levy collection rate (2016) | 63% | 100% | - |
| Average amount of collected PTA levy (2014–2016) | GHC 458.23 (GHC 567.72) | GHC 133.33 | GHC 115.00 |

Note 1: Average participation rate in SMC general meetings is calculated using school enrolment as the denominator and the average number of SMC general meetings in 2016 as the numerator.

Note 2: PTA levy collection rate is calculated using households who are expected to pay PTA levies as the denominator and those who actually paid PTA levies as the numerator.

Note 3: GHC 1 was worth 0.16 USD as of October 20, 2018.

Note 4: Ghanaian cedi (GHC), parent–teacher association (PTA), standard deviation (SD), school management committee (SMC), school performance appraisal meeting (SPAM).

Source: Headteacher questionnaire

school and school activities (i.e., the actions of the headteacher and teachers). The interviewees were nearly the same as in 2017 and 2018; thus, the author asked about changes during the past year. The author also conducted a documentary review of eight sets of PTA general meeting minutes (August 2011; October 2013; June and November 2014; February and October 2015; and February and June 2016) and one set of SMC/PTA executive meeting minutes (October 2016). All meeting minutes were available in English.

**Table 4. Summary of interviewees**

| School A | | |
|---|---|---|
| Interviewee | Number | Basic information |
| Headteacher | 1 | Man; age, 48 years; work experience as teacher, 19 years; appointed as headteacher for this school in March 2017 (first school as a headteacher); educational background, Bachelor's degree |
| Teacher | 5 | Sex: three men, two women. Qualifications: four qualified, one community-hired. Educational background: one Bachelor's degree, three diplomas, and one SHS. Age: four 20–30 years, one 30–40 years |
| SMC/PTA executive members | 12 | Composition: PTA chairperson, community representative, chief representative, PTA executive members, guardians. Occupation: 10 farmers. Sex: seven men, five women. Age: two, 30–40 years; seven, 40–50 years; two, 50–60 years; and one, 60–70 years. |

| School B | | |
|---|---|---|
| Interviewee | Number | Basic information |
| Headteacher | 1 | Man; age, 43 years; working experience as teacher, 18 years; appointed as headteacher for this school in 2014; educational background, Bachelor's degree. |
| Teacher | 2 | One man (age, 46 years; English teacher in JHS section; educational background, College of Education). One woman (age, 23 years; classroom teacher at grade five; educational background, Diploma in Basic Education). |
| SMC/PTA executive members | 3 | Composition: three guardians (two men, ages 70 and 26 years; one woman, age 49 years). Occupation: one farmer; educational background: JHS, SHS (currently enrolled). |

Note 1: Data as of September 2017.
Note 2: Junior high school (JHS), parent–teacher association (PTA), senior high school (SHS), school management committee (SMC).
Source: Author interviews

# 4. Findings

SMC general meeting minutes from the case study schools showed that guardians expected teachers to discipline pupils using a cane. However, in 2016, the Ghana Education Service issued a directive[6] that banned corporal punishment. As a result of that directive, corporal punishment was regarded as illegal, and teachers who conducted corporal punishment were penalised. At both SMC general meetings, participants discussed how to react to the directive. Their reactions differed greatly, as explained below.

## 4-1. School A

The geographical community surrounding School A had established its basic structure, levied financial resources from community members and provided labour for the renovation of school facilities. One SMC executive member explained their strong commitment to this school:

> This school belongs to this geographical community. The products (pupils) are good for the community.

With a strong commitment to school development, school communities had serious concerns about the previous headteacher's mismanagement of the school fund and his frequent absence without justifiable explanation. Guardians criticised his work ethic and practices. The school community agreed that they should meet the headteacher personally (General Meeting Minutes, February 2017). This issue was shared with a circuit supervisor at the district education office, who also participated in the general meeting. Subsequently, the headteacher retired voluntarily. School A was able to manage conflicts through dialogue and continued to mobilise resources for school improvement, despite the headteacher's mismanagement of the school funds. This was possible because the school community was buttressed by a geographical community who strongly supported school development. The geographical community then observed positive signs of change, initiated by the new headteacher.

Upon his appointment to the school, the new headteacher introduced several changes, with the aim of making the school enjoyable to pupils, by dividing grades one through six into three groups: red, green, and yellow. Pupils competed for reward marks by fetching water for washing tanks, cleaning classrooms and dressing themselves neatly. An SMC executive member commented on this activity:

> Through the pupils who attended school, the headteacher sent a message to the pupils who were not attending that school is enjoyable. He is doing his best. Before, pupils did not come to school consistently or on time. However, once the new headteacher took over and initiated this strategy, pupils began to return to school and were on time.

Thus, the geographical community felt obliged to commit themselves to developing the school and supporting the new headteacher's initiative. This generated a sense of empowerment and enabled the school community to continue their support for School A. At the general meeting in February 2018, the school community agreed to mobilise resources in accordance with the headteacher's appeal; they collected 496 Ghanaian Cedi, greater than the average collected PTA levy of 133.33 Ghanaian Cedi (2014–2016; general meeting minutes, February and May 2018, and interview with the headteacher in September 2018).

The school community of School A often discussed how to respond to pupils' lack of respect for their guardians at home and their lack of discipline as the main agenda at SMC/PTA general meetings (September 2017, February and May 2018). In particular, SMC/PTA general meeting minutes in May 2018 showed the possibility of conflicts among school-level stakeholders. For instance, some guardians requested that teachers use the cane when pupils misbehave; some argued that they would transfer their children away from the school to one where teachers disciplined children well, if the school adhered to the directive. Some teachers objected to the directive and referred to the Bible, which allowed necessary punishment for children, while others doubted the effectiveness of punishment without pain and objected to banning the use of the cane.

The headteacher opposed such ideas from guardians and teachers, insisting that disciplining pupils does not necessarily require the use of a cane. He advocated for guardians to have a positive relationship with the teachers. He also asserted that any corporal punishment was illegal and if teachers performed it, guardians could potentially sue teachers; thus, there was a need to identify ways to discipline pupils without the use of a cane. A circuit supervisor, who oversaw this school, also mentioned that any corporal punishment, including the use of a cane, was prohibited in Ghana. After the expression of such diverse and conflicting opinions by guardians, teachers, the headteacher and the circuit supervisor, everyone agreed that when children misbehaved, their guardians would be invited to the school and would be provided with an explanation as to why their children had been punished (based on an interview with SMC executive member, September 2018). This implied that the school community had come to an understanding in terms of pupils' discipline.

In this school (School A), the geographical community reinforced the agreed-upon actions of the school community toward pupils' discipline, without conducting corporal punishment. According to the interviewed SMC executive members, the school community at the general meetings selected the following actions to prevent a lack of discipline among the children, in terms of going out at night and watching TV. First, they requested that teachers provide additional homework for children to ensure that the children were more engaged with their studies. Second, they passed a resolution that children in the neighbourhood should not watch TV; neighbours who allowed children to watch TV would be sanctioned. Representatives from the geographical community participated in the SMC/PTA general meetings, and the same message was announced to guardians who were absent from the meetings, as well as to community members without children.

One guardian described teachers' contributions to pupils' discipline as follows:

Pupils greet parents and do their homework when they come home from school. This is because teachers have made a positive impression on their pupils, and the pupils are thus committed to working toward the expected responsibilities given to them by their teachers.

A pupil described discipline at this school as follows:

The discipline at this school is good. Pupils are attentive to teachers. Pupils come to school and sweep classrooms, fetch water and read English books before 8 a.m. when school assembly starts. Pupils greet community members as well.

Moreover, one of the teachers described pupil discipline as follows:

Pupils' attitudes are good, and they respect the teachers. Pupils come to school on time, and they are ready to learn.

Thus, School A was able to incorporate different opinions from all school-level stakeholders, such as guardians, teachers and pupils, and confirmed that pupils were disciplined without the use of a cane. Banning the use of a cane was presumed likely to generate possible conflicts; however, the stakeholders were able to discuss issues, and manage divisive conflicts by depending on each other, having high expectations, and performing their expected duties within the school community.

### 4-2. School B

According to the headteacher and teachers of School B, the relationships in the geographical and school community were cordial before 2013. A town development fund existed for the school.[7] The geographical community donated financial resources, and school renovation work in the JHS section was initiated using this fund.

However, divisions arose among the geographical communities owing to the chieftaincy issue; these divisions had a significant effect on the school community. The headteacher and teachers mentioned that some community members considered the SMC and PTA chairpersons to be supporters of the current chief; therefore, they did not participate in the general meetings, and the school community suspended collection of the PTA levy.[8] No financial resources had been mobilised to the town development fund for the school, due to the lack of accountability for the levy-collecting committee members. As a result, the JHS classroom renovation efforts were suspended.

Moreover, division among the geographical communities of School B undermined external support for the school. A local Member of Parliament, a United Kingdom-based businessman and a lawyer, all of whom had relations with the geographical communities, had planned to support the school by providing scholarships, textbooks, uniforms and a school library. However, guardians who considered these supporters to be in favour of the current chief did not show any interest in the plan and, in fact, refused to accept it. Therefore, division among the geographical communities undermined external support for the school community.

Such divisions within geographical and school communities and a lack of resource mobilisation for school development reduced motivation on the part of the headteacher and teachers who were engaged in daily school management. The headteacher emphasised the difficulty of school management in the context of inadequate resources, as follows:

> I take a risk in spending my own money to buy necessary materials before any capitation money comes.

He also explained the gravity of the situation in which teachers had been placed:

> Because of this issue, most teachers have requested a transfer, as they consider all of their efforts to be in vain.

School B exhibited serious conflicts, indifference, and a lack of motivation, in sharp contrast to School A.

The school community at School B, including all school-level stakeholders, guardians, the headteacher, teachers and pupils, regarded pupil discipline as an acute challenge. Periodic discussions at the general meeting addressed whether the school had an issue with adolescent pregnancy. Pupils said that some older pupils earned money by working as motorbike riders after school and did not respect teachers.

Due to the division among geographical communities, the school community overall had lost opportunities to discuss pupil discipline with the headteacher and teachers and had no agreement or general consensus as to how to address discipline at school. The headteacher insisted that guardians should care for their children at home and ensure that they do not go out at night or on weekends, or watch TV; he indicated that this would prevent adolescent pregnancy and improve the pupils' lack of discipline (general meeting minutes, June 2016). Despite the request by the headteacher, pupils' lack of discipline became worse. A teacher remarked:

> Pupils have the same mentality as their guardians. If guardians speak ill of teachers at home, pupils do not listen to the teachers at school. Teachers presumed that the division within geographical and school communities had accelerated the pupils' lack of discipline.

The government directive that banned corporal punishment sharpened conflicts over pupil discipline among school-level stakeholders. Teachers could no longer use a cane to discipline misbehaving pupils. As a result, there were differences of opinion between the teachers, who believed that disciplinary actions were necessary for pupils, and the headteacher, who was obliged to adhere to the directive due to his role in the local educational administration. One teacher recalled:

> I made female pupils who misbehaved stand outside the classroom; however, the headteacher said that I should not do this … If teachers do not receive the necessary support, then teachers hesitate to do what they think they should do.

The headteacher stated that teachers should not use a cane and communicated this to the pupils. He cautioned that some pupils would not come to school, due to the use of a cane. Teachers lamented that pupils did not attend morning classes and that this would continue without change. Therefore, pupil discipline greatly affected the teachers' motivation.

## 5. Discussion

This study investigated the process by which socioeconomically disadvantaged households and school communities manage pupil discipline through conviviality. This study demonstrated new findings from the perspective of conviviality in the field of community participation in school management, which has been discussed through the analytical lens of instrumental value for educational outcomes. However, the concept of conviviality has remained vague up to this point. For this reason, in this study the characteristics of conviviality in the field of community participation in school management were explored from the perspective of diversity and fragility, coexistence with conflicts, and living together through interdependency.

First, when conviviality works, consensual democracy is necessary to embrace diversity and fragility. The modality of consensual participation varies the ways in which people meet to discuss issues, contribute financial resources and provide effort in the decision-making process and implementation. Geographical communities have traditionally performed these tasks, as noted by Ajei (2001). Despite fragility shown by a less-endowed SES, School A showed a high level of collective participation. It is reasonable to assume that conviviality works when a diverse range of guardians can meet, discuss and reach consensus, rather than when a few elite or representative members make decisions. Fragility matters not just socioeconomically but also socioculturally. Both the parents and the teachers are vulnerable, with respect to the parent's invasion into a teacher's professional autonomy and the information asymmetry between parents and teachers. Such a fragility makes them depend on each other in the management of conflicts through dialogue for the benefit of the children.

Second, conviviality coexists with conflicts. School B showed a level of collective participation and active resource mobilisation on the part of geographical communities until the occurrence of the dispute regarding the legitimacy of chiefs in 2013. However, the extent of collective participation had declined sharply owing to the chieftaincy issue, and venues for conviviality had been minimised. Conversely, despite the questionable work ethic and practices of the previous headteacher and his financial management issues at School A, the school community had expectations for the new headteacher and mobilised resources for the school in response to expectations from the new headteacher.

Leadership by headteachers and community representatives can trigger changes to manage conflicts through conviviality. At School A, some guardians might have executed the exit strategy by transferring their children to other schools if School A had continued to obey the directives to ban the use of a cane. However, conflicts was resolved through discussion, where stakeholders realised that they should depend on each other to discipline pupils. The headteacher facilitated the conviviality embedded in the geographical and school communities, while community representatives urged other members to respond to the headteacher's call to collective action.

Likewise, School B faced serious conflicts over pupil discipline, which made teachers request for transfer. The headteacher at School B – who had nearly the same work experience as the headteacher at School A – could not manage the situation, despite his efforts to address the chieftaincy issue. This was potentially because the individuals who were involved in school management (i.e., the SMC and PTA chairpersons, as well as the headteacher and teachers) were regarded by the opposite party as supporters of the current chief, whom they did not support. This indicates that individual leadership can trigger changes in conviviality; however, such changes depend on politics within geographical communities, which are beyond the realm of particular individuals. These narratives suggest that conviviality always coexists with conflicts; however, it matters how the conflicts are managed through the headteacher and the school community's leadership.

Finally, conviviality appears to be embedded in both geographical and school communities, where stakeholders must live together through interdependency for the benefit of the community and the children. A school community alone cannot manage conflicts over pupil discipline, as observed in this study. Rather, geographical communities must be proactively convivial. However, as observed in School B, divisions among the geographical communities strongly affected the school community. Conversely, the geographical communities of School A provided a solid foundation for its school community. Specifically, conviviality within a school community is determined by the conviviality within geographical communities. Thus, conviviality exists in multi-layered communities that pursue life together through interdependency.

This study contributed to the literature by illuminating the relationship between individual households and the school community, which constitutes a universal challenge for both developed and developing countries. Gebre et al. (2017) argued that Western institutional settings focus on individuals, whereas African cultures consider the collective as the unit of social organisation. Nyamnjoh (2016) also asserted that not only Africa but also the world as a whole should employ conviviality as part of their citizenship development and move away from a fixed mechanism originating from Western modernised society to a kinetic one characterised by relationships, interconnectedness and networks. Participatory democracy, as elaborated by Putnam et al. (1993) in the context of developed countries, has been criticised with respect to the collectives of a community requiring equal membership and the burdens for its members, without consideration being given to diversity, fragility and need for flexibility (Selle and Kristin, 1999; Suetomi 2005). This appears to be related to 'African Potentials' in that even if individuals are socioeconomically vulnerable and socioculturally different, they can formulate collectives of communities to practise the kinetic arts of conviviality, to manage conflicts through mutual dependency.

# 6. Conclusion

This study posed the following research question: how do school communities manage conflicts over pupil discipline through conviviality? This study revealed that both case study schools experienced socioeconomic vulnerabilities, but differed significantly in their approach to disciplining pupils; these differences arose from the school communities' ability to implement conviviality. School A was able to manage pupil discipline through dialogue, bridge the divide in school-level stakeholder opinions and make the obligations meet the expectations between the school and the school community. Conversely, School B was not able to resolve pupil discipline without having venues for dialogue, owing to the dispute over the legitimacy of the chief. Literature on community participation in school management has highlighted conflicts, differentiation and alienation among school-level stakeholders; however, few have examined how stakeholders interact over the course of managing conflicts. This study contributed to acknowledging the potential of conviviality with regard to how stakeholders with socioeconomic fragility and sociocultural difference can live together and manage conflicts in the context of community participation in school management.

This study had the following challenges. The schools included in the study are in rural areas of Ghana, where cultural diversity is not evident and geographical and school communities overlap. Thus, cultural diversity in terms of ethnicity, religion, gender and age has not been studied. For instance, Komatsu (2014) analysed a situation in Bosnia and Herzegovina where different ethnic groups who had experienced civil war achieved social cohesion through school management. In addition, cultural diversity in developing countries is more evident in urban areas, in terms of ethnicity and religion. Moreover, as demonstrated in Cambodia by Shoraku (2008), community members in some cultures are subject to others who have authority. In countries where cultural diversity is more evident and community members are subject to authority, additional studies are needed to determine how the school community can operate under conditions of conviviality.

# Endnotes

[1] Nyamnjoh (2016) conceptualised conviviality based on a literature review that discussed how people manage conflicts and coexist in the context of community policing in Johannesburg, South Africa, as well as in diverse circumstances in London, United Kingdom.

[2] The primary education gross enrolment rates in 2017/2018 were 89.3 per cent (national), 87.8 per cent (Volta region) and 88.9 per cent (Akatsi South). The lower secondary education gross enrolment rates were 48.5 per cent (national), 43.1 per cent (Volta region) and 30.8 per cent (Akatsi South) (Ministry of Education, Ghana, Education Management System).

[3] This is a government administration under the District Assembly at the town or village level. In Kwahu South District, Eastern Region, 500 to 1,000 community members compose a 'unit' and 15 members represent each unit committee (Hirose 2011).

[4] The Ewe constitute 73.8 per cent of the population in the Volta region and 13.9 per cent in Ghana as a whole. Christianity and indigenous religion constitute 61.5 per cent and 26.5 per cent in Akatsi South, respectively (Ghana Statistical Service 2013, 2014b).

[5] School community socioeconomic status was determined from the answers of the headteachers to a multiple-choice questionnaire that investigated the geographical community from which the pupils of each school originated, based on the 2020 Population and Housing Census.

[6] The Ghana Education Service headquarters issued the directive dated 27 February 2016. The Volta regional education office sent a letter to each district education office to reconfirm that authorities needed to obey the directive. The author observed the letter on a notice board at the District Education Office, Akatsi South District, during the field survey in September 2018.

[7] According to guardians, in the past, 600– 800 Ghanaian cedi was collected monthly.

[8] According to the headteacher, the mobilised PTA levy in 2017/2018 was 85 Ghanaian cedi.

# Acknowledgements

This study was supported by JSPS KAKENHI (grant nos. JP16H06318 and JP17K04627). The author is especially grateful to Mr Adovor Yogha, the District Director of Education, Mr Clements Katsekpor, Akatsi South District Education Office, and Mr Fred Birikorang and Ms Junko Nakazawa, Ghana Education Service, for their support and advice during the field study.

# References

Ajei, O. M. (2001) *Indigenous Knowledge Systems and Good Governance in Ghana: The Traditional Akan Socio-Political Example, Occasional Papers, No. 30*, Accra: Institute of Economic Affairs.

Alhassan, A. B. (2013) 'School corporal punishment in Ghana and Nigeria as a method of discipline: A psychological examination of policy and practice', *Journal of Education and Practice*, Vol. 4, No. 27, pp. 137–47 (https://www.iiste.org/Journals/index.php/JEP/article/view/9890) (accessed: 3 December 2018).

Ampadu, E., Butakor, P. K. and Cole, Y. (2017) 'Working together to improve the quality of mathematics education and students achievements: Exploring the views of Ghanaian parents', *African Research Review*, Vol. 11, No. 1, pp. 11–27.

Andrews, R. G. (2017) 'A case study of parental involvement in basic education in rural Ghana', unpublished doctoral dissertation, University of Sussex.

Barrera-Osorio, F., Fasih, T., Patrinos, H. A. and Santibáñez, L. (2009) *Decentralized Decision-Making in Schools: The Theory and Evidence on School Cased Management*, Washington DC: World Bank.

Bruns, B., Filmer, D. and Patrinos, H. A. (2011) *Making Schools Work: New Evidence on Accountability Reforms*, Washington DC: World Bank.

Bryk, A. S. and Schneider, B. (2002) *Trust in Schools: A Core Resource for Improvement*, New York: Russell Sage Foundation.

De Grauwe, A. (2005) 'Improving the quality of education through school-based management: Learning from international experiences', *International Review of Education*, Vol. 51, No. 4, pp. 269–87.

Edwards Jr, D. B. and Klees, S. J. (2015) 'Unpacking "participation" in development and education governance: A framework of perspectives and practices', *PROSPECTS*, Vol. 35, pp. 483–99.

Essuman, A. (2013) *Decentralization of Education Management in Ghana: Key Issues in School-Community Relations*, Saarbrücken: LAP LAMBERT Academic Publishing.

Essuman, A. and Akyeampong, K. (2011) 'Decentralization policy and practice in Ghana: The promise and reality of community participation in education in rural communities', *Journal of Education Policy*, Vol. 26, No. 4, pp. 513–27.

Fujii, M. (2010) 'Educational development and decentralization policy', *Journal of International Development Studies (Kokusai Kaihatsu Kenkyu)*, Vol. 19, No. 2, pp. 79–86 (in Japanese with English abstract).

Gebre, Y., Ohta, I. and Matsuda, M. (2017) 'Introduction: Achieving peace and coexistence through African Potentials', in Y. Gebre, I. Ohta and M. Matsuda (eds) *African Virtues in the Pursuit of Conviviality: Exploring Local Solutions in Light of Global Prescriptions*, Bamenda: Langaa RPCIG, pp. 3–37.

Ghana Education Service (2012) *School Management Committee Resource Handbook*, Accra: Ghana Education Service.

Ghana Statistical Service (2013) *2010 Population & Housing Census, National Analytical Report*, Accra: Ghana Statistical Service (http://www.statsghana.gov.gh/docfiles/2010phc/National_Analytical_Report.pdf) (accessed: 22 November 2018).

———— (2014a) *Ghana Living Standard Survey Round 6 (GLSS6) Main Report*, Accra: Ghana Statistical Service (http://www.statsghana.gov.gh/docfiles/glss6/GLSS6_Main%20Report.pdf) (accessed: 22 November 2018).

———— (2014b) *2010 Population & Housing Census, District Analytical Report Akatsi South District*, Accra: Ghana Statistical Service (http://www.statsghana.gov.gh/docfiles/2010_District_Report/Volta/AKATSI%20SOUTH.pdf) (accessed: 22 November 2018).

Hirose, K. (2011) 'Traditional chieftaincy', in T. Takane and S. Yamada (eds) *47 Chapters to Understand Ghana*, Tokyo: Akashi Shoten, pp.166–71 (in Japanese).

Illich, I. (1973) *Tools for Conviviality*, New York: Harper and Row Publishers.

Komatsu, T. (2014) 'Does decentralization enhance a school's role of promoting social Cohesion? Bosnian school leaders' perceptions of school governance', *International Review of Education*, Vol. 60, pp. 7–31.

————— (2019) 'Integrated schools and social cohesion in post-conflict Srebrenica: Bosniak youths views of their schooling experiences', *Comparative Education Review*, Vol. 63, No. 3, pp. 398–417.

Lartey, N. L. (2019) '"Ban on caning in order; it makes students timid" – GNECC', *CITI Newsroom*, 31 January 2019 (https://citinewsroom.com/2019/01/ban-on-caning-in-order-it-makes-students-timid-gnecc/) (accessed: 8 February 2020).

Matsuda, M. (2016) 'African Potentials for conflict prevention: With a special reference to the reorganization of community policing in Kenya', in M. Matsuda and M. Hirano-Nomoto (eds) *Cultural Creativity for Conflict Resolution and Coexistence: African Potentials as Practice of Incompleteness and Bricolage*, Kyoto: Kyoto University Press, pp. 237–75 (in Japanese).

Mfum-Mensah, O. (2004) 'Empowerment or impairment? Involving traditional communities in school management', *International Review of Education*, Vol. 50, pp. 141–55.

Ministry of Education, Ghana, Education Management Information System (http://www.ghanaeducationdata.com/) (accessed: 22 November 2018).

Nishimura, M. (2017) 'Community participation in school management in developing countries', *Oxford Research Encyclopedia of Education* (https://doi.org/10.1093/acrefore/9780190264093.013.64) (accessed: 12 December 2020).

Nowicka, M. and Vertovec, S. (2014) 'Comparing convivialities:

Dreams and realities of living-with-difference', *European Journal of Cultural Studies*, Vol. 17, No. 4, pp. 341–56.

Nyamnjoh, F. B. (2016) 'Incompleteness: Frontier Africa and the currency of conviviality (translated by K. Kusunoki and M. Matsuda)', in M. Matsuda and M. Hirano-Nomoto (eds) *Cultural Creativity for Conflict Resolution and Coexistence: African Potentials as Practice of Incompleteness and Bricolage*, Kyoto: Kyoto University Press, pp. 311–47 (in Japanese).

Ogawa, M. (2017) 'Emerging inequity in the process of educational expansions in rural Kenya: Impact of the community on secondary school management', *Journal of International Development Studies (Kokusai Kaihatsu Kenkyu)*, Vol 26, No. 2, pp. 113–30 (in Japanese with English abstract).

Pellini, A. (2005) 'Decentralization of education in Cambodia: Searching for spaces of participation between traditions and modernity', *Compare*, Vol. 35, No. 2, pp. 205–16.

Pryor, J. (2005) 'Can community participation mobilize social capital for improvement of rural schooling? A case study from Ghana', *Compare*, Vol. 35, No. 2, pp. 193–203.

Putnam, R. D. (2000) *Bowing Alone: The Collapse and Revival of American Community*, New York: Simon and Shuster.

Putnam, R. D., Leonardi, R. and Nanetti, R. Y. (1993) *Making Democracy Work: Civic Traditions in Modern Italy*, Princeton: Princeton University Press.

Rose, P. (2003) 'Community participation in school policy and practice in Malawi: Balancing local knowledge, national policies and international agency priorities', *Compare*, Vol. 33, No.1, pp. 47–64.

Saito, K. (2013) 'Community participation in school management in Senegal: Differences between behavior and perception', *Comparative Education*, Vol. 46, pp. 80–101.

Sefa-Nyarko, C., Kyei, P. and Mwambari, D. (2018) *Transitions from Primary to Lower Secondary School: A Focus on Equity, Background Paper, Secondary Education in Africa: Preparing Youth for the Future of Work Series (SEA) of MasterCard Foundation*, Participatory Development Associate Ltd.

Selle, P. and Kristin, S. (1999) 'Organizational membership and democracy: Do we need to consider passive members seriously? (translated by A. Ogawa)', *Chiba Journal of Law and Politics*, Vol. 14, No. 1, pp. 143–66 (in Japanese).

Shoraku, A. (2008) 'A case study of parental participation in primary school education in Kampong Chhang Province, Cambodia', *Comparative Education*, Vol. 36, pp. 3–24.

Suetomi, K. (2005) 'Membership problems in public compulsory school as "club goods"', *Bulletin of the Japan Educational Administration Society*, Vol. 31, pp. 133–50 (in Japanese with English abstract).

Vigneswaran, D. (2014) 'Protection and Conviviality: Community Policing in Johannesburg', *European Journal of Cultural Studies*, Vol. 17, No. 4, pp. 471–86.

Volta Online (2018) 'Commercial use of motorbikes in Ghana; A convenient mode of transport or death trap?', *Volta Online*, 1 June 2018 (https://voltaonlinegh.com/2018/06/01/article-commercial-use-of-motorbikes-in-ghana-a-convenience-mode-of-transport-or-death-trap/) (accessed: 22 November 2018).

Yamada, S. (2011a) 'Linkage between the urban and the rural', in T. Takane and S. Yamada (eds.) *47 Chapters to Understand Ghana*, Tokyo: Akashi Shoten, pp. 205–9 (in Japanese).

———— (2011b) 'Social factors determining "Community Participation": The tradition of community school and school management committees in Oromia Region, Ethiopia', *Journal of International Development Studies (Kokusai Kaihatsu Kenkyu)*, Vol 20, No. 2, pp. 107–25 (in Japanese with English abstract).

# Chapter 8

## Community Schools Providing the Tools for Conviviality in Urban Kenya

### *Asayo Ohba*

Most community schools go the extra mile. They offer not only education but provide those kids with other basic needs. You find that some of our schools provide clothes and food at no cost. Some even pay for school fees through well-wishers. So we do more than what the government school does. If you look at the government school, they just teach and even charge for feeding programmes. Not all parents are able to pay for it. So if the government phases out all community schools, where do we take these children? (Manager, School 9).

## 1. Introduction

The number of pupils attending community schools in the urban slums of Kenya is on the rise due to insufficient numbers of public primary schools after the introduction of free primary education (Oketch et al. 2010a). Most community schools are officially unregistered, as they have not met the registration criteria set by the Ministry of Education (MoE) (Ohba 2013), and charge relatively low school fees (Tooley et al. 2010; Tooley 2017). Therefore, these institutions are referred to as unregistered or low-fee/low-cost private schools. According to Open Schools Kenya, a non-governmental organisation (NGO) that collects low-fee/low-cost school data in three Nairobi slums, there are 161 primary schools with 39,822 pupils in Kibera, 120 schools with 20,302 pupils in Mathare and 101 schools with 21,070 pupils in Kangemi (Open Schools Kenya website, as of April 2020). The presence of these schools is well known in Kenya and, as early as 2003–04, school census data suggested that about 36 per cent of primary pupils in

Nairobi attended such schools (Lauglo 2004: 38). Another study in two of Nairobi's slums in 2005–07 found that 43 per cent of pupils in their respective catchment areas were not enrolled in public schools, suggesting that they attended nearby community schools (Oketch et al. 2010a: 28). Thus, community schools are prevalent but there are no official data to indicate how many pupils they accommodate.

Many studies on community schools by educational researchers and practitioners (including myself) have paid attention to their academic performance and cost-efficiency compared with their public counterparts (e.g. Dixon 2004; Tooley and Dixon 2005; Srivastava and Walford (eds) 2007; Tooley et al. 2008; Rose 2009a; Oketch et al. 2010a, 2010b; Tooley et al. 2010; Akaguri 2011, 2014; Cameron 2011; Härmä 2011; Dixon et al. 2013; Ohba 2013; Srivastava (ed.) 2013; Amjad and MacLeod 2014; Heyneman and Stern 2014; Alcott and Rose 2016). However, little has been explored in terms of their role and potential beyond that of learning institutions. For example, it has not been determined why some schools with poor academic performance are still in relatively high demand despite the reasonable assumption that they would be closed down for not meeting the needs of parents and pupils, based on the assumption that only relatively well-performing schools would survive.

This Western ideology of school competition for better performance has driven the consumption of more and more education in the interest of a successful life; conversely, little or no education is considered a sign of failure in life (Illich 1971, 1973). In fact, if we consider the community school as a place only for academic performance, we would underestimate its role and potential for local inhabitants. As will be discussed below, some community schools function not only as a place of learning but also as a sanctuary and a source of food, clothes and shelter for poor and vulnerable children. For this reason, the present study explores how community schools meet the needs of children in the urban slums of Kenya and investigates the reasons for their prevalence.

The remainder of this chapter is organised as follows: the next section reviews the literature on the concept of conviviality and describes the Kenyan context in relation to the community school. This is followed by a description of the data collection, the findings and a subsequent detailed discussion. The last section presents the conclusions.

## 2. Conviviality and Schooling

### 2-1. Understanding Conviviality

The term 'conviviality' means 'festive' and is academically and basically understood as 'the capacity to live together' (Wise and Noble 2016: 423). Referring to Gilroy (2004), Wise and Noble (2016: 425) underscore that the English term 'conviviality' often refers to happy or fun forms of togetherness while the Spanish term *convivencia* encompasses a much wider meaning, including practice, effort, negotiation and achievement. Rodríguez (2020: 107) also points out that *convivencia* 'has moral implications as it emphasises a communal being in the world, one that is tied to a respectful and caring living together'. Owing to globalisation, migration and urbanisation, cosmopolitan urban populations encompass a mixture of people with diverse social and cultural backgrounds. Thus, Wise and Noble (2016: 424) see conviviality 'in a very specific way; a way that includes potential ambivalence at the heart of the everydayness of living together'. In this context, conviviality is regarded as the study of how different people live together through everyday negotiation. For this reason, when one explores conviviality, it is necessary to examine people's interactions, negotiation and relationships and the extent of their capacity to live together.

Similarly, Nyamnjoh and Brudvig (2014a: 217) state that '[c]onviviality rests on the nuances inscribed and imbibed in everyday relations—the micro-trends of socialisation'. Nyamnjoh and Brudving (2014a: 226) elucidate that conviviality emerges from everyday life through 'the frequent interplay between dynamics of group autonomy on the one hand and interdependent communalism of groups on the other hand'. Their emphasis is on urban cosmopolitan communities and interdependence among the

249

inhabitants. Referring to Mamdani (1996), Nyamnjoh and Brudvig (2014b: 341, original emphasis) state that '[c]onviviality may emerge from a resolution of frictions which, when negotiated into meaningful relationships, may actually facilitate mutual interests between individuals as "subject" and "citizens" or between individuals and the state'. Moreover, Nyamnjoh (2017a: 262) notes that '[c]onviviality is recognition and provision for the fact or reality of being incomplete', implying that one exists only in relation to others. This is actually an African philosophy embedded in society, as Gebre et al. (2017) explain: 'African society understands the self as "something incomplete" and has the potential power to create a symbiotic order of interdependence free from the mutual exclusion of others, who are similarly incomplete' (19–20, original emphasis). As will be discussed in this chapter, when examining schooling in the urban slums of Kenya, it is crucial to observe how they operate in relation to interactions with local people, on the one hand, and the authorities, on the other. As stated by Nyamnjoh and Brudvig (2014b), such interactions with both sides may be the result of emerging conviviality, which will be further discussed in the next subsection.

## 2-2. Schools for Conviviality

For those who study schooling in social science, the term 'conviviality' is also associated with the works of Ivan Illich who is globally known for publications such as *Deschooling Society* (Illich 1971) and *Tools for Conviviality* (Illich 1973). For Illich, a convivial society 'should be designed to allow all its members the most autonomous action by means of tools least controlled by others' (Illich 1973: 20). By 'tools' he means institutions such as schools, hospitals, banks, etc., which make individuals work for them. Illich (1973: 19) argues that '[e]ducation became the search for an alchemic process that would bring forth a new type of man who would fit into an environment created by scientific magic'. He claims that schools are factories that produce uniform people who are taught by qualified teachers using an authorised curriculum and textbooks. Pupils study in schools wherein entrance age and grade progression are fixed and receive

250

qualifications when study is completed (Illich 1971). He argues that this education industry reproduces the same types of people who fit into a man-made environment. He therefore claims that, while a minority of individuals climb the education ladder as far as they can benefit from the system owing to better 'qualifications', the majority fail or drop out in the middle of the ladder and are inevitably discarded as unfit or unprepared for life (Illich 1973: 19). Thus, such an education system cannot enlighten individual capabilities and fulfil self-realisation.

Just as Illich (1973) criticises the education system per se, so does Nyamnjoh (2012), albeit from a slightly different point of view, as he is concerned more with the present education curriculum in Africa as it originates from Western ideology (Nyamnjoh 2012, 2019a, 2019b). In his articles, Nyamnjoh (2012) emphasises the richness of endogenous epistemology African societies possess, and how such epistemology was overtaken by the colonial epistemology that values objective, observable, dual and dichotomous truth (Nyamnjoh 2013, 2017a, 2017b, 2019a, 2019b). He further states that '[t]he colonial epistemology has survived in the continent more because it suits the purposes of the agents of (neo)colonialism than because of its relevance to understanding African situations' (Nyamnjoh 2012: 146). Thus, Nyamnjoh claims the necessity of developing an education curriculum that is relevant to the local context and reflects its reality.

These two authors – Illich and Nyamnjoh – argue that the present education system is detached from the local context and call for the necessity of developing a school system that is rooted in the local context. As this study will present, on the one hand, the present education system in Kenya, which originates from the former colonial state, is the stereotypical system that emphasises academic success and is often detached from the local context. On the other hand, a growing number of community schools in urban slums have provided the tools for conviviality, whereby they perform multiple tasks beyond the conventional role. These multiple tasks include but are not limited to offering accommodation and providing meals and clothes for the majority of poor and vulnerable children, meeting the needs of parents and guardians, preparing children for becoming self-reliant individuals after school, reproducing a sense of community and belonging among members, and sustaining the schools by pulling financial resources from diverse stakeholders. As I present in the findings section, their role and functions far exceed what conventional authorised schools can offer.

## 3. Community Schools in Urban Slums of Kenya

Community schools in the urban slums of Nairobi have been operational since the 1970s as non-formal schools (NFSs) for children and adults who are otherwise unable to receive an education (MoE 2009). These schools are owned and managed by individual proprietors, religious organisations, community groups or charitable trusts (Tooley et al. 2008; Ohba 2013). Because such schools initially offered basic literacy and numeracy skills for those without a formal education, they were placed under the authorisation of bodies other than the MoE.[1] An earlier study found that, of twelve schools in Kibera, only four had more than 80 per cent qualified teachers (Ohba 2013: 771). Many schools hire local staff who are un- or underqualified as they are willing to work for fairly low salaries (Ohba 2013).

Although pupils who attended NFSs were able to graduate to formal secondary schools, the new guidelines developed by the MoE in 2009 officially indicated that they should register with the MoE by following the approved national curriculum and meet standards of school setup such as classroom and sanitation facilities.[2] Teachers are required to have a teaching certificate and register with the Teacher Service Commission.[3] Schools are also required to pay registration fees[4] (MoEST 2015). The intention of the MoE was 'to integrate the education and training institutions into the mainstream programme by ensuring that the "non-formal" education sub-sector is included in the national education statistics' (MoEST 2015: 8, original emphasis). For this reason, NFSs were requested to follow the registration criteria; otherwise, they were considered to be 'unregistered' or 'illegal'.

It is noteworthy that despite the registration policy developed by the government, this practice has ceased since 2017, without a sufficient explanation. Anecdotal evidence suggests that the government is concerned about the new Constitution of 2010 and the Basic Education Act No. 14 of 2013, which refer to basic education. In particular, article 43 (1) of the Basic Education Act states that there are only two categories of school: public and private (Republic of Kenya 2013). Thus, it is suggested that the government is unwilling to accept and recognise schools outside these two categories. This means that every school needs to be recognised as a formal school by meeting the regulations and guidelines. This move was further accelerated by an incident where eight pupils died on 23 September, 2019, when a school collapsed due to ill-constructed buildings in a Nairobi slum (Kakah 2019; Misiko et al. 2019). Immediately after the incident, the government ordered closure of some schools for unmet school setup standards. The owners of these schools have taken the government to court as they were forced to close down (Kakah 2019). As will be shown in the findings section, although they may look like they are confronting each other, these institutions are actually dependent on each other.

## 4. Field Study

### 4-1. Description of Mathare

Mathare sub-county in Nairobi was chosen for the study because it is one of the largest slums in the city and there is a proliferation of community schools. During the colonial era, the flood-prone east and south areas of the city centre, including Mathare, were mainly residential areas occupied by Africans and Indians (Muungano Support Trust et al. 2011). The first residents moved to Mathare in the 1920s and the village gradually expanded from the 1930s to the 1950s. Following independence in 1963, the population grew rapidly and the settlement pattern changed. It is estimated that the population of Mathare had reached 30,000 by 1969 (ibid.). This was in part due to the presence of land companies that constructed new housing. Owing to its location near the city and high rents paid by tenants, many companies invested in construction in Mathare,

253

resulting in uncontrolled housing (ibid.). Because these building companies failed to provide land titles and basic services such as drinking water and sanitation, the area has no systematic supply of basic services to date. It is estimated that Mathare had a population of 193,416 in 2009 (Nairobi City County 2014). The government owns part of the land while other areas are privately owned. About 83 per cent of residents are tenants and pay an average of 1,245 Kenyan shillings (12 United States dollars) per month in rent (Muungano Support Trust et al. 2011).

In terms of housing structure, most residential space consists of shacks, isolated or collected in large dwellings. In the latter case, each dwelling consists of six to eight units, a unit being about nine to twelve square meters without windows (Andvig and Barasa 2014). While most units have earthen walls with a corrugated iron sheet for the roof, there are some buildings of two or more storeys made of brick (ibid.). Because these buildings are often rented as community schools, some schools are made of brick and others consist of corrugated iron sheets only. Additionally, there are schools that are constructed with a mixture of earthen walls and corrugated iron sheets, and a very small number that are made of stone. Most of these structures do not have windows so they use electric lighting whenever affordable.

### 4-2. Data Collection

This study was conducted in August 2018, February 2019 and February 2020 for four weeks in total. The study included 21 primary schools – twenty community schools and one public school for comparison. Of the twenty community schools, ten were established and owned by incumbent teacher(s), and one was started by a retired teacher. There were also five schools initiated by community members and three schools established by churches. Only one school was set up by a businessperson. Although each school has its funder(s), managers and headteachers in the study considered their schools as belonging to the community.

In terms of establishment year, while the public school was founded in 1973, only four community schools started in the 1990s and the rest were established after 2000. This may be a result of greater numbers of migrants and growing demand for learning institutions near residential areas. In addition, the introduction of universal free primary education in 2003 seems to have had some influence on the prevalence of community schools (Tooley et al. 2008). The study interviewed school managers (or headteachers in the case of absence) on the reason for school establishment, the role and functions of the school, and some challenges.

## 5. Findings

### 5-1. Role and Functions of the Community School

Community schools are considered complementary to government schools (Rose 2009b). However, in-depth interviews with managers and headteachers clarified that their schools went much further to support their pupils. The following interview extracts reveal the way they operate in the community:

> As I told you, this is a faith-based school whereby we have some well-wishers from the church. Some church members become a guardian and financially support them. Actually, food at this school is provided by the church. So, those who stay at our dormitory – sixteen boys and twelve girls – take breakfast, lunch and dinner here. They need to feel like their parents are around. Those pupils who commute daily get porridge in the morning. We also have pupils who come from very poor families. Such pupils also take dinner with boarding pupils here. We give them free meals. This is one of our missions. We feed this village (Manager, School 8).

> And we also give them clothes. Church members bring their clothes from home and we give them to our pupils. ... So we are providing children shelter, food and clothes (Headteacher, School 8).

The above quotations clarify what schools actually offer community children. They provide not only learning opportunities but basic needs such as shelter, meals and clothes. This was echoed by managers and headteachers in other schools. When I asked why some schools with poor performance were still in demand, one school manager explained as follows:

> Now, you also need to look at the dynamics of our communities. There are ways of life. For some parents, schools including public are often expensive as they charge for lunch and exams. So, such parents have to find a school where they can afford payment. So, even when schools perform poorly, as long as parents are able to afford and their children are provided with lunch and learning, then parents take the child to that school. So, performance is one important aspect but not an absolute condition for surviving (Manager, School 1).

Another manager argued that the school is not merely a place for academic achievement:

> Basically, you have to look at [things] holistically. This child may not be talented academically but do well in other areas ... If we look at performance only, then we may bring up children who cannot do anything apart from academics. But we are concerned about life after school. They have to fit into our community. A child cannot fit into this community just by passing exams. The child needs to be disciplined and know how to socialise with other community fellows and create [his or her] own job. So, school is not all about performance (Manager, School 6).

These interview extracts present the ways that the schools serve children in this community. As several managers emphasised, without these schools, tens of thousands of children in Mathare would have nowhere to learn and some would have to go without proper meals and clothes. Although these schools are considered to be unauthorised, what they offer goes beyond the normal role of a school and they provide children with the opportunity to learn and socialise with their fellow children. As pointed out by the interviewees, it is apparent that performance is just one aspect of schooling; however, what community schools offer demonstrates the actual needs of local children. For schools to be inclusive for all children, these needs must be fulfilled.

## 5-2. Networking, Negotiation and Interdependence

Schools in Mathare are under negotiation with the government for official registration; otherwise, they are considered to be illegal, a position that all interviewees under study clearly stated was not what they wanted. While most schools are unable to meet the basic standards set for school registration, they try hard to meet as many standards as possible. The following interview extract exemplifies their efforts and dilemmas as well as how they negotiate with the government.

> And now the government … says, 'We appreciate you are there. We understand you are doing a great job for our kids. We are going to register you in the same status as other schools so long as you meet some criteria'. Then she told us: 'Can you have two-thirds of your teachers trained?' Some of us did. 'Can you have toilets?' We got them. 'Can you have the [recommended] ratio of desks to pupils?' We got the ratio of one to two or one to three. 'Can you have your classroom conducive [to learning]?' We tried as much as possible. 'Can you have running water with tanks?' Almost all schools did. So, we worked on a number of things the government raised and prepared towards registration only to find that those guidelines had not yet been signed by the then Cabinet Secretary to help our registration process! So, many of us were lobbying around. Our network chairman was on TV several times asking why the guidelines had not been signed. Whose fault is this? Is it us? Is it our kids? It's the government! She needs to come strongly to sign the guidelines and allow us to officially register (Manager, School 5).

As demonstrated in the above interview extract, I found great efforts had been made by the schools under study to meet the guidelines. For example, most schools had water tanks and electricity. All schools had at least two to three latrines for each sex, although this is one of the most commonly unmet criteria, as the guidelines recommend one latrine for every 30 learners. The total number of pupils in each school ranged from a minimum of 107 to a maximum of 878. Most schools thus had insufficient latrines according to the guidelines. However, it can be said that each school worked on what they could address within the limited environment and conditions.

Another standard required by the government is facility setup. As described in Section 4-1, while most schools are made of corrugated iron sheets and/or bricks, a very few schools are made of stone. The former building structure is particularly weak and unstable. This concern was urgently raised after eight pupils died on 23 September, 2019, when a school collapsed due to ill-constructed buildings (Misiko et al. 2019). Following this incident, government officials visited several slums and directed some schools to close down:

> Last year, many schools were closed down by the government but our school was acknowledged as a good school because we support needy children. The government staff came and found what we were offering. They accepted ... that if our school were closed down, children would suffer without a home to stay and food to eat. So they recommended our school and that's why we are still here (Headteacher, School 8).

This story is interesting as it illustrates how complex the situation is. On the one hand, the government stopped the registration process and most community schools, including School 8, remain unregistered. However, on the other hand, the government actually acknowledged and appreciated their efforts to provide what it could not supply for the local children. This clearly presents a dilemma for the government, in setting standards and jeopardising the presence of community schools on paper while actually showing its appreciation. While government double standards are the cause of this dilemma, because neither institution can completely meet the diverse needs of local children, this situation actually gives rise a growing number of community schools in Mathare. Thus, through their versatility and flexibility, the community schools actually provide the tools for conviviality.

## 5-3. Interrelationship and Reproduction

Throughout the field study, in relation to why individuals opened a school when income is unstable and running a school without funding is a considerable risk, one particular phrase reappeared among interviewees: '*kurudisha mkono*'. In Swahili, '*ku*' is a prefix to form infinitives or gerunds. The verb '*rudisha*' literally means 'repay' and the noun '*mkono*' means 'hand'. When these words are put together, it means to repay or return a favour, implying reciprocal goodwill. Although it has a flipside and is also used to describe unjust and corrupt practices, the cases found in this study represent the former. In fact, managers and headteachers echoed the spirit of paying back to the community. This concept of *kurudisha mkono* is deeply imbedded in everyday Kenyan life. I asked the interviewees why they thought of starting or supporting a school. The following interview excerpts illustrate how the founders arrived at the initiative:

I was born and raised here at Mabatini [community in Mathare Valley]. So, when I was attending school, I could see how other kids were doing without going to school. When I finished my college, I was recruited as a teacher by a school in another county. But I used to come back every weekend to see my mum. I had a passion in my heart to support these kids but I couldn't do it because I didn't know how to begin. So, I kept working as a teacher for five years. But in 2013, I made my mind [up]. … I returned and talked to many people such as village elders and pastors in this community about the need to establish a school. … After engaging with them, they were able to negotiate with the owner of this building and he was willing to rent us some rooms. … That's how I have started my school (Manager, School 9).

They [former pupils] have seen how we supported them. They feel, 'I want to support someone such as the school the way this school supported me'. So this is how the circle goes. We have some teachers who finished this school and are now back with us to teach our pupils or to financially support us (Manager, School 8).

I was supported by my teacher to finish secondary school. So if you

259

look at such experience, you feel you need to give back to the community. I need to hold someone's hands somewhere. That's why some of us are here. We want to give something back to the community and we also want to see a child progresses [sic] through your hands (Headteacher, School 13).

This local concept and practice represent the value of community and how people are related to each other. Most teachers teaching in the community schools are residents of Mathare and share similar experiences. This interrelationship is spread not only among these schools but also among community members through intergenerational networks. These vertical and horizontal interrelations are imbedded in Kenyan society and sustain learning opportunities for vulnerable children. Thus, as pointed out by Illich (1971), although the conventional education system may reproduce social inequality, the community schools offer tools for conviviality and function as a safety net to redress existing inequalities. I will further discuss this in the next section.

## 6. Discussion

The findings of this study show how the community school functions not only as a learning institution but as a shelter and a source of food. Some learners also get clothes and study at no cost. It also reveals that some teachers are graduates of the school who returned to pay back what they received through the school. In addition, the study shows the extent to which these schools are in negotiation with the government. Thus, their versatility and flexibility to adjust to local needs, on the one hand, and their perseverance in working with the authorities, on the other, are central to the survival for what Nyamnjoh (2017a) refers to as 'frontier Africans', and have provided the tools for conviviality.

Illich states that a convivial society 'should be designed to allow all its members the most autonomous action by means of tools least controlled by others' (1973: 20). In reality, however, there is not a single country where the government does not intervene in basic

260

education. Article 28 of the Convention on the Rights of the Child, which is ratified by 196 parties, states that it is the duty of the government to ensure free and compulsory primary education for every child (United Nations 1989). This means it is unavoidable that governments intervene in the primary education sector. Having said that, the role and functions of community schools recorded in this study clearly demonstrate the extent of their capacities and practices beyond acting as a mere learning institution. On the one hand, they are controlled by the government with respect to school curriculum and standards for school operation, while on the other they actually practise their versatility and flexibility by responding to local needs. Such needs include but are not limited to providing shelter, food and clothes. Often, free meals are provided for needy children. Moreover, many schools allow poor children to study at no cost. Thus, the relationship with the authorities is not necessarily mutually exclusive. Rather, they compensate for respective incompleteness and this is how the presence of and negotiation with the authorities reproduce the community school.

Because of the versatility and flexibility of the community schools, the findings also reveal that schooling reproduces interrelationships among community members. This is because some teachers who have grown up in the community are willing to repay the benefit they received from the community. There is a strong sense of community that is deeply rooted in African culture. The philosophy of reciprocal benevolence imbedded in the community is what local people call *kurudisha mkono* – to repay or return a favour. Thus, while a school may actually and negatively function as a reproduction of inequality (Illich 1971), as learners attending community schools come mostly from poor families, they also reproduce the tools for conviviality and strong interrelationships within community members. Findings from the present study reveal that community schools in cosmopolitan urban slums function as the tools for conviviality, which reproduces a sense of community belonging through everyday school experiences.

Community schools are also interconnected as they must negotiate with the government if they are to be recognised. As shown in this chapter, it is imperative for them to be recognised because they will otherwise be regarded as illegal institutions. This dichotomy between authorised and unauthorised, which is rooted in ontological and epistemological positions of the West, continues through labelling the latter institution an inappropriate and incongruent entity. Assié-Lumumba (2016: 15) notes that '[t]he colonial philosophy and goals led to methods that created a binary and hierarchical system, which severely undermined Africans' struggle for equality'. In relation to the dichotomy, Matsuda (2020) mentions that the binary opposition between the African and the Western constitutes two sides of the same coin that can no longer stand independently as they are already part of African society. Thus, as shown in this chapter, unrecognised community schools actually demonstrate their full capability by meeting the diverse needs of local children while also negotiating with the authorities for recognition. If schools are to meet the diverse needs of cosmopolitan urban inhabitants who come from different backgrounds, community schools are imperative for creating an inclusive learning environment.

As highlighted by Nyamnjoh (2017a, 2017b), the above situation shows the incompleteness of each side and the extent of negotiation required to reach a compromise between them. Neither the government nor the community school offer a complete solution to the problem of providing learning opportunities for vulnerable children. Thus, each has to work together instead of negating the other. It is crucial for the government to make mutual concessions as it is apparent that tens of thousands of children would be left without learning opportunities if there were no community schools. The study also shows how important it is for conventional schools to be as flexible as possible to meet different needs. The actions of the community schools show their potential and strength with regard to collective action and their flexibility in meeting local needs. For this reason, these schools have provided their pupils with the tools for conviviality. These actions are imbedded in traditions, and are often routes taken by African communities, as has been discussed in other fields (see Matsuda 2017 for community policing). I earlier referred to Rodríguez (2020) to explain the Spanish term *convivencia* and, similarly, the present study also reveals that conviviality actually entails mutual respect and caring about living together in the Kenyan context.

## 7. Conclusions

This study explored how community schools function to bridge the gap between the Kenyan education system focused on academic performance, on the one hand, and local needs for learning and surviving in the cosmopolitan urban slums of Nairobi, on the other. The findings revealed that, despite the fact that these schools are unrecognised by the government, because they have not met standard criteria for school setup, they offer what the government schools cannot. This includes giving vulnerable children a place to stay, eat and obtain clothes at no cost, demonstrating that the community school is not merely a place for academic achievement. If there were no such schools, tens of thousands of children would have no place to learn, resulting in the creation of a yet more unjust and unequal society between the haves and have nots. Because of the existence of these schools, children are at least able to continue learning. The study also explored the interrelationships among the schools as well as the community members. The fact that the intergenerational relationships actually function as a safety net to support many vulnerable children demonstrates that community schools provide the tools for conviviality.

In addition, the study revealed how these vulnerable schools are interconnected with each other to form a network for negotiation with the government. In fact, the government is faced with a dilemma. While the government sets standards and jeopardises the presence of community schools on paper, it has actually stated its appreciation for the work of community schools in supporting vulnerable children. This illustrates the incompleteness of each position and the imperative interdependence between them. While the study does not necessarily support the present education system, as it reproduces learning gaps between the rich and the poor, what it does support is the role and function of community schools and their provision for local children. As global society converges toward a schooled society and mobility is further accelerated, a conventional education system is unavoidable. However, we must critically examine the role and function of contemporary schools and the extent of their relevance to the local context. We also need to support learning opportunities for poor and vulnerable children. Thus, recognising the presence of community schools and supporting these institutions are what the government actually needs to address, as community schools have significant capacities and potential to reduce further socioeconomic inequality, beyond acting as a learning institution.

### Endnotes

[1] In the 1980s and 1990s, NFSs were placed under the Ministry of Culture and Social Services. After the presidential election in 2002, this was reformed as the Ministry of Gender, Sports, Culture and Social Services. With a new government in 2007, it was restructured again as the Ministry of Gender, Children and Social Development.

[2] The education office checks the school setup and environment, for instance, the distance to the nearest school and the sustainability of the site. Primary schools in urban areas should have a minimum of 0.5 acres of land and a minimum classroom size of 8 metres × 6 metres for 40 pupils. The public health office scrutinises the sanitation of the environment such as the number of latrines according to enrolment. The ratio is one per 30 learners (except during initial school setup).

[3] All teachers, including the headteacher and manager in a primary school, should have a P1 qualification, which can be obtained from a teacher training college.

[4] While public schools pay 1,000 Kenyan shillings (10 United States Dollars) for provisional and re-registration, private schools pay 10,000 Kenyan shillings (100 United States dollars) for provisional registration and 5,000 Kenyan shillings (50 United States dollars) for re- or full registration. Religious-based schools pay 4,000 Kenyan shillings (40 United States dollars) (MoE 2011). Exchange rate utilised in this chapter: 100 Kenyan shillings is equal to 1 United States dollar.

## Acknowledgement

This work was supported by JSPS KAKENHI Grant Number JP16H06318.

## References

Akaguri, L. (2011) *Quality of low-fee private schools for the rural poor: perception or reality? Evidence from Southern Ghana, CREATE Pathways to Access Research Monograph No. 69*, Falmer: University of Sussex.

————— (2014) 'Fee-free public or low-fee private basic education in rural Ghana: How does the cost influence the choice of the poor?', *Compare*, Vol. 44, No. 2, pp. 140–61.

Alcott, B. and Rose, P. (2016) 'Does private schooling narrow wealth inequalities in learning outcomes? Evidence from East Africa', *Oxford Review of Education*, Vol. 42, Issue 5, pp. 495–510.

Amjad, R. and MacLeod, G. (2014) 'Academic effectiveness of private, public and private-public partnership schools in Pakistan', *International Journal of Educational Development*, Vol. 37, pp. 22–31.

Andvig, J. C. and Barasa, T. (2014) *A Political Economy of Slum Spaces: Mathare Valley, NUPI Working Paper 838*, Oslo: Norwegian Institute of International Affairs.

Assié-Lumumba, N. T. (2016) 'Evolving African attitudes to European education: Resistance, pervert effects of the single system paradox, and the Ubuntu framework for renewal', *International Review of Education*, Vol. 62, pp. 11–27.

Cameron, S. (2011) 'Whether and where to enrol? Choosing a primary school in the slums of urban Dhaka, Bangladesh', *International Journal of Educational Development*, Vol. 31, Issue 4, pp. 357–66.

Dixon, P. (2004) 'The regulation of private schools serving low-income families in Hyderabad, India: An Austrian economic perspective', *Economic Affairs*, Vol. 24, No. 4, pp. 31–6.

Dixon, P., Tooley, J. and Schagen, I. (2013) 'The relative quality of private and public schools for low-income families living in slums of Nairobi, Kenya', in P. Srivastava (ed.) *Low-Fee Private Schooling: Aggravating Equity or Mitigating Disadvantage?*, Oxford: Symposium Books, pp. 83–103.

Gebre, Y., Ohta, I. and Matsuda, M. (2017) 'Introduction: Achieving peace and coexistence through African Potentials', in Y. Gebre, I. Ohta and M. Matsuda (eds) *African Virtues in the Pursuit of Conviviality: Exploring Local Solutions in Light of Global Prescriptions*, Bamenda: Langaa RPCIG, pp. 3–37.

Gilroy, P. (2004). *Postcolonial Melancholia*, New York: Columbia University Press.

Härmä, J. (2011) 'Low cost private schooling in India: Is it pro poor and equitable?', *International Journal of Educational Development*, Vol. 31, Issue 4, pp. 350–56.

Heyneman, S. P. and Stern, J. M. B. (2014) 'Low cost private schools for the poor: What public policy is appropriate?', *International Journal of Educational Development*, Vol. 35, pp. 3–15.

Illich, I. (1971) *Deschooling Society*, Harmondsworth: Penguin Books.

———— (1973) *Tools for Conviviality*, London/New York: Marion Boyars.

Kakah, M. (2019) 'Owners of informal schools sue State over "illegal" forced shutdowns', *Daily Nation*, 8 October 2019 (https://nation.africa/kenya/news/owners-of-informal-schools-sue-state-over-illegal-forced-shutdowns-211414) (accessed: 4 July 2020).

Lauglo, J. (2004) *Basic Education in Areas Targeted for EFA in Kenya: ASAL Districts and Urban Informal Settlements*, a consultancy report prepared for the Ministry of Education, Science and Technology in collaboration with the Nairobi office of the World Bank.

Mamdani, M. (1996) *Citizen and Subject: Contemporary Africa and the Legacy of Late Colonialism*, London: James Currey.

Matsuda, M. (2017) 'Everyday knowledge and practices to prevent conflict: how community policing is domesticated in contemporary Kenya', in Y. Gebre, I. Ohta and M. Matsuda (eds) *African Virtues in the Pursuit of Conviviality: Exploring Local Solutions in Light of Global Prescriptions*, Bamenda: Langaa RPCIG, pp. 275–308.

———— (2020) 'Conclusion: Creativity, collectivity and conviviality: Towards African Potentials', in Y. Ofosu-Kusi and M. Matsuda (eds) *The Challenge of African Potentials: Conviviality, Informality and Futurity*, Bamenda: Langaa RPCIG, pp. 229–54.

MoE (Ministry of Education) (2009) *Policy for Alternative Provision of Basic Education and Training*, Nairobi: Government Printer.

———— (2011) *Basic Standard Requirements for Registration of Educational and Training Institutions in the Ministry of Education*, Nairobi: Government Printer.

MoEST (Ministry of Education, Science and Technology) (2015) *Registration Guidelines for Alternative Provision of Basic Education and Training (APBET)*, Nairobi: Government Printer.

Misiko, H., Wako, A., Kahongeh, J., Kabale, N. and Okeyo, V. (2019) '7 pupils die after classroom collapses in Nairobi school', *Daily Nation*, 23 September 2019 (https://nation.africa/kenya/counties/nairobi/7-pupils-die-after-classroom-collapses-in-nairobi-school-206450) (accessed: 13 May 2020).

Muungano Support Trust, Slum Dwellers International, University of Nairobi, University of California, Berkeley (2011) *Mathare Valley in Nairobi, Kenya, 2011 Collaborating Upgrading Plan* (http://healthycities.berkeley.edu/uploads/1/2/6/1/12619988/matharevalley_report_ucb_2_25_2012_final.pdf) (accessed: 1 August 2019).

Nairobi City County (2014) *Nairobi County Integrated Development Plan 2014*, Nairobi: Government Printer.

Nyamnjoh, F. B. (2012) 'Potted plants in greenhouses: A critical reflection on the resilience of colonial education in Africa', *Journal of Asian and African Studies*, Vol. 47, Issue 2, pp. 129–54.

———— (2013) 'From quibbles to substance: A response to responses', *Africa Spectrum*, Vol. 48, No. 2, pp. 127–39.

———— (2017a) 'Incompleteness: Frontier Africa and the currency of conviviality', *Journal of Asian and African Studies*, Vol. 52, Issue 3, pp. 253–70.

———— (2017b) 'Incompleteness and conviviality: A reflection on international research collaboration from an African perspective', in Y. Gebre, I. Ohta and M. Matsuda (eds) *African Virtues in the Pursuit of Conviviality: Exploring Local Solutions in Light of Global Prescriptions*, Bamenda: Langaa RPCIG, pp. 339–78.

————— (2019a) 'Amos Tutuola as a quest hero for endogenous Africa: Actively anglicising the Yoruba language and yorubanising the English language', keynote address, *2019 SAALT and SAALS Conference on Indigenous Languages in Contemporary African Societies*, 30 June–4 July, 2019, University of Pretoria.

————— (2019b) 'Decolonising the academy: A case for convivial scholarship', keynote address, *Conference on Africa and the Academy in the 21st Century*, 1–2 November 2019, Basel, Switzerland.

Nyamnjoh, F. B. and Brudvig, I. (2014a) 'Conviviality and negotiations with belonging in urban Africa', in E. Isin and P. Nyers (eds) *The Routledge Handbook of Global Citizenship Studies*, Routledge: London and New York, pp. 217–29.

————— (2014b) 'Conviviality and the boundaries of citizenship in urban Africa', in S. Parnell and S. Oldfield (eds) *The Routledge Handbook on Cities of the Global South*, Routledge: London and New York, pp. 341–55.

Ohba, A. (2013) 'Do low-cost private school leavers in the informal settlement have a good chance of admission to a government secondary school? A study from Kibera in Kenya', *Compare*, Vol. 43, Issue 6, pp. 763–82.

Oketch, M., Mutisya, M., Ngware, M., Ezeh, A. C. and Epari, C. (2010a) 'Why are there proportionately more poor pupils enrolled in non-state schools in urban Kenya in spite of FPE policy?', *International Journal of Educational Development*, Vol. 30, Issue 1, pp. 23–32.

————— (2010b) 'Free primary education policy and pupil school mobility in urban Kenya', *International Journal of Educational Research*, Vol. 49, Issue 6, pp. 173–83.

Open Schools Kenya (2020) website (http://openschoolskenya.org/) (accessed: 3 April 2020).

Republic of Kenya (2013) *Basic Education Act No.14 of 2013*, Nairobi: Government Printer.

Rodríguez, E. G. (2020) 'Creolising conviviality: Thinking relational ontology and decolonial ethics through Ivan Illich and Edouard Glissant', in O. Hemer, M. P. Frykman and P.-M. Ristilammi (eds) *Conviviality at the Crossroads: The Poetics and Politics of Everyday Encounters*, Cham: Palgrave Macmillan, pp. 105–24.

Rose, P. (2009a) 'Non-state provision of education: Evidence from Africa and Asia', *Compare*, Vol. 39, Issue 2, pp. 127–34.

——————— (2009b) 'NGO provision of basic education: Alternative or complementary service delivery to support access to the excluded?', *Compare*, Vol. 39, Issue 2, pp. 219–33.

Srivastava, P. (ed) (2013) *Low-Fee Private Schooling: Aggravating Equity or Mitigating Disadvantage?*, Oxford: Symposium Books.

Srivastava, P. and Walford, G. (eds) (2007) *Private Schooling in Less Economically Developed Countries: Asian and African Perspectives*, Oxford: Symposium Books.

Tooley, J. (2017) 'Low-cost private schools: What we need to know, do know, and their relevance for education and development', in S. McGrath and Q. Gu (eds) *Routledge Handbook of International Education and Development*, London and New York: Routledge, pp. 227–40.

Tooley, J. and Dixon, P. (2005) *Private Education is Good for the Poor*, Washington DC: Cato Institute.

Tooley, J., Dixon, P. and Stanfield, J. (2008) 'Impact of free primary education in Kenya: A case study of private schools in Kibera', *Educational Management Administration and Leadership*, Vol. 36, Issue 4, pp. 449–69.

Tooley, J., Dixon, P., Shamsan, Y. and Schagen, I. (2010) 'The relative quality and cost-effectiveness of private and public schools for low-income families: A case study in a developing country', *School Effectiveness and School Improvement*, Vol. 21, Issue 2, pp. 117–44.

United Nations (1989) *Convention on the Rights of the Child*, General Assembly resolution 44/25, United Nations, 20 November 1989.

Wise, A. and Noble, G. (2016) 'Convivialities: An orientation', *Journal of Intercultural Studies*, Vol. 37, Issue 5, pp. 423–31.

# Chapter 9

## Examining International Aid and Community Self-Help Initiatives from a Conviviality Perspective: Unrecognised Low-Fee Private Schools in a Slum Area of Nairobi, Kenya

*Nobuhide Sawamura*

## 1. Introduction

This chapter examines the relationship between international aid and self-help initiatives undertaken by the local population from a conviviality perspective and aims at understanding the dynamics between donors and recipients on the ground. Although the reason and the necessity for international development and cooperation on the country level have been studied extensively, the focus has been on international cooperation based on bilateral relationships between countries or multilateral organisations' interests. Individual dynamics have been neglected and conviviality, the main point of discussion in this chapter, was not an important issue.[1]

Much developmental aid is provided on the premise that people in developing countries lack the proper knowledge and appropriate technology, and do not make the necessary efforts to tackle their own problems. Traditional technical cooperation often underestimates the capabilities of local communities because aid organisations rarely spend sufficient time with beneficiaries to understand their circumstances fully. In light of such shortcomings, NGOs with strong on-the-ground collaborative activities are increasingly becoming major players in community-based programmes.

This study aims at rethinking the relationship between international aid and self-help initiatives led by the local population by investigating two unrecognised low-fee private schools, 'School A' and 'School B', both of which are located in the Kibera slum of

Nairobi, Kenya. It observes the formation and operation of these schools and a series of negative events prompted by international aid.

School A was opened in 2009 by C's own initiative. It started to receive aid from an American NGO two years later, allowing for financial stability, the construction of new school buildings, and the enrolment of more students. C was then suddenly accused by the NGO of funds misappropriation and was removed from the school.

Only two weeks after C was dismissed, he found another place to rent and started a new school, School B. The school's expenses exceeded its income, bringing it to the brink of a serious deficit. School fees constituted the majority of School B's income, but only 20 per cent of students paid their tuition, with most not paying in full. Despite the critical situation, C did not seem particularly concerned. He filled teaching roles with younger friends from the slum who had graduated from secondary school, though they were not regularly paid. Why did they behave in such a manner? The situation could have been understandable had the school been run by a foreign charitable enterprise, but that was not the case.

I met C for the first time in 2014 after an introduction by a student's mother. He was 32 years old at the time (born in 1982). He went to a school in the slum until grade four and then moved to the Western Region near Lake Victoria where his grandmother lived. It was there that he graduated from secondary school in 2002. He said, 'life was hard' and to raise money for school fees, he had to wake up very early in the morning and help in the field before going to school. He had only one school uniform and one pair of shoes. Starting in 2004, he worked nights at a security company while going to a community development college for two years in Nairobi, graduating in 2006. He also worked at a printing company, but inspired by the situation in the slum, he decided to work for the community and in 2008, he joined a community organisation to which he devoted his life. While pursuing this career and gaining experience, he decided to start and run a school after seeing so many children without educational opportunities.

In light of the school's financial instability, I did not initially believe C's story. The key to understanding it, however, appears to lie in 'conviviality', a concept that was strongly advocated by Ivan Illich decades ago and, more recently, by Francis Nyamnjoh.

Fieldwork was carried out from February 2015 to March 2020 for at least one week per year. Adding to semi-structured interviews with teachers (largely involving C), questionnaire surveys were conducted with teachers and sixth and seventh-grade students to collect their views on fellow students and teachers and the living environment in Kibera.

This study presents the case of two schools, to gain a deeper understanding of the steady rise in the popularity and role of low-fee private schools in Kenya. I first detail the circumstances surrounding the opening of School A, its financial situation, and the background of its teachers and students, followed by the events that led to the founding of School B, its financial situation, and the strategies used to hire its teachers. This observation is then used to understand the reasons for operating such schools from the perspective of conviviality.

## 2. The Boom of Low-Fee Private Schools

### 2-1. Low-Fee Private Schools That Support Formal Education

The Kenyan Government enthusiastically worked towards achieving the universalisation of primary education by 2015, one of the UN Millennium Development Goals (MDGs). Lacking the necessary financial means to achieve this goal meant that the government had to rely on international aid, with many aid agencies willing to assist.

In recent years, Kenya experienced a tremendous increase in the number of private schools – at a rate far higher than public schools (Table 1). The majority of private schools are small and, while public schools are tuition-free, private schools are not. Many parents, even from low-income households, nevertheless chose to send their children to private schools. One reason is the large class sizes at public schools, especially in urban areas that often reach up to 100 students or more. Another is that, while public schools do not explicitly charge school fees per se, they nonetheless impose charges under other labels, such as payments for Parent Teacher Association (PTA) teachers and remedial classes. Given that low-fee private schools often perform better than public schools and take good care of their students, many households choose private schools after judging the costs and benefits. The popularity of private schools seems to stem from the strong emphasis Kenyan culture places on academic records. For instance, getting good marks at the Kenya Certificate of Primary Education (KCPE) is necessary for entering a good secondary school that will then afford a greater chance of being accepted to the best higher education institutions.

**Table 1. The number of primary schools in Kenya (2014-2018)**

| Year | 2014 | 2015 | 2016 | 2017 | 2018 |
|---|---|---|---|---|---|
| Public | 21,718 | 22,414 | 22,939 | 23,584 | 24,241 |
| | | (3.2) | (2.3) | (2.8) | (2.8) |
| Private | 7,742 | 8,919 | 10,263 | 11,858 | 13,669 |
| | | (15.2) | (15.1) | (15.5) | (15.3) |
| Total | 29,460 | 31,333 | 33,202 | 35,442 | 37,910 |
| | | (6.4) | (6.0) | (6.7) | (7.0) |

Note: the increase for each year is shown in brackets (%)
Source: KNBS (2019: 225)

Much of the literature points to the existence of low-fee private schools and the role they play in developing countries such as India, Ghana, or Nigeria (e.g. Tooley and Dixon 2005; Srivastava (ed.) 2013). These studies show that, in addition to their great contribution to the attainment of universal primary education, those schools have better educational performance than public schools. This implies they do not necessarily provide low-quality education to the poor.

Schools A and B are unrecognised schools that do not appear in government statistical data. Since private schools are booming, their numbers would be much higher if they were included in the government database. The discrepancy shown in the next section suggests that there is a significant number of such schools in urban areas like Nairobi. Why is this the case? The government is not promoting the construction of private schools, and the pursuit of profit alone does not explain the tremendous increase in the number of private schools.

## 2-2. Unrecognised Private Schools in the Urban Area

Two types of primary school enrolment data are collected in Kenya. The first is based on the Educational Management Information System (EMIS), a census conducted by the Ministry of Education at the school level. The second is based on the Demographic and Health Survey (DHS), which is a household sample survey. A comparison of the two databases, that were expected to be similar, produced very different figures. While there is no significant difference in the average at the country level, EMIS shows fifteen percentage points lower enrolment than DHS for Nairobi County (Table 2). Moreover, a comparison of the NER (Net Enrolment Ratio) between Nairobi County and the country average shows that Nairobi County is ten percentage points lower in EMIS and seven percentage points higher in DHS. The EMIS data are often inflated because schools tend to report higher numbers to take advantage of capitation grants, but the figure for Nairobi County is the other way around.

**Table 2. Comparison of primary school enrolment ratios between EMIS and DHS data (in %, for the year 2014)**

| Area | | EMIS | | | DHS | | |
|------|------|------|--------|-------|------|--------|-------|
|      |      | Male | Female | Total | Male | Female | Total |
| Nairobi | NER | 77.7 | 77.9 | 77.8 | 92.3 | 93.2 | 92.8 |
|         | GER | 84.3 | 83.7 | 84.0 | 105.7 | 101.2 | 103.3 |
| Country | NER | 90.0 | 86.4 | 88.2 | 84.8 | 86.7 | 85.7 |
| average | GER | 105.6 | 101.4 | 103.5 | 109.2 | 105.5 | 107.3 |

Notes: EMIS data are from the Ministry of Education. DHS data are from the Bureau of Statistics. NER stands for Net Enrolment Ratio. GER stands for Gross Enrolment Ratio and is the number of students enrolled in a given level of education, regardless of age, expressed as a percentage of the population in the relevant official age group. Therefore, the value of GER can exceed 100%, while that of NER cannot.
Source: MoEST (2015); KNBS et al. (2015)

The reason for such a discrepancy is rooted in the large number of children enrolled in unrecognised private schools. For instance, when household surveys ask about enrolment, whether a school is recognised does not matter to the investigator or the family being surveyed. On the other hand, only recognised schools that are formally registered are included in the Ministry of Education surveys. As a consequence, the government rarely counts children who are enrolled in unrecognised schools.

### 2-3. Unrecognised Private Schools in the Kibera Slum

It is estimated that 60 per cent of Nairobi's population (roughly 2 to 3 million people) live in slums or informal settlements that occupy as little as six per cent of Nairobi's total area. Of the ten slums in the city, Kibera has the largest population of half a million. It is said to be the largest urban slum in Africa. No substantial data or relevant information on the number or situation of schools in Kibera were available at the Nairobi County Education Office. But they know that there are many of them.

Data produced by the NGO Map Kibera Trust helped to fill this gap. The NGO spent nine months, from August 2014 to April 2015, investigating schools in the Kibera slum (Map Kibera Trust 2015). According to their database, there are 335 schools (144 preschools, 147 primary schools, 31 secondary schools, and 13 vocational schools) in Kibera (including the private property area), 81 per cent of which are recorded as unrecognised schools (ibid.).[2] There are 29,047 children enrolled in primary schools in the Kibera area, of which 13,056 go to public schools around the slum. In looking at the map, I identified 92 schools inside the slum out of the 147 primary schools in Kibera at large.

The characteristics of, and comparisons between, public and private schools in Kibera based on the Map Kibera Trust database are summarised in Table 3. It shows that there are twelve times more private schools than public schools. Private schools are significantly smaller than public schools, with ten times fewer students and more than four times fewer teachers. The student-teacher ratio is 2.4 times greater at public schools than private schools. Female teachers are predominant, with a more striking difference at public schools. More than half the students (55 per cent) are enrolled at private schools. No gender difference is found in students at either type of school.

**Table 3. Comparison between public and private primary schools in the Kibera area**

|  | School category | |
|---|---|---|
|  | Public | Private |
| Number of schools | 11 | 136 |
| Total number of students | 13,056 | 15,991 |
| Male | 6,418 | 7,831 |
| Female | 6,638 | 8,160 |
| Number of students per school | 1,187 | 118 |
| Total number of teachers | 274 | 791 |
| Male | 52 | 314 |
| Female | 222 | 477 |
| Number of teachers per school | 24.9 | 5.8 |
| Number of students per teacher | 47.7 | 20.2 |

Source: Calculated from Map Kibera Trust (2015) data

Around half of all school children are enrolled at private schools. The student-teacher ratio at private schools is smaller than at public schools, which could indicate high-quality teaching and learning. A study on the comparison of test scores between private schools in the slum and surrounding public schools shows that private schools are performing better than public schools in Kiswahili and Mathematics, and conversely in English (Dixon et al. 2013).

Even after the promotion of free primary education in 2003, parents are enthusiastically choosing unrecognised private schools (Oketch et al. 2012). Academic performance and expenses are more important factors than government recognition in influencing school choice (Ohba 2011). In other words, unrecognised schools do not necessarily provide low-quality education for the poor.[3]

## 3. The Establishment and Operation of School A

### 3-1. Establishment and Financial Situations

School A started in 2009 when C acted on his own initiative. He took care of 30 children (5 males and 25 females) in difficult circumstances such as street children. The number of students from preschool (3 years old) to grade two reached 182 in 2011. They rented a small workroom or a hall depending on the number of children, then moved to a newly constructed building with six classrooms and a kitchen in 2012 after meeting members of an American NGO while playing football with the children and subsequently receiving funding from them. In 2014, a second building was constructed 50 metres away from the first one. It had four classrooms, a staff room, a headteacher's office and a storeroom. By 2015, the school had seven grades and a total of 341 enrolled students (171 males and 170 females).

The school collected 500 shillings (approximately USD 5) per month in tuition fees, which was mainly allocated to teacher salaries and food for the students. But in 2015, only 100 out of the 340 students paid in full, and about 80 students did not pay at all. Assuming a fee of 250 shillings per student, the school only collected around 90,000 shillings in tuition for the year. In addition to the 60,000 shillings per month provided by the NGO for teacher salaries, their total income for the year was around 150,000 shillings. With eighteen total employees (13 teachers and 5 non-teaching staff members including a social worker, a nurse, and a cook) earning 6,000 shillings per month, the school's expenditures totalled 108,000 shillings per month, not accounting for the monthly 90,000 shillings for school lunches.

### 3-2. Teachers and Students

As of September 2018, School A had a total of fifteen teachers (six males and nine females), all from the Kibera slum. Excluding a 58-year-old female teacher, their average age was 29. Four were born in the slum and the others moved there between 2005 and 2016 at around 15 to 35 years of age. Six graduated from Teacher Training College (TTC) and nine finished only secondary school. Despite living in the same slum, the teachers had a 20 to 40-minute commute. All belonged to one of two predominant ethnic groups in the area, Luo or Luhya.

According to the questionnaire survey conducted in September 2018, there were three primary motivations for the teachers to work at the school: (1) The importance of taking the responsibility of teaching to the children, (2) The unity among the staff and the cooperation between them, (3) Stable and regular income. Interviews with the teachers readily revealed their strong sense of responsibility and deep sympathy for the children. They asserted the need for perseverance. Such a strong relationship is uncommon at many public schools and can be attributed to the fact that they experience the same life in the same community as the children. One of the teachers stated that 'teachers are also encouraged by the students.' They know the families of their students and the difficult circumstances they face, and teachers personally get involved in their lives. Some teachers even give food or money to the families. Many teachers believe that students can be role models for their families, and that if students can change for the good through their schooling experience, then their families can also change.

Despite the apparent pride in what they were doing, most of the teachers had left School A by March 2020. Only the headteacher and two additional teachers remained. As stated by a female teacher who moved from School A to School B, many teachers left the school because the new headteacher, who succeeded C, started to keep secrets and was not trustworthy. She said that a good salary is not the only reason teachers choose their workplace; relationships with other teachers, as well as mutual trust, are also important. Another female teacher stressed that she left because a new Sister who managed the school started to command the teachers.

Most students live with their parents and siblings in a household of six to eight people in one room, most of the time separated only with curtains or plywood boards. Most said that what they dislike the most about Kibera is the unpleasant environment such as sewage and garbage. Conflict, fighting, theft, and crammed shanty houses were also problems for students. On the other hand, most of them pointed out the conveniences of living in the slum. They said that there are schools, clinics and churches, and that they have access to electricity and clean water. They also emphasised mutual help and the thriving economic activity owing to the large number of shops.

During the investigation in September 2015, interviews were conducted with all of the seventh-grade students (8 males and 11 females) in School A. Most of the students spend 20 to 30 minutes to commute to school. Besides the good quality of education in terms of test results, teachers and infrastructure, the children tended to choose School A mostly because they are the relatives of the teachers. More than 90 per cent of them are Luo or Luhya as are the teachers. It is worth mentioning that almost all of the children affirm to be proud of the quality of the teachers and enjoy learning. For those children, being a good teacher is so simple: come every day and teach properly.

## 4. The Founding Process and Management of School B

### 4-1. Removal from School A and Establishment of School B

School A showed steady development from the local population's self-help initiative. Both teachers and students from the same community worked hand-in-hand to enhance their school, making it attractive for NGOs because they could see the short-term impact of their aid. As a result, full-fledged support began in 2012, with solid school facilities built in concrete. The number of students increased, teachers' salaries could be paid on a regular basis, and the management of the school was stable. As a founder, C was satisfied, as were other teachers. This prosperous honeymoon period continued for four years but ended suddenly. On 4 January 2016 (at the beginning of the first term), C was locked out of the school after being accused of fraud by a staff member of the NGO. According to C, the accuser was corrupt, and observing C's behaviour to date seems to indicate that he was right.[4]

On 18 January, only two weeks after being fired, C established and opened School B, just 500 metres away from School A. C was able to attract 33 new students to School B in addition to twelve seventh-grade students (two males and ten females) who trusted him to move from School A to School B. The initial size of 45 students soon increased to 60 by September 2016 and 80 as of March 2017.

Despite a rent increase from 5,000 to 8,000 shillings, School B moved to a better place near the main road in January 2018. The new location allowed them to have up to 126 students. Judging from the number of students, the school seemed to be functioning well, but the collection of tuition fees was again a critical issue. For example, in May 2018, only a small part of the tuition fees was collected and a look at the cashbook showed that only 27 students (21 per cent) paid tuition. The number of students then decreased to 81 in March 2020, which was likely to be due to the government's announcement that children should not attend unrecognised schools. On the students' side, family breakdowns and conflict between families are prevailing. Many parents do not or cannot properly take care of their children, and in one instance, an eighth-grade female student did not see her mother for two months, forcing her to bounce from one friend's house to another.

### 4-2. Finances and Teacher Recruitment

In March 2017, School B said that its total monthly income was about 6,000 to 7,000 shillings (about 60 to 70 USD). With 80 students each paying 500 shillings per month in tuition fees, the school should have collected 40,000 shillings. With rent alone costing 5,000 shillings per month, this meant that their expenditures would largely exceed their income. As a result, neither rent nor teachers' salaries had been paid since January of that year. How could the school survive under such conditions? The limited income made it difficult to provide the children with lunch. C did not seem to have the financial resources to sustain the school by himself. How did he manage to keep the school running?

Teachers not receiving their salary regularly could be a reason. Commonly, one would move to another job or stop working if the salary is not paid. It certainly looks like a volunteer activity since they are energetically working together for the school. For the landlord, however late the rent is, it is difficult to request strict payment. They all seem to share common values that bind them to protect and educate the children in the area.

By September 2018, there were four teachers (two males and two females) apart from C. They were all between 20 and 30 years old and finished secondary school but did not go to TTC. Three of them started teaching in January 2017. With the low pay, only two of the four teachers (both male) remained as of March 2020. Neither appeared to be dissatisfied with their small salaries. When asked about their livelihood, one of them (25 years old) said he worked as a waiter and sometimes as a cook at a restaurant in town at night to earn an additional 7,000 shillings per month. He said that if he worked full-time at the same restaurant, he would earn 15,000 shillings, but he wanted to continue working as a teacher. The other (27 years old) cleaned offices for about one or two hours during the day to earn an additional 3,500 shillings per month.

When asked why he worked as a teacher even though the salary was low and not regularly paid, the first teacher said that he stayed because of the good relationship between the teachers and C was a reliable person and a role model who often encourages him and gives him advice. He added that he was proud to bring his contribution however small it is because he felt profound gratitude towards C who supported him when he went to secondary school. Moreover, since he struggled as a child, he wants to help children the best he can. He said that with money, he could surely help people but since he had nothing but his knowledge, he wanted to help contribute to children's education by being a teacher.

Despite its extremely low income, School B hired two new teachers in January 2020. Both were friends of C and had just finished secondary school in 2019. They were suggested to work at School B because there were no other jobs at the time. When asked why they hired new teachers despite their financial situation, C responded that the more teachers there are, the more lively the school is, which is positive for the school. The two new teachers did not seem to expect much of a salary but wanted to contribute to the development of the community. During a staff meeting, C encouraged them to 'just continue the same spirit.' As he says, 'schools are for children, for teachers, and for communities.'

## 5. Understanding School Management: Insights from Conviviality

### 5-1. The Advantages of Being an Unrecognised School in the Slum

Although the particulars of the schools examined in this study cannot lead to generalisations, it is nonetheless the case that unrecognised private schools in Kenyan slums have distinct ways of management and operation that are not seen in public schools. Analysing the features of these types of schools leads to the following four conclusions.

First, schools in slums are often established by local people who live there. People mobilise to build schools and autonomously run them in places where the government's provision of education does not reach. Living in the same area allows teachers and children to develop strong mutual trust. Flexible school management is possible owing to the lack of complicated administrative procedures and the ability of teachers to work regardless of qualifications.

Second, it is possible to manage schools in a way that considers the poorest of the poor. For instance, School B sometimes receives children who cannot continue their education elsewhere because they cannot pay tuition fees. Although School B urges parents to pay, rarely will it use lack of payment as a reason to prevent children from attending school. The school easily gives up on collecting money, simply rationalising that they do not have it. This kind of tolerance and sympathy for those who do not pay can be understood as a guarantee of education opportunities.

Third, schools serve as platforms to help their communities. At School A, for instance, each teacher tries to establish a connection with the families of their students. C said that 'providing quality education to ten children entails changing ten families' lives.' Some teachers even provide food for households experiencing serious difficulties. Mutual help happens on a daily basis when poor people support one another. Such schools foster connections and social safety nets to support the most vulnerable.

Finally, teachers who live in the same community as the children they teach feel a strong sense of duty that strengthens their willingness to work. Feelings of solidarity and trust are especially strong among teachers who live close to one another, both physically and mentally. This is one of the reasons why teachers continue working despite their meagre salaries. They cherish their relationships with other teachers, appreciate the teamwork, and are proud of the sense of unity. Compared to public schools, these teachers appreciate the importance of what they do and also understand the benefits they themselves receive. This is one of the reasons why quality education is being provided despite the harsh environment in the slum.

## 5-2. School Management from a Conviviality Perspective

I believed that C was sympathetic to children who could not afford to pay tuition fees because of his sense of solidarity owing to them living in the same community. But the lens of conviviality may offer an even deeper understanding. Nyamnjoh asserts that people are interdependent and that, by working as a group instead of pursuing their own profits, they place a priority on conviviality. He expresses this interdependence as follows:

> Acknowledgement and appreciation should be reserved and room created for excellence, especially for individuals who demonstrate how well they are ready to engage with collective interests. Individuals who refuse to use their endowments towards enhancing their community are most likely to be denied the public space to articulate their personal desires, and, like Cinderella, find themselves dependent on external agents and muses, or confined to singing their little songs in their little corners: 'In my own little corners in my little chair I can be whatever I want to be' (Nyamnjoh 2002: 116).

Such a perspective allows us to understand C's insistence on running a school in the same slum in which he resides, despite his own difficulties. C leads the school but also relies on the support of other teachers. People in the slum live in a close relationship with others who share the same difficulties, which makes it easy to understand why they do not forcibly urge parents to pay tuition fees.

On the other hand, the following statement from Illich about individuals' interdependence and freedom accords with Nyamnjoh's: 'I consider conviviality to be individual freedom realised in personal interdependence and, as such, an intrinsic ethical value. I believe that, in any society, as conviviality is reduced below a certain level, no amount of industrial productivity can effectively satisfy the needs it creates among society's members' (Illich 1973: 11).

The idea that the disappearance of conviviality from society makes it harder for the individual's desires to be satisfied is also linked to what Nyamnjoh terms 'incompleteness'. Education, which is an 'intangible commodity', is part of what Illich calls 'tools' (Illich 1973: 20).

Illich's famous work, *Deschooling Society* (originally published in 1970), is critical of institutionalised education that follows the progress of industrial societies. He refers to the *Tools for Conviviality* in the following passage: 'Not only has the redefinition of learning as schooling made schools seem necessary. It has also compounded the poverty of the unschooled with discrimination against the uneducated' (Illich 1973: 19), and 'A convivial society does not exclude all schools. It does exclude a school system which has been perverted into a compulsory tool, denying privileges to the dropout' (ibid.: 24).

However, Illich was critical of schools institutionalised to be places for children to 'be taught and made learn'. Indeed, test scores are of critical importance, and children who do not have education through schooling are discriminated against and labelled as uneducated. In other words, it is exactly because of the existence of such rigid school systems that people with the same convictions as C establish and continue to run schools in slums. Of course, not all behaviours can be explained by conviviality, as there are also advantages to living in the slum, for example, the unlawfulness of land ownership that makes rent cheaper along with people's strong sense of unity and solidarity as a community. Unrecognised schools can be shaped by the will of those building them since they exist outside the purview of the government's regulations, standards and administrative procedures.

### 5-3. Incompleteness and Interdependence

I personally support School B by providing funds (which are negligible compared to what NGOs generally provide). We have never exchanged documents stipulating the use of my financial support.[5] C uses the funds appropriately, taking into consideration my intention as an aid provider. The money is usually spent on urgent items, such as rent and food. Despite not being asked for proof, C typically sends photos of the items and the corresponding receipts. Just before the start of each school term, he sends an email expressing appreciation for the support received thus far and asking for further assistance with new needs.[6] Thanks to the internet, it is possible to connect whenever it is needed.

There was a time when our ideas completely diverged on the issue of sustainable funding. In the aid community, projects are started on the premise that assistance will end in the near future. As a result, ownership of a project is essential, and aid providers are concerned about their sustainability. When I asked C about his plan to develop School B autonomously and sustainably, he answered: 'Of course, I understand. I will continue to rely on you.' For C, the sustainability of relationships matters most. When asked about the difference between me and other supporters, C replied: 'You come every year but the others, they never come again.' This was an unexpected response from the perspective of regular international aid. I was at first surprised by C's intention to continue relying on my financial support; however, in a society that positively perceives interdependence with others, interconnections among people are not only unavoidable but preferred.[7] If we think there is an independent individual at the very centre of deep interdependence with others, it becomes possible to understand C's reaction. Conviviality appears to help one make a living, however difficult, which could be a foundation for resilience.

Nyamnjoh suggests that, as an individual is an incomplete being, there are infinite possibilities. He describes 'Frontier Africa' as the

286

African characteristics of having flexible viewpoints on identity and a sense of belonging. Speaking of the possibilities arising out of interdependence, he says that, 'Myriad interconnections, inextricable entanglements and creative interdependencies, despite persistent hierarchies at global and local levels, afford Africans the opportunities to explore the fullness of their potentialities without unduly confining themselves with exclusionary identities' (Nyamnjoh 2017: 259).

International aid without sustainable development is problematic. However, if a society has the values described by Nyamnjoh, along with Illich's ethical values, continuously receiving aid can be understood as a form of interdependence and, therefore, not to be criticised and considered negative. Interdependence is always a rationale for aid policies, however, interdependence in this sense refers to the dependence of a developing country on a developed country's resources, not interdependence between people. Sustainability and interdependence in a convivial society appear to be different from what is seen in an aid-linked society.

Nevertheless, the potential of African people to demonstrate conviviality stems from the incapacity of governments to respond to the growing disparity between the rich and the poor. An unjust and unfair society is itself a problem, so we are cautioned not to overestimate conviviality in African societies. If African governments could provide a welfare system, such as social security, and guarantee the protection of a minimum livelihood, pecuniary interdependence would be significantly lower than it currently is.

In the following excerpt, Nyamnjoh himself expresses conviviality in a more explicit way:

Conviviality is recognition and provision for the fact or reality of being incomplete. If incompleteness is the normal order of things, natural or otherwise, conviviality invites us to celebrate and preserve incompleteness and mitigate the delusions of grandeur that come with ambitions and claims of completeness. Not only does conviviality encourage us to recognise our own incompleteness, it challenges us to be open-minded and open-ended in our claims and articulations of identities, being and belongings. Conviviality encourages us to reach out, encounter and explore ways of enhancing or complementing ourselves with the added possibilities of potency brought our way by the incompleteness of others (human, natural, superhuman and supernatural alike), never as a ploy to becoming complete (an extravagant illusion ultimately), but to make us more efficacious in our relationships and sociality (Nyamnjoh 2017: 262).

Since each individual is an incomplete being, they move towards conviviality through interdependence with others. There is no such thing as a complete human being, making it possible to achieve deep relationships with others. Motoji Matsuda, one of the pioneers of anthropological studies in Nairobi slums, summarises Nyamnjoh's arguments as follows:

> Once one believes in one's 'completeness', intolerance and attack towards anything else are justified as the duty of justice to 'save those who lag behind'. On the other hand, African societies consider themselves as 'incomplete beings' and do not reject others who are equally 'incomplete'. Instead, they depend on one another and hold the key to imagining a conviviality driven system. Nyamnjoh pointed out that, by connecting the incomplete being with others, mingling them and complementing one another, the strength for conviviality lies in the heart of African cultural potentiality (Matsuda 2016: 16, translated by the author).

## 6. Conclusion

The reasons for building schools, and for teachers working hard despite earning small salaries, is intimately linked to schools being built inside the slums. Teachers are motivated by a sense of duty to contribute to their communities by supporting the children who live in these harsh environments. A school is a place where they can positively affirm their existence and play a key role in their community as educated people. The emotional proximity between teachers and students in the unrecognised private schools of the slums is rarely seen in public schools, particularly in urban areas. While it is not possible to teach at a public school without proper qualifications, at unrecognised private schools, it is. Young secondary school graduates who become teachers at these private schools not only influence children's growth but also contribute to the development of their communities. Building trust, which is difficult in the slums, can boost the self-esteem of teachers, making both students and teachers the mutual beneficiaries of unrecognised private schools.

What happens when a big donor gets involved where conviviality is part of people's everyday life? Accepting the assistance of a donor means following the organisation's principles and reasonably losing one's autonomy. When the 'incomplete' beneficiary and the 'complete' donor work together, a master-servant relationship emerges rather than one of interdependence. Even if having ownership by a recipient is encouraged on paper, the recipient cannot be equal to the donor. Therefore, new possibilities suggested by Nyamnjoh become likely impossible to achieve.

Five years have passed since the establishment of School B and its operation without international aid. While C hopes to find donors and realises their importance, he also understands the problematic nature of this kind of relationship and the difficulty to come to a common understanding of the value of 'being connected'. What they need is faith in their mission and being trusted for the implementation of the projects.

My support for School B is feasible when done on an individual level but impossible when it comes to organised entities such as NGOs, for whom it is unthinkable to entrust fund management to the recipient alone. Unlike dealing with public funds, where accountability is a major issue, providing support on a personal level with a small amount of funding requires nothing more than a certain level of mutual trust. The primary reason I decided to support School B was the respect for C and the other teachers,[8] but these kinds of subjective personal emotions and judgments cannot be influencing factors for government aid agencies that must ensure transparency. With today's growing internet access making long-lasting relationships of mutual trust possible between individuals across international borders, human, rather than institutional ties may enable conviviality to become the mainstream for international development and cooperation in the future.

**Endnotes**

[1] Nowadays, development presupposes 'human-centred development' or 'human security'. With such concepts first appearing around the 1990s, development never truly considered 'humanity' until that particular period.

[2] Government recognition is not necessarily bestowed by the Ministry of Education. Recognition sometimes comes from other ministries not as education institutions but under other labels. For example, more than 90 per cent of the 92 low-fee private primary schools in the slum are likely to be unrecognised by the Ministry of Education.

[3] Unrecognised schools received harsh criticism in the 2017/2018 Global Education Monitoring Report (UNESCO 2017), which stated that they were unaccountable and in urgent need of government regulation. It is perhaps a fair argument under normal circumstances, but the expansion of regulation when the government cannot guarantee access to quality education is of concern and may generate outcomes that are not in line with the intended purpose.

[4] Corruption is not uncommon in Kenya and exists across different levels of government and in private organisations. For instance, C said that half of the NGOs working in the Kibera slum only exist on the internet to make money and do not engage in on-the-ground activities. Schools are a common place for such fraud and are becoming 'hustling points'. NGOs use people, and when you are no longer needed, 'you are dumped'. During my fieldwork in March 2020, an international NGO visited School B and proposed to get involved with a project that offered mentoring for young girls. According to C, the NGO randomly wrote names on a list to inflate the numbers and receive extra funds to keep for themselves. It is clear that people have an awareness of how corruption plays out in their everyday lives.

[5] My desire to provide support to C and School B comes from my

experience working in a Japanese government aid agency from the mid-1980s to mid-1990s (from the age of 26 to 37). It was a world where even a small project required hundreds of thousands of USD. We worked hard to make effective and efficient use of funds, but almost none of the aid we provided showed a direct impact on the poorest people. In contrast, the one thousand USD I provide annually to C covers one year's rent and serves 100 children in school. Reflecting on my experience in the past made me realise that such a contribution is far more efficient and effective than any kind of governmental aid, even if the impact is limited to a small number of people.

6 It is also common for people in difficult circumstances to use cell phones (smartphones) as an important means of communication. No maintenance cost is incurred, and prepaid cards are used to pay only what is needed, when it is needed. Transactions such as remittance, withdrawal, savings, and even loans are possible.

7 There are many studies on the relationship between lenders and borrowers (or gift-exchange), particularly in anthropology. Matsumura (2017) offered insightful observations and analyses on the ethical values emerging among aid-givers by means of 'guilty feelings'. However, this chapter takes the perspective of aid-receivers, not aid-givers. In this regard, C does not say anything about aid or assistance but, instead, speaks in terms of support or help. He took the lead in receiving my support in accordance with their actual needs. I helped him out of respect for his commitment to working on behalf of the community, not from an ethical consideration arising out of disparities.

8 Osaka University started a Doctoral Program for Multicultural Innovation in 2012 with the goals of enhancing multicultural understanding and changing society for the better. As the program is primarily aimed at nurturing competencies out of respect for others, they use the acronym RESPECT (Revitalising and Enriching Society through Pluralism, Equity, and Cultural Transformation).

## Acknowledgements

This work was supported by JSPS KAKENHI Grant Numbers JP16H06318 and JP19H00620.

# References

Dixon, P., Tooley, J. and Schagen, I. (2013) 'The relative quality of private and public schools for low-income families living in slums of Nairobi, Kenya', in P. Srivastava (ed.) *Low-Fee Private Schooling: Aggravating Equity or Mitigating Disadvantage?*, Oxford: Symposium Books, pp. 83–103.

Illich, I. (1973) *Tools for Conviviality*, London: Marion Boyars Publishers.

KNBS (2019) *Economic Survey 2019*, Nairobi: Kenya National Bureau of Statistics (KNBS).

KNBS, Ministry of Health, National AIDS Control Council, Kenya Medical Research Institute, National Council for Population and Development and ICF International (2015) *Kenya Demographic and Health Survey 2014*, Nairobi: Kenya National Bureau of Statistics (KNBS).

Map Kibera Trust (2015) *Kibera Schools Map* (http://openschoolskenya.org) (accessed on 1 May 2020).

Matsuda, M. (2016) 'The social and cultural characteristics of "African Potentials"', in M. Matsuda and M. Hirano-Nomoto (eds) *Cultural Creativity for Conflict Resolution and Coexistence: African Potentials as Practice of Incompleteness and Bricolage*, Kyoto: Kyoto University Press, pp. 1–28 (in Japanese).

Matsumura, K. (2017) *Anthropology of Guilty Feelings*, Tokyo: Mishimasha (in Japanese).

MoEST (2015) *2014 Basic Education Statistical Booklet*, Nairobi: Ministry of Education, Science and Technology (MoEST).

Nyamnjoh, F. B. (2002) 'A child is one person's only in the womb: Domestication, agency and subjectivity in the Cameroonian grassfields', in R. Werbner (ed.) *Postcolonial Subjectivities in Africa*, London: Zed Press, pp. 111–138.

——————— (2017) 'Incompleteness: Frontier Africa and the currency of conviviality', *Journal of Asian and African Studies*, No. 52, Issue 3, pp. 253–270.

Ohba, A. (2011) 'A comparison of low-fee private primary schools in relation to school choice: A slum case study in Nairobi, Kenya',

*Journal of International Cooperation in Education,* Vol. 14, No. 1, pp. 15–28 (in Japanese with English abstract).

Oketch, M., Mustiya, M. and Sagwe, J. (2012) 'Do poverty dynamics explain the shift to an informal private schooling system in the wake of free public primary education in Nairobi slums?', *London Review of Education,* Vol. 10, No. 1, pp. 3–17.

Srivastava, P. (ed.) (2013) *Low-Fee Private Schooling: Aggravating Equity or Mitigating Disadvantage?,* Oxford: Symposium Books.

Tooley, J. and Dixon, P. (2005) *Private Education is Good for the Poor: A Study of Private Schools Serving the Poor in Low-Income Countries,* Washington DC: Cato Institute.

UNESCO (2017) *Global Education Monitoring Report Summary 2017/18: Accountability in Education: Meeting Our Commitments,* Paris: UNESCO.

# Part IV

# Knowledge Acquisition as a

# Subjective Process

# Investigating Mathematical Activities in Zambian Children's Play from the Perspective of Mathematics Education

*Nagisa Nakawa*

## 1. Introduction

As a mathematics educator, I believe that every culture has developed its own mathematical activities. For instance, in Africa, people knit a basket with straw, they measure beans, sugar or powder using a same-sized tin in the market or draw geometrical figures on the ground. These unique culturally embedded mathematical activities have been intensively discussed in the field of ethnomathematics in mathematics education (D'Ambrosio 2016). The concept of ethnomathematics and its development has been useful for developing mathematics education curriculum. The concept of ethnomathematics was proposed in 1980s and developed further by D'Ambrosio, a Brazilian mathematic educator, in the field of mathematics education research. It is fundamentally a broad research programme (Rosa and Gavarrete 2017) holding philosophical and theoretical orientations for curriculum development as well as development of teaching and learning materials in a practical way. The background of ethnomathematics is well explained by Rosa and Gavarrete (2017): 'Our own culture and society considerably influences the way in which we understand mathematical ideas, procedures, and practices' (3–4). Thus, ethnomathematics respects the unique mathematical activities seen in different parts of the world and helps in using these mathematical activities for children's learning of mathematics in school. According to the principles of ethnomathematics, each child has a unique understanding of mathematical phenomena, being influenced by the environment and other people culturally and socially. Over the last three decades, studies on ethnomathematics have developed broadly. For instance, Carraher et al. (1985) showed that Brazilian children's performance in computing problems related to daily-life situations was better than the ones they were asked at school. This implies that the degree of children's understanding of mathematics is heavily dependent on the context. Recent discussions in ethnomathematics have centred on languages, pedagogy, classroom applications, cross-cultural situations and theoretical bases (e.g., Rosa et al. (eds) 2017).

In this chapter, investigating children's play can be a good starting point to consider ethnomathematical curriculum development, because play occurs in a natural setting in children's lives and hence probably influences their mathematical skills. Thus, the chapter seeks for harmonisation between children's knowledge, experiences and skills in daily-life situations and their learning at school. Considering the case of Zambia, young children engage in various types of play that can be used for school education, but not much academic research has been done on this aspect, particularly from the standpoint of mathematics education. Therefore, this chapter aims to bridge this gap by contributing to the discussion from a cultural perspective related to ethnomathematics in developing effective mathematics education for African children.

There have been African studies emphasising how children's play outside school offers informal and meaningful learning, which can also be connected to formal learning (e.g., Mukela 2013; Nkopodi and Mosimege 2009). In Zambia, several studies have examined children's play from the perspective of anthropology and education (e.g., Mukela 2013; Mtonga 2012); the current chapter adopts a similar methodology to collect data. Furthermore, new attempts can be added to the academic accumulations from a mathematical perspective. The chapter, therefore, aims at examining Zambian children's play, the types of play they engage in as well as the characteristics of these games from the perspective of mathematics education. Particularly, I seek to shed light on cultural discussions, such as those developed by Alan Bishop on universal activities. The research question addressed here is twofold: (1) What kinds of play do children engage in? (2) What are the characteristics of these games from the perspective of mathematics?

## 2. Key Conceptual Terms

### 2-1. Ubuntu and the Cultural Perspective of Mathematics Education

Various perspectives of education that embrace African values, beliefs and cultural components have been recently discussed in relation to the concept of ubuntu (Assié-Lumumba 2016; Brock-Utne 2016). Brock-Utne (2016) connects the ubuntu paradigm with education focusing on curriculum, language of instruction and assessment, and explaining that the concept of ubuntu is an African worldview, rooted in the character of African life. Odora (1994) is concerned about the inappropriateness of the Western style of education for African children, mentioning that while Western children do acquire various kinds of knowledge and skills at school, they tend to focus less on 'our' and 'we', which are at the core of the concept of ubuntu. The concept of ubuntu as a philosophy could be applied in education in a broader sense (Makalela 2015; Brock-Utne 2016), particularly in curriculum development and pedagogy for African mathematics education. Ubuntu can embrace the development of cultural perspectives in the field of mathematics education, including ethnomathematics, because, as Odora (1994) and other scholars of Africa insist, it contains the African worldview. Nyamnjoh (2019) adds that it espouses a deep allegiance to the collective identity, including deep rootedness in the community. This idea, which starts from a person's actions and thinking in a context, has the same foundation of discussion in ethnomathematics. The concept supporting the ethnomathematical viewpoint can start from African children's actions and characteristics, their so-called children's play, while the current curriculum is much influenced by Westernised mathematics education. The need for a cultural perspective stemmed from a critical view of the Western-centric contents of school mathematics (D'ambrosio 1985, 1998, 2016). The curriculum in non-Western countries is relatively similar to the so-called Eurocentric mathematics curriculum, but local children often have difficulty understanding the context of the school mathematics curriculum in relation to its relevance. To overcome this challenge, ethnomathematics, a field that developed in the 1980s, connected multiple mathematical activities with uniquely rich contexts from different socio-cultural perspectives, such as drawing pictures in sand and designing baskets, buying and selling in a market, and the geometrical patterns in the coloured textiles in African contexts (e.g., Huylebrouck 2019; Eglash 2007; Zaslavsky 1999). This is an opportunity to reconsider school mathematics in the context of school education by questioning its validity for children from varying socio-cultural backgrounds. Zaslavsky's renowned book, *Africa Counts* (1999), explains and discusses numerous African art and crafts related to geometry, measurement methods, playing and the number counting system. The book attempts to identify the role of mathematics in a range of groups, areas and nations. Types of children's play are also included as culturally unique activities that are symbolic of mathematics. In this chapter, observational data from children's games are collected first; the chapter draws inspiration from anthropological studies such as Mtonga (2012). The procedure will be explained in detail later. The investigations from the standpoint of mathematical education are also connected to the heart of ethnomathematics. Part of Bishop's discussion in *Mathematical Enculturation* (1997) is closely connected to the development of ethnomathematics. Bishop's noteworthy contributions to mathematics education include the collection of not only various mathematical phenomena and actions in different parts of the world, including Africa, but also universal mathematical activities found in any place that has developed on inhabitation by humans. In this chapter, I modify and apply Bishop's universal activities to the investigation of children's play.

## 2-2. African Children's Play and Education

Several studies have touched on children's play (including games) and its importance (Nyota and Mapara 2008; Serpell 1993), with some connecting play and games to education, particularly pedagogy in subjects such as music (Kekana 2016; Dzansi 2004) and mathematics (Nkopodi and Mosimege 2009; Tatira et al. 2012) considering cases in the sub-Saharan African countries. South African studies have shown that education received at school is not well connected to children's daily lives (Nkopodi and Mosimege 2009; Tatira et al. 2012). In these discussions, implementing play is considered a possible way for children to understand subjects, connecting them to their culture and communities (Tatira et al. 2012; Nyota and Mapara 2008). In South Africa, Nkopodi and Mosimege (2009) introduced an indigenous game into a mathematics class for better pedagogy. Tatira et al. (2012) also explore 31 cultural games in South Africa to connect them to pedagogy in mathematics education. Some of the games mentioned in the South African cases are also observed in Zambia (Tatira et al. 2012; Mukela 2013). In music education, Dzansi (2004) compares the differences in music performances observed in class and the community, and conclude that the degree of children's participation is very different in both: in the community, children were free and confident. Kirkby (1992) states that play can help children learn mathematical knowledge and skills.

## 2-3. Zambian Children's Play and Cognition

Serpell (1993) describes the rich folk traditions of games, riddles, and songs among the children of the Chewa people in Zambia. Children play and engage in multiple activities, such as 'hide and seek', reasoning games, complicated sand painting games and so on. He defines intelligence as a competency in specific situations and the ability to deal with social responsibilities (as in the case of rural Zambia), which is related to the development of children's non-cognitive and social skills. In describing children's play in the Eastern Province of Zambia, Mtonga (2012) collected more than 150 games and discussed child development education and schooling. He also mentioned the counting systems of two ethnic languages in Zambia. From the perspective of music education, Mukela (2013) studied the role of indigenous music and play in promoting cognitive development in Zambian children. Mukela (2013) also mentions perceived cognitive attributes, such as concentration, speed and accuracy, and perceived social processes, such as cooperation and socialisation, in children's play leading to non-cognitive skill development during play. In childhood education, Kalinde (2016) focused on cultural play songs and found that play song activities could be connected to an effective pedagogy at that stage of learning. Traditional games are also linked to physical education (Sport in Action 2004). Recently, Takagi (2018) compared children playing in an urban area of the Southern Province and a rural area in the Central Province in Zambia. She finds that children in the urban area are more engaged with their smart phones or preferred watching television together while children in the rural area used locally available resources such as stones, wires and bottle caps to make up their own play. Children in rural areas were found to be good at discovering things around them, thus proving the decline in opportunities for children in urban areas to experience indigenous knowledge and skills. These studies show not only the types of games children played and how they had a positive impact on their informal learning, but also their applications in formal educational settings. A cross-sectional analysis of the relationship between play and mathematics is not discussed in these studies, while a few of the chapters (e.g., Mukela 2013; Mtonga 2012) introduced mathematically related contents in play.

## 3. Method of Analysis

### 3-1. Data Collection
I observed children's play and interactions in my fieldwork and participated in some of their games when I was offered the opportunity. During my fieldwork in March 2019 in Mazabuka, the Southern Province of Zambia, I recorded children's play using a tablet and took memos during and after observing their conversations and play.

### 3-2. Mathematical Activities as an Analytical Lens
I classified children's play by following the structure of the five universal activities related to mathematics, as proposed by Bishop

(1997). Bishop's five universal activities included counting, locating, measuring, designing and explaining. In the original chapter, playing was added to these five activities, thus resulting in six universal activities. These six activities, according to Bishop (1997), interact with each other and are observed in numerous cultures for the advancement of mathematical ideas. In this chapter, I would like to analyse the mathematical properties of each game, because even in play, fundamental mathematical activities may be included explicitly and implicitly. This investigation will be the foundation toward better pedagogy in mathematics education, particularly for early childhood and lower primary education. Table 1 describes five mathematical activities with examples.

Bishop (1997) explains each mathematical activity in detail emphasising several points in his book. First, counting is the most apparent activity with a long history for mathematical development. Locating is related to determining the importance of the spatial environment in the search for universal activities but is less documented compared to counting. Measuring is the third activity and involves comparing, ordering and quantifying objects. Bishop (1997) uses the word 'designing', rather than 'making', because it includes not only the actual properties of things but also the imagined and perceived shapes and the spatial relationships between objects, which is more related to mathematical development. Explaining, the last activity, seems the most significant in the field of mathematics education; It emphasises the experiences around the environment related to abstractions and formalisations. In these activities, people ask 'Why?' rather than 'What?', 'How to?', and so on.

I apply this framework for analysing children's play to identify what kind of mathematical basis each type of play has, rather than focusing on the classification of areas in mathematics, such as number, measurement, geometry and language/logic. This is because the framework respects the cultural aspect more than the classic one, which originally emerged through the development of Western-centred mathematics.

**Table 1. Five universal mathematical activities**

| Mathematical activity | Description | Example |
|---|---|---|
| Counting | • Associated with numbers and objects with numbers | • Different counting systems<br>• Representation of numbers |
| Locating | • Code and symbolise the spatial environment by searching and identifying positions in different geographical locations | • Route-finding<br>• Spatial orientation<br>• Navigation |
| Measuring | • Compare, order, and quantify qualities that are valuable and important | • Units of measurement using hand breadths or a finger<br>• Number words of order (first, second, third, etc.), and the objectification of the quality (e.g. 'heavy', 'heaviest', and 'weight') |
| Designing | • Describe a widespread activity in shaping the environment<br>• Position oneself and other objects within the spatial environment for different purposes in one's life<br>• Transform a part of nature | • To plan/structure/create things such as houses, villages, gardens, fields and cities using natural materials such as wood, clay, or earth<br>• Shapes and patterns |
| Explaining | • Associated with experiencing the environment<br>• Answer complex questions 'Why?'<br>• Focus on relationship concerns and similarities/differences | • Classifications (the same, similar, or different) |

Source: the author, referring to Bishop 1997

## 4. Fieldwork

I interacted with young female students and took part in the play they engaged in outside their homes (Figure 1).

**Figure 1. Research participants: Female students in Mazabuka**

I was in Mazabuka in mid-March 2019. I happened to meet these young girls in my Japanese friend's house. My friend was a JOCV (Japan Overseas Cooperation of Volunteers) - JICA (Japan International Cooperation Agency) volunteer. Children often visited her home and played with her after school. These children belonged to the ethnic group Bemba. They spoke English, Bemba and Nyanja.

In Mazabuka, Tonga is considered an ethnic language, because the Southern Province is called 'Tonga land' as many Tonga live there. Nyanja is spoken widely in Lusaka and its surrounding areas. Mazabuka is also close to the capital, and thus Nyanja is also often used in daily conversations, particularly by the younger generation. The children all live within one compound, close to the biggest sugar company in the sub-Saharan African region, where approximately 2,000 seasonal workers come from different areas of Zambia to work and live. Their living standard is better compared to the compounds of the other townships of Mazabuka because of the company for which they work. Children gather at someone's house after school and spend time together chatting and playing. Girls take care of their smaller siblings and others do household chores after school. When they finish their duties at home, they stroll around, go to the market and sometimes go back to school or to others' houses to play. All the girls were in the 7th grade in primary school and were between ten and fourteen years of age. While participating in the various games and activities with the children, I made continuous observations. All data were video-recorded, and the memos noted and analysed qualitatively.

## 5. Results and Discussion

### 5-1. Children's Games

The following seventeen types of play were observed.[1] I classified these games according to the places where I observed them:

(i)  At home: (1) 'Chiato', (2) 'Pada', (3) 'Fashion', (4) 'Spell your name', (5) 'Go neighbour', (6) 'September', (7) 'My boyfriend gave me an apple', (8) 'Knock, knock, knock' (including 'Bad girl', a similar one), (9) 'Bubble gum' (similar to hiding), (10) 'Lengu lengu' and (11) 'Rubber jump'
(ii)  At church: drums and dances
(iii)  Outside school and in open spaces: (1) 'Tyres and blanco', (2) 'Somersault', (3) 'Wrestling', (4) 'Tug of war', and (5) 'Hide and seek'.

First, the rules and procedures will be explained, and second the classifications of these games from the perspective of five mathematical activities will be discussed. When the lyrics of a song are written in English, it means that the song is sung in English.

306

## 5-2. 'Chiato'

'Chiato' is a popular game in Zambia; people from different places in Zambia and from different generations play this game. The name of the game varies from place to place among the different ethnic groups. Smaller and younger children play 'Chiato' in their free time. They draw a circle on the floor, 20–30 centimetres in diameter and place stones inside the circle. The number of stones varies. The game can be played by many people. The game is also mentioned by Mukela (2013) as 'Muyato' on another research site in the Western Province. Since this is a popular game among all generations, the rules vary from place to place. In Mukela (2013), the game has four types of rules (Mukela 2013: 38); however, in this case, the girls mentioned only one version. In the other study, 'Chiato' was often used and observed in preschool mathematics classrooms (Nakawa 2018). In my observation, as shown in Figure 2, the players, in turn, throw a stone up in the air, and while the stone is in the air, they take another stone from the centre of the circle and move it outside the circle.

**Figure 2. Playing 'Chiato'**

This is repeated until there are no stones in the circle or if a player fails to catch the thrown stone. When every stone is outside the circle, the player throws the stone again and starts to move all the stones back into the circle, one by one, in the same way. When all the stones are moved back to the centre of the circle, the person wins the game. They sometimes extend the game using two stones thrown or two or more stones moved. The changes in rules are left to the group. A variety of rules exist.

### 5-3. 'Pada'

'Pada' is a floor game. This is also a popular game in Zambia. In Figure 3, different rectangles are drawn on the ground, and there is a starting point and an ending point: a house. 'Pada' is called 'Poda' and it is one of the three parts of a big game called 'Kaseko' (Sports in Action 2004). Thus, the name varies in different parts of Zambia.

**Figure 3. A game called 'Pada'**

When a player throws a stone into one of the rooms (rectangles), s/he jumps from one rectangle to another, except the one containing the stone, by hopping on one foot and ending on both feet, depending on how many rectangles are drawn. (There were only one or two rectangles arranged as shown in Figure 2). When the player reaches the house, s/he turns back to the starting point, following the same path within the rectangles. S/he then picks up the stone and comes back to the starting point, after which the stone has to be thrown into the next rectangle, and the same pattern continues until s/he stamps on any of the lines of the rectangles by mistake. Earlier, a tiny piece of wood or bone, instead of a stone, was used. The game can be played by any number of children, and the minimum number of children required for play is two. I observed three children playing together. The number of houses (rectangles) can be extended in another version of the same game.

### 5-4. 'Fashion'

Four to six children can play this game. They form a circle and sing an English song. When the song finishes, they stop and stand still in any pose without moving. The first player to start to move even slightly, loses the game. The loser can be punished by the others, who hit his/her arm with two fingers.

### 5-5. 'Spell Your Name'

Four to six children can play this game. Two children stand opposite each other and clap their hands above their heads and the other two clap their hands below in rhythm with a song sung at a fast pace.

The leader: Spell your name, Love (a girl's name), spell your name, Love (a girl's name).

Love: L, O, V, E, Love. Spell your name, Mapepe, spell your name, Mapepe.

Mapepe: M, A, P, E, P, E, Mapepe. Spell your name, Diana, spell your name, Diana.

Diana: D, I, A, N, A, Diana.

Each child who is pointed out in the song has to spell out his/her name with the rhythm and at the same time continue to clap. 'Name' can be sometimes changed to 'Surname'. The loser is the one who spells the name wrong. There is no punishment if anyone fails. On the other hand, my friend told me that some children who lose can be chased out from the circle when there are too many players.

### 5-6. 'Go Neighbour'

Four to six children can play this game. They form a circle and clap their hands and tap their thighs rhythmically, and sing a song, as below:

Leader of the play: One, two, three, let's go. Go neighbour.
Another girl (1): Pragya (Any girl's name).
Leader of the play: Pragya, who says?
Everyone: Pragya.
Leader of the play: Oh, she says?
Another girl (2): Abi (Any girl's name).
Leader of the play: Oh, she says?
Everyone: Abi.
Leader of the play: Oh, who says? (Continue the song)

As seen, girls' names have to be given out quickly, while singing and clapping their hands and patting their thighs simultaneously. This goes on until one fails to say a name. There is no punishment for the loser.

### 5-7. 'September'

This is similar to 'Knock, knock, knock', but it needs two stones. Five to six children form a circle; two stones are randomly given to two girls, standing facing each other, and the children pass the stone to the neighbour repeatedly. A song with a rhythm like 'Knock, knock knock' is sung: 'One, two, three, let's go. With 'September', I only remember, I only remember <u>from, if you are</u>' (the underlined part was not very clear to catch). At the end of the song, two children are left holding a stone each and they stand with their backs together. When the others say 'The teacher says, one, two, three, four! And do?', the two children move their neck to the right or left. If they move in the same direction, they kiss or hug, and the game is over. There is no punishment, but the last action could be a sort of a soft

310

punishment, because everyone is excited to see them doing it.

### 5-8. 'My Boyfriend Gave Me an Apple'

This can be played by any number of children. The loser in the game is one who makes a mistake in his or her actions during the song. However, there are no strict rules, and it is mostly played for fun. The song goes like this: 'My boyfriend gave me an apple, a rotten one, and my boyfriend gave me a pen, my boyfriend gave me a kiss on my cheek, and I pushed him down the stairs, and I told him to wash the dishes, and I told him to wash the plates, and I told him to wash the baby's bum, and I pushed him down the stairs'. Everyone sings together and when the song finishes, they jump and cross their legs and open them with the next song, 'In 1964, the soldiers are going for the hole. (inaudible) in 1964'. The singing continues until one fails to perform the correct movement. There is no punishment for this either.

### 5-9. 'Knock, Knock, Knock' (Including 'Bad Girl', Which is Similar to This)

This game can be played by four to six children. Players form a circle; both hands are stretched outward with palms facing upward. A stone is passed from the left palm of a player to the right palm of the player next to him or her, and so on while the leader of the play sings 'Knock, knock, knock, who is the policeman, I want to send a letter, so get it from me, and shoot your friend, she or he must die'. The person who has the stone when the song ends will be the shooter and she or he can choose whom to shoot, including themselves, the heaven (the sky), or hell (the ground). The person who is shot is out of the game, and the game continues until only one remains. If the sky is shot, everyone can come back to the game and continue the same again. If the ground is shot, everyone will die, which means the game is over. The song used varies. Another one I heard is 'Bad girl', using the same rule, in which the lyrics are 'Bad girl, bad boy, what are you gonna do? What are you gonna do and it's time for you'. The rhythm and the way to pass the stone are exactly the same as in 'Knock, knock, knock'. There is a similar game called 'Amadamao'.

311

In the arrangement of a circle, between two children with legs forward, the middle one jumps backward instead of clapping hands, while the leader sings a song: 'Amadamao tuzi a amadamao', 'Amadamao tula amadamao' (The words are not very clear). Amadamao is difficult to continue, unlike 'Knock, knock, knock' and 'Bad girl'.

### 5-10. 'Bubble Gum'

This is a game similar to 'Knock, knock, knock', but it continues longer than 'Knock, knock, knock'. A small stone is passed around in the circle in rhythm with the song until the song ends in a question: 'Bubble gum, bubble gum in a dish, how many bubble gums do you eat per day?' The player who has the stone can come up with any number, for instance, 'Ten'. Ten players are counted and the person who is at number ten will have to do whatever the group decides. The decision making is useful in playing as a group. This game can be played when there are many children.

### 5-11. 'Lengu Lengu'

This is a complicated game with hand clapping and dances (Figure 4). This game is popular throughout Zambia (Sport in Action 2004); however, the rules described were different from the ones I observed. Many children can play this game together simultaneously. They form a circle while standing, and sing a song as follows:

Leader of the play: Lengu, lengu, lengu lengu (Clapping hands).
Another girl (1): Lengu.
Leader of the play: Ah lengu (at the end of the word, clapping above the head and bringing the hands down).
Leader of the play: Oh lengu (again clapping above the head and bringing the hands down).
(Continuing the same actions)

Hands are clapped above the head in the rhythm of the song. When one player stops or makes any mistakes of the patterns, the game is stopped. There is no punishment, and it is played just for fun.

**Figure 4. A game called 'Lengu lengu'**

## 5-12. 'Rubber Jump'

This is a popular play among girls. It requires at least three children. Two children stand face-to-face holding lengths of elastic. The third will jump and cross the elastic. The height can be changed and there are various ways to jump.

## 5-13. 'Tyres and Swing'

These games can be discussed together. These are very popular forms of play in school playgrounds and open spaces. At the school where I observed children's play, there were tyres half embedded in the ground. Primary school children stood on them and jumped from one tyre to another. Outside school, near the market by the house where I visited, there were swings (Figure 5). Children were usually found swinging on them after school.

## 5-14. 'Somersaults'

During break at school, children played outside. When they saw a slab or a small hill, they performed acrobatic movements, including

313

'Somersaults'. I have never seen girls perform such actions during my stay in Zambia. Only boys do this. In my observation, grade six boys enjoyed this.

**Figure 5. Children swinging by the market side**

### 5-15. 'Wrestling'

In wrestling, children draw a circle on the ground; two children stand inside the circle and start to push and pull until one is pushed out of the circle. In my observation, sixth-grade boys enjoyed this game, although girls also participate in wrestling.

### 5-16. 'Tug of War'

This involves children standing in two lines facing each other, and the child in the front is held by the ones behind him/her. The first two from each group start pulling each other; there is a line drawn on the ground, which should not be stamped or crossed by either group. The group that gets pulled to the other side of the line loses the game.

### 5-17. 'Hide and Seek'

This is another common game, played even by Japanese children. All children hide while the seeker tries to find them. They determine who is the seeker by singing the song 'Bubble gum' (see 5-10.) and play the game as previously mentioned.

# 6. Classification of the Play from the Perspective of Mathematical Activities

I excluded some of the games for further analysis because they were unrelated to mathematical activities. Considering the rules and procedures of the play, the classification of five mathematical activities is as shown in Table 2.

**Table 2. Analysis of games from the perspective of the five universal mathematical activities**

| Name of play | Five universal mathematical activities | | | | |
| --- | --- | --- | --- | --- | --- |
| | Counting | Locating | Measuring | Designing | Explaining |
| *Chiato* | ✔ | ✔ | | ✔ | ✔ |
| *Pada* | ✔ | ✔ | ✔ | ✔ | |
| Spell your name | ✔ | | | ✔ | |
| Bubble gum (similar one, hiding) | ✔ | | | | ✔ |
| *Lengu lengu* | ✔ | | | ✔ | |
| Rubber jump | | ✔ | ✔ | ✔ | |
| Wrestling | | ✔ | ✔ | ✔ | |
| Tug of war | ✔ | ✔ | | ✔ | |
| Dance-related games: Fashion/Go neighbour/ September/ My boyfriend gave me an apple/Knock, knock, knock/*Lengu Lengu*/Drums and dances | | | | ✔ | ✔ (September) |

(Note: dance-related games are many)

315

## 6-1. Mathematical Structures Related to Universal Mathematical Activities

My observations revealed that the rules of some games and actions required were complicated. Bishop (1997) mentioned that playing itself has a certain structure of mathematics, because games have rules, procedures, tasks and criteria. He admits that the actions of following these formalised and ritualised patterns are similar to mathematics. Thus, 'to play what they know' is already embedded as a mathematical action for children. This is a significant proposition from my data. Here, I would like to analyse the characteristics of the mathematical activity in each of these types of play comprehensively, comparing them to the discussions in Bishop (1997). At the observation level, some of the games do not have any mathematical characteristics, but I included them in case they have implicit mathematical activities, for further development.

### 6-2. Counting

Bishop (1997) showed a variety of counting systems in different regions. For example, in the African context, the belief regarding counting certain objects or numbers was mentioned in his book. In line with this, Mtonga (2012) also introduced children's counting games in ethnic languages spoken by different ethnic groups such as the Chewa and Tumbuka. On the other hand, my observations revealed that counting did not demonstrate Zambian characteristics; rather, as children are educated in school, they counted in English. 'Chiato', compared to the other games, offers more chances for children to count. Although I did not see children counting the stones, they compared the numbers of stones to decide the winner. Furthermore, while playing 'Chiato', they increased the number of stones as it progressed, requiring players to count to confirm. 'Pada' does not explicitly involve counting; in this play, when children make a house, they measure the dimensions of the rectangles that are drawn as they may get tired if the squares are too long. Therefore, counting is indirectly included in 'Pada'. 'Spell your name' also implicitly involves counting. I did not observe children counting during play; however, it can be developed by counting the number of words. 'Bubble gum' explicitly includes counting from one to twenty. Both 'Lengu lengu' and 'Tug of war' do not explicitly involve counting, but can be played by numerous children, and then, children would be involved in counting. During play, players count the number of children participating. Additionally, 'Tug of war' includes counting as children first count the number of participants to divide them equally into two teams. Thus, I did not observe the cultural counting system that is unique to the Zambian context. Zambian children in the target areas are accustomed to using the universal counting system. In summary, a few games explicitly include counting, whereas others include it indirectly.

To sum up, the children's play that I observed had a few specific tendencies in terms of counting. Explicit counting games were not observed, but in their rules and structure, some of the play demonstrates aspects of counting implicitly. Counting is done in English, which is not the same as seen in the literature reviews. This could be because the results were dependent on the site of the data collection. Mazabuka is a small town, but it is close to the capital. The number of English speakers is more here than in towns in the rural areas. Moreover, every child I met went to school; therefore, they were used to counting in English.

### 6-3. Locating

In 'locating', it is crucial to consider the spatial environment. Bishop (1997) mentioned that compared to counting, locating-related activities are less frequently found in different areas; nonetheless, locating is a fundamental activity that may lead children to develop their understanding of mathematics. Locating in the sense of mathematics is related to geometrical notions. 'Chiato' physically requires children to sense where to place the stones, within/outside the circle while playing, which enables children to consider the shape of a circle as well as the boundary of the surrounding space. While throwing a stone in the air, players also perceive the spatial environment. Furthermore, they need to estimate the time taken for the thrown stone to fall, which is related to their spatial thinking. 'Pada' also involves an activity in which a child throws a stone into a rectangle, followed by the child jumping and stepping into each rectangle. These actions require children's ability to perceive two dimensions as well as three dimensions, which is fundamental for understanding space (Bishop 1997). 'Rubber jump', 'Wrestling' and 'Tug of war' are more physical activities than hand-clapping games and include locating activities. In 'Rubber jump', children must estimate the height to be jumped according to the height of, and their distance from, the elastic, and in 'Wrestling' and 'Tug of war', they must determine the distance between a drawn circle and line. These actions are related to measuring.

### 6-4. Measuring

Zaslavsky (1999) discussed the measuring systems used in Egypt, Ethiopia and Swahili-speaking regions, and reported various ways commonly followed in market areas to measure things using parts of the human body. Although measuring is commonly observed in African contexts, few measuring-related games were observed among the ones I collected, as compared to counting. As mentioned before, 'Pada', 'Rubber jump' and 'Wrestling' implicitly included measuring for structures and procedures. In 'Pada', when players construct a house out of boxes that they consider a house, they need to measure the length of the entire house. In 'Rubber jump', when a child jumps, they must determine the relationship between the height of the rubber and the jump, which involves measuring. In wrestling, players need to know the distance between themselves and the boundary of the circle drawn. Therefore, these types of play involve measuring.

### 6-5. Designing

In relation to children's play in her book, Zaslavsky (1999) stated that African music with its dance beats greatly contributed to world art, especially African drumming. I classified children's hand-clapping play, dance-like play, drums and dancing in this category. I inferred that these games are, as mentioned above, implicitly related to measuring, because some games require players to check whether they need to stand up to play, maintaining an appropriate distance from the others. For instance, games such as 'Go neighbour', 'Knock,

knock, knock' and 'Lengu lengu' contain repetitions of body movements and rhythmic dancing in harmony. The actions of moving their bodies as well as singing a song with complexity create sophisticated patterns, which lead children to thinking and operating in the space in three dimensions around them. It is interesting to note that these games for girls do not have actual designed objects like wire toys, one of the common toys for boys in Zambia; instead, the girls shape their environment in the space. They are ephemeral. A few studies also mentioned a similar piece of work in Africa (Huylebrouck 2019; Zaslavsky 1999), and Bishop (1997) stated that designing activities in Africa revealed many geometrical properties. In my observations, this was applicable only in 'Pada'. The play explicitly includes the aspect of designing in preparation for the play. The players need to design and draw a house on the ground, which is significant as the players will be stamping on each rectangle within a house. Thus, 'Pada' involves the designing of two-dimensional figures.

Consequently, many hand-clapping plays, drumming and dancing activities were found to be connected to designing the space, compared to the other four activities. Children pay more attention to space and patterns, without creating physical artefacts such as toys. This result supports the idea of the importance of African drumming and dancing art (Zaslavsky 1999). Presmeg (1998) also stated that various patterns, rhythms, chord progressions and melodies that are found in music are a part of ethnomathematics. This supports the idea that girls' singing and dancing when playing can be connected to the foundations of mathematics. This, however, could also be influenced by the type of children I observed: I mainly observed girls. During my fieldwork, I found boys were engaged in these designing games, but I inferred that these games are played more by girls. In mathematics education, it is assumed that children learn two-dimensional shapes first and then acquire understanding of three-dimensional shapes (Clements and Sarama 2014). By contrast, the result here supports the idea that Zambian children's play contains invisible patterns created by voices and body movements and is related to three-dimensional space. These games would definitely influence children's cognitive development, and thus, we need to investigate further how they can be utilised in the context of school education.

### 6-6. Explaining

'Explaining', according to Bishop (1997), includes classifications of objects, followed by a certain rule. I did not observe many games with explanation. From the perspective of classification of objects, 'Chiato', 'Bubble gum' and 'September' include explanation. 'Chiato' is a popular game in Zambia, which means that its rules vary from group to group. Therefore, it includes more parts requiring explanation in its rules. The play can also be considered from the perspective of classification. The fundamental classification here is distinguishing between similar-looking stones that are inside the circle and those outside. In 'Bubble gum' one player is selected by counting the number of children for classification. 'September' has two stages of selection in its structure. First, the group determines two players who will continue the play. In the second stage, it determines the actions that these two players are required to perform. To conclude, all the games have a simple structure of classification for different purposes. The analysis showed that children's play does not show much evidence of explaining activities; however, a few games included classification of players. Of course, during their play, children discussed many things verbally, which might be included in this category, but this will be discussed intensively in the context of children's interactions in a different chapter.

## 7. Conclusions

Educators can always learn important lessons from children. The message of ubuntu is that children's actions in a community should be carefully observed and their collective experiences and knowledge should be elicited in a practical manner. My data collection and analysis showed that children's play contains an inherent sense of mathematics. The following two significant findings from the analysis could be used in school mathematics education and curriculum development in Zambia. First, referring to Bishop's argument, games that involve hand clapping and singing songs are complicated and make children think and act logically. This can be connected to the beginning of learning in school mathematics and can support curriculum development for early childhood and primary school mathematics, emphasising children's play. A detailed pedagogy creation and evaluation would be the next step. For instance, how can teachers support children's play for effective learning? Or should teachers leave children to play as they naturally learn the logical aspect of the play? These questions require answers for school mathematics.

Second, dealing with three-dimensional space through play may help children grasp the fundamental notions of space, perhaps at the same time as they learn two-dimensional geometrical shapes. In the current early childhood mathematics education, there is no content on three dimensions at all (Ministry of Education, Science, Vocational Training and Early Education 2013); on the other hand, Zambian children have already acquired an understanding of three-dimensional shapes and space in their play. The results and the suggestions are different from those required of a Eurocentric curriculum; therefore, this can be a unique finding from a cultural perspective. These games can also be used to understand the notion of 'Classification' in the mathematics curriculum, particularly for three- to four-year-old year children. In the current curriculum, children are encouraged to play with blocks; by contrast, Zambian children can understand rhythmic patterns through play. The perspective of ethnomathematics could be effectively used to make the current curriculum more child friendly. This can be an academic contribution to mathematics education.

The data I collected have some limitations as well. The results were limited to girls in an urban area in modern times. The actual implementations or pedagogical aspects of play are not discussed, which should be a challenge for future studies. In addition, children's interactions during play are not covered here. This aspect is significantly related to tackling the pedagogical issue and to incorporating them, as well as the philosophy of ubuntu, into

321

educational practice. However, the study offers an opportunity to examine the characteristics of Zambian children's play in the modern era. A fascinating result is that children have developed spatial awareness, a fact that needs to be investigated further and can be an aspect of ubuntu; it might open a new path for children's mathematics learning than that they derive from the existing curriculum in Zambia. The analytical lens to identify the fundamental mathematical activity contributed to identifying the characteristics of children's play.


**Endnote**

[1] Except for the commonly known English games, for any particular name of the games, the author put the single quotations with them.


**Acknowledgements**

I wish to express my appreciation of the Zambian children who taught and welcomed me to play with them during my fieldwork. I would like to thank Mr Musonda, the former headmaster of Nakambala Primary School, Ms Nonaka Hikari, a former JOCV-volunteer, working at the same school, and Mr Shambweka, who supported me in translating their interactions into English. My fieldwork was financially supported by the project 'African Potentials' and JSPS KAKENHI Grant Number JP16H06318.

# References

Assié-Lumumba, T. N. (2016) 'Evolving African attitudes to European education: Resistance, pervert effects of the single system paradox, and the Ubuntu framework for renewal', *International Review of Education*, Vol. 62, Issue 1, pp. 11–27.

Bishop, A. (1997) *Mathematical Enculturation: A Cultural Perspective on Mathematics Education*, Dordrecht: Kluwer Academic Publishers.

Brock-Utne, B. (2016) 'The Ubuntu paradigm in curriculum work, language of instruction and assessment', *International Review of Education*, Vol. 62, Issue 1, pp. 29–44.

Carraher, N. T., Carraher, W. D. and Schliemann, D. A. (1985) 'Mathematics in the streets and in schools', *Developmental Psychology*, Vol. 3, Issue 1, pp. 21–9.

Clements, H. D. and Sarama, J. (2014) *The Learning Trajectories Approach*, Oxford: Routledge.

D'Ambrosio, U. (1985) 'Ethnomathematics and its place in the history and pedagogy of mathematics', *For the Learning of Mathematics*, Vol. 5, No. 1, pp. 44–8.

——————— (1998) *Ethnomathematics: The Art or Technique of Explaining and Knowing* (translated by P. B. Scott), ISGEm International Study Group on Ethnomathematics.

——————— (2016) 'An overview of the history of ethnomathematics', in M. Rosa, U. D'Ambrosio, D. C. Orey, L. Shirley, W. V. Alangui, P. Palhares and M. E. Gavarrete (eds) *Current and Future Perspectives of Ethnomathematics as a Program (ICME-13 Topical Surveys)*, Cham: Springer International Publishing, pp. 5–10.

Dzansi, M. (2004) 'Playground music pedagogy of Ghanaian children', *Research Studies in Music Education*, Vol. 22, Issue 1, pp. 83–92.

Eglash, R. (2007) *The Fractals at the Heart of African Designs*, TED Global (http://www.ted.com/talks/ron_eglash_on_african_fractals.html) (accessed: 27 July 2020).

Huylebrouck, D. (2019) *Africa and Mathematics*, Cham: Springer International Publishing.

Kalinde, B. (2016) 'Cultural play songs in early childhood education in Zambia: In and outside of classroom practice', unpublished PhD thesis, University of Pretoria.

Kekana, M. S. (2016) 'Indigenous songs and games in the classroom', *International Journal of Scientific Research in Education*, Vol. 9, No. 3, pp. 151–65.

Kirkby, D. (1992) *Games in the Teaching of Mathematics*, Cambridge: Cambridge University Press.

Makalela, L. (2015) 'Introduction', in L. Makalela (ed.) *New Directions in Language and Literacy Education for Multilingual Classrooms in Africa*, Cape Town: CASAS (Centre for Advanced Studies of African Society), pp. 1–14.

Ministry of Education, Science, Vocational Training and Early Education (2013) *Early Childhood Education Syllabus*, Lusaka: Curriculum Development Centre, Ministry of Education, Science, Vocational Training and Early Education, Zambia.

Mtonga, M. (2012) *Children's Games and Plays in Zambia*, Lusaka: University of Zambia Press.

Mukela, R. M. (2013) 'The role of indigenous music and games in the promotion of cognitive development in Zambian children in Senanga and Shangombo districts of Western Province', unpublished MA dissertation, University of Zambia.

Nakawa, N. (2018) 'Current situations and challenges on mathematics lessons in early childhood care, development and education in urban areas of Lusaka, Zambia', *Africa Educational Research Journal*, No. 9, pp. 23–38 (in Japanese).

Nkopodi, N. and Mosimege, M. (2009) 'Incorporating the indigenous game of marabaraba in the learning of mathematics', *South African Journal of Education*, Vol. 29, No. 3, pp. 377–92.

Nyamnjoh, B. F. (2019) 'Ubuntuism and Africa: Actualised, misappropriated, endangered and reappraised', *Africa Day Memorial Lecture*, University of the Free State, Bloemfontein, 22 May 2019.

Nyota, S. and Mapara, J. (2008) 'Shona traditional children's games and play: Songs as indigenous ways of knowing', *The Journal of Pan African Studies*, Vol. 2, No. 4: pp. 189–202.

Odora, C. (1994) 'Indigenous forms of learning in Africa with special reference to the Acholi of Uganda', in B. Brock-Utne (ed.) *Indigenous Education in Africa (Report. No. 7)*, Oslo: Institute for Educational Research, University of Oslo, pp. 61–72.

Presmeg, N. C. (1998) 'Ethnomathematics in teacher education', *Journal of Mathematics Teacher Education*, Vol. 1, pp. 317–39.

Rosa, M. and Gavarrete, E. M. (2017) 'An ethnomathematics overview: An introduction', in M. Rosa, L. Shirley, M. E.

Gavarrete and W. V. Alangui (eds) *Ethnomathematics and Its Diverse Approaches,* Cham: Springer International Publishing, pp. 3–19.

Rosa, M., Shirley, L., Gavarrete, M. E. and Alangui, W. V. (eds) (2017) *Ethnomathematics and Its diverse Approaches for Mathematics Education,* Cham: Springer International Publishing.

Serpell, R. (1993) *The Significance of Schooling: Life-Journeys in an African Society,* Cambridge: Cambridge University Press.

Sport in Action (2004) *Sport in the Development Process, Leadership Manual* (https://www.sportanddev.org/en/document/manuals-and-tools/sport-action-sport-development-process-leadership-manual) (accessed: 13 December 2020).

Takagi, A. (2018) 'Children living in urban and rural areas in Zambia', The 29th JASID (Japan Society for International Development) Annual Conference, University of Tsukuba, 23–24 November 2018.

Tatira, B., Mutambara, L. H. N. and Chagwiza, J. C. (2012) 'The Balobedu cultural activities and plays pertinent to primary mathematics learning', *International Education Studies,* Vol. 5, No. 1, pp. 78–85.

Zaslavsky, C. (1999) *Africa Counts: Number and Pattern in African Cultures (3rd edition),* Chicago: Chicago Review Press.

# Chapter 11

## Bringing Ali Mazrui's Epistemic Eclecticism into Classroom Praxis: Morero as Pedagogic Eclecticism for Teaching African Potentials

*Sethunya Tshepho Mosime*

## 1. Introduction: *African Potentials* at the Height of #RhodesMustFall — An Epistemic and Existential Crisis for Botswana–Japan Potentials

The first draft of this chapter was presented as a paper at the International Forum on 'Comprehensive Area Studies on "*African Potentials*" to Develop Alternative Methods of Addressing Global Issues', held in November 2017 at Rhodes University in Grahamstown (now Makhanda), South Africa. Across Africa and internationally, universities have responded in various ways to this call for decolonisation, from responses I could call 'add the word decolonisation and proceed as normal' to radical demands for pulling down all residual colonial physical and ideational infrastructure as in the case of South Africa since 2015. Just the year before the 2017 African Potentials meeting, the host, Rhodes University, was the site of a student protest going by the hashtag #RhodesMustFall, demanding the physical and symbolic removal of the very founding architecture of colonialism and racial discrimination. Although the history of students' protests is much longer in South Africa, since 2015, universities became spaces for student-led protests and demands for all things neo-colonial and neo-liberal to fall; starting with #FeesMustFall to address the neo-colonialism in education and its resultant disparities in access to education, to epistemic violence in education that obliterated African ways of knowing.

Botswana is a southern African country, one and a half times the size of Japan, home to a small population of about 2.4 million, compared to Japan's 126.5 million. It was one of the countries in the world hardest hit by HIV and AIDS in the 1990s, and one of the most unequal societies with a GINI coefficient ranging between 53 and 64.7 in the last 35 years (Index Mundi 2019). The World Happiness Report has consistently ranked Botswana as one of the unhappiest populations in the world (World Happiness Report 2020), although the same report finds the score anomalous as the country has higher performance on some of the key variables.

Even with the above challenges, Botswana is celebrated as one of Africa's most stable democracies, with steady economic growth, some the lowest levels of corruption on the continent, good governance and higher levels of transparency. Contexts such as Botswana that are not associated with a history of, or presence of, on-going violent conflict are often left out in discussions around peace building, conflict and post conflict recovery. This is despite the country's long and successful history of being a player in regional and continental peace efforts and missions since the days of the Non-aligned Movement in the late 1970s. Botswana's former presidents have presided on a number of mediation processes in the region, notably in Angola, Lesotho, Somalia and the Democratic Republic of Congo.

At the time of the 2017 African Potentials meeting, it felt as if Botswana was at the margins of this potentially transformative discourse of decolonisation. With the raging demands for decolonisation, if we were not at the forefront of the struggle, what potential alternative methods of addressing global issues could Botswana provide? As I will demonstrate in this chapter, many African Potentials exist between Botswana and the rest of Africa to share avenues for culture as praxis towards decolonisation of the curriculum, thus advancing the infinite possibilities in the shared value of ubuntu.

Addressing global issues seemed even more daunting. What conversations could exist between this small African economy and Japan, in the co-creation of knowledge? Yet, upon further reflection, it became apparent that similarities do exist between Botswana and

Japan. Japan faced similar epistemic and existential challenges and opportunities vis à vis the decolonisation project. Where Botswana is often set apart as an exceptional African democracy with a small but strong economy, Japan is often clustered together with major world capitalist economies of the USA and Western Europe, yet culturally often set apart from them. Additionally, although the two contexts are economically unequal, they do not have a history of domination of one over the other, especially domination of one over another's social and political thought.

For both countries, the post-war period was of rapid growth in literacy levels. Although Japan had significantly more people with literacy by the 1960s than Africa with nine per cent of population with post-secondary education, by the 1990s, literacy and tertiary education numbers in both contexts had grown exponentially. Both contexts have also had to strive for their universities to grow from unknowns into global rankings, again with drastically varying levels of success. Another similarity is their divergent but familiar history of Western cultural hegemony, while at the same time, both being strongly associated with stronger cultural ties. While recognising the economic advantage that Japan has over Africa, by drawing from their non-hegemonic cultural capital, the two contexts have more opportunities to make African Potentials a reality. For that to happen requires for Japan to observe the preferential consideration for African epistemologies and pedagogies, so as to avoid the project of African Potentials from becoming an entry point for Japanese cultural hegemony over Africa. As both are non-Western societies, Mazrui saw potentials for what he called horizontal interpenetration, partnerships among countries that while culturally different, have many things in common.

## 2. Botswana's Rich Reiterative Consensus Building Tradition through *Morero*

Bertha Osei-Hwedi argues that Botswana has kept its relative peacefulness through infusing indigenous norms and institutions of the Tswana traditional culture with modern democratic institutions.

329

The 'grafting' of 'Western' notions of democratic participation into an already existing local notion of participatory decision making through an old tradition of *kgotla* has been in some quarters credited for Botswana being one of the most stable democracies in Africa. Osei-Hwedie (2010) describes this as 'modern democratic institutions such as civil society and the judiciary; and socio-economic development for conflict resolution and prevention, and governance'. Much attention to Botswana indigenous norms and institutions of the Tswana traditional culture has been given to the *kgotla*, followed in close tow by *botho* – the local term for ubuntu (Ntseane and Chilisa 2012; Steyn 2012; Ngwenya 2002). Here I propose that what makes the *kgotla system* sustainable over time is how its philosophy of open debate becomes operationalised through its lesser known theory of power that informs the critical process, *morero* – loosely translating to consensus building. While the *kgotla* provides the epistemic frame for families, communities and the national government to participate to some extent in decision making, *morero* provides modalities for praxis among multiple pedagogies; pedagogies of the oppressed, pedagogies of liberation and, increasingly so, pedagogies of cultural inclusiveness. *Morero* is central to the performance of all ritualised activities at family, national and, increasingly, international engagements in Botswana and many southern African communities. Virtually all rites of passage are carried out through attempts at careful attention to *morero* protocols.

Richard Werbner's 1977 work on 'Small Man Politics and the Rule of Law' (Werbner 1977), and Isaac Schapera's work before him have long made the point that, among the Tswana, consensus building is valued more than establishment of patron–client relations. He noted that *morero* – that he translated to 'a moot', was one of the 'small' but important building blocks towards consensual decision making in local politics (Werbner 1977). Consensus building is used in every part of the world in different ways for different purposes, such as mediating industrial relations disputes, urban and rural planning, environmental impact assessments and many other areas where collective effort and buy-in are needed to proceed with projects and processes. *Morero* has similar outcomes to other consensus building approaches (CBA), of bringing together communities around a common cause, assigning roles and responsibilities in order to reach an agreement and hold people to their commitments (Sills 2018). However, *morero* differs from other CBAs in that, although it might provide collaborative problem solving, that is not its central aim.

*Morero* is both epistemic and pedagogic; it is an epistemic philosophy for how indigenous knowledge systems have mobilised power to arrive consensus outside the logic of winners and losers, and also a pedagogical set of ritualised methods that are used in practical ways to arrive at consensus. *Morero* is done to primarily to maintain and sustain existing consensus mechanisms, not to invent them. Consensus is thus taken for granted, to be sustained through continuous, critical and reiterative and everyday lived experience. Whereas most consensus building processes are intermittent and built to address specific social problems through manufacturing consent, *morero* is not a mediation and/or arbitration process to decide which of the parties is right or wrong, or what each party may have to concede in a given conflict. Should conflict resolution become necessary, the methodology of *morero* is to bring back parties to a recognition of their inalienable socially prescribed and ascribed roles, and the ethics that the responsibility comes with. *Morero* draws from existing bonds of mutual consent, and therefore has inbuilt sustainability. It is a living process that requires continuous maintenance through open-ended participatory appraisal and review. When engaging parties arrive at the *morero* table, they are already recognised as occupying inalienable, reciprocal, altruistic and ethical responsibilities towards the larger group, determined by their socially ascribed statuses.

*Morero* cannot proceed except on mutual respect and understanding of the boundaries and scope of each participant's role. Central to the proceedings is whether or not the actions being taken are within the 'rights and responsibilities' of the role an actor maybe playing in the larger group, and in that particular context. These 'rights and responsibilities' are not assigned to persons by their social roles. They are not entitlements but assignments. For example, among the different ethnic groups in Botswana, a maternal uncle plays a different role from that of a paternal uncle, depending on whether the rite of passage in progress is a marriage or a funeral. A maternal uncle may have more responsibility and influence during marriage rituals of their nephew or niece, but play a lesser role in their burial rites. To gain recognition and leadership in processes of *morero,* one must exhibit outstanding consistency in the performance of any role they may be ascribed depending on the occasion, in line with the commonly held understanding of the scope of the role, albeit constantly shifting. And because no two events are ever exactly identical, nor the parties involved and their roles ever exactly the same, *morero* remains open-ended, continuously negotiable and therefore adaptable to different contexts and dynamics.

The efficacy of *morero* beyond rites of passage and governance internally is yet to be fully tried and tested in Botswana's international relations. However, evidence points to it potentially playing a role in Botswana's diplomatic relations, as well as in the country's success in regional and continental conflict resolution processes. Thus far, *morero* has come to be used as part of the country's international branding through its embassies' websites across the world. It is placed as one of the unique features about Botswana culture and society in a number of the embassies of Botswana homepages across the world, including Japan and Zambia. Described as *'Consultation and Consensus Building',* Botswana's diplomatic missions present *morero* to the rest of the world as one of the core values of the people of Botswana,

> People of Botswana strongly believe in the value of consultations within the society to ensure peace through consensus. The process of *MORERO* (consultation) at inter-personal, family, and community levels is considered an invaluable asset in the ability to reach and sustain agreements. Communities and even Government consult at the *KGOTLA* (Embassy of Botswana in Japan 2018).

*Morero* has the potential to help provide sustainable and consensus-building approaches to African and global problems. *Morero* has already played a significant role in regional and continental conflict resolution, through its mobilisation by successive presidents

332

of Botswana in different peace processes, particularly at the funeral of Botswana's second head of state, Sir Ketumile Masire in 2017, which I attended. A representative from Angola recounted how he was humbled and impressed by the way Sir Ketumile Masire approached a very daunting task in the mid-1980s of peace talks with UNITA 'rebel' leader, Jonas Savimbi. Masire arrived in Luanda expecting to meet with the UNITA leader in the capital city, but Savimbi would not come down from the mountains deep in the countryside and very far from the capital city to meet Masire as had been agreed. Coming from a *morero* culture, Masire would have understood that, for the negotiations to be successful, he as the mediator, would have to respect that, while engaged towards a particular outcome, Savimbi occupied a socially sanctioned role that entitled him to respect. If it was a *morero* marriage negotiation, he, Sir Ketumile Masire, came to ask for UNITA's 'hand in marriage', and representing the groom's family, the onus was on him to prove to Savimbi that he came in peace and with good intentions. Apparently, in a similar fashion as *morero* would have prescribed, Masire asked to be driven all night into the mountains, with minimal comfort and security, to meet Savimbi and, needless to say, the meeting was successful.

Again, during the leadership of Masire, the Botswana Defence Force (BDF) troops were deployed to Lesotho on the night of 22 September 1998, following an election-related unrest. Although the legitimacy of this intervention by South Africa and Botswana was highly contested as not having been duly sanctioned by either SADC or the UN Security Council, through *morero*, the ordinary people in Lesotho highly praised the conduct of the BDF. The manner in which the BDF and the South African National Defence Force approached the intervention was remarkably different, as recalled by both locals and political analysts; Botswana landed with a white flag to indicate a peace-keeping agenda while South Africa immediately pounded the Royal Palace and some military barracks with ammunition. At the end of the exercise, the BDF received very positive reviews from locals in Lesotho. Botswana had other successful deployments in Somalia and Democratic Republic of

Congo.

Within the country, especially in the mid-1990s as many minority groups, including the Khoisan and Yei, began to demand for land rights and cultural autonomy from more dominant Tswana groups. The economically and cultural Tswana-centric state was put to task through a combination of what Lydia Nyathi-Saleshando (Solway 2011) called lawfare, and demands for *morero*. In order to deliver on the *morero* promise, a Presidential Commission of Inquiry in terms of sections 77, 78 and 79 of Botswana's Constitution was sent around the entire country to solicit views on the proposed reforms to give all tribes equal standing in the *Ntlo ya Dikgosi*, and remove reference to eight principal tribes with permanent hereditary seats in the House. Known as the Balopi Commission, the *morero* exercise fortuitously coincided with the launch of Botswana's national television, BTV, and the proceedings were publicly televised. According to Jacqueline Solway, between television, print media and radio, the Commission saturated the public sphere to a degree virtually unprecedented, and heightened consciousness around minority issues (Solway 2011: 223). As a result, although the said sections were not removed, *morero* helped minorities to express their sense of oppression and for ethnic diversity to become recognised firmly as a feature of Botswana (Solway 2011), replacing the narrative of homogeneity. *Morero* is thereby able to circumvent, although not always completely, hegemonic impetus towards appropriation of culture to secure oppression. It is beyond a counter-hegemonic discourse; it is an anti-hegemonic discourse.

In the quest to prove the scientific nature of African knowledge systems, some African philosophers have proposed that the Euro-centric and therefore epistemic individualism of Western social science be replaced by an epistemic pluralism that would be inclusive of non-Western types of rationality. Proponents of epistemic pluralism such as Lesiba Teffo fully recognise the negative impact of colonisation on the ways of knowing among conquered communities in ways that was tantamount to denying their humanity. To this end, they seek to reverse the colonial experience by bringing back a universal humanity where all human beings are seen as endowed with a scientific rationality, so that African ways of knowing are no longer relegated to superstition or alternative to science. For this reason, their proposed remedy is a 'holistic' and universalistic epistemology that affirms the humanity of the African person, by which they mean that 'the African voice and the African genius [and] his/her existential experiences and conditions are incorporated and mainstreamed in the general corpus of scientific knowledge' (Teffo 2011: 25). Therein lies the problem. By drawing from Aristotle, Plato, Descartes, Locke and other Western philosophers, the epistemic launching pad of African epistemic pluralists is already compromised. They take for granted the completeness and internal consistency of Western rationality, except that African and other rationalities have not been given a fair chance to prove themselves to be similarly rational.

In the quest to explore alternative models of power sharing that are rooted within African cultures, methods that can unlock *African Potentials*, I share my own eclectic experience in the teaching of a course on *African Social Thought*, which I have taught since 2011 in the Department of Sociology, University of Botswana. Among other learning outcomes of the course is to critically engage with colonialism and its attempts at cultural hegemony over African cultural autonomy.

At the same time as I was beginning to teach African Social Thought, I also started to work on a project on Young Women's Leadership (YWL) at the University of Botswana, using Feminist Action Research (FAR). The project was supported by the Africa Gender Institute (AGI) in Cape Town, South Africa, and funded by the Ford Foundation focused on young women in several southern African universities, and their daily survival strategies to resist the strongly patriarchal university cultures. I also use my experience with it to explore the potential for *morero* as an eclectic pedagogy to enable intersectional and intergenerational conversations.

Before sharing my experiences of an attempt at *morero* as a potential for an eclectic pedagogy of teaching African Social Thought and doing feminist action research towards *African Potentials*, in the next section, I discuss in the broader debates about the place of culture in the decolonisation of the curriculum, particularly since former South African President Thabo Mbeki's call for an African Renaissance.

## 3. Decolonising the Curriculum through the Turn to Culture: From Mbeki's African Renaissance through Ubuntu to Agentic and Eclectic Pedagogies of Emancipatory Culture

As African countries reach more than half a century of the end of formal colonisation, and yet remain socio-economically fragile and dependent on external resources, a clarion call for decolonisation has been made to decolonise every aspect of social life, from curriculum to the economy, to methodologies and all aspects of knowledge production and consumption. The most significant post-independence shift happened with the restructuring of the former Organisation of African Unity (OAU) into the African Union in 2002, with the third generation of African presidents that attempted to re-think Pan Africanism from a political movement to a potential vehicle for economic growth and social development (Mboup 2008). Thabo Mbeki, the former President of South Africa led this transition, with the support of Presidents Olesegun Obasanjo of Nigeria, Abdoulaye Wade of Senegal and Abdel Aziz Bouteflika of Algeria. Significantly, Mbeki bequeathed the new direction of Pan Africanism with the idea of an African Renaissance built on an African philosophy of ubuntu. These two concepts of an African Renaissance and ubuntu have come to dominate developmental, philosophical, epistemic and pedagogical debates around what Africa's futures can look like if we are to re-enter the global systems of economic and knowledge production, not as subjects, but as equals. Although the idea of an African renaissance was initiated by Nelson Mandela, it was Thabo Mbeki that gave it a greater impetus, starting with his famous poem, 'I am African' (Tomaselli 2003).

For this reason, Thabo Mbeki has been heralded as a philosopher of liberation by William Mpofu of the University of the Witwatersrand Centre for Diversity Studies in South Africa. Mpofu argues that, contrary to his detractors would have us believe, Mbeki has a 'critical understanding of the whole world and the human

336

condition, from the perspective of the oppressed', and from the organic experience of his people (Mpofu 2017). Mpofu asserts that such philosophers of liberation are able to 'resist the hegemonic epistemic impositions of the North, and prefer a dialogue of civilisations rather than a clash'. Tomaselli and other scholars have warned of the possible danger of an essentialised and quintessential mobilisation of 'African cultures' by political leaders in the project of an ubuntu-based African Renaissance. This could potentially rob notions such as ubuntu of their potential revolutionary edge, whereas the European Renaissance was in fact a counter hegemonic movement against authority (Tomaselli 2003). Yet, its proponents argue on the contrary that ubuntu is able to transcend cultural barriers because it is 'within the heart' (Pitsoe and Letseka 2016).

With specific reference to pedagogy, the pursuit of the African Renaissance through curriculum development and delivery has been centred around the notion of decolonising the curriculum through ubuntu as a humanising pedagogy akin to Paulo Freire's *Pedagogy of the oppressed*, and as liberation pedagogy (Pitsoe and Letseka 2016). Moeketsi Letseka, speaking in 2016 at the Ali Mazrui Centre for Higher Education Studies at the University of Johannesburg on 'Indigenous African Epistemologies: Focus on ubuntu', argued that it was 'a notion of African communal justice and fairness, as a signifier of identity, and as a pedagogical principle' (Letseka 2016).

## 4. Re-Thinking Ali Mazrui: From Epistemic Eclecticism to Pedagogic Eclecticism

According to Sabelo Ndlovu-Gatsheni, Mazrui's illustrious writings incited either cult-like reverence of the man that South Sudanese scholar Dustan M. Wai coined as 'Mazruiphilia', or quite the opposite, 'Mazruiphobia' – an aggressive anti-Mazruism (Ndlovu-Gatsheni 2014). Ndlovu-Gatsheni himself called Ali Mazrui an 'encyclopedic' academic and an 'intellectual pluralist' whose scholarly contributions not only transcended traditional academic disciplinary boundaries but also broke bondages of academic 'tribalism' (Ndlovu-Gatsheni 2014). Although he does not use the term eclecticism to describe his work, Ndlovu-Gatsheni describes Mazrui as an iconoclast that challenged cherished ideas and a maverick in that he 'did not easily fall into either Marxist, Gramscian or Foucaldian descriptions' (Ndlovu-Gatsheni 2014).

Mazrui was deeply invested in a kind of knowledge production that celebrated African autonomy in modern conditions; of resilient African traditional values and their role in how Africa has contended with imperialism, liberalism and capitalist values, the rise of modern nationalism, and what he considered a fascination with Marxism among black intellectuals. He concluded that what was needed was a creative eclecticism, a careful and genius selection and synthesis of these disparate ideological and epistemic elements. This could provide an alternative that opens up for Africa an altogether independent intellectual trajectory, that engages the participation of the Other in its production but remains autonomous (Mazrui 1975). Mazrui's creative eclecticism was epistemic, and in this chapter, we explore the possibility of translating this epistemological approach into classroom practice, to propose a creative pedagogical eclecticism. Such classroom strategies should contribute to the bigger debate of decolonising the curriculum; providing an autonomous and engaged teaching towards African Potentials, that at once draws from the resilient African traditional values as it creatively weaves in existing teaching and learning strategies that are often pragmatically – but not necessarily eclectically – adapted from elsewhere. By taking Mazrui's eclectic epistemology to inform pedagogy – the mode of delivery of the known to inform action – Mazrui's legacy may continue to influence the project of decolonisation in practical and accessible ways.

Mazrui explained the postcolonial condition of Africa to be that of predicaments and instabilities that were a 'symptom of cultures at war', arising from an eclectic triple heritage of indigenous, Islamic and Western forces. He found these to be in constant flux, between 'fusing and recoiling, at once competitive and complimentary' (Mazrui 1986: 21). Mazrui identified six paradoxes of postcolonial Africa that were happening at the same time, that Africa is at once a cradle of humankind as it is a site of humiliation by slavery,

338

imperialism and colonialism, and racial discrimination. It is a place of cultural domination by others and a place of underdevelopment in the global capitalistic system. It suffered retardation as fragmentation prevented unity, and while perfectly geographically located, it remained marginalised in the global political economy. And all of these are compounded by a leadership crisis.

Critical African feminist scholar, Obioma Nnaemeka, has warned about the fact that 'how we construct, teach, and disseminate knowledge of the Other', can be challenging. Epistemologically, Nnaemeka asks of us to seriously question our constructions of knowledge or text – 'how the information and data in the texts came into being and are articulated', whether written, oral or visual. Pedagogically, the teaching of the knowledge of the Other involves what Nnaemeka calls a risky interaction among the text, the teacher and the student (Nnaemeka 1994). She explains the risk in this way: that the 'text cannot defend itself against use, misuse, and abuse'. Hence, the choice of texts used in a course is dependent upon the teacher's own often incomplete knowledge of all available texts on the subject matter, but more dangerously, the teacher's prejudices. Thus, at the pedagogical level, the 'course syllabus not only demonstrates how much the teacher knows but also betrays the teacher's limitations and prejudices'.

Nnaemeka based her observations on experiences of African women in classrooms outside Africa. For African women in African classrooms at home, teaching of the knowledge of their Othered self – Othered both internally and externally – pedagogy is inherently as act of deviance, defiance and risk taking. To overcome this, one important first step, according to Nnaemeka is to recognise that 'we enter other cultures with our own cultural baggage' (Nnaemeka 1994). For African women, taking up the challenge of decolonising the curriculum requires that we recognise the patriarchal 'baggage' that comes into play.

However, approached as 'baggage', culture may be seen as something we are trapped by and, as Nnaemeka herself acknowledges, this can undermine efforts towards strategic alliances (Nnaemeka 1994). The same is true for the project of African

Potentials. To succeed, the project must intentionally make efforts towards strategic alliances between Africa and other sites of knowledge production by unlocking and extending existing spaces for critical but mutually supportive frames for meaningful knowledge production and exchange. *Morero* as I will demonstrate, provides an opportunity for praxis, bridges the gap between epistemology as philosophy and pedagogy as philosophy in action. It is a set of practical methods for engagement among parties that bring with them inalienable but constantly fluid rights.

## 5. *Morero*: Toward an Ubuntu Theory of Power as Eclectic Connectedness

Bagele Chilisa (2019) has argued that, when mobilised with the aim is to achieve social, economic and climate justice, African cultural practices have the potential to contribute towards inclusive global justice; as such, there are many lessons yet to be learnt from the margins (Chilisa 2019). Chilisa explains that in the particular context of Botswana, ubuntu – locally referred to as *botho* – humanness is understood as connectedness among people, the earth and all its inhabitants, celebrated through taboos and totems. Webs of relations and interconnectedness, rather than hierarchies are organised around ubuntu as consensus building that takes plurality seriously. 'When an Ubuntist reads solidarity and consensus, s/he therefore also reads alterity, autonomy, and cooperation', (Louw 2001: 6, cited in Chilisa 2019: 235). To be truly transformational, ubuntu must contain within it, a radical approach to power as a resource that can be equitably shared. Ubuntu must also provide for a co-existence with Others than displaces the tendency towards abusing our differences as a basis for oppression. According to Chilisa (2019: 235), 'Ubuntu incorporates dialogue, preserving the Other in their Otherness, in their uniqueness, without letting the Other slip into distance'.

Question to self then is, from my personal experience, can I call myself an ubuntist? Great as ubuntuism sounds, it has to make sense as a sociology of everyday life. Are African women's experiences of ubuntu of it as an inclusive web that has unlocked both bodily autonomy and consensus-based connectedness with others? Put differently, in my experience, a Botswana woman in a global context, is this claim to interconnectedness, something I've experienced? Or have I ever only experienced exclusion, injustice, discrimination and violation? For the most part yes, especially as a result of the neo-liberal economy that thrives on widening income and livelihood gaps. With a GINI co-efficient that can range between 53 and 64 out of 100, Botswana is one of the most unequal societies in the world (Mosime and Kaboyakgosi 2017), with women as the face of the intersection among gender, ethnic, resource, social, economic and climate injustice.

Yet I've also experienced validation and agency within the same space that can be oppressive; as an expert in African studies, as a gender activist, a choir stage performer, a union leader, an aunt, a mother, a wife and a head of an academic department, among other roles and responsibilities. I've increasingly enjoyed some degree of autonomy to subvert hetero-normative and patriarchal restrictions, yet not in ways that are antagonistic to culture. Sylvia Tamale, leading Ugandan African feminist, has found culture to be a very potent vehicle for what she calls an *African Feminist Renaissance* that turns towards 'culture' for emancipatory potential to enhance women's lives. This is notwithstanding that 'culture' can be oppressive, colonised, exploited, submerged and deprecated (Tamale 2006).

If culture can be oppressive, how can it also be emancipatory? What the African Renaissance turn to cultures of ubuntu proffers, I find, is an epistemic framework for recognising that inclusion and connectedness, despite the colonial trauma, have always existed in Africa. However, ubuntu and therefore the project of African Renaissance, does not provide with it a theory of power. In the search for African Potentials within ubuntu to imagine mutually enriching cultural exchange with others that would simultaneously heal the trauma of colonialism, I came across a project that Samuel M. Makinda (2017) and others have embarked on to expound on the work of Ali A. Mazrui's 1975 paper titled, 'Eclecticism as an ideological alternative: an African perspective'. Mazrui's explained eclecticism as an epistemological framework, 'through which a

341

theorist constructs a coherent analytical approach by utilizing, synthesizing and reflecting on insights from disparate paradigms' (Makinda 2000: 398, cited in Makinda 2017). Makinda (2017) thus proposes that 'eclecticism, if properly constructed, should provide an opportunity for non-European, including African, perspectives to play a role in shaping the production of knowledge', particularly by avoiding the tendency towards becoming another paradigm competing to have 'its own boundaries and discourse … with exclusive practices and hegemonic ambitions'. Eclecticism, according to Makinda, must remain 'dynamic, inclusive, and emancipatory' (Makinda 2017: 222). In this way, eclecticism opens up for what Ali Mazrui (1975: 484, cited in Makinda 2017) described as 'vertical cultural integration'.

Mazrui never fully developed this thesis of an eclectic epistemology in his later works, though he never abandoned it in practice. There are several schools of thought about eclecticism, both its epistemic and pedagogic meanings and implications and relevance to African Social Thought and African Philosophy. One strand of the debate is between particularistic African ethno-philosophers who argue that African ways of knowledge production and consumption must be free of 'foreign ideas', and those arguing for an eclectic or convivial lending and borrowing among cultures. The fear against eclecticism by the particularists is not so much about the purity of African cultures or philosophies but, as University of Zimbabwe ethno-philosopher Fainos Mangena warns, that African Philosophy is often the one that keeps needing to borrow from other world philosophies (Mangena 2014).

Pedagogic eclecticism should not be confused with epistemic pluralism; for it does not call for a simple add and stir of African ways of sense making and knowledge production into the pot of global epistemologies. Secondly, epistemic pluralism is also compromised by its instrumentalism or pragmatism in its efforts to be more 'democratic'. With all its half-hearted attempts to be inclusive and to provide more options, epistemic pluralism cannot do away with the historicity from which has emerged, of the audacity of knowledge imperialism, where only certain ways of knowing where given the status of being rational 'theoretical frameworks', while others failed the litmus test of 'logic' and 'coherence', and are therefore aberrant. These are the hallmarks of racism and other forms of Othering that excluded imagined others from full humanity and, therefore, as analytically irrelevant.

Pedagogic eclecticism must be founded on epistemic eclecticism. Before we can embrace epistemic pluralism, we must first insist on giving preferential consideration of epistemic perspectives from Africa above the already hegemonic epistemologies. This should not be conditional upon presenting any unity among African epistemologies, and so, eclecticism as mutually respectful celebration of different logics operating at the same time must be non-negotiable. This should not be understood to mean that eclecticism is itself a matter of negotiation, but that its negotiation processes must be protected and defended at all times. By taking a decidedly eclectic foundation, we avoid the pitfall of treating Africa as a homogenous entity, but a site of multiple pedagogies that may be mutually exclusive or mutually complimentary. Eclecticism, at both epistemic and pedagogical levels, provides a possibility to have a conversation and debates among disparate discourses for comparability and dissonance, without forcing any internal coherence among them. This way, cultural relativism, which often paralyses the deepening of cross-cultural conversations under the pretext of incomparability of cultures, can be avoided. At the same time, any comparative analysis would not use any one culture as a yardstick of another; thus avoiding parochialism and tendency towards epistemic and pedagogic hegemonic regimes.

The idea of a preferential epistemic consideration of oppressed groups has been proposed by Phia S. Salter and Glenn Adams (Salter and Adams 2019) as a first and provisional strategy and decolonising consciousness in the United States. Using a kind of 'law of displacement', a new normal can be reached by displacing hegemonic accounts with accounts from the margins as a standpoint for understanding everyday events, in the course of a long term project of interrogating existing hegemonic tools of knowledge production that have normalised racism. Salter and Adams insist that, by providing a context-sensitive, normalising account of the Other that had hitherto been rendered abnormal, we may be able to reach a new normal that is deracialised and decolonised (Salter and Adam 2019).

While inspired by both Mazrui and Makinda's eclectic ideological practices, I locate my own take on eclecticism a discursive practice that is distinctly located in Botswana's rich reiterative consensus-building tradition, known as *morero*. I argue that *morero* can provide what ubuntu lacks, a theory of power as eclectic; where its tendency to create hegemonic hierarchies is constantly and reiteratively countered by the centrality of consensus, coupled with the fluidity of roles in brokerage towards the consensus. *Morero* thus makes power and powerlessness unstable and impermanent, giving ubuntu its capacity to remain a dynamic, inclusive and yet personal quality. Traditionally used as a methodology of organising through negotiation of consent among various family and community interests in the handling of all rites of passage, *morero* has remained indispensable to keeping together Botswana's social fabric; traversing ethnic, religious and cultural diversity. It has served interactions and meaning making beyond the family and into Botswana's global reputation. It is eclectic in the way that it mobilises power, sustaining a constant redefinition of seemingly static and emic cultural norms and values, yet within each's own internal logic. Through reiterative negotiation and redefinition of disparate norms and values, *morero* is never fully completed, it remains open-ended. In this way, it is able to enable negotiating parties to come to the table from their various ways of knowing, and leave the table with a new negotiated understanding that harvests from their often mutually exclusive internal logics. With different ways of knowing, *morero* accomplishes a successful completion of a rite of passage, each time depending on the particular eclectic combination of negotiating parties and logics. At every meaning making or negotiation table, a new settlement is reached, yet always fitting within the internal logics of all participating voices. Inclusion is reached from diversity. Conclusions are arrived at by continuous expansion and contraction of logics. It thus provided possibility of a pedagogy that better captures the *incompleteness* of the project of African thought, where room always exists for reinterpretation and re-examination of previously agreed standpoints.

## 6. Teaching of African Social Thought in African Universities: A Case for Re-Thinking Mazrui's Eclecticism

Although Sociology has been taught in most African universities since their foundation, mostly in the 1960s and 1970s, and sociological analysis of African contexts has been a staple, it was only in the 1990s that calls for African Sociological thinkers started to be heeded, and even then, very reluctantly. In the University of Botswana, it was only in the mid-1990s that a proposal for the introduction of African Social Thought was made to 'enable upper level students to understand and appreciate the contributions that African Scholars and writers have made to social thought in general, and sociological issues and concerns in particular'. The course was first taught in the year 2000, following a programme review of the sociology undergraduate programme that was part of the Faculty of Social Sciences submissions into the Botswana's Eighth National Development Plan (NDP8), to justify why the sociology programme remained relevant to the human resources needs of the country.

The original draft course description contained in the Department of Sociology report for the 'Revision of Current Undergraduate Programme in Sociology' submitted for approval by university structures read as thus:

African intellectuals have attempted to understand and explain social phenomena by developing and debating social-philosophical perspectives of the world. Although it is arguably the case that social thought originated from Africa with the writings of Ibn-Khaldun (1332–1406), this [course] concentrates in assessing contemporary debates in African social thought. Contemporary African perspectives started by developing alternatives to colonial perspectives, for example: colonial 'ethno-philosophy', colonial conceptions of social and structural 'backwardness'; the nature of colonial society, economy and state. At the same time, African social thought has often combined

345

discourses on culture and representation with those on society, political economy and politics and it is not always possible or advisable to disentangle the two. The 'negritude' intellectual movement (of which Senghor was the most well-known proponent) is perhaps the best known initial attempt to search for an 'African identity' denied by the coloniser. It was followed by Nyerere's 'Ujamaa' and many other attempts to understand the essence of 'Africaness'. More recent intellectual developments have stressed not only Africa's essential uniqueness, but also its multi-faceted nature as well as its contributions to world social thought. This course will assess such debates through the works of cultural writers such as Cesaire, Senghor, Diop, Mazrui and more recently Hountondji and Mudimbe, as well as socio-political theorists such as Nkrumah, Nyerere, Rodney, Cabral, Fanon, Biko, Samir Amin and Mahmooh Mamdani. In all cases, theories and perspectives will be related to the changing historical conditions of their production.

The final version of the course description in the Departmental Handbook, read as thus:

This course will examine discourses on African Philosophies, worldviews, belief systems, cultures, personhood, identities and representations. Given past tendencies towards denying Africa and Africans any creativity or rationality, the course will focus especially on the writings of African thinkers, leaders and academics on the continent or in the diaspora. Different African philosophies and symbolic representations will be analysed in historical perspective, and their contribution to the African social thought highlighted. Among thinkers, scholars and leaders whose works and ideas will be critically discussed are: Cesaire, Senghor, Diop, Fanon, Biko, Samir Amin, Mahmood Mamdani, Soyinka and Mbembe. In all Cases, theories and perspectives will be related to the changing historical, political and economic circumstances of the continent.

The initial concept for the course was written in 1997 by one of Botswana's leading sociologists, Onalenna Selolwane, and she was later joined by one of the leading African anthropologists, Francis Nyamnjoh, and each of them taught it between 2000 and 2010. They stated the objectives of the course as to 'acquaint students with the ideas of important African thinkers and, secondly, 'to provide a critical understanding of the main debates in African social thought'. The prescribed textbook for the course was a book edited by Emmanuel Chukwudi Eze (1997), *Postcolonial African Philosophy: A Critical Reader*, published by Blackwell, Oxford. Upon the departure of both of them from the department at various times, I took over teaching the course from 2011.

It has come very clear in my teaching of African Social Thought many local African attempts at alternative modes of thinking such as Julius Nyerere's *ujamaa* were very quickly declared failed. Perhaps in a classic case of throwing out the baby with the bathwater, during the lifetimes of the now acclaimed African Social Thinkers, their ideas were often dismissed. This often led to a waning popularity of the leaders, especially those that used public office to experiment with such alternatives. Almost all of them, Cesaire, Senghor, Nkrumah, Nyerere and Cabral either suffered coup d'états or lost elections. Only after many years, and often posthumously, did many of them gain acclaim as African Social Thought leaders. Waves of nostalgia and revisionist African revivalism, through narratives such as African Renaissance, Afro-optimism and Africa Risings, had their detractors. Sylvia Tamale makes the point that, this is often because African 'cultures' are often unfavourably pitted against Western human 'rights' or modes of knowing.

Important as a philosophical approach to African Social Thought was, it in many ways trapped the course on a validation mission; to prove to the imagined Other that African philosophies were as rational as other philosophies if understood within their cosmologies. Strikingly, the inclusion and therefore the structured absences in whose thoughts were worth paying attention to was heavily skewed against women, youth, minorities, marginalised groups, LGBTQ and other equally important facilitators of knowledge construction such as artists, new social movements and 'organic intellectual'. It appeared to me that what I chose to called the 'project' of African

347

Social Thought was already at risk of becoming the very thing it emerged to address: parochialism. It was also at risk of becoming from the outset a very patriarchal undertaking and very elitist and exclusive to a particular African men's network.

Taking into account the demographics of the audience the course was designed for, of young people confronted by huge socio-economic inequalities and neoliberalism's mixed messages of a future of identities crafted around consumer culture in the face of poverty, the list of African men listed on the course – dead or alive – seemed disconnected from them. From my media studies background, I realise that audience analysis is crucial. Reception of information is understood as a dynamic process that largely depends on pre-existing points of reference on the part of audiences, so that as they choose their own ways of making sense of what is being presented, they have material from which to make inferences. Deeply informative as the selected scholars and thinkers were – to the extent that there was no resonance between the students and the content of the course – then the process could become purely academic and devoid of transformative potential. *Morero,* consultation and consensus building with the learners would to me have to be the first step towards an inclusive and meaningful course design that could be responsive to everyday lived realities of young Africans.

A *morero* approach to pedagogy must in the first place be ingrained in the teaching philosophy. Although the University of Botswana (UB) senate approved a learner-centred '*Learning and Teaching Policy*' in February 2008, teaching has largely continued instructor-centred. This has been in part due to limited resources to retrain instructors to implement the policy, but largely due to the absence of decolonisation as an intentional teaching and learning outcome of the policy. The policy defined 'learner-centredness' as 'learning and teaching processes [that] should adapt existing methods and techniques, adopt new ones and adjust to the learners' styles and pace of learning, and focus on the achievement of learner outcomes'. Emphasis was however on providing students with timeliness and quality of feedback in assessing students, rather than in transforming relations of learning and pedagogies for doing so (University of

348

Botswana 2008). The relations between learner and teacher remained unchanged and top-down.

Bringing together UB's Learning and Teaching Policy efforts at learner-centredness and my own epistemic eclecticism, I have experimented in the teaching of African Social Thought to make it more inclusive of more knowledge-production processes than was initially intended. It has not easy to bring learners who are products of an education system that has elsewhere been characterised as that of 'vocal teachers and silent Pupils'(Fuller and Snyder Jr 1991). Classrooms in Botswana have tended to be teacher-centred, and the students who reach tertiary education levels are truly survivors. They mostly should have successfully internalised schooling as a necessary evil that requires learned personal invisibility and inaudibility.

## 7. Employing *Morero* in Feminist Work

Feminist Action Research (FAR), demands co-creation as a non-negotiable in the production of knowledge. FAR also takes it as a given that knowledge that has been produced and reproduced through pedagogies and research methodologies that sustain existing power relations is inherently oppressive. Co-creation of knowledge can only be arrived at if any inequalities in power relations are acknowledged, addressed and removed. Such a process must be determined and led by the oppressed.

Young Women's Leadership (YWL) at the University of Botswana, that I have been the academic co-investigator for since 2010, uses Feminist Action Research (FAR) as a strategy for bringing together faculty members as participant-facilitators of a process where young female students unpacked their experiences with patriarchy at the University of Botswana through their daily lived realities. Drawing from the feminist mantra that the personal is political, students and faculty staff body mapped to locate any discomfort they might experience within the nexus among campus life and their gendered bodies to the wider socio-economic environment. Together with between five and twenty young women, we started our research projects by creating a safe space within which we could check in with

349

one another by answering as honestly as we can the question, 'how are you?' We shared how we were; mentally, financially, physically, academically and emotionally.

With an age gap of between 15 and 35 years between students and myself and two other colleagues as participant-facilitators, it was interesting to discover how the experiences of being female at the UB campus changed and yet remained the same. Among all of us, we would at different times and in different ways experience the campus as a site of assault against our bodily autonomy and denial of our sexual reproductive health rights. Sexual harassment, gender-based violence, disregard for specific needs of female identifying students remained a reality as it was when the facilitators had been students. At the same time, a lot had changed. The university no longer provided residence accommodation for all students without families in Gaborone. Many off-campus students were tenants in tented accommodation within a radius of about 50 km from campus, which presented a different set of circumstances including co-habitation with intimate partners and very often, gender-based violence and precariousness of accommodation for students. From these personal-political encounters, we would develop platforms for action and healing, including awareness campaigns, demands for policy reforms around sexual harassment, flash mobs, panel discussions, art therapy, drama therapy, academic papers and other interventions.

The YWL process enriched my approach to the classroom, inasmuch as my teaching experience was also employed in YWL projects. Until I came across the work of Samuel Makinda, I had not found a framework with which to justify this unusual assemblage of my personal as political, along with an appraisal of moments and ideas in and of Africa that are simultaneously disparate as they are connected. The construction and assemblage of what qualifies as 'thought' in the Euro-Western disciplinary traditions were already beyond redemption, but through a conscientious pedagogy, it was possible to avoid similar pitfalls, of using knowledge production for imperialist outcomes.

Although Bagele Chilisa (2019) does not invoke the concept of *morero*, but calls it 'ceremony', she argues that to achieve ontological and educative authenticity that is guided by a postcolonial indigenous framework requires 'acknowledging relationships that people have with each other and the environment, as well as the moral and spiritual-based obligation that they have for each other, the community, and the environment at large' (Chilisa 2019). This should include relations between learner and teacher in all postcolonial learning environments. Feminism, borne out of frustration with patriarchy's disregard for mutuality of relations among men and women, has been at the forefront of demands to deconstruct, decolonise and indigenise knowledge production.

The first and most important step in engaging students in *morero* as a teaching and learning strategy is to give them hearing. At the beginning of every semester and with every new group, I shared the course outline from the year before. It was used as talking point to begin the conversation about what ideas students might have about what African Social Thought could be and whose voices they thought could be included. To get into those questions, it was imperative that we first acknowledge one another as legitimate co-creators along with the other thinkers we might wish to invite into our think space.

From the YWL experience, I came to know that, from the 2010s, it had become part of the university culture that most students had 'side hustles' alongside their schooling life. Hustles ranged from selling beauty products, printing t-shirts for sale, bake sales, chicken sales, pyramid schemes, tutoring and more recently, online presence as bloggers, influencers and brand ambassadors, among many other things. The YWL ice breaking occurred around the question 'How are you?' For African Social Thought, it occurred around the question 'What's your hustle?'

Once acknowledged as bringing into the classroom experiences from their hustles, it became easier to revise the draft course outline around what their hustles could benefit from the course and benefit the course. *Morero* could then proceed with an understanding that they are not coming as empty slates to absorb information that they will later reproduce in a test, but that they have a moral and spiritual-based obligation to their hustles and their real and imagined communities. The course was designed around two major trajectories.

The first trajectory was of an archaeology of the very notion of an African Social Thought. We explored the construction/constructedness of African Social Thought, as both resistance against hegemonic forces and an affirmation of Africa's diverse but interconnected encounters with imperialism, colonialism, nationalism, Pan Africanism, liberation struggles, African Renaissance and neo-colonialism. The second trajectory was to critically engage with the thinkers that the course was originally designed in mind with, but to also to recognise the structured absence of 'thought' of women, minorities, popular culture and queer Africa, among others. We explored the notion of 'thought' as both political and gendered. Using the lens of African Feminism(s), we drew from struggles for gender equality to imagine African Social Thought, not just as African alternative, but as a global alternative to how 'thought' can break away chains of patriarchy and parochialism. We also sought to challenge all forms of privilege in knowledge production, and to listen to non-academic and non-institutionalised, non-canonised thought. In this way, African Social Thought becomes as much an archive as it is a movement.

## 8. Conclusion

African Potentials is inherently a project of synthesising all that has intersected with the geographical, ontological location known as Africa. It is inherently eclectic, by which Ali Mazrui means a process arrived at by 'synthesising and utilising values from different traditions', resisting uncritical adoption of external influences while at the same time critically appropriating those that make sense and enhance what already exists (Makinda 2017). It should be by definition anti-canonical and anti-colonial. Being anti-canonical, the project towards African Potentials must abhor any attempt to close out some voices over others. Because African Potentials have suffered brutal asphyxiation by 'western canons' a pedagogy for African Potentials must guard against reproducing the same gate-keeping that privileges closes and canonises some voices at the expense of others. As an inherently postcolonial exercise, a pedagogy based on *morero* to unlock infinite African Potentials must critically analyse the import of colonisation in its meaning making processes, and consciously guard against the incessant attempts of neo-colonialism to limit the potency of African Potentials.

## Acknowledgements

This work was supported by JSPS KAKENHI Grant Number JP16H06318. The educational and research activities on which this chapter was based were made possible with the financial support of the Bill & Melinda Gates Foundation.

## References

Chilisa, B. (2019) *Indigenous Research Methodologies* (second edition), Los Angeles: Sage Publishing.

Embassy of Botswana in Japan (2018) 'Culture and history', Embassy of Botswana in Japan (https://www.botswanaembassy.or.jp/tourist.php?La=E&Show =2) (accessed: 30 November 2020).

Eze, E. C. (1997) *Postcolonial African Philosophy: A Critical Reader*, Oxford: Wiley-Blackwell.

Fuller, B. and Snyder Jr, C. W. (1991) 'Vocal teachers, silent pupils? Life in Botswana classrooms', *Comparative Education Review*, Vol. 35, No. 2, pp. 274–94.

Index Mundi (2019) 'Botswana - GINI index (World Bank estimate)', Index Mundi (https://www.indexmundi.com/facts/botswana/indicator/SI.P OV.GINI) (accessed: 28 December 2019).

Letseka, M. (2016) 'Indigenous African epistemologies: Focus on Ubuntu', seminar presentation, The Ali Mazrui Centre for Higher Education Studies at the University of Johannesburg, Johannesburg, South Africa, 22 September 2016.

Louw, D. J. (2001) 'Ubuntu and the challenges of multiculturalism in post-apartheid South Africa', *Quest*, Vol. 15, No. 1-2, pp. 15–36.

Makinda, S. M. (2017) 'Eclecticism as a theoretical approach: The pillar of Ali A. Mazrui's intellectual legacy', in K. Njogu and S. Adem (eds) *Critical Perspectives on Culture and Globalisation: The Intellectual Legacy of Ali Mazrui*, Nairobi: Twaweza Communications, pp. 213–26.

————— (2000) 'Reading and writing international relations', *Australian Journal of International Affairs*, Vol. 54, No. 3, pp. 389–401.

Mangena, F. (2014) 'In defense of ethno-philosophy: A brief response to Kanu's eclecticism', *Filosofia Theoretica: Journal of African Philosophy, Culture and Religions*, Vol. 3, No. 1, pp. 96–107.

Mazrui, A. A. (1975) 'Eclecticism as an ideological alternative: An African perspective', *Alternatives*, Vol. 1, No. 4, pp. 465–86.

————— (1986) *The Africans: A Triple Heritage*, Boston and Toronto: Little, Brown and Company.

Mboup, S. B. (2008) 'Conflicting leadership paradigms in Africa: A need for an African Renaissance perspective', *International Journal of African Renaissance Studies*, Vol. 3, No. 1, pp. 94–112.

Mosime, S. and Kaboyakgosi, G. (2017) 'Botswana: Africa's democratic developmental state or outright flattery? Towards inclusive democratic states', in G. Kanyenze, H. Jauch, A. Kanengoni, M. Madzwamuse and D. Muchena (eds) *Towards Democratic Developmental States in Southern Africa*, Harare: Weaver Press, pp. 106–34.

Mpofu, W. (2017) 'Thabo Mbeki: Understanding a philosopher of liberation', *African Historical Review*, Vol. 49, No. 2, pp. 48–71.

Ndlovu-Gatsheni, S. J. (2014) '"My life is One Long Debate": Ali A Mazrui on the invention of Africa and postcolonial predicaments', Lecture in Memory of Professor Ali A. Mazrui, Centre for African Studies, University of the Free State (UFS), 30 October 2014 (https://www.ufs.ac.za/docs/librariesprovider20/centre-for-africa-studies-documents/all-documents/mazrui-lecture-2032-eng.pdf?sfvrsn=f836fb21_0) (accessed: 9 September 2020).

Ngwenya, B. N. (2002) 'Gender, dress and self-empowerment: Women and burial societies in Botswana', *African Sociological Review*,

Vol. 6, No. 2, pp. 1–27.

Nnaemeka, O. (1994) 'Bringing African women into the classroom: Rethinking pedagogy and epistemology', in M. R. Higonnet (ed.) *Borderwork: Feminist Engagements with Comparative Literature*, Ithaca and London: Cornell University Press, pp. 301–18.

Ntseane, P. and Chilisa, B. (2012) 'Indigenous knowledge, HIV, and AIDS education and research: Implications for health educators', in L. M. English (ed.) *Adult Education and Health*, Toronto: University of Toronto Press, pp. 76–89.

Osei-Hwedie, B. Z. (2010) 'Botswana: Indigenous institutions, civil society and government in peace building in Southern Africa', *Journal of International Development and Cooperation*, Vol. 16, No. 2, pp. 115–27.

Pitsoe, V. and Letseka, M. M. (2016) 'Ubuntu driven ODL student assessment', in M. Letseka (ed.) *Open Distance Learning (ODL) through the Philosophy of Ubuntu*, New York: Nova Publishers, pp. 93–105.

Salter, P. S. and Adam, G. (2019) 'Provisional strategies for decolonizing consciousness', in F. Blake, P. Ioanide and A. Reed (eds) *Antiracism Inc.: Why the Way We Talk about Racial Justice Matters*, Santa Barbara: Punctum Books, pp. 299–324.

Schapera, I. (1955) *A Handbook of Tswana Law and Custom*. 2nd ed., Oxford: Oxford University Press.

Sills, P. (2018) 'Consensus building – Introduction', Paul Sills (https://paulsills.co.nz/consensus-building-introduction/) (accessed: 4 December 2020).

Solway, J. (2011) '"Culture fatigue": The state and minority rights in Botswana', *Indiana Journal of Global Legal Studies*, Vol. 18, No. 1, pp. 211–40.

Steyn, G. (2012) 'The influence of "botho" on social space in Botswana since independence', *South African Journal of Art History*, Vol. 27, No. 3, pp. 112–29.

Tamale, S. (2006) 'African feminism taking a "cultural turn"', Presentation on the Occasion of the Launch of the African Feminist Forum, Accra, Ghana, pp. 1–14.

Teffo, L. (2011) 'Epistemic pluralism for knowledge transformation',

*International Journal of African Renaissance Studies*, Vol. 6, No. 1, pp. 24–34.

Tomaselli, K. (2003) 'Dialectical intellectuals, essentialism and the African renaissance', *Journal of Cultural Studies*, Vol. 5, No. 1, pp. 1–34.

University of Botswana (2008) 'Learning and teaching policy', University of Botswana (https://kitsiso.ub.bw/documents/learning-and-teaching-policy-approved-senate-20-2-08) (accessed: 14 December 2020).

Werbner, R. (1977) 'Small man politics and the rule of law: Centre-periphery relations in east-central Botswana', *Journal of African Law*, Vol. 21, No. 1, pp. 24–39.

World Happiness Report (2020) (https://worldhappiness.report/) (accessed: 13 December 2020).

# Index

#FeesMustFall 86, 91, 327

3.8 Generation 180

the generation of post-independent expectation 182–184

the genesis of ICBT from the 184–188

#RhodesMustFall 19, 56, 61–62, 86, 91, 327

## A

Aari 10, 157, 160–165, 167, 171–174

the educational environment in 158–160

affirmation 7, 114, 352

places of belonging, connection and 108–113

African children's play and education 300–301

African phenomena 1–4

African Potential/s 1-4, 7, 9–10, 69

African Renaissance 336–337, 341, 347, 352

African Social Thought 18, 335, 342, 351–352

teaching of 345–349

African socialism 5, 27

Afrikaners 6, 53, 57–58, 60–62

Ali Mazrui *see* Mazrui

alienation 7, 88, 91, 108, 112, 114, 219, 221, 239

places of exclusion and 101–107

apartheid 6–7, 30, 66, 76–77, 83, 85, 90–92, 113, 185–186

apprenticeship/s 5, 127, 137–138, 150

Arusha Declaration 30, 32, 34, 37

autonomy 2, 91, 219, 223, 236, 249, 289, 334–335, 338, 340–341, 350

## B

Bantu education 6, 53–68

basic education 11, 32, 128–130, 136, 139, 141–142, 145–146, 149, 215, 222, 226, 229, 253

belonging 7, 252, 254, 261, 287

and exclusion 83–115

connection and affirmation
108–113

constructing places of 83–115

places of 108–113

black South African/s 6–7, 53–54, 91, 107

an overview of education history for 57–62

Botswana 18, 76, 327–349

Botswana–Japan Potentials 327–353

boundary/ies 2, 4, 6, 93, 101–102, 151, 218, 317–318, 331, 337, 342, 272

# C

campus 7–8, 34, 56, 61, 83–114, 349–350

capitalism 26, 29, 42

career/s 9, 11, 128, 132–134, 143–146, 149–151, 179, 184, 204

choice 133–135

factors affecting 133–135

paths 146–148

CBA *see* consensus-building approaches

CCM *see* Chama Cha Mapinduzi

*Chama Cha Mapinduzi* 29, 34–35

children's games 300–320

children's play 17–18

African 300–301

and cognition 301–303

and education 300–301

from the perspective of mathematics education 297–322

Zambian 301–303

classroom praxis 327–353

collective identity 5, 299

colonial rule 7, 27, 29–30, 61–62

colonialism 7, 53, 83, 107, 251, 327, 335, 339, 341, 352–353

coloniser/s 4, 346

community participation 12, 216, 219, 221, 225, 236, 239

in school management in Ghana 221–224

policies and practices of 221–224

community school/s 13–14, 215, 248–249, 260–263

in urban slums of Kenya 252–253

role and functions of the 255–257

conflict/s 12–13, 65, 200, 279, 281, 328, 330–332

within school communities in Ghana 215–240

consensus-building approaches (CBA) 330–332

continuing education 9, 149

conviviality 2–3, 8, 13–15, 19, 26, 42, 151, 220–221

    community participation in school management and 217–221

    community schools providing the tools for 247–264

        focusing on the art of 215–240

        insights from 283–288

        perspective 271–291

corruption 25, 31, 60, 290, 328

credentials versus knowledge for use 8–11, 125–212

crisis/es 29, 58, 198, 339

    an epistemic and existential 327–329

    for Botswana–Japan Potentials 327–329

cultural capital 5, 329

cultural games 301

cultural integration 18, 342

cultural practices 10, 174, 340

culture/s 1, 18, 27, 74, 76, 86–87, 91, 106, 238–239, 261, 274, 297, 301, 303, 328–330, 332, 335, 339, 341–343, 346–348, 351–352

decolonising the curriculum through the turn to 336–337

curriculum/s 5, 8, 16–18, 33–34, 37, 87, 128, 130, 151, 195, 250–252, 261, 297–300, 321–322, 328, 335, 338–339

    decolonising the 336–337

**D**

decolonisation 61, 86, 327–329, 335–336, 338, 348

Demographic and Health Survey (DHS) 275

donor/s 11, 131, 271, 289

**E**

eclecticism 18

    a case for re-thinking Mazrui's 345–349

        epistemic 327–353

        pedagogic 337–340

economic development 29, 192, 330

economic growth 132, 151, 194, 198, 205, 328, 336

education

    African children's play and 300–301

    and employment 179–207

and future careers 143–146

and social structure in Africa 1–19

as a mode of transmitting values 4–8, 23–24

establishing an agricultural association and 163–172

formal 6, 39, 42, 139, 142, 147, 157, 159, 252, 302

from the perspective of the marginalised 75–77

further expansion 158–160

higher 87–90, 191–194

history 57–75

mathematics 297–322

on *ujamaa* and UDSM 32–35

rehabilitation in primary 188–191

system 221–222

technical and vocational 127–152

transformation in South Africa 85–87

visual research methods in 92–94

Education for All 11, 130, 191, 215

Education for Self-Reliance (ESR) 32–33

educational development 12–13, 130

Educational Management Information System (EMIS) 275

elite/s 5, 12, 58, 85, 194, 196, 219, 236

employment 9–10, 130–133, 137, 141, 149–150, 158–159, 224

education and 179–207

for the post-war generation 188–197

under jobless growth 198–199

enrolment/s 91, 132, 138, 140, 146, 150, 157–159, 190–191, 193, 222–223, 228

entrepreneurship 10, 133

epistemology 2, 251, 335, 338, 340, 342

ESR *see* Education for Self-Reliance

Ethiopia 10, 157–160, 162, 170, 195–196, 218, 318

school education in 158–163

ethnomathematics 18, 297–300, 319, 321

exclusion/s 7–8, 105

and alienation 101–107

constructing places of belonging and 83–115

360

**F**

Feminist Action Research (FAR) 335, 349

financial situation/s 273, 282

    establishment and 277–278

formal education 6, 39, 42, 139, 142, 147, 157, 159, 252, 302

    low-fee schools that support 273–275

formal schooling 5, 10, 26, 32, 142, 157

formal sector/s 10, 133, 143, 180, 186, 198–200, 205

**G**

Ghana

    labour market and youth skills development in 131–133

    the TVET system in 136–141

globalisation 7, 14, 85, 249

graduate/s 9–10, 33, 37, 127, 129–133, 136, 138, 149–150, 181, 183, 191, 205, 252, 260, 289

graduation 9–10, 138, 141, 143–144, 148, 165, 181

**H**

headteacher/s 12, 216, 219, 222, 2227–238, 254–256, 259, 278–279

hegemony 329, 335

higher education 7, 10–11, 18, 34, 66, 83, 85, 92–93, 113, 139, 158, 175, 179, 181, 184, 188, 191, 194, 197, 203, 205, 221, 274, 337

    drastic expansion of 191–194

    research into students'

experiences in 87

    space and research into 87–90

    transformation in South Africa 85–87

humanity/ies 95, 290, 334–335, 343

**I**

ICBT *see* informal cross-border trade

identity/ies 4–7, 61, 76, 83–85, 90, 93–94, 97–98, 101–103, 107, 110, 112–114, 287–288, 299, 337, 346, 348

ideology/ies 6, 25–29, 32, 34–35, 40–42, 88, 96, 248, 251

Illich 2, 8, 18, 151, 180, 204, 220, 250–251, 260, 273, 285, 287

IMF *see* International Monetary Fund

imperialism 338–339, 342, 352

incompleteness 2, 18–19, 26, 77, 261–263, 285, 344

    and interdependence 286–288

inequality/ies 7–8, 14, 25, 31, 69, 83, 85, 88, 96, 113, 133, 191, 260–261, 264, 348–349

informal apprenticeship/s 5, 130, 132, 138

informal cross-border trade (ICBT) 11, 180–182, 201, 204–205

informal sector/s 10–11, 132–133, 141–143, 150, 181, 184, 186, 199, 205

interdependence 3, 15, 249–250, 263, 284–285, 289

    incompleteness and 286–288

    networking, negotiation and 257–258

international aid 14, 271–291

International Monetary Fund (IMF) 31, 183, 198–199


**K**

Kenya 13–14, 202, 218, 220, 273–274, 283

    community schools in urban slums of 252–253

    conviviality in urban 247–264

Kibera 14, 247, 252, 271, 273, 276–279

knowledge

    acquisition as a subjective process 15–19, 295–356

    and views of Tanzanian youth regarding *ujamaa* 25–45

    education and social structure in Africa 1–19

    local 10, 18, 157–176

    school credentials versus 8–11, 125–212

Kumasi 9, 135–136

Kumasi Polytechnic (KP) 9, 129, 139–142, 145–149

Kumasi Senior Technical High School (KSHS) 9, 129, 139, 141–142, 146–150

Kumasi Technical Institute (KTI) 9, 128–129, 138–142, 146–149

Kumasi Vocational Training Institute (KVTI) 9, 129, 138–142, 147–149

KVTI *see* Kumasi Vocational Training Institute


**L**

language of instruction 6, 61, 159, 299

362

leadership 15, 30, 108–109, 217, 237–238, 332–333, 339

legitimacy 12–13, 74, 151, 218, 224, 237, 239, 333

Lesotho 328, 333

liberation 6–7, 29–30, 54, 65–66, 69, 72, 75–76, 330, 336–337, 352

literacy 54, 63, 66, 69, 71, 74–75, 135, 203–204, 252, 329

local knowledge 10, 18, 157–176

low-cost/fee private school/s 13–14, 247, 273–275

    the boom of 273–277

    unrecognised (in Nairobi, Kenya) 271–291


**M**

marginalisation 53, 83, 86, 91, 105

Masire 333

mathematical activities 297–322

mathematics education 17, 297–322

Mazabuka 17, 302, 305–306, 317

Mazrui 329, 337–340, 342, 344, 346, 352

Mbeki 336–337

migration 14, 185–187, 221, 223, 249

Millennium Development Goals 11, 189, 191, 215, 273

minority/ies 5, 54, 58, 69, 75–76, 150, 251, 334, 347, 352

mission school/s 6, 54–55, 57–60, 64, 67

motivation/s 3, 15–16, 69, 129, 133, 151, 234, 236, 279

Mozambique 10–11, 180, 188, 191, 193–195, 197–199, 205

    genesis of highly educated informal workers in 179–207

Musoma 33–34


**N**

Nairobi 13–14, 247–248, 252–253, 263, 271-291

Namibia 6–7, 53–58, 62–70, 72–76

nation building 5, 75, 180, 186

nationalism 27, 58, 338, 352

neoliberalism 7, 42, 85

NER (net enrolment ratio) 275

Nyamnjoh 2–3, 5, 216, 220, 238, 249–251, 260, 262, 273, 284–289, 299, 347

Nyerere 5, 7, 25, 27, 29, 31–41, 346–347

    and *ujamaa* 29–32

**O**

Ohangwena 53, 56, 75–76

the history of education for the San in the 69–75

Ovawambo 6, 53–54, 70–72, 74, 76

the history of education for the 62–69

**P**

Parent Teacher Association (PTA) 218, 222–223, 228–229, 231–232, 234, 237, 274

parochialism 343, 348, 352

patriarchy 349, 351–352

pedagogy18, 298–303, 321, 335, 337–340, 344, 348, 350, 352

play 17–18, 297-322

pluralism 334, 342–343

post-secondary education 9, 34, 144, 146, 149, 189, 329

primary education 58, 66, 73, 157, 159, 191, 247, 255, 261, 273–274, 277, 303

rehabilitation in 188–191

primary school /s 14, 17, 33, 36–37, 129, 132, 158, 164, 189, 221, 247, 254, 274–277, 306, 313, 321

private school/s 13–14, 247

in the Kibera slum 276–277

in the urban area 275–276

that support formal education 273–275

the boom of low-fee 273–277

unrecognised low-fee 271–291

privilege/s 7–8, 58, 83, 85, 88, 94, 96, 114, 128, 252, 285, 352

PTA *see* Parent Teacher Association

public school/s 12–13, 248, 254, 273–274, 276–277, 279, 283–284, 289

punishment 224, 230, 232, 235, 309–312

**R**

recruitment 33, 170

finances and teacher 281–283

role model/s 204, 279, 282

**S**

San 7, 53–56, 66, 75–77

the history of education for the 69–75

Savimbi 333

school education 6, 9–10, 25–26, 33, 36, 42–43, 127, 130, 295, 300, 320

establishing an agricultural association and 163–172

experiences of 157–176

in Ethiopia 158–162

modern 161–162

the medium of instruction for 53–78

school fees 138, 145, 147, 215, 247, 272, 274

school management 13, 215–216, 221-224, 228–229, 234, 236–237, 239

community participation in 217–223

from a conviviality perspective 284–286

in Ghana 221–224

understanding 283–288

School Management Committee/s (SMC) 12, 215, 228–229

secondary school 27, 33, 36–38, 68, 128, 158, 164, 179, 182–183, 189, 221, 223, 259, 272, 274, 278, 282, 289

self-help initiative/s 14

examining international aid and community 271–291

from a conviviality perspective 271–291

senior technical certificate 9, 137–139, 149

skills development, 127–152

slum/s 13–14, 253, 283–284

area of Nairobi, Kenya 271–291

Kibera 276–277

SMC *see* School Management Committees

social organisation 7, 54, 57, 62, 238

social structure 26

knowledge, education and 1–19

socialisation 16–17, 219, 249, 302

socialism 5, 26–27, 31–42, 182

evolution of 27–29

South Africa 6–7, 54–58–66, 72–73, 76, 83, 85, 88, 90, 92, 106, 131, 183–188, 200, 203–204, 220, 301, 327, 333, 335–336

higher education transformation in 85–87

South West Africa 6, 54, 63, 65–66

spatial environment 303–304, 317

student/s

affect and identity 83–115

at the University of Dar es Salaam 25–45

characteristics of the 141–143

knowledge and views of 36–42

knowledge of *ujamaa* 36–39

perceptions about their education and future careers 143–146

teachers and 278–280

views of *ujamaa* 39–42

subjective process 15–19, 295–256

subjectivity/ies 8, 10, 17, 87–89, 134, 146, 151

sustainability 15, 286–287, 331

Swahili 5, 25, 37, 259, 318

## T

Tanganyika African Nationalist Union (TANU) 29–30, 33–35

TANU *see* Tanganyika African Nationalist Union

Tanzania/n 6, 25–26, 29, 34, 40–43

teacher/s

and students 278–280

recruitment 281–283

Technical and Vocational Education and Training (TVET) 9, 127–152, 191

technology 2, 140, 165, 169, 174, 195, 271

tertiary education 138, 182, 188–189, 205, 329

textbook/s 6, 10, 26–27, 36–37, 42–43, 67, 234, 250, 347

transformation 8, 61, 85, 87, 89, 91–93, 114, 340

higher education 85–87

Tswana 329–330, 334

## U

ubuntu 299–300, 320–322, 328, 330, 336–337, 340

theory of power as eclectic connectedness 340–345

*ujamaa* 5–6, 31, 51–52, 346–347

education on 32–35

history of 29–35

President Julius Nyerere and 29–32

students' knowledge of 36–42

University of Botswana 18, 335, 345, 348–349

University of Cape Town (UCT) 7, 56, 61, 85, 88, 90, 94–95, 102, 106

    study context 90–92

University of Dar es Salaam (UDSM) 6, 25–45

    education on *ujamaa* and 32–35

    history of *ujamaa*, education and the 29–35

    knowledge and views of students at 36–42

unrecognised schools 274, 277, 281, 285

**V**

value/s 2, 4–6, 9–10, 15, 127, 129, 132, 134, 151, 196, 219, 236, 251, 260, 275, 282, 285, 287, 289, 299, 328, 332, 338, 344, 352

    education as a mode of transmitting 4–8, 23–124

villagisation 31, 39

vulnerable children 14, 248, 251, 260, 262–264

**W**

white/s (people) 7, 59, 61–62, 64–66, 70, 83, 85–86, 88, 90–91, 95, 102, 104, 108–109, 113

**Y**

Young Women's Leadership (YWL) 335, 349–351

**Z**

Zambia 17, 298, 301–302, 306–308, 312, 314, 319–322, 332

www.ingramcontent.com/pod-product-compliance
Lightning Source LLC
Chambersburg PA
CBHW060021030426
42334CB00019B/2132